The Present and Future of Music Law

The Present and Future of Music Law

Ann Harrison and Tony Rigg

BLOOMSBURY ACADEMIC
NEW YORK • LONDON • OXFORD • NEW DELHI • SYDNEY

BLOOMSBURY ACADEMIC
Bloomsbury Publishing Inc
1385 Broadway, New York, NY 10018, USA
50 Bedford Square, London, WC1B 3DP, UK
29 Earlsfort Terrace, Dublin 2, Ireland

BLOOMSBURY, BLOOMSBURY ACADEMIC and the Diana logo are trademarks of Bloomsbury Publishing Plc

First published in the United States of America 2021
This paperback edition published 2023

Copyright © Tony Rigg and Ann Harrison, 2021

Each chapter copyright © of the contributor

For legal purposes the Acknowledgments on p. ix constitute an extension of this copyright page.

Cover design: Louise Dugdale
Cover image: Sound Studio / Petrovich12 © Adobe Stock

All rights reserved. No part of this publication may be reproduced or transmitted in any form or by any means, electronic or mechanical, including photocopying, recording, or any information storage or retrieval system, without prior permission in writing from the publishers.

Bloomsbury Publishing Inc does not have any control over, or responsibility for, any third-party websites referred to or in this book. All internet addresses given in this book were correct at the time of going to press. The author and publisher regret any inconvenience caused if addresses have changed or sites have ceased to exist, but can accept no responsibility for any such changes.

While every effort has been made to locate copyright holders the publishers would be grateful to hear from any person(s) not here acknowledged.

A catalog record for this book is available from the Library of Congress.

ISBN: HB: 978-1-5013-6777-9
PB: 978-1-5013-6967-4
ePDF: 978-1-5013-6779-3
eBook: 978-1-5013-6778-6

Typeset by Deanta Global Publishing Services, Chennai, India

To find out more about our authors and books visit www.bloomsbury.com and sign up for our newsletters.

Contents

List of illustrations	vii
Special thanks must go to	ix
Editors and Foreword	x
List of contributors	xi
Foreword: Music law: Music and the law *Peter Hook*	xv
Reflection on the Foreword *Tony Rigg*	xix
Introduction: Music law: Unravelling complexities *Tony Rigg* and The perspective of a legal practitioner *Ann Harrison*	1

Part One Tensions between the rights of copyright owners and the freedom to create

1	Copyright, royalties and industrial decline *Richard Osborne*	27
2	Sampling practice: The threat of copyright management to its future (and past) *Justin Morey*	46
3	Emerging frontiers: Platform regulation of mashups in and beyond an EU context *Alan Hui*	64
4	Music copyright, creators and fans: Enemies or friends in the digital domain? *Paul G. Oliver and Stefan Lalchev*	82
5	Piracy: Past, present and future: How the recording industry can disrupt, mitigate and innovate in troubled waters *James Brandes*	100

Part Two Responding to the needs of the music business

6	Mediation and arbitration: An alternative forum for transnational dispute resolution in the music industries *Metka Potočnik*	127
7	The acoustic trademark *Katarzyna Krupa-Lipińska*	148
8	The derivative work right and the creative epistemologies of the other: Working towards a legal framework for remix *Lesley Model*	173

9   The US compulsory licence: A lesson in technological
    development and legislation shaping the music market
    Ralph W. Peer   190

Part Three The developing commercial landscape

10 Blockchain: Hero or hindrance for the music industry from a legal
    perspective   *Charlotte O'Mara*   209
11 Greening the live music industry   *Teresa Moore*   229
12 Branding and endorsement: The growing importance of branding
    and the developing legal framework   *Emma Harding*   247
13 The artist/manager relationship   *Jules O'Riordan, a.k.a. Judge
    Jules, and Les Gillon*   263

Index   277

Illustrations

Figures

3.1	Blocking requests for webpages on Mashup Site A's old domain from Google Transparency Report. Photo courtesy of Alan Hui	68
3.2	Request to take down webpage on Mashup Site A's new domain from Google Transparency Report. Photo courtesy of Alan Hui	70
3.3	Sample licensing in action. Photo courtesy of Alan Hui	73
7.1	EUTM no. 001312008. Available at: https://euipo.europa.eu/eSearch/#details/trademarks/001312008	153
7.2	EUTM 003553261. Available at: https://euipo.europa.eu/eSearch/#details/trademarks/003553261	153
7.3	EUTM no. 013823539. Available at: https://euipo.europa.eu/eSearch/#details/trademarks/013823539	155
7.4	EUTM 002984912. Available at: https://euipo.europa.eu/eSearch/#details/trademarks/002984912	159
7.5	EUTM 011301082. Available at: https://euipo.europa.eu/eSearch/#details/trademarks/011301082	160
7.6	EUTM 010265486. Available at: https://euipo.europa.eu/eSearch/#details/trademarks/010265486	160
7.7	Polish trademark R.155520. Available at: https://ewyszukiwarka.pue.uprp.gov.pl/search/pwp-details/Z.227333	160
7.8	Polish trademark R.300795. Available at: https://ewyszukiwarka.pue.uprp.gov.pl/search/pwp-details/Z.438707	161
7.9	EUTM no. 005170113. Available at: https://euipo.europa.eu/eSearch/#details/trademarks/005170113	163
7.10	EUTM no. 005090055. Available at: https://euipo.europa.eu/eSearch/#details/trademarks/005090055	164
7.11	WO 1215169. Available at: https://euipo.europa.eu/eSearch/#details/trademarks/W01215169	166

7.12 WO 1291399. Available at: https://euipo.europa.eu/eSearch/#details/trademarks/W01291399	168
10.1 How blockchain works. Diagram courtesy of www.blockgeeks.com	210
11.1 Summarises the hierarchy of regulation and self-regulation currently in place. Image Courtesy of Teresa Moore	236
11.2 The Circular Economy. Image Courtesy of Teresa Moore	242

Special thanks must go to

The University of Central Lancashire, The School of Arts and Media, The School of Justice, Jane Anthony, Andrew Churchill, Georgina Gregory, Vivienne Ivins, Ewa Mazierska and Simon Price.

John Rigg, Dorothy Rigg, Sophie Rigg, Ava Rigg and Anna Rigg, Joanne Smith, Max Smith, Lucilla Green and Johnny Jay.

Particular thanks must go to Glen Woodroffe.

Disclaimer: The Publisher and Editors cannot be held responsible for errors or any consequences arising from the use of information contained in this volume; the views and opinions expressed do not necessarily reflect those of the Publisher and Editors; The Publisher, Editors and contributors are not providing legal advice by providing this product. The information contained herein is not a substitute for the advice of a lawyer. If you require legal or other expert advice, you should seek the services of a competent lawyer or other professional.

Editors and Foreword

Ann Harrison is a Partner at SSB Solicitors Limited, a leading boutique law firm that specialises in music law, wider entertainment law, sponsorship and branding. She is a highly experienced lawyer who is well known across the UK music industry and regarded as an expert in all aspects of music business contracts, copyright, protection of IP rights, etc. Ann is the author of *Music: The Business* (8th Edition, pending 2021), the key textbook on all music business further education courses in the UK. She is a guest lecturer at many UK further education institutions and a Leader in Residence at the University of Central Lancashire. Ann is recognised as a leading practitioner in the Chambers and Partners 2021 Legal Services Guide.

Tony Rigg is a Music Industry Practitioner, Business Consultant and Educator affiliated with the University of Central Lancashire where he leads the Master of Arts Programme in Music Industry Management, and also Head of Music Business Education at the School of Electronic Music. He has occupied senior management roles in market-leading organisations including Operations Director for Ministry of Sound, overseen the management of more than one hundred music venues and delivered thousands of music events. As an artist/producer he has a chart pedigree with tracks featured on chart-topping and gold-selling albums. His other notable publications include *Popular Music in the Post-digital Age: Politics, Economy, Culture and Technology* (2018), *The Future of Live Music* (2020) and *The Evolution of Electronic Dance Music* (2021), which he co-edited with Ewa Mazierska and Les Gillon.

Peter (Hooky) Hook is a singer, songwriter, multi-instrumentalist, record producer and author. In a career spanning five decades, he has been involved with many music-related projects, but is best known as a founding member of two of Britain's most influential bands, Joy Division and New Order. Today he continues to work with innovative projects, having instigated orchestral collaborations with the Hacienda music brand and more recently the Joy Division catalogue. He performs live all over the world with his band 'Peter Hook and the Light' and is the author of *The Hacienda: How Not to Run a Club*, (2009), *Unknown Pleasures: Inside Joy Division* (2012) and *Substance: Inside New Order* (2016).

Contributors

James Brandes is Managing Director at the Digital Copyright Consultancy. It was set up in 2010 to combat digital piracy in the creative industries. His legal qualifications include an LLB (Hons) in Law, a Postgraduate Diploma in Legal Practice, an LL.M in International Business Law and an MSc (Econ) in International Business Management. His knowledge of intellectual property law has facilitated the removal of over twenty million infringing URLs for clients within the recording industry. James and his business have provided internet anti-piracy services for eighteen Number 1 chart-topping albums and over seventy Top 40 chart albums worldwide.

Les Gillon is a Principal Lecturer at the University of Central Lancashire. He writes on popular music and is active in practice-based music research that explores composition and improvisation, the use of non-Western music traditions and interdisciplinary collaboration. In addition to his research in the field of music, he also writes on aesthetics and the visual arts. His monograph *The Uses of Reason in the Evaluation of Artworks* (Palgrave, 2017) uses the Turner Prize as a case study, to explore fundamental questions about the nature, purpose and value of art.

Emma Harding is a Senior Associate at music law firm SSB Solicitors which is based in London and represents a global client base which includes recording artists, songwriters, producers, FMCG brands, managers and independent record labels.

With expertise in drafting commercial agreements with a music content, intellectual property and/or branding focus, Emma particularly enjoys, and specialises in, negotiating endorsement and brand ambassador agreements between platinum selling recording artists and global brands. Emma is a regular guest speaker at BIMM Institute and a guest lecturer at Hertfordshire University.

Alan Hui is a Postdoctoral Research Fellow at the RITMO Centre at the University of Oslo, Norway. His research with the MASHED project at RITMO considers how music platforms and copyright laws – particularly in North American and

European legal contexts – regulate mashups. His PhD thesis, *99 Problems but a Riff Ain't One* (2018), focused on the Anglo-American concept of originality in the context of music sampling, while his forthcoming journal publications focus on the copyright exceptions of free use, quotation and parody as well as prices in music streaming. He is an active musician, particularly in improvised theatre.

Katarzyna Krupa-Lipińska is Assistant Professor at the Law and Administration Faculty of Nicolaus Copernicus University in Toruń, Poland, and a practicing patent and trademark attorney in the Polish Patent Office and the European Union Intellectual Property Office. She graduated in both Law (2007) and Administration (2007) and obtained a PhD with distinction (2016) at NCU in Toruń, Poland. Her research interests focus on industrial property law and civil law and, in particular, trademark law, design law, and causation in civil law. She has published over thirty publications, including books, book chapters and articles on civil law and intellectual property law. Her most recent book is *Związek przyczynowy jako przesłanka odpowiedzialności z tytułu czynów niedozwolonych* (Causation as a prerequisite to liability in tort law) (2020).

Stefan Lalchev is a PhD candidate, who also teaches in the London College of Music at the University of West London, UK. His research interests focus on music management and artist development in the context of the current music industry environment. His most recent publication is a chapter on the role of contests and talent shows in artist development, as part of the book *Innovation in Music: Future Opportunities* (2021).

Lesley Model: After fourteen years of lecturing in the Media School at the London College of Communication (University of the Arts, London), Lesley Model is now focusing on her PhD research in the Department of Media, Film and Music at the University of Sussex. Her research brings postcolonial theory and principles of decolonisation to assessing the discord between copyright and non-European conventions in musical creativity and art.

Teresa Moore is Director at A Greener Festival, co-founder of Green Events and Innovation (GEI) Conference and co-founder of Green Operations Europe, a Think-Do Tank for sustainable events. She is an author, researcher and contributor to a number of books and industry reports including *Berridge G., Moore T., and Ali-Knight J., Promoting and assessing sustainability at festivals* (2019), *Bristol Live Music Report* (2016), *The Show Must Go On Report* (2020,

2015), *Editor New Purple Guide* (2014), *Why Festival Goers Leave their Tents Behind* (2013). She is undertaking a PhD on pro-environmental behaviour change at live events.

Justin Morey is a Senior Lecturer in Music Production and the Music Industries at Leeds Beckett University, UK. His main research interest is in sampling as a creative practice within British dance and electronic music, which has been the focus of the majority of his published work. He has a background in sound engineering and music production, having set up and run a recording studio in London from 1995 to 2003. As a co-writer and producer of dance and electronic music, he has had records released through labels including Acid Jazz, Ministry of Sound and Sony.

Paul G. Oliver is a Lecturer in Entrepreneurship in the Business School at Edinburgh Napier University, UK. He has degrees in both popular music and business and management, as well as a PhD in music management. His research interests focus on music copyright, DIY culture and entrepreneurship within the music industry, as well as digital pedagogy. His most recent publications include a pedagogical paper about innovation in the virtual classroom as well as a book chapter on the role of contests and talent shows in artist development.

Jules O'Riordan has over thirty years of experience across the entire spectrum of the music industry and is a Partner at Sound Advice solicitors, a respected London-based firm specialising in all aspects of music law. Jules's clients include artists, management companies, record labels, songwriters, event promoters, producers, music tech businesses, production companies, live agents, music publishers and DJs.

Jules's industry experience includes nearly a decade as an A&R for the Universal umbrella of labels, fifteen years as a presenter on BBC Radio 1, over 150 record releases and remixes in his own capacity as a recording artist, plus a thirty-year career as one of Britain's best-known globally travelled DJs, with over 5,000 gigs under his belt, plus extensive experience as an event promoter and artist manager at the highest level.

Charlotte O'Mara is a music and media lawyer with gunnercooke LLP UK. She specialised in music and entertainment law after qualification, building on an already established career in the music industry, and her clients include artists, songwriters, managers, producers, independent record labels and music publishing companies, among others. Charlotte advises on, drafts and negotiates contracts in all areas of the music, media, broadcast, and entertainment and creative industries and related intellectual property rights. She regularly lectures and holds tutorials on music and media law throughout the UK.

Richard Osborne is a Senior Lecturer in Popular Music at Middlesex University. He is the author of *Vinyl: A History of the Analogue Record* (2012); co-editor, with Zuleika Beaven and Marcus O'Dair, of *Mute Records: Artists, Business, History* (2018); and co-editor, with Dave Laing, of *Music by Numbers: The Uses and Abuses of Statistics in the Music Industries* (forthcoming). He publishes widely in the field of popular music studies, including the blog 'Pop Bothering Me' (http://richardosbornevinyl.blogspot.com/).

Ralph W. Peer works in music publishing in London as an intellectual property practitioner. His research interests include the intersection of music, technology and finance. He holds an MSc in Finance and Financial Law from SOAS, University of London, a Graduate Diploma in Law from City University, London, and an LLM from Columbia Law School, New York.

Metka Potočnik is a Senior Lecturer in Law at the University of Wolverhampton, UK. Her research interests focus on the critical investigation of intellectual property law through a feminist lens; and she has published in the area of intellectual property law, arbitration and foreign direct investment. Her most recent publication is a research monograph *Arbitrating Brands* (2019). She is also on the Board of Directors of the F-List for Music CIC, which focuses on gender equality in the music industry.

Foreword

Music law: Music and the law

During my legal case one of the most depressing things I heard throughout the whole torturous ordeal was when my barrister, in one of my many 'How can they get away with this!' outbursts, replied simply . . .

'I'm afraid that the Law and Justice are just about on nodding terms, Peter!'

So bear in mind what we are talking about here is 'The Law' not 'Justice'; you have to use the Law to get to Justice. The law these days is mainly about how much money you have, which, in my view, directly relates to how close you will get to Justice. So my advice about 'The Law' right from the beginning of anything to do with it is to make sure you do NOT do anything rash, you do NOT do anything stupid, you do NOT do anything without fully knowing the consequences of your actions. By signing that piece of paper, the consequences could outlast you, your children and your children's children.

It is that important!

Not only will you have to live with it forever, you will also have to live with the financial problems, and the mental health consequences that could very much affect you and your family when you try and fight your way out later. In my case it made me more determined than ever to succeed on my own, and with the support of my family and friends we have done it.

You must ensure as much as you can that the Law cannot be used against you. Do not do what I did in the past and leave it to chance or trust, because, believe me, unlike Albanian hitmen, justice for the rest of us can be very difficult to get.

When I became a musician in 1976, I did not see how these two, Music and Law, would ever have anything in common. I would learn later how much they actually did and sadly I am still learning. I have a wonderful game with my lawyer where he shows me a piece of paper, spelling out some awful deal and tragic scenario (mainly moneywise) for me that lasts forever, literally forever!

I say, 'What idiot would sign that?'

He turns over the piece of paper, and smirks!

'It's you again, Peter'.

Personal guarantees, terrible lifelong contracts, property leases, company formations, partnerships, you name it, I signed it. I digress. . . . So as I said before, when I became a musician all I was interested in was playing music, wherever and whenever I could. If I had to sign a piece of paper to do it, I would. I would laugh, never caring about the consequences.

My first 'legal' rip-off was our first-ever appearance on a physical record. This was one of the first Punk Samplers, seven Bands, eight tracks, a collective deal for all of us which said, 'All bands shall receive 2% of the royalties earned' – this was for both record royalties and publishing royalties earned on the sale of this ten-inch record. Unusual to include publishing but we were all unsigned bands so basically didn't have a clue what we were doing.

We all duly signed. Later we found out that it meant that we would all receive 2% between the seven different artists. The record went on to sell hundreds of thousands. The record company earned a fortune but we got a couple of hundred each! Insult to injury for us after our success grew, meaning it even came out re-released with a sticker proudly proclaiming 'Featuring Joy Division'.

I remember when we signed to London Records after Factory (our Manchester record label) went bankrupt. Our manager was desperate to get the money to prop up our ailing nightclub (Please see my first book 'The Hacienda: How Not To Run A Club' for details) and the limit of our due diligence was our singer asking the head of London Records if he was going to rip us off. When he replied he would never do that ever, as if any Record Company had ever done that to a musician, perish the thought, again we duly signed. Now in that case he didn't, London worked out very well for us as a group, but after two sets of London (the place, not the label) lawyers negotiating the contract for months and months you would expect it to go smoothly, wouldn't you?

Our lawyer phoned me on a Friday to tell me that after months and months and hundreds of thousands of pounds in legal fees, our new record deal was finally done.

'I have the finished signing copy here. I will send it up to you'.

After a couple of days it had still not arrived. I phoned him back.

'Peter, glad you rang. I just thought on Saturday as I had a couple of hours to spare I would read it. I got a Gin and Tonic and got stuck in!'

No mean feat – this thing was hundreds of pages long.

'As I read, I realised that they had somehow added five more clauses in right at the end, none of them in your favour. It's gone back to them for their "mistake" to be rectified'.

I could regale you with hundreds of these stories – I realise now they are all part of having a job in this business.

I have paid fortunes to accountants, to lawyers, bought managers sports cars, even paid musicians, more bad than good. I know for a fact that three of Manchester's greatest bands will never play together again because of their legal battles. Any book you read about your musical heroes will undoubtedly contain many of these tales also, although I have noticed most do not go into much detail. Legal pitfalls are endemic in this business.

You have to be very, very careful. Check, check and then ask a lawyer for advice, ask your mum and dad, ask your mates, ask your contemporaries, even ask me. Now I hope you have that warning very firmly in place. If anyone asks you to sign anything, you should get it checked by as many people (impartial, independent experts and professional advisers, and people you know you can trust) as possible. Otherwise like me, you and your descendants will be suffering from these mistakes forever, I cannot stress that enough. Thankfully these days, 'In Perpetuity' deals are frowned upon. If you are short you can have a couple of mine.

Now, Groups.

This working together business is very difficult. Unfortunately, you generally find out only after you've been dragging your arse round every s***hole in England for a long, long time, and are just about to get that wonderful first taste of success that the best friend you formed the group with has, in your opinion, of course, now turned into a combination of Mrs Doubtfire, Cruella De Ville and Margaret Thatcher, which probably isn't true, it's probably very much how it feels to you. It could just be that your hopes and ideals for the group have changed, and like in any relationship over time people do change. Now, what can you do about it? Nothing much ... Split the band, leave or do what most do and moan to the other members of your beleaguered group, or your roadies, or your harassed management (who are probably listening to everyone else telling them you're a b*****d too ... and agreeing with them).

So most of us usually get on with just signing our lives away along with all our rights to publishing and record royalties etc., and mainly forgetting about them all until that dreadful moment when you've had enough of him or them and they or you eventually split the group. Then .... Oh how those rash moments could come back to haunt you.

In my opinion in this industry we need a prenup! Let's call it 'The Hooky Prenuptial Agreement for Band Members' entered into when everything is rosy and you love each other, and everything is still great.

A friend of mine got a great gig managing a very big English group. Let's call them Skunkville. They were going places, huge even to begin with. A massive stadium band in England already. As soon as he got the job he sat them all down and said,

'Right, let's sort out what happens between you when it all goes wrong and the Group splits!'

They all laughed. 'But we love each other!' they cried in unison.

Now I am telling you there was a very good chance that two of them were lying. But that is how it is in most groups. You swallow the beefs for the fame, the adulation and hopefully the money and the freedom you know it can bring, and don't care what happens legally or otherwise. I am here to tell you, you should care, more than ever these days. This book will give you a sense of the complexities of music law and the business of music. Question everything and consider carefully who has your best interests at heart. Before I finish, don't forget industry trade associations like the Musicians' Union. They are great for advice and resources like contracts, partnership agreements, etc. that members can use free of charge at the start of any endeavour.

If you are really desperate e-mail me on peterhookenquiries@outlook.com. I will do my best.

Good luck,
Peter Hook

Reflection on the Foreword

Peter Hook's Foreword provides a look through the eyes of a seasoned music industry professional, in particular offering the perspective of 'music maker'. Drawing on his long and eventful time in the music industry, he raises a number of fundamental issues.

Early in his career, Hook was exposed to the culture and approaches to business of Factory Records, described more as 'a collective of like-minded individuals than a structured business' (Robertson 2006: 10), with a 'freewheeling approach to the business of running a record label' (Robertson 2006: 10). Tony Wilson who was central to the label described it as 'a laboratory experiment in popular art' (quoted by Robertson 2006: 10) with its survival 'propped up by the success of its major acts Joy Division, New Order and the Happy Mondays' (Robertson 2006: 10). By Wilson's own admission in the foreword of Robertson's book, regarding the labels as a distinctive and often lavish approach to presenting music, he said, 'We just did what we wanted to do. And then post-rationalised it' (Wilson in Robertson 2006: 9). In the case of Peter Hook this may or may not have contributed to his lack of attention to, or appreciation of the importance of the business arrangements earlier in his career. In this he is not alone. Either way, having suffered the consequences and benefiting from hindsight, he now has a very different view. Despite the relative youth of key stakeholders and the apparent deprioritisation of the commercial agenda at Factory, clearly these circumstances enabled a creative and business legacy that is still being talked about decades later. Moreover, Hook's creative output throughout his career generated significant revenue. Understandably, at some point, one might reflect on what happened to this money if it didn't come to him. He gives accounts of two different record deals, one that resulted in low value being attributed to the music early in their career. The high value of the recording in question had not been established at the point of signing the agreement. However, this example raises issues relating to the nature of the relationship between new artists and record labels. It also demonstrates the potential for language to be misinterpreted and hence, arguably, to be misleading. We see later on, in Hook's account of his dealings with London Records that, no doubt warranted by demonstrated commercial potential, there was significant investment in legal support with part of the negotiation process being engineered through contract revisions. In this case the relationship between band and label went on to be positive and productive.

One point of particular contention for Hook is the potential for the breakdown of relationships between band members, and he offers suggestions for how such situations may be avoided. Profiling this concern in itself should serve as an important message to those starting out or those who are working creatively with other people and have yet to formalise relationships. We continue to expand on some of the matters he raises in the introduction, with further insight being provided in the subsequent chapters. Clearly, much can be taken from Peter Hook's experiences and we would like to thank him sincerely for his contribution to this book.

Tony Rigg

Reference

Robertson, M. (2006). *Factory Records: The Complete Graphic Album*. London: Thames and Hudson Ltd.

Introduction

Music law

Unravelling complexities
Tony Rigg
and
The perspective of a legal practitioner
Ann Harrison

In the music industry it is generally understood that 'music law' is an overarching term incorporating a range of legal subjects which are applicable to music and the business of music such as, but not exclusively, intellectual property law, contract law, defamation law, competition law, employment law, and others. Each of these subject areas are substantial and complicated, consequently they are all typically examined separately in literature. To illustrate, publications we may draw on to illuminate UK copyright law in relation to music might include *Copinger and Skone James on Copyright* (Harbottle, Caddick and Suthersanen 2020) and *Intellectual Property Law* (Bentley et al. 2018). While such specialist publications are clearly pertinent to music, it is important to note that copyright law and the other aspects of law that relate to music are not exclusive to the music industry; hence, it is also advantageous to look beyond to review the application of the laws to the specific requirements of the music industry.

In the world of academia, while much has been written examining the philosophical and cultural significance of music, its creation, (music) business and law individually, up to now, there has been relatively little literature dedicated to the study of 'music law'. To illustrate this point, it was as recent as 2014 that Desmond Manderson, in his extended review of Sara Ramshaw's *Justice as Improvisation: The Law of the Extempore*, acknowledged music and law as a new interdisciplinary field, with each having the potential to illuminate the other

(Manderson 2014: 311–12). With a view to expanding the literature available in this new area, this edited collection is dedicated to the interdisciplinary study of 'music law', its subfields of music, law and business, and how they correlate, thus providing a basis for expansion of discourse within the field.

One of the ideas explored in this introduction is the notion that different functions within the music industry result in different perspectives and outlooks. One of the editors of this collection, Ann Harrison, is a leading UK music lawyer working at the top of the industry, with a broad spectrum of clients and almost forty years of experience within music business and legal practice. The other, Tony Rigg, is a music industry practitioner and business consultant with a history of senior management roles in market-leading entertainment, music and lifestyle organisations such as Operations Director for Ministry of Sound. Both are active in education and have significant publications to their names, with Harrison having written the popular practical guide to the music industry, *Music: The Business – the Law and the Deals* (7th edition 2017, 8th edition 2021) and Rigg having co-edited a number of academic music-related texts published by Bloomsbury including *Popular Music in the Post-digital Age: Politics, Economy, Culture and Technology* (Mazierska, Gillon, Rigg 2018), *The Future of Live Music* (Mazierska, Gillon and Rigg 2020) and *The Evolution of Electronic Dance Music* (Mazierska, Gillon and Rigg 2021). This introduction embraces the different approaches of the two editors: Rigg's perspective of the music industry is from outside legal practice and Harrison's perspective is from within, though it is important to note that in order to be successful in these particular roles, an understanding of the connecting disciplines is a requisite, particularly for acting in the role of professional adviser, which is a key aspect of both legal practice and business consultancy. The perspectives of 'music makers' and their relationships with music business and music law are also considered in this collection. This is in part explored in the foreword by seminal musician Peter Hook (co-founder of the bands Joy Division and New Order), which presents a look through the eyes of an accomplished and seasoned music creator who has observed industry practices since 1976, enabling us to draw on his experiences and consider how they have influenced his perception and relationship with music business and music law. These are relationships that, for Hook, have continued to evolve throughout his career, as his experience and knowledge grew. At the beginning Hook had a manager, but as his career matured this also evolved into 'managing his managers', namely using them to organise his artistic life while being in charge of his overall strategy' (Mazierska and Rigg 2018: 152).

Acknowledging the three macro perspectives of *music maker*, *music business* and *legal practitioner*[1] highlights the interdisciplinary nature of the agents within the music industry and also facilitates reflection on the intersections where roles can overlap.

In this introduction we present an overview of music law and identify some of the challenges endemic to the international music industry that music law has to deal with, including its susceptibility to external factors, complexities in ownership and the complimentary but also confrontational nature of the relationships between its stakeholders. It concludes with Harrison's thoughts from her perspective of working at the cutting edge of music law, correlating a number of the topics explored in this collection within the context of the commercial music industry.

This collection has been designed to accommodate a wide-ranging readership, framing the fundamental aspects of music law for readers new to the subject area but expanding into deeper technical and philosophical investigation for experienced practitioners and academics. The contributors examine pertinent topics that are resonating within the music industry and academic discourse today. There are instances where the opinions of the contributors do not necessarily reflect the views of the editors, however; this demonstrates the complex nature of the music industry and music law along with its susceptibility to differing interpretations and understanding. Indeed, the debate of legal points as such, is characteristic to legal practice. Thus, we feel the inclusion of such views is an important part of the conversation and likely to contribute to a deeper insight into sometimes opaque-seeming music business practices.

Music law and practice

The modern music industry is a complex environment made up of many different agents, organisations and institutions and is susceptible to the impact of transient external factors, including cultural change and technological innovation. It falls upon music law and its legal practitioners to provide a framework, the

---

[1] We are viewing these as overarching perspectives and it should be acknowledged that there are many contingent functions and roles, examples of which in *music business* include A&R, label manager, artist manager, booking agent and so on.

mechanisms and the foundations for functionality, and a means to resolve matters, should they go wrong. To do this music legal practitioners primarily draw on intellectual property law and contract law, to identify and assess issues in the context of the industry, along with the needs of the client and prospects of success, applying knowledge of the law to arrive at strategies that will achieve an optimum outcome for the client. To become a legal practitioner, prospective lawyers will have to undertake substantial education and training and, in order for career progression, it is typically necessary to accumulate significant practical experience and demonstrate success. While the role of a professional adviser is to advise, clients are under no obligation to take this advice and it is not a foregone conclusion that they will. Indeed, the practice of music law can be frustrated by a range of factors including human nature and behavioural traits people may exhibit, such as manifestations of ego and greed, the transient nature of the music industries due to their susceptibility to external factors, the complexities of ownership and copyright and furthermore the transnational nature of the music industries and the many differences in jurisprudence from territory to territory. Consequently, many things can, and do, go wrong; however, when business is conducted ethically and rigorously (which cannot be taken for granted in any business where significant sums of money are involved), sustainable careers and enduring art can result. Conversely, a misunderstanding, one overlooked word on a contract that can change its meaning and an ill-considered pen stroke or e-signature can have significant and unfortunate consequences. In the event of an error being made, there is a doctrine of rectification that can in certain circumstances allow for correction, but failure to understand the implications of a contract and its potentially long-term effect on an artist's career can lead to artists entering into agreements which they later come to regret. It is a key role of a music lawyer to ensure that what is in the contract correctly conveys the client's instructions and that the client understands what they are signing up to. While manifest mistakes can often be rectified through the courts if necessary, ill-judged signings are much harder to untangle.

The influence of external factors on music law

The music industry is multifaceted, traditionally comprised of three converging key sectors, the recording industry, the publishing industry and the live music industry (Rethink Music 2013). However, in the light of the recent and continuing development of new practices and their growing importance, there is an argument for 'branding-, sponsorship- and endorsement-related' activities to be acknowledged in their own right along with the three core elements of the traditional music industries. Each of these industries is susceptible to factors beyond its control, in particular political, economic, sociocultural and technological change. The trends within the music industries over the last twenty years clearly demonstrate this, as do the industries' responses. Global recording industry revenues declined from $24.4 billion in 2001 to $14.2 billion in 2014, largely as a consequence of progressive digitisation and technologically enabled 'free' music consumption. This was a major challenge to the future survival of the recording industry; however, the industry embraced that challenge and returned to a growth of $21.5 billion in 2019 (Watson 2020), largely due to the monetisation of the streaming of music. Study of these macro-environmental factors and their impact on business provides a framework for analysis and reflection, which was explored in the 1967 publication by Francis Aguilar 'Scanning the Business Environment'. The acronym for the 'P.E.S.T.' (Political, Economic, Social and Technological) analysis, originally 'E.T.P.S' (Economic, Technical, Political and Social Influences) (Frue 2017) subsequently became subject to further additions and expanded to P.E.S.T.L.E. to incorporate legal and environmental factors, thus suggesting that law is something that sits beyond the control of most businesses or at least that it is a framework that must be given due consideration. The issue of the effect of live concerts on the environment is considered by Teresa Moore in Chapter 11. The UK Government Select Committee of the DCMS is also hearing evidence on the 'Future of UK Music Festivals' where stakeholders have been making a case for government interventions in support of the live industry including its many freelancers, as a consequence of factors such as the UK leaving the EU and the effects of prolonged periods of lockdown. These factors profoundly impact on the mode and manner of music creation, how it is disseminated/ distributed and how it is consumed, and thus music business must adapt to the changing circumstances to ensure its practices are relevant. With the law being so integral to the music industry's functionality, it is also necessary for the legal framework to keep pace, but law itself is also subject to influence from political, economic, sociocultural and technological forces. With both the music industry and law being prone to these forces, this creates an intersection where regimes can on one side of the scale be dynamic, or on the other side, rigid. The fundamental premise of how law works is that it is typically oriented towards being reactive rather than proactive. However, it does raise the question: is it possible for the law to anticipate, and be ready for, change? This is dependent on many factors including the sources of law that impact on the music industry on a transnational basis. These include major pieces of legislation and policies governed by lawmakers such as UK's Copyright, Designs and Patents Act 1988 and its subsequent amendments, international treaties such as the Berne Convention for the Protection of Literary and Artistic Works or the WIPO Copyright and Performances and Phonograms Treaties Implementation Act, et al – thus there are numerous regimes and dynamics within the legal sphere.

Sometimes law already has a solution. It may exist for a different purpose but have the potential to be used in new and different ways, an example being the 'acoustic trademark', a subject examined by Katarzyna Krupa-Lipińska in Chapter 7.

Case law, which is the product of court judgements, is by nature typically reactive as it will relate to something that has already happened, although, particularly in complex and protracted cases, judges have the scope to make forward-thinking judgements, bearing in mind that case law provides a legal premise to inform future judgements.

Contracts (a form of private law) can also be used to affect change by establishing agreement between two or more parties but are, however, subject to the regimes of contract law which can vary from jurisdiction to jurisdiction. The recording, publishing, live industries and 'branding, sponsorship and endorsement' activities all draw heavily on contract law, with contracts detailing the specific nature of the agreements between stakeholders, addressing matters that are complex in nature such as ownership and copyright. Contracts need to be comprehensive and comprehensible so that it is clear what the parties have agreed to. In order to do this sufficiently, contracts have typically been substantial documents. For example, an exclusive recording contract of a significant term, for a major record label, could consist of between sixty and seventy A4 pages,[2] although, this may be subject to change as, for example, in 2020 Universal Music

---

[2] In practice, non-major label deals will typically be shorter, at circa thirty to forty pages, arguably suggesting the more relaxed culture, typically associated with independent label deals. Non-exclusive deals or, for example, a licence for use on a compilation, are likely to have a contract of no more than ten pages, reflecting the fact that they do not have clauses addressing exclusivity, and there may be fewer secondary income provisions and less complicated royalty provisions. In the instance of 'one-off' digital distribution licences with, for example, a company such as AWAL, the documents are often made available as essentially a non-negotiable document with a digital signature process, to facilitate a quick turnaround and uniformity in deals done for administrative purposes.

Group announced to lawyers their intention to review practice with regard to long-form contracts, proposing modifications to practice in 2021. In practice, as means of exploitation change, so do the deals and the contracts evolve to reflect these changes. Consequently, clauses are introduced to cover new provisions and definitions, as was the case at the time of the adoption of the three hundred and sixty degree deals circa 2010, when secondary income provisions had to be accommodated. Whenever a high-profile music case or a new law is introduced, contracts will often be modified to take such developments into account, for example, the addition of clauses on rights reversion for non-exploitation following the well-publicised dispute between George Michael and his then record label, *Panayiotou v Sony Music Entertainment (UK) Ltd.* [1994]. As it stands, a publishing contract with a major label may be between thirty to forty pages,[3] a contract between a promoter and artist for a live show may be five to ten pages (though provision for cancellation and force majeure have received new attention in the wake of Covid-19). 'Branding, sponsorship and endorsement' deals can run to circa forty pages because they have to deal with matters such as exclusivity; scope of services; rights granted; and what happens should things go wrong. More can be read about the growing importance of branding and contractual considerations in Chapter 12 of this collection written by music lawyer Emma Harding. Clearly, the flexibility afforded by contracts and contract law holds the potential to recognise new developments and facilitate change; however, this requires all parties to be on the same page, so to speak.

Where legislation can be formed through democratic means, industries can lobby lawmakers such as parliamentarians and governments; arguably there is also potential for law to synchronise with innovation. However, crucially there has to be an understanding amidst lawmakers about the changes and innovations that are occurring, which the law should take into account. Thus, the ability of the music industries to understand the implications of new developments and effectively communicate these to policymakers is a key factor in the law's ability to meet the needs of the industry. That said, as previously mentioned, the music industry is comprised of a number of different perspectives and what is in the interest of one stakeholder may not be in the interest of another. Lobbying will often draw on the expertise of the public relations industry, which can

---

[3] In practice, the major record labels on both recording deals and publishing are typically investing and hence risking more, and are therefore likely to be more detailed in setting out agreed terms. Independents will tend to be investing less but also to some extent relying on the relationship with their artists and writers to sort things out if a problem arises.

sit in between industry and the policymakers; thus it is advantageous to have money and it is the more powerful that tend to have access to such resources. Furthermore, the agendas of the policymakers can impact on the prospects for change and these can vary from territory to territory. Hence in cases where the music industries make greater contributions to the economy, such as, for example, the UK with an estimated £5.2 billion contribution in 2018 (UK Music), they may be prioritised, whereas in territories where the contributions to the GDP[4] are less significant, the music industries may not have the same extent of lobbying power or have the same level of importance placed on their requirements.

A further complication is that the law that shapes the music industry is not exclusive to the music industry. It can also be influenced by other arguably more powerful agents. To illustrate, the music industries share intellectual property law with many other industries including tech giants such as Microsoft, Apple and Google, and consequently it also has to effectively deal with technology-oriented considerations such as databases, algorithms, and so on. It was reported that Warner Music Group in June 2020 had a market capitalisation value of circa $15.36 billion after a significant lift due to a successful flotation (Ingham 2020), whereas Forbes reported that in January of the same year Google's parent company Alphabet had exceeded its market value of one trillion dollars (Klebnikov 2020). Clearly, there is a significant difference in the value of these two organisations and thus the scale of the business and potential influence may vary. Hence it is feasible that changes to music law could be brought about by the lobbying influence of richer industries and as a consequence hold the potential to impact negatively on the music industries. Conversely, if a tech giant were to absorb a key music institution, that could, indeed, impact favourably on law for the music industry should strategic agendas align. How realistic is such a prospect? It is worth noting at the time of writing that Chinese tech giant Tencent, owner of circa 9 per cent of Spotify, was also seeking to exercise an option (via a consortium) to lift its existing stakeholding in Universal Music Group, from 10 to 20 per cent (Sweney 2020).

We should also acknowledge that as well as impacting on music business and law, the political, economic, sociocultural and technological environments have an influence on creativity and consumption, thus impacting on how music is presented, how it sounds, what it says or has said, and its role in everyday

---

[4] Gross Domestic Product is the total value of services and goods produced by a country in one year.

life. Cultural and political discourse has often served as a muse for musicians, for example, in the 1970s inspiring John Lennon's 'Give Peace a Chance', which sought to bring about cultural and political change. In the 1980s the 'Red Wedge' collective's activities were influential in bringing about a change in young people's political views. Artists associated with the movement, such as Heaven 17, produced topical songs including 'Crushed by the Wheels of Industry'. It is important to recognise the challenges law has to deal with as a consequence of music being a cultural product; as Jacques Attali observes, music 'runs in parallel to human society and changes when it does' (Attali 2014: 4). It is important to recognise the potential for conflict and complement and how interconnected all of these elements can be.

Ownership and copyright

A key factor intrinsic to the nature of music which presents challenges within the area of music law is the notion that music composition stems from ideas. It is spiritual, malleable and increasingly collaborative in nature. Music is not conducive to simplicity when it comes to the matter of ownership, a situation further complicated because of the nature of its exploitation. It is easily reproduced and can have many creators. As music creation and consumption, and associated technologies, have evolved, so have methods of consumption, exploitation, and associated practices. A significant challenge to the recorded music industry has always been that of 'piracy' and even more so after music was digitised and liberated from physical formats, requiring the music industry to find ways of protecting its intellectual property assets, a subject area explored by James Brandes in Chapter 5 of this collection. Furthermore, the democratisation of technologies for making music and the means to disseminate materials have given rise to more active modes of consumption or fans 'consuming by doing'. Understandably, consumers are often oblivious to matters such as copyright infringement and consequently modify and publish materials derived from the intellectual property of others. Whether fan-uploaded content is a positive or negative development is examined by Paul Oliver and Stefan Lalchev in Chapter 4.

Before technological advances enabled the capture and reproduction of music via mechanical devices and sound recordings, the prospects for exploiting music were relatively few. Composers and musicians would rely largely on commissions and performances for wealthy individuals. The printing press ushered in the age of mechanical reproduction enabling an additional opportunity to produce and sell sheet music, something notably Beethoven and other composers of his and subsequent eras were able to benefit from. Up to the 1920s, the sole owner of the music was the composer and the rights of the performers of music weren't recognised (Schiffer 2009: 78).

When phonographs started to be mass produced, the composers of popular songs began signing contracts with performers to record them, a practice also adopted by the budding record companies. Rivalry between the live and recording industries ensued. Initially, the composers would sell their work to as many performers as possible, as it served to increase their income, and boost the sale of sheet music. At this time, it was commonplace for the recording industry to release several different versions of the same song, caring little about the revenue of their own artists (Cooper 2009). The same song would have a number of different versions, for example, a piano recital or a rendition played by a band. In due course, however, the recording companies discovered the commercial potential of investing in and promoting a specific artist's performance of specific works. Thus, the concept of an *original* as opposed to the *cover version* became a key notion in the discourse of popular music. Original music was not only that composed by X or Y, but also that performed by Z. Consequently, performer's involvement and rights needed to be recognised in addition to the work of a composer – as was the case with the master rights associated with the sound recordings and other mechanical playback methods such as player pianos. This resulted in the creation of additional copyright dimensions and arguably dilution of the ownership of popular music. Music no longer belonged exclusively to the composer, but also to the record company, and the performers on the recordings.[5]

Inevitably, the more stakeholders that are involved with a specific piece of music, the more scope there is for dispute: between both the people engaged in the creative process and those facilitating the production and distribution of this music. Such disputes often cannot be solved by the artists themselves. They need a specific legal framework and lawyers to establish who has the rights to the musical work: its copyright. The more complex music is, and the more the intermediaries that exist between its producers and consumers, the more

---

[5] It is worth noting for temporal context that the Performing Rights Society (PRS) was formed in 1914 to cover the UK EIRE and the British Empire, and the MCPS the Mechanical Copyright Protection Service in the UK was formed in 1924 by a merger between Mecolico and the Copyright Protection Society (CPS)

the need for the intervention of lawyers to help make sense of how ownership of music should be divided and what to do in case the rules are not followed. From this perspective, the advent of electronic music and the introduction of digital technologies are of particular importance, presenting further challenges of how to protect the rights of musicians whose work is sampled or used in mashups, subjects further explored by Justin Morey in Chapter 2 and Alan Hui in Chapter 3, later in this collection.

Cultural shifts can also be seen influencing matters of ownership. Returning to John Lennon, for more than forty years after its release, 'Imagine' had solely been credited to John Lennon. In an interview in 1980, Lennon acknowledged that it 'should be credited as a Lennon–Ono song'. 'A lot of it – the lyric and the concept – came from Yoko', (Lennon quoted by Savage 2017). This matter was revisited in 2017, when the National Music Publishers Association sought to remedy this, by recognising Ono as co-writer and changing the credit to a 'Lennon–Ono song'. As Yoko Ono was already a beneficiary that development did not significantly alter the distribution of royalties. It would, however, delay the passing of the song into the public domain thus extending the period of time it will generate income for the rightsholders which in many of the major jurisdictions, including the UK, currently runs for seventy years from the end of the year in which the death of the last surviving creator occurs. While money is clearly a very important consideration and a key motivating factor when it comes to establishing the rights and ownership of music, finance is another one of a number of value-systems. Legacy-related matters can also be contentious, as was evident when Paul McCartney sought to change songwriting credits from Lennon and McCartney to Paul McCartney and John Lennon for songs McCartney wrote, on his 2002 Live album, resulting in Ono threatening legal action (Savage 2017) and thus McCartney continuing with the established Lennon and McCartney tradition.

Further compounding issues relating to ownership of popular music, in recent times we have been seeing a significant increase in the number of composers per track, described by Dorian Lynskey as 'Hyperinflation' in songwriting credits. In his article published in GQ magazine, he compares the craft of traditional songwriters of the seventies, eighties and nineties, in particular Billy Joel who, without the involvement of collaborators, quickly wrote the key elements of the hit record 'New York State of Mind' (1976) to 'Sicko Mode' (2018) by Travis Scott feat Drake 'which credits no fewer than 30 writers' (Lynskey 2019). Lynskey continued to write, 'Rather than risk the time, cost and reputational damage of a trial, potential defendants take the pragmatic route of offering a share of songwriting in advance', offering an explanation that the increasing number of credited songwriters may be serving as a means to mitigate the risk of prospective claims of plagiarism – a notion also reinforced by a Music Week article stating 'credits for samples and adding writers to avoid plagiarism claims all continue to proliferate' (Music Week 2019). The number of writers credited as working on the top 100 records in recent times has continued to grow from 4.03 in 2016, increasing to 4.84 in 2017 and again to 5.34 in 2018 (Music Week 2019).

Copyright infringement is an inherent risk for any songwriter, inadvertent or otherwise. The old industry adage of 'Where there's a hit, there's a writ' may seem like hyperbole; however, as previously mentioned, music is a cultural product in the sense that all of the music that is being written and released today will in some way be informed by the experience of its creator or composer and music they have previously listened to or heard and thus, by its very nature is derivative.

There have been many instances of successful copyright infringement actions such as *Bright Tunes Music Corp. v Harrisongs Music, Ltd.* (relating to the Chiffon's 'She's So Fine' and George Harrison's 'My Sweet Lord'), as well as many unsuccessful actions as in the case of *Campbell v Acuff-Rose Music*, Inc. (relating to Roy Orbison's 'Pretty Woman' and the 2 Live Crew parody), and many out-of-court settlements as in the dispute between Queen, David Bowie and Vanilla Ice. Forensic musicologist Joe Bennett, in Michael Hann's article, alludes to the nature of pop music and the potential for approaches to its creation to be derivative:

> popular song is a constrained art form, with a palette of statistically predictable phrase lengths, song forms, scale and chord choices, lyric tropes and song durations. These norms are largely defined by market forces, through massed listener preferences over time affecting the kind of creative decisions that songwriters are likely to make. (Bennett quoted by Hann 2020)

It is, however, important to recognise that it is very difficult for music creators to escape these forces. When it comes to litigation, it falls on the law to determine where the boundaries of influence, homage and infringement lie, based on the facts of each case and the applicable laws, which can vary from territory to territory. That said, it is not a foregone conclusion that established arguments will hold fast as was evident in the 'Blurred Lines' case *Marvin Gaye Estate v Robin Thicke and Pharrell Williams*, a US case which for the first time found that the 'feel' of a record was something that could be copyrighted. The concept of music as a cultural product and its derivative nature, with particular focus on modes of expression associated with Afrodiaspora, are themes explored further by Lesley Model in Chapter 8, as is the notion that intellectual property law of itself does not take into account all aspects of the creative processes associated with musical composition. The 'Blurred Lines' case has become a veritable Pandora's Box and raises many questions. It seemed to undermine music-making traditions typical within genres. There is a school of thought that the outcome of this case would have been different had it been heard outside the United States with a different jurisprudence influencing the outcome, thus illustrating the potential for transnational discrepancies. At the same time, however, given the global nature of the music business, a case decided in another jurisdiction may well, sublimely at least, have an effect on the creative process in another jurisdiction.

The challenges that legal practitioners have to overcome, posed by different jurisprudences in different territories are, indeed, of great significance. To illustrate, there are numerous notable instances where practice in the United States is different than in other territories: one example of such practice is the 'Compulsory License', which is examined by Ralph Peer in Chapter 9.

When looking at how music law litigates and deals with matters when disputes arise, particularly transnational disputes, possible solutions include mediation and arbitration, a topic explored by Metka Potočnik in Chapter 6.

Clearly, it is not possible to examine the issues presented by different jurisprudences in different territories to any greater extent in this collection; however, we would like to profile this subject as an area for further research, moving forward.

Stakeholders: Friends or enemies

In recent times, the democratisation of the tools to create, release and promote music have enabled music makers to take greater control of the business of music, though arguably music law has yet to become as accessible. There are a growing number of music makers who are demonstrating significant prowess at business including seasoned artists such as Peter Hook and contemporary artists such as Stormzy. This is further evidenced by the rapid growth in the number of artists who are bypassing the traditional record labels and seeking to retain control of the distribution process, explored in more detail in Harrison's section, which follows. However, historically and still to a significant degree, the roles of music maker and music business can be quite separate and thus result in diametrically opposing perspectives, each with a different mindset and a distinctly different end goal. Music creators produce music, arguably with a view to making the best music possible. Music business serves as the interface between creator and consumer, coordinating these activities with the fundamental aim of commercial gain.[6] There is an argument that approaches to creating a 'hit' record and making a 'great' record are different, as one prioritises commercial success over an artistic agenda and the other vice versa, respectively. It should be acknowledged that without profiting from the music creator's artistic endeavours, the commercial sustainability of either role is compromised. Clearly, it would be wrong to suggest that all music creators are only interested in making music for its own sake as it is not uncommon for music makers to seek fame and fortune, too. Furthermore, it is not uncommon for artists to pursue action to secure more favourable terms or to address financial discrepancies, as was the case with the Dixie Chicks[7] in 2001. According to the Los Angeles Times, the dispute began after the Dixie Chicks commissioned an audit of the accounts pertaining to their activities, at which point:

> the trio sent a letter notifying the corporation that the act would no longer record for Sony. Sony responded weeks later by suing them, alleging it was owed damages for five undelivered albums, the value of which the company estimated at more than $100 million. A month later, the music group countersued, accusing Sony of engaging in 'systematic thievery' to 'swindle' recording artists out of royalty earnings. (Philips 2002)

The suit alleged 'breach of their recording agreement, fraud, breach of fiduciary duty and violation of the federal Racketeer Influenced and Corrupt Organization Act' (Dansby 2001), claiming that Sony Music Entertainment had withheld $4.1 million in royalties. The dispute between the Dixie Chicks and Sony raised issues relating to both ethical and technical matters despite the basis for the relationship being fairly typical, in so much as both parties had at the onset entered into a legally binding agreement requiring mutual consent. However, the Los Angeles Times reported that

> The performers' suit called into question the 'unconscionable" terms that young artists are required to accept when signing a standard industry recording

---

[6] The extent to which this is prioritised can vary depending on the status and culture of the organisation.
[7] In 2020 the Dixie Chicks became the 'Chicks'.

contract. Like most entry-level artists, the trio had no bargaining power when its first contract was drafted, the suit said, allowing Sony to treat its standard offer as nonnegotiable. (Philips 2002)

Despite these disputes, the matters were concluded with the Dixie Chicks appearing to have reconciled differences with Sony and entering into a new deal reported to have more favourable royalty rates for the former.

While the Dixie Chicks dispute related largely to the 'business of music', the potential for tensions and conflict between the artistic agenda and the business agenda are also difficult to dispute – an example being the case of English folk singer-songwriter Lucy Rose, who felt she had to compromise her artistic vision when writing her second album, due to pressure to write 'more upbeat and radio-friendly songs' (Peirson-Hagger, 2020). That said, it is possible to find a middle ground, but these relationships require careful management if they are to work, even in the short term. Music companies often make significant investments in an artist, and it is surely not unreasonable that they have a fair chance of recouping on their investment. The chances of doing that are less if the artist insists on recording something which is not commercial. The recording contract seeks to protect the record label's investment. The artists are often quite willing to accept such restrictions at the outset, only to find them constricting as they progress through their career. And, of course, record labels are not always right about what is commercial. Harrison tells a story of how an artist's managers had to fight hard for the record label to release a track as a single that the managers (and artist) believed would have huge commercial success. The record label did not see it (or perhaps I should say 'hear it') and resisted its release. Thankfully for the artist, the managers prevailed and the track in question went on to sell many millions of copies. The ideal situation is where all parties are working to a common goal; hence, as well as arrangements making sense for all parties, clear communication and management of expectations are also conducive to harmonious and lasting relationships. Another key, and long-established music business role, is that of the Artist Manager: a relationship with the potential to be both conflicting and complementary. We do not have to look very hard to find examples of this relationship becoming contentious or manifesting in disputes. The management relationships of high-profile artists such as the Killers and Britney Spears were both reported to be the subject of legal disputes (Lindvalle 2009). Conversely, there are clearly a significant proportion of artist/manager relationships that are remarkably successful and stand the test of time.

Jules O'Riordan and Les Gillon examine, in Chapter 13, the artist–manager relationship and its evolution, in more detail.

While the case of the Dixie Chicks was pertinent to the circumstances of 2001, at a time when the medium for music was still the physical product (primarily CDs), much has changed since then and whereas the consumption model was oriented towards buying and ownership of music, streaming and subscription to streaming services have become the most common means of consuming recorded music today. Richard Osborne, in the opening chapter of this collection, traces key developments in the dissemination and consumption of music, exploring some of the ways in which technological changes have been well served by the law as well as some where tensions and lacunae still exist.

At the time of writing, the Department for Digital Culture, Media and Sport (DCMS) in the UK was pursuing an inquiry into the impact of Digital Service Providers (DSPs)[8] on the music industry. This area is another key battleground with music makers seeking to address concerns relating to fair payment and the response of the DSPs being seen as not going far enough. We can clearly see some of the key music industry perspectives at play here, namely music makers, record labels and streaming services in conflict, with policymakers presiding over the issue. In this case, the pressure for a review came out of a collaboration between trade associations (the Musicians' Union and The Ivors Academy), together with members of the music-making community who gave evidence at the hearings in late 2020, including Tom Gray of Gomez, Nadine Shah, Guy Garvey of Elbow and Ed O'Brien of Radiohead, who lobbied policymakers with the '#FixStreaming' campaign (Paine 2020). While royalties received by musicmakers from streaming was already a contentious matter, this became particularly prominent when Covid-19 decimated the live music industries, thus bringing into more urgent focus concerns that musicmakers were not being fairly rewarded from streaming activities. While in the UK performance royalty payments had been healthy when the campaign began, due to the retrospective nature of payment cycles administrated by the UK royalty collections services such as PRS and PPL, there were fears that publishing revenues, due to the absence of the social consumption of music in live venues during the pandemic, would lead to a worsening picture and further constriction of income for musicmakers. As of the date hereof that has not proved to be the case, with distributions to members having held up well thus far. However, it is thought

---

[8] A term that incorporates music-streaming services such as Spotify and Apple Music.

that the impact of no live performances will start to be felt from the end of the first quarter of 2021. To some extent greater radio and online streaming of music has offset some of these losses but it is yet to be established to what degree the anticipated shortfall has been mitigated. The timeline between the start of the campaign in May 2020 and the start of the committee in November 2020 gives an indication of the time frame involved in this case. However, as previously mentioned many factors can have an influence on both time frame and outcome. Paine alludes to the complexities and challenges for presiding non-music experts, in her article for Music Week, reporting one MP saying, 'I'm trying to understand, and following along, it's complex' (Paine 2020), thus raising another potential problem, namely the suitability of the arbiters. Undoubtedly, the skill and knowledge of the legal practitioners involved with this case will play an important role in the resolution of these matters. In the case of the DCMS review of streaming we can clearly see conflicting agendas of stakeholders and the law in action, as it seeks to adapt to facilitate a fair and sustainable music industry. With so many moving parts and complexities, some of which are unravelled in this introduction, and others in the chapters of this collection, resolving such matters are far from straightforward.

While music law applies to all music, its creation, dissemination and consumption, for law makers, or legal practitioners to become actively involved, typically this will occur when it is considered that the financial prospects warrant such activity. In the next part of this introduction, we offer a concluding overview of the developing commercial music industry picture, through the eyes of a legal practitioner working at the cutting edge of music law and practice, Ann Harrison.

The perspective of the legal practitioner Ann Harrison

As outlined earlier, there are many factors at play when considering the general topic of music law and its constituent parts. A key element of this is the law in practice and what follows is a personal view from the perspective of a legal practitioner.

Harrison qualified as a lawyer in 1982. At that time and for decades afterwards there was no specific training for a music lawyer in the UK. Her work for music business clients and ultimately her career as a music lawyer came about by happy accident and on-the-job training.

In the late 1990s a planned career as a music lawyer began to be possible, around the time that record labels and music publishers began to re-evaluate their intellectual property assets and started to deal with them like any other property, including mortgaging or securitising them in the commercial marketplace. When the finance world took an interest, so too did the commercial lawyers.

The involvement of non-music players in the business of music took a leap forward with the digitising of the product. Suddenly the tech people were on board. Initially they were clearly often bewildered by the hugely complex range of rights and the number of different bodies involved in organising and exploiting those rights. Their extreme scepticism as to how they could even begin to function efficiently led lawyers to look more closely at what they were doing, and the professionalisation of the industry began to take hold in the early 2000s.

At the same time there were great changes being introduced in tertiary education in the UK under a Labour Party that seemed to see getting a degree as being every child's right. Music courses teaching both performance and business sprang up. Legal education also adapted to fill the need and offered options and learning outcomes geared to those who wanted to make a career in music business and law.

The tech world was also responsible for the introduction of a degree of democratisation in the way music was to be consumed, taking up the reins from the proliferation of independent labels that had sprung up in the 1980s and 1990s. The reduction in the number of major record labels through mergers and acquisitions meant that fewer major league signings were taking place, and the global financial crisis of 2008 exacerbated the problem of how to get your music heard. The combination of better-educated and clued-up artists, and a more affordable route to the market in the form of online distribution, coupled with easily accessible marketing outlets in the form of social networks meant that being your own record label came within the reach of almost every artist. To be clear this was not to the exclusion of the old guard. Traditional major and independent record labels still had their place and may always do so, but these DIY alternatives now sat alongside them: perhaps as the first step on the ladder to a bigger deal or as a step sideways when being signed to a major label or publisher began to pall.

New business models sprang up to service these new outlets with label service companies supplying online distribution and project management. Feeding into this were new technological developments intended to help ease the process of collection and distribution of revenues such as blockchain, which is examined in more detail in Chapter 10 by Charlotte O'Mara.

It was but a small step from there to companies seeking to be not only a record label but also a music publisher or vice versa. They were tapping into the desire for one-stop licensing being demanded by the internet platforms. Label services and DIY releases represent the biggest change affecting the work of a lawyer in the last five years, following rapidly on the heels of digital distribution and dissemination through technical advances.

After being in the throes of despair during the period of rampant music piracy, file-sharing and illegal downloading which threatened to finish off the music business, along came streaming. Industry representatives undoubtedly made missteps at the beginning, either alienating new streaming services through over-aggressive litigation or selling the goods too cheaply. But now, the music business is firmly in the sight-lines of major corporations and investors from outside the music business who have cottoned on to the 'long tail' of the internet (Anderson 2004) and to an asset in intellectual property that has a seventy-years-plus lifespan, with little or no manufacturing, warehousing or physical distribution costs to get in the way of profits.

Enter the venture capitalists (VCs), the latest in a long run of outsiders who have taken an interest in this corner of the commercial world. And music really must be a good bet for investors if these VCs are prepared to ramp up the multiples of earnings that they are willing to pay for these copyrights by two or three times what music industry veterans are willing to pay for those same assets. It has felt at times a little like a new gold rush out there.

And then came 2020 and a global pandemic. The recording music and publishing arms of the industry have held up well so far in the most challenging trading period ever. However, the lack of live performance income, which has not been fully offset by the increased online consumption of music during the various lockdowns, will undoubtedly start to be felt from the first half of 2021 onwards. If live events can restart on some scale in 2021, the industry will weather this too, but at the time of writing in late 2020 it is still very uncertain as to when acts will start touring although there are encouraging signs with big ticket names announcing multi-country and multi-date tours from June 2021. Government support may need to be provided to ensure that certain key events like 'Glastonbury' can begin the lengthy preparations needed to run a festival in mid-2021.

The ability of the music business and of creative people to reinvent themselves in response to challenges is well documented. We have seen off many threats over the last fifty years from radio (a threat to the live industry and record sales); video games (fears that players would not want to buy music); piracy (both physical and online – still a major threat) and global economic collapses. But adaptation usually takes time to get all the pieces in place to monetise, collect and police. Covid-19 meant that the live industry had to pivot on its axis overnight and adapt quickly like never before. For about two to three months from March 2020 the live side of the music business just shut down. Tens of thousands of jobs vanished, and a significant number of self-employed freelancers saw their livelihoods disappear. But then we began to see some interesting things. First came a clearer realisation of the damage our lifestyles had been doing to our environment: the beauty of our world becoming obvious only when everything else stopped. The principles behind greener festivals suddenly made much more sense to many more people. These and other issues are addressed in Teresa Moore's Chapter 11. Then came survival and the need to both make money and satisfy the urge for public performance and enjoyment of the live performance. Music lawyers and deal makers such as managers and agents had to learn quickly how to apply the existing legal framework to new platforms like Instagram Live, Mixcloud, Tik Tok, Driift and a myriad of other platform deals to stream live or 'as live' concerts. Podcasts came into their own and performers played from their living rooms for tips. Some lawyers did pro bono work to keep their clients afloat while still protecting their rights.

And alongside these new methods of performance came new means of filling the huge financial gap left when a performer could not tour or sell tour merchandise. This fortunately coincided with brands looking to shift their focus when no one was out socialising or going to the gym. Branding and sponsorship deals had begun to be a lucrative source of additional income for higher profile artists some years prior to this but now the deals multiplied, and the numbers involved were often very large. Most times the artists did not need to leave their hometowns or even their homes. Deals for bloggers and vloggers and other online influencers were also a growth area for music business law firms. The merchandise being promoted may have been that of a third party but the artist as brand was still benefiting as was the small army of support personnel who made these deals work.

Albums were recorded and released during periods of intense lockdown. More artists learnt to appreciate what it took to get a record to the marketplace, and some may well begin to embrace the whole DIY ethos. If they do, then they will need good business partners. Some have begun to re-evaluate the role of one of their closest advisers, their manager, and we are starting to see the relationship of manager/client evolving in some cases into one of more equal partnerships in a joint venture.

So far, the legal infrastructures we have in place have proved elastic enough to adequately cover the bundle of rights and these new means of exploitation. Of course, at the end of December 2020 the UK entered into a new trade agreement with the EU marking the end of the country's transition period after leaving membership of the EU. There is undoubtedly likely to be more red tape involved in doing business with the EU in future, but the legal changes may not be as great as some feared, and we are encouraged by the commentators at the UK's Intellectual Property Office who see copyright as bigger than the EU. It is a global issue governed by international treaties. We may find some areas which do not work quite as well or as smoothly as before, but in the short term at least it should be largely business as usual in the areas of recording and publishing. Live music will still face significant challenges in moving individuals and their equipment across EU countries. A return to the carnet and individual VAT registrations for each country visited looks to be a likely prospect.

The topic covered by this book is so large that it is impossible to deal with everything in one volume. The changing role of collective rights management organisations and monetisation of the 'neighbouring right' of performers are two areas that are not dealt with in great detail, but overall we believe that the contributors have addressed the key issues and given us much to think about.

Ann Harrison
December 2020.

References

Anderson, C. (2004). 'The Long Tail', *Wired*, 10 January 2004, https://www.wired.com/2004/10/tail/, accessed 8 January 2021.

Attali, J. (2014[1977]). *Noise: The Political Economy of Music*, trans. Brian Massumi, Minneapolis: University of Minnesota Press.

Cooper, B. L. (2009). 'Charting Cultural Change, 1953–1957: Song Assimilation Through Cover Producing', in George Plasketes (ed.), *Play It Again: Cover Songs in Popular Music*, 43–76. Farnham: Ashgate.

Dansby, A. (2001). 'Dixie Chicks Sue Sony', *Rolling Stone*, 28 August 2001, https://www.rollingstone.com/music/music-news/dixie-chicks-sue-sony-236628/, accessed 29 Nov 2020.

Frue, K. (2017). 'Who Invented PEST Analysis and Why It Mattered', *Pestanalysis.com*, 8 May 2017, https://pestleanalysis.com/who-invented-pest-analysis/, accessed 31 January 2020.

Hann, M. (2020). 'A Hit, a Writ: Why Music Is the Food of Plagiarism Law Suits', *The Guardian*, 26 March 2020, https://www.theguardian.com/law/2020/mar/26/a-hit-a-writ-why-music-is-the-food-of-plagiarism-lawsuits, accessed 31 December 2020.

Ingham, T. (2020). 'Warner Music Group Started Today with a $12.8bn Valuation. It's Now Worth $2.6bn More', *Music Business Worldwide*, 3 June 2020, https://www.musicbusinessworldwide.com/warner-music-group-started-today-with-a-12-8bn-valuation-its-now-worth-over-2bn-more/, accessed 4 December 2020.

Klebnikov, S. (2020). 'Google Parent Alphabet Passes $1 Trillion in Market Value', *Forbes*, 13 January 2020, https://www.forbes.com/sites/sergeiklebnikov/2020/01/13/google-parent-alphabet-set-to-hit-1-trillion-in-market-value/, accessed 4 December 2020.

Lindvalle, H. (2009). 'Behind the Music: When Artists and Managers Fall Out', *The Guardian*, 19 March 2009, https://www.theguardian.com/music/musicblog/2009/mar/19/artist-manager-relationship, accessed 2 January 2020.

Lynskey, D. (2019). 'How Many People Does It Take to Write a Hit Song in 2019', *GQ*, 2 November 2019, https://www.gq-magazine.co.uk/culture/article/long-songwriting-credits, accessed 2 November 2020.

Manderson, D. (2014). 'Towards Law and Music: Sara Ramshaw, Justice as Improvisation: The Law of the Extempore' (Oxford: Routledge, 2013), *Law and Critique*, 25: 311–17.

Mazierska, E. and Rigg, T. (2018). The Adaptive Musician in Mazierska, E. Gillon, L. and Rigg, T. (eds), *Popular Music in the Post-digital Age: Politics, Economy, Culture and Technology*, 152. New York: Bloomsbury.

Paine, A. (2020). 'MPs' Inquiry into DSPs: Can Artists Shift the Economics of Streaming?' *Music Week*, 24 November 2020, https://www.musicweek.com/digital/read/mps-inquiry-into-dsps-can-artists-shift-the-economics-of-streaming/082018, accessed 4 December 2020.

Music Week (2019). 'Hit the Roof: Number of Writers on Biggest Hits Soars Again – but Is Ceiling in Sight?', *Music Week*, 20 May 2019, https://www.musicweek.com/publishing/read/hit-the-roof-number-of-writers-on-biggest-hits-soars-again-but-is-ceiling-in-sight/076239, accessed 31 December 2020

Peirson-Hagger, E. (2020). '"I Lost My Identity": The Artists Who Left Major Record Deals To Form Their Own Indie Labels', *Newstatesman.com*, 8 July 2020, https://www.newstatesman.com/culture/music-theatre/2020/07/i-lost-my-identity-artists-who-left-major-record-deals-form-their-own, accessed 12 November 2020.

Philips, C. (2002). 'Dixie Chicks, Sony End Feud With a New Deal', *Los Angeles Times*, 17 June 2002, https://www.latimes.com/archives/la-xpm-2002-jun-17-fi-dixie17-story.html, accessed 29 November 2020.

PRS for Music (Undated). 'History', *PRS for Music*, https://www.prsformusic.com/about-us/history#B5099316-0464-411A-B95B-9213E222363F, accessed 1 December 2020.

Ramshaw, S. (2013). *Towards Law and Music: Justice as Improvisation: The Law of the Extempore*. Oxford: Routledge.

Savage, M. (2017). 'Yoko Ono Added to Imagine Writing Credits', *BBC News*, 15 June 2017, https://www.bbc.co.uk/news/entertainment-arts-40286790, accessed 30 November 2020.

Schiffer, S. (2009). 'The Cover Song as Historiography, Marker of Ideological Transformation', in George Plasketes (ed.), *Play It Again: Cover Songs in Popular Music*, 77–98. Farnham: Ashgate.

Sweney, M. (2020). 'Chinese Tech Firm Increases Stake in Universal Music to 20%', *The Guardian*, 18 December 2020, https://www.theguardian.com/music/2020/dec/18/chinese-tech-firm-increase-stake-in-universal-music-to-20-percent-tencent, accessed 31 December 2020.

UK Music (2019). 'Music Industry Contributes £5.2 Billion to the UK Economy', 20 November 2019, https://www.ukmusic.org/news/music-industry-contributes-5-2-billion-to-uk-economy, accessed 4 December 2020.

Watson, A. (2020). 'Global Recorded Music Revenue from 1999 to 2019', *Statista*, 25 August 2020, https://www.statista.com/statistics/272305/global-revenue-of-the-music-industry/, accessed 4 December 2020.

Part One

Tensions between the rights of copyright owners and the freedom to create

1

Copyright, royalties and industrial decline

Richard Osborne

Writing in 1988, Simon Frith stated that, for the recording industry, 'the age of manufacture is now over. Companies (and company profits) are no longer organised around making *things* but depend on the creation of *rights*' (Frith 1988: 57. Emphasis in original). Record companies were able to reach this position because, as well as owning sound recordings, they were the usual owners of sound recording copyright. The 'rights' that Frith refers to are the exclusive controls that belong to a copyright owner and which address the different ways in which their work can be employed. These include the *reproduction* right (at the time Frith was writing, this right would primarily have addressed duplicative manufacture, that is, physical media such as vinyl and cassette tapes) and the *performing* rights (prior to the 1988 Copyright, Designs and Patents Act (CDPA) these rights encompassed the right to perform the work in public and the right to broadcast it; the broadcast right has subsequently been recast as the 'communication to the public' right, which in addition to covering broadcasts addresses the right of 'making available to the public'). Frith was not suggesting that record production was coming to an end; his point was that the recording industry was thinking of recordings in a different manner. Rather than focusing on them as physical products, it was conceiving them as a 'basket of rights' (Frith 1988: 57). He maintained that the job of a contemporary record company was 'to exploit as many of these rights as possible, not just those realised when it is sold in recorded form to the public, but also those realised when it is broadcast on radio or television, used on a film, commercial or video soundtrack' (Frith 1988: 57).[1]

---

[1] In UK law, this list of activities triggers only two of the exclusive rights. Although 'sync right' is regularly used as a term for the embedding of a sound recording in a film, television programme, commercial or video soundtrack, there is no such right in law. This activity falls under the reproduction right, instead. The use of recordings in television programmes and radio broadcasts additionally triggers the communication to the public right.

In many ways Frith's work was prescient. He paved the way for academics to conclude that the recording industry is a *copyright* industry' (Wikström 2009: 17. Emphasis in original). This approach has been accepted by governments. In 1994, Britain's Monopolies and Mergers Commission (later replaced with the Competition Commission) stated that copyright 'is central to the operations of the record industry' (MMC 1994: §1.4). The Congress of the United States has listed the recording industry as one of the 'core copyright industries' (CBO 2004: 3). This is also the opinion of representatives of the recording industry. In 2014, the global trade body, the International Federation of the Phonographic Industry (IFPI), declared that the principal task of record companies is to invest in copyright (2014: 4). Today, it is common practice among business analysts to refer to these companies as 'rights holders' (AIM 2019).

Yet there are also ways in which Frith's prognosis can be questioned. In the first instance, manufacture (and the associated right of reproduction) remained the recording companies' primary focus long after the period in which he was writing. In 2001, according to the IFPI's global revenue figures, physical sales were still accounting for 98 per cent of recording industry revenues (IFPI 2020: 13).[2] Moreover, it was only in 2013 that the accumulated revenues from downloading, streaming, broadcast, public performance and synchronisation overtook revenues from physical products for the first time (IFPI 2020: 13).

Secondly, now that the manufacture of physical products has finally been eclipsed, it has become apparent that Frith's dictum can be turned on its head. Downloading and streaming have been successively prosperous. Downloading achieved a 32 per cent global market share in 2014, and at one point it looked set to overtake physical sales (IFPI 2020: 13). It was superseded by on-demand streaming, which became the leading global revenue source for recorded music in 2017. By 2019, streaming was responsible for over 50 per cent of the recording industry's global revenues (IFPI 2020: 13). It should have been relatively easy for record companies to equate these means of delivering content with the

---

[2] It should be noted that the IFPI's figures are incomplete. They did not tally performing rights revenues until 2001, despite the fact that revenues for the activity were first collected in the 1930s. Similarly, they did not tally synchronisation until 2010, despite it being a feature of the recording industry since the invention of 'talking' pictures. These omissions are nevertheless indicative of the fact that it was only with the decline of manufacture in the early twenty-first century that the recording industry's global trade body began to think in terms of a basket of rights. Moreover, it should be noted that the IFPI categorises revenues by licensing or sales activity rather than by rights per se.

creation of rights. Streaming and downloading are not 'physical' and they are not formats per se. They are also multi-layered in respect of the rights involved. The terms describe complex processes that between them trigger a number of copyright controls. Yet the recording industry has not conceptualised streaming or downloading as baskets of rights. It has chosen to equate them with physical products.

This can be witnessed at a number of levels. Despite the fact that online services lend themselves to the access of individual tracks, the recording industry still retains a focus on albums, a format that makes most sense in the physical domain. The industry has in addition preserved a physical rationale for its popularity charts and its award certifications. Here the access model of streaming, paid for by subscription and advertising, is made equivalent to 'sales' (Osborne 2020a: 28–35, 2020b: 47–51). This physical orientation is also in evidence in legislative practice. The advent of downloading and streaming resulted in the creation of the 'making available' right, an exclusive control that addresses interactive services in the digital domain. This right has served two purposes: first, to ensure that all activities relating to online access are encompassed within legislation and second, to avoid plurality. It was designed so that it would sit alongside and operate in a similar manner to the reproduction right.

For the recording industry, 'manufacture' and 'copyright' have not been separate conceptions; rather, it is from the creation of physical products that the industry's legislative strength has been derived. Therefore, just as it sought to prolong the trade for physical recordings in the face of digital developments, the industry aimed to extend the copyright methodology for these products to the online domain. This is the subject of the first section of this chapter, which addresses the rationale for the development of the 'making available' right. The second section of the chapter addresses the limits of this exercise. The recording industry has not been able to ignore the fact that streaming and downloading are different in nature to the manufacture and sale of physical products. Consequently, the industry's practices have been questioned and to a certain extent transformed. The business activities of recording artists have simultaneously expanded, putting some of them in a position of greater power vis-à-vis record companies. Artists' situations are nevertheless diverse. While some are better off in this environment than they were previously (due to improved royalty rates and ownership of rights), there are plenty who complain about their situation (bemoaning royalty payments and the categorical quirks of copyright law), while others have a weary sense of déjà vu (being subject to contracts that were drafted in the age of manufacture).

Making things the same

Sound recording copyright is different from most other forms of copyright. The ownership of literary, dramatic, musical and artistic works is accorded to authors in respect of their original creative work. In contrast, the international copyright agreements for sound recordings grant ownership to the 'producer' (WIPO 1961 art. 10, 1996 art. 11). This term does not refer to studio personnel. In UK legislation, this producer is, instead, defined as 'the person by whom the arrangements necessary for the making of the sound recording are undertaken' (CDPA 1988: §9.2aa). It is the financing and organisation of the industrial, technical and artistic procedures of record creation that matter. As a result, this right has 'nearly always' belonged to record companies (Stewart and Sandison 1989: 228).

To a certain extent, the idea that record companies should have ownership has come first and the justifications for this designation have come afterwards. The World Intellectual Property Organization (WIPO) has stated that sound recordings 'are not works and their producers are not authors' (WIPO 1992: 32). Their 'purpose' has been 'to have the producer of the sound recording to be the person or legal entity in whom or in which the protection vests' (WIPO 1992: 39). The rationale for according ownership to record companies has nevertheless varied by territory and has changed over time. Britain's first legislation to recognise sound recordings, the 1911 Copyright Act, awarded authorship to the 'owner' of the recording. This was on the basis that 'ingenuity' could be discerned in studio and manufacturing processes (CA 1911: §19(1); Gorrell Committee 1909: 26). Conversely, there has been a refusal to recognise sound recordings as creative works, typified by the suggestion that there is 'a great measure of what is only technical and industrial in [a record's] manufacture' (Gregory Committee 1952: 86). Britain's subsequent Copyright Act of 1956 was influenced by the neighbouring rights philosophy of Continental Europe and granted ownership to the industrial 'maker' of the recording (CA 1956: §12(1)). By the time of the 1988 CDPA there were numerous record companies which created recordings but did not manufacture their discs. More pertinently for the recording industry, there were companies that manufactured discs, but did not contract musicians or develop their recordings. Hence it was expedient to have legislation that accorded ownership to the 'producer' who made the arrangements for the recording to take place. In the United States, where sound recordings are legislated for as creative works, record companies have nevertheless been able to assume ownership on economic grounds. This is due to 'work made for hire' rules, which grant copyright to employers and commissioners on the basis that they hire artists to undertake the work (Committee on the Judiciary 2000).

Michael Jones has argued that, for as long as the recording industry has a production process, musicians will be made to 'fit this production process' (Jones 2014: 55). He adds that by 'seeking "deals" the effort of musicians can be argued to be expended within the ideological boundaries of an industrial system' (Jones 2014: 55). The effects of this system are not only ideological, however. Industrial processes have also been responsible for musicians' rates of pay. It is manufacture and distribution that have constituted the greatest share of record company costs. From the late 1970s through to the end of the 1980s, the British Phonographic Industry (BPI) calculated that between 30 to 40 per cent of their dealer price revenues would be taken up by this expenditure (Scaping and Hunter 1978: 118; Scaping 1989: 50).[3] Recording artists' royalty rates for record sales were calibrated accordingly. By the late 1980s these were averaging at around seventeen and a half per cent of the dealer price, kept down to this amount because of the making of 'things' (Scaping 1989: 50).

Industrial manufacture is captured by the reproduction right. This is the area where record companies have had their greatest legislative strength, being granted an exclusive right that is oriented towards their activities. Their performing rights have traditionally been weaker. Legislators have taken into account the fact that broadcast and public performance are 'ancillary' to the main manufacturing activities of the recording industry (Gregory Committee 1952: 65). Moreover, there has been a reluctance to believe that record companies deserve significant compensation for these activities. This is because performances of recordings operate in the interest of the industry: they provide valuable publicity that helps to generate record sales. Musicians, on the other hand, have not regarded broadcast and public performance as being ancillary. This use of recordings has the potential to provide an inexpensive alternative to

---

[3] The dealer price is the amount that the record company charges the retailer to purchase the recording. It is therefore devoid of the retailer's markup and Value Added Tax.

their live appearances. Consequently, musicians have sought protection against and compensation for the broadcast and public use of recordings.

In Continental Europe it is most common that record companies will not be granted exclusive performing rights. Rather than having the power to set licensing rates or determine royalties, they are, instead, granted 'equitable remuneration' (WIPO 1961: art. 12). Handled by collective management organizations (CMOs), the revenues tend to be split equally between record companies and artists, thus offering performers a considerable improvement on the royalty rates for record sales. The UK has been unusual in that it grants exclusive performing rights to 'producers'. However, following the implementation of the Rental and Lending Rights Directive in the European Union (EU) in 1992 (EEC 1992), British record companies accepted the division of royalties suggested by equitable remuneration rules. In the United States, there were no performing rights for sound recordings until 1995, at which point they were introduced for 'digital audio transmissions' only (Digital Performance Right in Sound Recordings Act 1995: §2(6)). The American legislation encompasses online subscription and interactive services but does not cover free-to-air broadcasts, whether analogue or digital. Although the 1995 Act does not use the term 'equitable remuneration', it nevertheless stipulates that for 'non-interactive' digital broadcasts revenues will be divided evenly between companies and artists. As with European practice, the licensing rates are not negotiated in the free market. They are, instead, overseen by Copyright Royalty Judges and administered by a CMO (17 USC: §114). Moreover, in each of these territories the broadcast remuneration for recording artists stands outside of standard recording contract provisions. Most notably, it cannot be recouped in order to help pay back record company advances.

Given that manufacture has been central to the recording industry's economic, legislative and contractual power, this industry was always going to be troubled by the development of online services. In addition to having the potential to displace the sales of physical recordings, they would set in play different types of right. As early as 1993, the IFPI was flagging the threat posed by 'electronic delivery services' (Committee on the Judiciary 1994: 45). Two principal types of delivery were already being envisioned: music could be made available for download and it could also be streamed (Witt 2015: 13). While these activities entailed some form of reproduction, it was clear they triggered other exclusive rights. When it came to downloading, there was disagreement on whether it activated the communication to the public right or the distribution right.[4] In respect of streaming, it was clear that this activity represented a form of communication to the public. Thus these services combined the reproduction right, over which the record companies had control, with a performing right, which had the potential to reduce their influence and remuneration. The industry's legal response was twofold. It sought to preserve its manufacturing trade by prosecuting 'illegitimate' file-sharing services, adopting a variety of laws and methods in the process. While this activity has received much attention and has been widely criticised, the industry's other action has tended to be overlooked. It sought an exclusive control for online services that would clone its reproduction right.

Despite its attempts to thwart the development of online services, the recording industry was aware that these services might surpass physical sales. The United States' trade body, the Recording Industry Association of America (RIAA), noted in 1993 that computerised networking 'may soon become the means of making music accessible to the public, thus eroding and perhaps even one day eliminating the sale of recorded music' (Committee on the Judiciary 1994: 40). As a result, the industry fretted about the possible imposition of equitable remuneration. IFPI's Director General and Chief Executive, Nicholas Garnett, demanded that any legislation for online services should have 'more in common with provisions relating to reproduction' (Committee on the Judiciary 1994: 30). Exclusive controls would be required so that phonograph producers could 'establish price structures for the phonogram',[5] 'control the ways in which individual phonograms are released into the market', 'correct distortion of the market from unauthorised diffusion' and 'coordinate releases of phonograms between different markets around the world' (Committee on the Judiciary 1994: 36–7).

Garnett's agenda overlapped with the interests of WIPO. Since 1970, this organisation had been responsible for administrating the major international copyright treaties, including the principal agreement for sound recordings, the

---

[4] It was the United States' music industries that were most in favour of the distribution right. This was, in part, because the country did not as yet have any performing rights for sound recordings and also because the American recording industry was opposed to equitable remuneration. Conversely, European countries looked more favourably towards the 'communication to the public' right because many of them had no distribution rights (Samuelson 1997: 393–4).

[5] 'Phonogram' is a term that has been adopted in international legislation for sound recordings. It is defined in the Rome Convention as 'any exclusive aural fixation of sounds of a performance or of other sounds' (WIPO 1961: art 3(b)). The term 'phonogram' also provides the initial for the (P) symbol, which signifies the owner of sound recording copyright (WIPO 1961: art 11)

1961 Rome Convention. In November 1991, WIPO gathered delegates at Geneva for the initial meeting of a committee of experts, who would discuss the effects of 'technological developments' on copyright law (WIPO 1992: 42). In respect of digitalisation, WIPO believed that the protection provided by the Rome Convention was 'no longer high enough' (WIPO 1992: 39). They suggested that in addition to having 'the exclusive right of reproduction', phonogram producers should enjoy an exclusive 'communication to the public' right (WIPO 1992: 39).

In the summer of 1993 WIPO presented a draft for a new 'Performances and Phonograms Treaty' which contained a digital rights proposal that was 'virtually identical' to Garnett's (Committee on the Judiciary 1994: 49). Equitable remuneration would be retained for analogue broadcasting but would not apply 'in the case of digital communication to the public of phonograms' (WIPO 1993: 20). WIPO stated that this right must be exclusive, 'otherwise, the necessary control over this means of exploitation may not be guaranteed' (WIPO 1993: 15). This view received support in the United States, where the RIAA was campaigning for an exclusive 'communication to the public' right both at home and abroad (Committee on the Judiciary 1994: 10, 44, 55).[6] Other nations had different views. WIPO found that 'opinions on whether an exclusive right was warranted for digital broadcasting were divided' (WIPO 1994a). There was also debate among delegates whether such a right might combine exclusivity with equitable remuneration (WIPO 1994b: 252, 1995: 375–6).

At first there was discussion about the need to control all forms of digital transmission, thus encompassing online broadcasting as well as downloads and streams. As discussions progressed, the focus was honed to the 'on-demand, interactive digital delivery of phonograms' (WIPO 1994b: 252). In 1996 the European Commission made a proposal for a right that would make 'a clear distinction [. . .] between the traditional right of communication to the public and the interactive parts of the right' (WIPO 1999: 677). The resulting 'making available' right was enshrined in WIPO's Performances and Phonograms Treaty, which was agreed on in December of the same year. It provides phonogram producers with 'the exclusive right of authorizing the making available to the public of their phonograms, by wire or wireless means, in such a way that members of the public may access them from a place and at a time individually chosen by them' (WIPO 1996: art. 14). Countries are entitled to create a distinct 'making

---

[6] It should be noted that United States copyright law does not use the term 'communication to the public'. It, instead, embraces communication to the public and public performance under a single performance right (17 USC: §106).

available' right or they can introduce its provisions via the distribution right (which the United States has chosen for downloading) or the 'communication to the public' right (which the United States has chosen for on-demand streaming and which the EU has suggested for all interactive services).

Making a difference

In respect of online services, the IFPI achieved its legislative aims. The 'making available' right operates in tandem with and is hard to distinguish from the reproduction right. It is an exclusive right and therefore record companies have a free hand to negotiate licensing terms with service providers. This has enabled them to restrict the providers' share of revenues to a level that matches the retailers' share for physical record sales. In addition, the music publishing share has been calibrated to a level similar to that of the mechanical royalties for physical goods, albeit this sector's share is higher for streaming than for downloading.[7] There is no equitable remuneration for interactive services. As such, companies have contractual freedom to negotiate royalty rates with artists.

After an early period in which record companies provided higher royalty rates for downloads than they did for physical sales, they began to move towards equivalence as this form of service developed. There was some justification for doing this, as download sites have had much in common with, and provided a replacement for, traditional record shops. Although recordings are being 'communicated to the public', the principal action is the purchase of duplicated files. On-demand streaming is different. It has at least as much in common with radio broadcasting as it does with reproduction. In Britain, the Beggars Group reflected this position. In 2012, they were offering their artists a 50 per cent royalty rate for on-demand streaming. In their opinion, they 'couldn't justify it as a "sale"' and therefore impose rates drawn from the retail of physical recordings (Ingham 2012: 1). Similar policies were adopted by other labels at this time, including the Universal Music Group for 'some' of its artists (Ingham 2013: 2).

[7] In the UK, the publishing sector's royalty share is 8.5 per cent of the dealer price or 6.5 per cent of the retail price for physical products; 8 per cent of the gross revenues of download services (split 75:25 between the reproduction and 'making available' rights); and circa 15 per cent of the overall revenues for streaming services (split 50:50 between the reproduction and 'making available' rights). In the United States, the publishing share for physical products and downloads is the same: 9.1c in every dollar. The US Copyright Royalty Board has determined that the rate for streaming should rise from 11.4% of the revenue in 2018 to 15.1% of the revenue by 2022. This is split fairly evenly between the reproduction and performing rights.

In 2012, on-demand streaming was only worth 6.7 per cent of the recording industry's total global revenues, however (IFPI 2020: 13). Within two years the situation had changed. The revenues for streaming had doubled and it was apparent they would continue to multiply. The Beggars Group backtracked on their policy, stating that because streaming was now 'core income', it would have to 'bear its share of all our costs' and therefore physical retail rates should be applied (Smirke 2014). This policy chimed with views the RIAA had expressed in 1993. They argued that record companies could tolerate a lower share of online revenues if the services were 'ancillary to a sale', but this would not 'be sufficient' if they were to become a primary medium for recorded music (Committee on the Judiciary 1994: 50).

The record companies' position is questionable nonetheless. In the first instance, the royalty rates for physical products have been calibrated in relation to the expenses of industrial manufacture and physical distribution. These costs are absent in the online world. To counter the claim that digital royalties should reflect this, the record companies have suggested that 'in the wider scheme of things [. . .] manufacture and distribution was a small part of the budget' (Cooke 2016: 35). However, as late as 2013, it was still being calculated that these costs absorbed around a quarter of record sales' revenues (Donovan 2013). Moreover, these are not the only costs that have been reduced in the online domain. There is minimal expenditure on design and packaging, whereas for physical products 5 per cent of revenues were traditionally absorbed by this expenditure (Scaping and Hunter 1978: 118; Scaping 1989: 50). In addition, approximately 10 per cent of the dealer price for each physical record sold has been devoted to composers and publishers for their 'mechanical' royalties. When it comes to on-demand streaming, it is the service providers who bear this cost.

Another factor determining traditional royalty rates had been artists' contractual weakness and the lack of options available to them. In the physical era, the possibilities for artists to finance, distribute and gain publicity for their own recordings were circumscribed. As such, it was unlikely that they would be able to create professional sounding recordings without record company funding. They would also need to turn to a record company to initiate promotion for their work. The digital environment is more open. The recording process can be inexpensive and is relatively straightforward. Artists are able to communicate direct-to-fan and build followings online. Rather than hiring a record company for publicity or distribution, they can avail of independent services who will fulfil these tasks.

The result is that some artists have gained greater bargaining power. They are also being provided with a wider range of options. An increasing number are choosing to forgo traditional record contracts. Some are undertaking the entire recording and marketing activity themselves, merely engaging an aggregator to administer engagement with service providers. Others employ label services companies. The artist will fund the project, but the label service company will provide marketing expertise, distribute the recordings and administer the rights. In both situations the artists will own the sound recording copyright, as they are effectively making the arrangements for the recording to take place. In addition, they will be receiving a considerably higher share of the revenue generated than available through exclusive record company contracts. Some aggregators will charge a fixed commission fee only; others might charge a percentage fee, varying from 10 to 30 per cent of the artist's revenue (Voogt 2019). Rates for label services companies also vary, but in many instances an artist royalty of at least 70 per cent can be 'assumed' (MMF n.d.).

Artists signed to 'traditional' record companies are also gaining improved terms. It is more common for an artist to have initial ownership of the copyright, and to licence the rights to the recording company for a set number of years. In fact, it is claimed that 'the idea of a major [owning] a modern star's rights in perpetuity is pretty much dead' (Ingham 2018b). Royalty rates for streaming are also increasing. By 2017, artists signed to major labels were gaining on average 18 to 19 per cent royalty rates (Ingham 2018a), albeit that the UK Musicians' Union was advising recording artists that 'Anyone who signs a deal for less than 30 points on streaming needs their head examined' (Sexton 2017: 12). This figure appeared within reach by 2019, when major labels indicated that average artist royalties for streaming were now 25 per cent (Ingham 2019). There are nevertheless artists who are agreeing to streaming royalty rates that are little higher than those for physical sales. Here 'arrangements' and costs again come into play. In these instances it will be the record company that is driving the project rather than the artists themselves. In addition, the companies have argued that their expense of manufacture has been replaced with increased expense on marketing, particularly for artists who wish to escape the long tail of the Internet to become major stars.

This variety of options is most readily available to new artists, those renegotiating their terms, or those who have been released from their recording contracts. The situation for 'heritage' artists who have not renegotiated their 'legacy' contracts is different (Cooke 2016: 6). In the majority of cases the reproduction and 'making available' rights in their recordings will be owned by record companies for the life of copyright. In addition, they will commonly be in receipt of physical retail royalty rates for downloads and streams. There are nevertheless some signs of change. It was the record companies' risky investments in manufacture and recording that first entitled them to copyright, but these risks are reduced in the online world. Little investment is required to make the companies' back catalogues available from service providers. In response, recording artists with old contracts are seeking new rights. The European Council's Copyright Directive of 2019 provides a 'contract adjustment mechanism' that entitles performers to claim 'appropriate and fair remuneration [. . .] when the remuneration originally agreed turns out to be disproportionately low compared to all the subsequent relevant revenues' (EC 2019: art. 20). Due to its departure from the EU, these measures are unlikely to be implemented in the UK. Some record companies are acting on their own initiative, however. The Beggars Group has revised its contracts so that 'most heritage artists' receive a 25 per cent royalty rate for streaming (Ingham 2020b). In 2020, following the death of George Floyd and the reignition of the Black Lives Matter movement, BMG pledged to 'review all historic contracts' of black artists and address 'inequities or anomalies' (Ingham 2020c).

Another category of recording artists is campaigning on its own behalf. One of the quirks of equitable remuneration is that 'non-featured artists' (otherwise known as session musicians) often gain a share of the royalties, whereas for other areas of activity they receive fee payments only. Outside of the United States, this performing rights share is rarely established in law and has, instead, arisen from negotiations between CMOs, recording industry trade bodies and musicians' unions. In the UK, non-featured artists are entitled to 17.5 per cent of the performing rights revenues. These non-featured artists now feel doubly deprived. On the one hand, the 'making available' right is carving them out of equitable remuneration for online services. On the other hand, if on-demand streaming acts as a replacement for radio, its popularity will lead to a reduction in their broadcast royalties.

This situation has led legislators in Croatia, Lithuania and Spain to apply equitable remuneration to some of the revenues from interactive services. It has also mobilised musicians' unions in other European countries to campaign for a general change in the way that on-demand streaming is legislated. The International Federation of Musicians' (FIM) put forward a proposal that on-demand streaming should be regarded as representing a fifty/fifty split between the reproduction right and the 'making available' right, with the latter element being made subject to equitable remuneration (Trubridge 2015). This proposal has fed into the Fair Internet for Performers (FIFP) campaign. Launched in May 2015, FIFP is an alliance of performers' organisations that seeks equitable rights legislation for streaming services within EU law. Their crusade initially coincided with an EU programme to modernise copyright laws, including an investigation into the 'contentious grey area' of the making available right (European Commission 2015: 9). FIFP had limited success, however. When the EU introduced its Copyright Directive in 2019, it made no mention of the 'making available' right or of equitable remuneration. The Directive, instead, contains the 'fair remuneration' of its contract adjustment mechanism, which FIFP have suggested 'may prove useless in practice and not help those performers who are most in need' (FIFP 2017a: 2).

As can be expected, FIFP's campaign has not received the backing of record companies. Recording artists have also had differing opinions in respect of its worth. FIFP claim to speak on behalf of the '95% of performers who simply transfer all their rights to the producer for a single payment' (FIFP 2017b). They are talking of the non-featured performers, not the signed recording artists. The 5 per cent of artists who are on exclusive contracts have been slower to rally behind this cause. This is because the imposition of equitable remuneration might not be the best financial route for them. Its main benefit is that it cannot be recouped from advances; its weakness is that it may not offer the highest returns. If it were imposed upon on-demand streaming, featured artists would dilute their royalties by sharing them with session musicians. In addition, they would have to pay an administration fee to a CMO.[8] The position of the UK's Featured Artists' Coalition (FAC) has therefore been different to that of the Musicians' Union. They have argued, in alignment with record companies, that exclusive rights are 'stronger and better' than equitable remuneration (Aguilar 2018: 170).[9]

---

[8] In Britain, the performing rights CMO, Phonographic Performance Ltd., is owned by the record companies. They have elected to devote a share of revenues to anti-piracy campaigns. The fact that performing rights income is being used to combat an issue that more commonly affects the reproduction right provides further evidence of the recording industry's preoccupation with manufacture.

[9] There are signs that this position might change, however. At the time of writing (December 2020) the UK's Department for Digital, Culture, Media & Sport is conducting an inquiry into the 'Economics of Music Streaming'. Set against the background of the Covid-19 pandemic and its shutdown of revenues from live music, there has been renewed focus on the returns that artists are gaining from on-demand streaming. This has witnessed musicians of different statuses and different levels of

Conclusion

In his 1988 article, Simon Frith suggested that record companies were replacing a focus on manufacture with a focus on copyright. It is the case, however, that the recording industry's strength as a copyright industry has been derived from its strength as a manufacturing industry. The corollary of this is that, as the record companies' industrial practices have declined, there has been increased potential for recording artists to campaign for their own rights. This is leading some authorities to suggest that the age of manufacture has been replaced, not with an age of copyright, but, instead, by the 'age of the artist' (Mulligan 2020). There is a new generation of performers who 'are helping forge a reshaped industry built upon new, more-equitably balanced contracts and deal structures' (Mulligan 2020).

Mark Mulligan has stated that the 'combination of streaming, social media and artist distributors mean that artists can find global audiences without the need for a label' and that as a result they can 'either make a start for themselves or even never rely on a label's marketing muscle at all' (Mulligan 2020). François Passerard and Phillip Cartwright have also charted this transformation. Recording artists were divorced from the physical distribution process; it was record companies who, instead, acted as business-to-consumer operations. This process has been reversed. The turn to online services has meant that it is the companies who operate at a remove from audiences. Meanwhile, by creating 'interactive experiences with their fans, artists can keep fans engaged' (Passerard and Cartwright 2019). This has resulted in the companies carving out a new role. For those artists who do choose to engage them, they 'mainly serve as financial and marketing companies' (Passerard and Cartwright 2019). Rather than focusing on the needs of audiences, their orientation is 'business-to-artist' (Passerard and Cartwright 2019). Moreover, this applies to traditional record companies just as much as it does to label service providers.

Some caution should be urged, nonetheless. Although the record companies' power over recording artists has declined, the industry nevertheless retains a considerable hold over its licensees. The 'making available' right has enabled it to successfully transfer business practices that were developed for physical products to the online environment of downloads and streams. The revenues from the

income rallying together for legislative change. The first two oral evidence sessions for the inquiry have witnessed featured artists speaking in favour of equitable remuneration.

latter area, in particular, are returning the recording industry to profitable ways. In 2019, global revenues from streaming amounted to US$11.4bn (IFPI 2020: 13). By 2020, the major record companies globally were generating over US$1m from streaming every hour (Ingham 2020a).

It should also be restated that the position of recording artists is widely uneven. Some new artists and renegotiating performers have been able to negotiate strong contractual terms, but there have been few examples yet of heritage artists successfully having their contracts revised. Session musicians are feeling particularly disempowered. There has been an expansion of 'communication to the public' activity, but the 'making available' right has denied them the chance to partake of the royalties. More generally, the consensus among many recording artists appears to be that, while record companies are celebrating their streaming dividends, their own royalties remain paltry. Moreover, it should not be forgotten that those artists who are gaining ownership of their rights are doing so for their business acumen rather than for their artistic activity: sound recording copyright continues to be awarded to the 'producer'. It will be some time yet before its industrial legacy is dismantled.

References

Aguilar, A. (2018). '"We Want Artists to be Fully and Fairly Paid for their Work": Discourses on Fairness in the Neoliberal European Copyright Reform', *JIPITEC*, 9: 160–78.

Association of Independent Music (AIM) (2019). *Distribution Revolution*. London: Association of Independent Music.

Committee on the Judiciary (1994). *Performers' and Performance Rights in Sound Recordings*. Washington: US Government Printing Office.

Committee on the Judiciary (2000). *United States Copyright Office and Sound Recordings as Work Made For Hire, Hearings, One Hundred Sixth Congress, Second Session, Serial No. 145*. Washington: US Government Printing Office.

Congressional Budget Office (CBO) (2004). 'Copyright Issues in Digital Media', August, https://www.cbo.gov/publication/15911, accessed 18 July 2019.

Cooke, C. (2016). *Dissecting the Digital Dollar, Part Two: Full Report*. Headley Brothers: Music Managers Forum.

Copyright Act (CA) (1911). *Legislation.gov.uk*, https://www.legislation.gov.uk/ukpga/Geo5/1-2/46/contents/enacted, accessed 26 August 2020.

Copyright Act (CA) (1956). *Legislation.gov.uk*, https://www.legislation.gov.uk/ukpga/1956/74/contents/enacted, accessed 26 August 2020.

Copyright, Designs and Patents Act (CDPA) (1988). *Legislation.gov.uk*, http://www.legislation.gov.uk/ukpga/1988/48/contents, accessed 20 June 2020.

Copyright Law of the United States and Related Laws Contained in Title 17 of the United States Code (17 USC) (2016). *Copyright.gov*, https://www.copyright.gov/title17/, accessed 20 June 2020.

Digital Performance Right in Sound Recordings (1995). *Copyright.gov*, https://www.copyright.gov/legislation/pl104-39.html, accessed 26 August 2020.

Donovan, N. (2013). 'If CDs cost £8 Where Does the Money Go?', *BBC News*, 26 August, https://www.bbc.co.uk/news/magazine-23840744, accessed 28 April 2020.

European Economic Community (EEC) (1992). *Council Directive 92/100/EC of 19 November 1992 on Rental and Lending Right and on Certain Rights Related to Copyright in the Field of Intellectual Property*, https://eur-lex.europa.eu/legal-content/EN/ALL/?uri=CELEX%3A31992L0100, accessed 20 June 2020.

European Commission (2015). *Towards A Modern, More European Copyright Framework*. Brussels: European Commission.

European Council (EC) (2019). *Directive (EU) 2019/790 of the European Parliament and of the Council of 17 April 2019 On Copyright and Related Rights in the Digital Single Market*, https://eur-lex.europa.eu/legal-content/EN/TXT/?uri=CELEX%3A32019L0790, accessed 20 June 2020.

Fair Internet for Performers (FIFP) (2017a). 'Comments on the Proposed Directive on Copyright in the Digital Single Market', www.aepo-artist.org, accessed 20 June 2020.

Fair Internet for Performers (FIFP) (2017b). 'Europe's Performers Call on MEPs to Rebalance Copyright and Guarantee a Fair Remuneration from Streaming and Download Services', 11 January, https://www.fair-internet.eu/europes-performers-call-on-meps-to-rebalance-copyright-and-guarantee-a-fair-remuneration-from-streaming-and-download-services/, accessed 24 July 2019.

Frith, S. (1988). 'Copyright and the Music Business', *Popular Music*, 7, no. 1: 57–75.

Gorrell Committee (1909). *Report of the Committee on the Law of Copyright*. London: His Majesty's Stationery Office.

Gregory Committee (1952). *Report of the Copyright Committee, 1951*. London: Her Majesty's Stationery Office.

Ingham, T. (2012). 'Given Half a Chance', *Music Week*, 16 March, 1, 3.

Ingham, T. (2013). 'Editorial: Clearing up a Spot of Bother', *Music Week*, 19 July, 2.

Ingham, T. (2018a). 'How Much will Artists Get Paid from the Major Labels' Spotify Profits?', *Music Business Worldwide*, 5 April, https://www.musicbusinessworldwide.com/how-much-will-artists-be-paid-from-the-major-labels-spotify-profits/, accessed 2 May 2020.

Ingham, T. (2018b). 'Sony Music Isn't Robin Hood – It's Being Much Smarter Than That', *Music Business Worldwide*, 15 June, https://www.musicbusinessworldwide.com/sony-music-isnt-robin-hood-its-being-much-smarter-than-that/, accessed 20 June 2020.

Ingham, T. (2019). 'Streaming Platforms are Keeping More Money from Artists than Ever (and Paying Them More, Too)', *Rolling Stone*, 9 April, https://www.rollingstone.com/music/music-features/streaming-platforms-keeping-more-money-from-artists-than-ever-817925/, accessed 2 May 2020.

Ingham, T. (2020a). 'It's Happened: The Major Labels are Now Generating over $1m Every Hour from Streaming', *Music Business Worldwide*, 25 February, https://www.musicbusinessworldwide.com/its-happened-the-major-labels-are-now-generating-over-1m-every-hour-from-streaming/, accessed 20 June 2020.

Ingham, T. (2020b). 'Could Music Companies Help Black Artists by Adjusting Old Record Deals?', *Rolling Stone*, 8 June, https://www.rollingstone.com/pro/features/music-black-artists-old-record-deals-1011447/, accessed 20 June 2020.

Ingham, T. (2020c). 'BMG Pledges to Review Historical Record Contracts "Mindful of the Music Industry's Shameful Treatment of Black Artists"', *Music Business Worldwide*, 11 June, https://www.musicbusinessworldwide.com/bmg-to-review-historic-record-contracts-mindful-of-the-music-industrys-shameful-treatment-of-black-artists/, accessed 20 June 2020.

International Federation of the Phonographic Industry (IFPI) (2014). *Investing in Music: How Record Companies Discover, Nurture and Promote Talent*. London: IFPI.

International Federation of the Phonographic Industry (IFPI) (2020). *Global Music Report: The Industry in 2019*. London: IFPI.

Jones, M. L. (2014). 'Revisiting "Music Industry Research": What Changed? What Didn't?'. In L. Marshall and D. Laing (eds), *Popular Music Matters: Essays in Honour of Simon Frith*, 45–60. Farnham: Ashgate.

Monopolies and Mergers Commission (MMC) (1994). *The Supply of Recorded Music: A Report on the Supply in the UK of Pre-recorded Compact Discs, Vinyl Discs and Tapes Containing Music*. London: HMSO.

Mulligan, M. (2020). 'Welcome to the Age of the Artist', *MIDiA*, 27 February, https://www.midiaresearch.com/blog/welcome-to-the-age-of-the-artist, accessed 20 June 2020.

Music Managers' Forum (MMF) (n.d.). *Digital Deals Comparison Calculator*, https://themmf.net/digitaldollar-comparisoncalculator-form/, accessed 20 June 2020.

Osborne, R. (2020a). 'At the Sign of the Swingin' Symbol: The Manipulation of the UK Singles Chart'. In R. Osborne and D. Laing (eds), *Music by Numbers: The Use and Abuse of Statistics in the Music Industries*, 20–38. Bristol: Intellect.

Osborne, R. (2020b). 'The Gold Disc: One Million Pop Fans Can't be Wrong'. In R. Osborne and D. Laing (eds), *Music by Numbers: The Use and Abuse of Statistics in the Music Industries*, 39–55, Bristol: Intellect.

Passerard F. and P. Cartwright (2019). 'Business-to-Artist: Record Labels and Sub-labels in the Digital Age', *The Conversation*, 1 July, https://theconversation.com/business-to-artist-record-labels-and-sub-labels-in-the-digital-age-118950, accessed 20 June 2020.

Samuelson, P (1997). 'The U.S. Digital Agenda at WIPO', *Virginia Journal of International Law*, 37, no. 2: 369–440.

Scaping, P. (1989). *BPI Yearbook 1989/90: A Statistical Description of the British Record Industry*. London: BPI.

Scaping, P. and N. Hunter (1978). *BPI Yearbook 1978: A Review of the British Record and Tape Industry*. London: BPI.

Sexton, P. (2017). 'State of the Union', *Music Week*, 24 July, 10–12.

Smirke, R. (2014). 'Beggars Group's Martin Mills on Why He's Abandoning the 50/50 Streaming Split', *Billboardbiz*, 2 May, https://www.billboard.com/biz/articles/6077399/beggars-group-martin-mills-streaming-money-reduction-spotify-revenue, accessed 24 July 2019.

Stewart, S. M. and H. Sandison (1989). *International Copyright and Neighbouring Rights*, 2nd edn, vol. 1. London: Butterworth & Co.

Trubridge, H. (2015). 'Safeguarding the Income of Musicians', *WIPO Magazine*, May, https://www.wipo.int/wipo_magazine/en/2015/02/article_0002.html, accessed 24 July 2019.

Voogt, B. (2019). 'The Indie Musician's Guide to Digital Distribution', *Heroic Academy*, 31 December, https://heroic.academy/indie-musicians-guide-to-digital-distribution/#, accessed 2 May 2020.

Wikström, P. (2009). *The Music Industry: Music in the Cloud*. Cambridge: Polity Press.

Witt, S. (2015). *How Music Got Free: What Happens when an Entire Generation Commits the Same Crime?* London: The Bodley Head.

World Intellectual Property Organization (WIPO) (1961). *Rome Convention for the Protection of Performers, Producers of Phonograms and Broadcasting Organizations*, https://www.wipo.int/treaties/en/ip/rome/, accessed 20 June 2020.

World Intellectual Property Organization (WIPO) (1992). 'Preparatory Document for and Report of the First Session of the Committee of Experts on a Possible Protocol to the Berne Convention for the Protection of Literary and Artistic Works (Geneva, November 4 to 8, 1991)', *Copyright*, 2 February, 30–53.

World Intellectual Property Organization (WIPO) (1993). *Committee of Experts on a Possible Instrument for the Protection of the Rights of Performers and Producers of Phonograms, First Session, Geneva, June 28 To July 2, 1993*. Geneva: WIPO.

World Intellectual Property Organization (WIPO) (1994a). 'Committee of Experts on a Possible Instrument for the Protection of the Rights of Performers and Producers of Phonograms. Second Session, Geneva, November 8 to 12, 1993', *Copyright*, 2 February, 44–55.

World Intellectual Property Organization (WIPO) (1994b). 'Preparatory Document for the Third Session of the Committee of Experts on a Possible Instrument for the Protection of the Rights of Performers and Producers of Phonograms, Geneva, December 12 to 16, 1994', *Copyright*, 11 November, 241–76.

World Intellectual Property Organization (WIPO) (1995). 'Committee of Experts on a Possible Instrument for the Protection of the Rights of Performers and Producers of Phonograms Fourth Session, Geneva, September 4 to 8 and 12, 1995', *Industrial Property and Copyright*, 10 October, 363–96.

World Intellectual Property Organization (WIPO) (1996). *WIPO Performances and Phonograms Treaty*, https://www.wipo.int/treaties/en/ip/wppt/, accessed 20 June 2020.

World Intellectual Property Organization (WIPO) (1999). *Records on the Diplomatic Conference on Certain Copyright and Neighboring Rights Questions*. Geneva: WIPO.

2

Sampling practice

The threat of copyright management to its future (and past)

Justin Morey

This chapter first explores copyright law in relation to sampling with a focus on the letter and interpretation of UK law, but with an awareness of the influence of US law and how the major rightsholders in the global music industry handle copyright management accordingly. The particulars of sample clearance are explored, with consideration given to how terms and deals may have changed in the last decade, and to the responses by producers and artists to an industrial climate where the use of phonographic samples has become increasingly costly in the last twenty years, in particular the use of sample replays. Finally, some thought is given to the potential aura of the phonographic sample, and how far current industrial practice may be diminishing the work of sampling producers and the established canon of sample-based music. The chapter applies research[1] conducted between 2011 and 2020 into developments in the industrial management of copyright in respect of sampling, sample replays and sample clearance. Some of this research is taken from qualitative data resulting from interviews conducted with ten artists and producers,[2] a sample replay specialist (Mark Summers)[3] and a sample clearance specialist (Saranne

---

[1] Elements of this chapter are adapted from the author's PhD thesis, 'A Study of Sampling Practice in British Dance Music, 1987–2012' (Leeds Beckett University, 2017).
[2] Richard Barratt (DJ ParrotSweet Exorcist, Add N to X, All Seeing I); Bob Bhamra (WNCL); Andy Carthy (Mr Scruff); Denney (artist and DJ); Paul Hammond (Ultramarine); Aston Harvey (Freestylers, Sol Brothers); Dean Honer (All Seeing I, I Monster, Eccentronic Research Council); Alex Paterson (The Orb); Martin Reeves (Krafty Kuts); Jez Willis (Utah Saints). While all of these interviewees helped with the author's understanding of UK sampling practice and practicalities, not all have been referenced directly in this chapter.
[3] Mark Summers is a DJ and producer who has been creating sample replays under his company name, Scorrcio, since 1996.

Reid)[4] between 2011 and 2017. Both Summers and Reid were re-interviewed in 2020 to ascertain the extent to which their parts of the industry had changed, and in addition the music lawyer Jules O'Riordan[5] was interviewed for his perspective both as a UK music law specialist and an experienced DJ, artist and A&R person.

The period from 1987 to 1991 was one where a combination of factors, among them affordable digital sampling technology and the influence on UK composers and producers of a range of US dance music, from hip-hop to Chicago House and Detroit techno, led to an explosion of UK sample-based or sample-dependent dance and electronic music. Significant early tracks included what Simon Reynolds describes as the 'DJ record fad' of 1987/8 including releases such as 'Pump Up The Volume' by M/A/R/R/S, 'Theme From S'Express' by S'Express and 'Beat Dis' by Bomb The Bass (Reynolds 2013: Location 6886). The rave scene expanded in the United Kingdom in the late 1980s and early 1990s, and a range of UK forms of dance music emerged that were reliant on sampling, including hardcore, drum and bass and, later in the 1990s, big beat and breakbeat, while music within genres developed in the United States (hip-hop and house), and mainland Europe (EDM) also regularly employed samples. As sampling became an established creative practice within the music industry, processes for the management of the required copyright licences from rightsholders (sample clearance) also evolved. While the body of the case law directly related to musical copyright infringement in the UK is relatively small, and smaller still in consideration of sampling,[6] a significant number of disputes both in United Kingdom and United States have been resolved in favour of rightsholders, which in turn has led to increased difficulties and costs for artists and producers wishing to use samples in their work, resulting, in many cases, to changes in their sampling practice.

This chapter is concerned with sampling as a creative practice and the factors that encourage and shape that practice, and one of the chief pillars of its theoretical framework is Csikszentmihalyi's Systems Model of Creativity. To summarise this briefly, an *individual* is inspired and influenced by work in a particular *domain*, in this instance electronic and dance music, and as he/she develops his/her practice will gain an understanding of and also draw influence

---

[4] Saranne Reid, founder of her company, Sample Clearance Services, has been arranging sample clearances for clients for over twenty years.
[5] Jules O'Riordan (more widely known as Judge Jules) is a DJ, presenter, artist and former A&R person. He has been a music lawyer since 2015, and is currently practising at the firm, Sound Advice.
[6] See (Harrison 2017: chapter 13) for discussion of UK cases concerning sampling and plagiarism.

from the *field*, which we can think of as the sub-cultural gatekeepers, in this case DJs, artists, producers, club promoters, music journalists and record labels, for example. If the *individual*'s work is sufficiently novel, but also recognisable as belonging to this *domain* of dance and electronic music, then it will be accepted by the *field* and become part of the *domain* (Csikszentmihalyi 1988, 1999). This model was later adapted by Susan Kerrigan to amend *creativity* to *creative practice* in order to underline that a similar creative process occurs even if the resulting output does not become absorbed into the domain. In addition, Kerrigan recognised the collaborative nature of such practice in the arts by replacing *individual* with *agent* or *agents* (Kerrigan 2013). The concepts of *domain* and *field* imply certain boundaries as to what can be achieved by an *individual* or *agent* within a given *domain*, as well as certain possibilities, and another part of the theoretical framework used here is the idea of affordances and constraints, taken from Donald Norman (1998), who applied Peter Gibson's related work in this area concerning human perceptual systems (1966) to product design. In terms of sampling and sample-based dance music, affordances and constraints are especially useful when considering sampling technology, copyright law and the industrial management of sampling and sample clearance, and when thinking in terms of creative practice, constraints should not necessarily be considered as negatives. When limitations are imposed on an activity, creative individuals come up with interesting solutions; for example, early samplers had very limited sample time, and it was a common practice to sample a drum break into the machine at as high a pitch as the turntable would allow, and then play it back at a lower pitch in order not to run out of sampling memory.[7] While this was a constraint placed on users, the by-product was a sonic quality to the sampled break, due to sample aliasing,[8] which was used fruitfully by many producers who found the resulting effect pleasing and appropriate in their work. Similarly, with copyright, the constraints placed on the ease with which samples can be cleared and used have led to a number of developments to sampling practice by way of mitigation.

---

[7] See (Morey 2012: 58) for further discussion of this.
[8] Aliasing is harmonic distortion, particularly noticeable in early samplers with low sample rates and bit depth, and relatively rudimentary analogue to digital converters, where additional harmonics become added to the signal as a result of the sampling process. It is particularly noticeable in early models such as the EMU SP-12, where in order to play a sample back at a lower pitch, the machine would simply output it using a lower sample rate. In Carthy's example, pitching up a break on a record deck to save sample time would result in it having to be played back several semitones lower by the sampler, which would emphasise the harmonic distortion further. However, in the case of the EMU SP-12, the effect of this is 'quite musical. Like a bitcrusher but a hell of a lot warmer' (Morey and Carthy 2011).

Sampling and copyright law

A 'sample' can be used to describe three different but related methods of appropriating and adapting pre-existing musical ideas: a direct sample of a pre-existing recording, usually via digital sampling or digital recording technology; an interpolation, where phrases, melody and/or lyrics are taken from a pre-existing composition but without any attempt to copy the sound or timbre of the original recorded performance;[9] and a replay which recreates part or parts of an existing record with the intention of sounding as close as possible to the original. If using a direct, or phonographic, sample in a new piece of music, there are two copyrights and two sets of clearances required: the copyright of the musical work (the song, including the lyrics,[10] or composition – referred to in industry as the 'publishing copyright' or 'publishing') and the copyright of the recording sampled (the 'master copyright' or 'master'). When employing either an interpolation or a sample replay, only the copyright in the musical work needs to be cleared, and an explanation of the implications of this in terms of the difference between the publishing and master copyrights follows later in this chapter. There has never really been a question of doubt over whether a substantial sample infringes either of these copyrights, and even hip-hop records made before the widespread availability of digital samplers, and which recreated rather than sampled an original recording, can be seen to be credited to the authors of the source material.[11]

Although a small number of cases regarding sampling have reached the UK courts, they have been settled prior to a verdict being reached (Harrison 2017: 6633–48). This is not because disagreements over copyright do not occur in the UK, with Jules O'Riordan reporting that he regularly deals with sampling and other copyright disputes, but because the costs of going to trial (between £20,000 and £40,000 at county court level, higher still for the High Court) will generally far outweigh the costs of any agreement that is reached, meaning 'the incentive to settle is pretty enormous' (Morey and O'Riordan 2020). There have been a number of cases in the United States which have led

---

[9] An example of an interpolation is the adaptation by Coolio of the chorus melody and lyrics of 'Pastime Paradise' by Stevie Wonder for his record, 'Gangsta's Paradise'.
[10] Technically, a song is a combined musical and literary work, and publishing was split 50/50 between music and lyrics historically.
[11] For example, 'Rappers Delight' by The Sugarhill Gang released in 1979 replayed aspects of 'Good Times' by Chic, and the authors of 'Good Times', Bernard Edwards and Nile Rodgers, are also the only credited authors of Rapper's Delight.

to a verdict and created case law, and while the two countries are governed by their own copyright laws, these cases are relevant when considering sampling in the United Kingdom because the United States is the world's largest recorded music market, and the largest source of repertoire (IFPI 2016: 44) and industrial practices in regard to sampling adopted by the major record companies in the country are largely matched, as far as local law permits, by those companies in other territories. In addition, the Anglo-American view of copyright is argued to have been designed more to protect the interests of rightsholders than those of authors and creators (Laing 2004: 73–5) and there are important similarities in spirit if not in letter. It was possible to get samples cleared for relatively small upfront fees and percentages of publishing once digital sampling became prevalent in the mid to late 1980s, but this changed from 1991 after the Irish singer-songwriter Gilbert O'Sullivan sued the rapper Biz Markie for sampling his record 'Alone Again Naturally'.[12] The presiding judge in this case, The Honourable Kevin Thomas Duffy, found in favour of O'Sullivan, beginning his judgement with the words 'thou shalt not steal' (Collins 2006: 289). After this case, costs of sample clearance and percentages of publishing required for clearance increased steadily throughout the 1990s and 2000s (McLeod 2002; McLeod and DiCola 2011: 269–77). The decision by the United States Court of Appeals for the Sixth Circuit in a subsequent landmark case, *Bridgeport Music v Dimension Films* in 2004 was that the recording copyright is 'fixed in the medium'(2004 FED App. 0279P (6th Cir.), Section 2), meaning that '*any* sampling of a master, even if it's *unrecognizable*, is an infringement of copyright' (Passman 2011: 334). In spite of considerable criticism of the reading of US copyright law that led to the *Bridgeport* decision[13], this bright-line ruling[14] created significant increases in the costs of both master clearance and publishing clearance because it abolished the *de minimis*[15] defence of sampling; questions of substantiality were no longer admissible, and rightsholders had to do no more than demonstrate that a recording they owned had been sampled for any claims of copyright infringement to be upheld. McLeod and DiCola looked at

---

[12] *Grand Upright Music Limited v Warner Bros. Records, Inc.*, 780 F.Supp. 182 (S.D.N.Y. 1991).
[13] See for example: (Brodin 2006; Ponte 2006; Webber 2007).
[14] A bright-line ruling is one which seeks to provide clear and unequivocal guidance on a particular point of law.
[15] In legal terms, *de minimis* means something that is too insignificant or minimal to be taken into account, and a *de minimis* defence is used to argue against the prosecution of cases where there is a technical breach of rules, the impact of which is negligible. In terms of sampling, this could be applied to a short or transformed sample, the source of which would be very difficult to recognise without being advised of its use.

current costs (at their time of writing in 2011) of clearing two sample-heavy albums from the so-called 'golden age' of hip-hop of the late 1980s and early 1990s, 'Fear of a Black Planet' by Public Enemy and 'Paul's Boutique' by The Beastie Boys, and concluded that the total bill for clearance would result in net losses per album sold of $4.87 and $7.87, respectively, in terms of master copyrights, while the combined demands from publishers for their shares of the musical works would require between 200 per cent and 400 per cent of the available publishing (McLeod and DiCola 2011: 269–77). Clearly, the record labels that released these albums (Def Jam and Capitol, respectively) were able to derive sufficient economic benefit after clearance and at the time of release for the whole process to be worthwhile, suggesting a more than 400 per cent increase in publishing clearance requirements, and an increase of over 750 per cent in the costs of master clearance over approximately a thirty-year period. Public Enemy producer Hank Shocklee argued as far back as 2002 that it would be unfeasible to try to make such albums at that point, a position echoed by the artist Beck Hansen in a 2005 interview after the *Bridgeport* ruling (Shocklee is quoted by McLeod 2002; Hansen is quoted by Fink 2005). The creation of music using multiple samples, to the extent practiced by artists such as The Beastie Boys and Public Enemy has, then, become a commercial impossibility for most of this century. Although the *Bridgeport* decision led to the end of the idea that some small or fragmentary samples are potentially too insignificant, or *de minimis*, to infringe copyright, a more recent decision by the United States Court of Appeals for the Ninth Circuit, concerning the sampling of the horn stabs in Madonna's 'Vogue'[16] from an earlier record, upheld the notion of *de minimis* in favour of the defendants, meaning that there is now a circuit split on this concept in the United States;[17] while a Court of Appeals' decision is binding only in its particular jurisdiction, it is also considered as *persuasive* outside of that jurisdiction, meaning that these opposing decisions on the validity of a *de minimis* argument offer hope to those who may wish to argue a legal defence against established industrial practice. However, very few defendants will have the financial resources and/or desire to argue this point in the courts, and the

---

[16] *VMG Salsoul, LLC v Ciccone*, 824 F.3d 871 (9th Cir. 2016).
[17] There are thirteen United States Courts of Appeals in the United States, with each of these courts' rulings being binding within its particular federal jurisdiction. The United States Court of Appeals for the Sixth Circuit, which ruled in the *Bridgeport* case, is based in Cincinnati and has jurisdiction over areas of Kentucky, Michigan, Ohio and Tennessee, whereas the Court of Appeals for the Ninth Circuit, which ruled in *VMG Salsoul, LLC v Ciccone* is based in San Francisco and has a jurisdiction covering California, Alaska and a number of Western states.

industrial management of copyright in regard to sampling appears to have remained unchanged in spite of this circuit split.

UK copyright differs from US law in that it is not as clear-cut as the *Bridgeport* decision, which determined that a sound recording is physical rather than intellectual property. According to the relevant UK law, the Copyright, Designs and Patents Act of 1988 (hereafter CDPA), in order for infringement to occur, copying would be considered 'in relation to the work as a whole or any substantial part of it' (s.16(3) (a) CDPA), meaning in theory that the qualitative and quantitative substantiality of a sample, both in relation to its source and in relation to the new recording that it became part of, would need to be considered before deciding whether or not infringement had occurred. However, as with US copyright law, you only infringe the recording copyright if you directly sample the record, but not if you make a sound-alike of that recording. Under UK law, while there is no theoretical difference between the recording copyright and the publishing copyright in terms of the level of copying that would be considered infringement according to the letter of the CDPA, UK industrial practice tells a very different story, as attested to by sample clearance specialist Saranne Reid:

> On the recording side, even if you sample a second, we need to clear it. It's someone's master, and any element you use of that master is a copy of that master. On the publishing side of things, you have to be able to show that you've copied someone's skill and labour at such a substantial level that it becomes infringement. (Morey and Reid 2012)

Industrial practice would seem to be at odds with the letter of copyright law, and one explanation of this would be that the UK music industry has simply fallen in line with the requirements of the US industry to maintain a consistent approach to rights management internationally and to avoid any problems with exports. However, UK law has been read in such a way as to make a distinction between the copyright of the musical work and that of the sound recording; in terms of the musical work (the content), infringement occurs only if substantial and original aspects are copied (you cannot copyright a chord sequence for example), but any aspect of the recording (the medium) is infringed by direct sampling (Arnold 2001: 272; Toynbee 2006: 85). Richard Osborne summarises the idea thus:

> If songwriting copyright is thick, it is also loose. Composers are generally free to incorporate rhythms, timbres, chord changes and production techniques from previous works. They can even borrow melodies and lyrics if they are shown to be commonplace. Sound recording copyright, meanwhile, is thin but rigid. On

the one hand, you can *mimic* huge swathes of previous recordings. On the other, it is not legally permissible to use even the smallest element of a recording unless you pay for it. This is very much a *property* law: trespassers will be prosecuted. (Osborne 2017)

Although the letter of the CDPA may appear distinct from the interpretation of US copyright law[18] in regard to sound recordings as formulated in *Bridgeport*, these readings argue that all aspects of recordings are protected from direct sampling in the UK, and this consideration therefore informs the process and scope of sample clearances.

Sample clearance in practice

The procedures and costs of sample clearance are well established. If using a direct sample from an existing record, a composer or producer, or their representatives, will need to present the sample in the context of the completed new record and negotiate master clearance with the owners of that master (generally a record label), as well as agreeing on a percentage of ownership of the new work with the rightsholders of the composition that was sampled (Harrison 2017: 6684–756; Passman 2019: 250–1). Unlike recording a cover version, where the owners of the new master can purchase a compulsory mechanical licence for an agreed royalty to cover the usage of the composition, using a sample of a work in a new record is an adaptation of that work, and therefore one that needs to be agreed to by the rightsholders. The writer(s) and/or their publisher, if one is administering those rights therefore has the option to refuse clearance, and as such, the rightsholders of the composition can choose to demand most or even all of the publishing revenue in the new work if they wish.[19] Given that ideas of substantiality and originality are considered when reviewing potential plagiarism of a composition, in theory it would be possible to argue a case of no infringement of the original if, for example, a simple chord sequence was all that was used. However, Saranne Reid was not aware of any instances of this argument being attempted in her experience of sample clearance (Morey and Reid 2012).

---

[18] Copyright Act of 1976, 17 U.S.C. § 107.
[19] A successful crossover record by one of my interviewees included a replay of a bassline from a record by a well-known 1980s British pop band. While the bassline was a distinctive feature of both records, the interviewee and his fellow artists had written entirely different verses and choruses (both lyrically and melodically) over the bassline. However, in order to agree to the use of the bassline, they had to cede 90 per cent of the publishing revenue.

Assuming rightsholders agree in principle to clearance,[20] a fee, which is an advance on the potential royalties earned by the new record, will need to be paid to clear the master. This can often be substantial and will mean that the artist whose record contains the sample will share their agreed royalty rate (historically a percentage of PPD – the wholesale price of the record, CD or digital download) with the rightsholders of the sampled master. A royalty rate for a new artist can be as much as 20 per cent or as little as 15 per cent (Harrison 2017: 2279; Passman 2019: 92), while the royalty rate for the sample can typically be in the range of 2 per cent to 8 per cent, but much higher for substantial and/or very recognisable samples (Passman 2019: 251; Morey and Reid 2020). Assuming the record is successful enough to pay off the advance on royalties for the sample clearance, the rightsholders of the sample will continue to earn revenue from the new record based on their royalty rate. Although the sample clearance for the new recording is always in perpetuity, there will be additional negotiations for other usages like synchronisation (or 'sync' – use of the new record in film, TV or other visual media), such as whether or not the rightsholders of the new record will be able to agree to sync deals without gaining fresh permissions,[21] and what percentage of revenue from sync will flow back to the rightsholders of the sample (Morey and Reid 2020). In addition to this, the musical performers on the sample will be entitled to a share of performer royalties on the new record.[22] Clearly, if you decide to use samples in your records and get them cleared, third parties can have considerable control over how and where that record may be used and will derive a significant share of any royalties that it earns.

Saranne Reid was interviewed again in 2020, to find out if the structure or terms of sample clearance deals had changed since the first interview in 2012. There had been significant change to the deals for master rights due to streaming becoming the dominant format for the way in which recorded music is consumed and therefore its most significant revenue stream. Whereas deals were formerly struck on the basis of a percentage of PPD as discussed earlier, this has begun to change to a percentage of an artist's net receipts from streaming

---

[20] Featured artists on a recording, like writers of a work, also have a right of veto over sample clearance.
[21] This was the issue that led to the *Bridgeport Music v. Dimension Films* case. The hip-hop artists NWA obtained clearance for the use of a sample of 'Get Off Your Ass And Jam' by Funkadelic for commercial release of their record '100 Miles And Runnin' but failed to seek additional permission for a sync deal, at which point Bridgeport Music sued for copyright infringement.
[22] In the UK, performers' royalties are administered by PPL (Phonographic Performance Limited) and paid to performers and master rightsholders when a record is played on radio and TV. These performers' rights, also referred to as neighbouring rights, are an area that Jules O'Riordan believes requires further clarification in terms of which portion of the royalties the original performers on a sample are entitled to (Morey and O'Riordan 2020).

(Morey and Reid 2020). There has also been a growing difference between the kind of terms demanded by rightsholders in the United Kingdom and those in the United States, with one of the major record companies and its publishing arm being described as 'particularly avaricious' (Morey and Reid 2020). 'Harsh' terms that Reid has encountered include an advance on publishing income (in some instances, on deals where 100 per cent of publishing rights was required for clearance)[23] and master clearance deals based on a label's net receipts of streaming income, rather than artist's net receipts:

> In the US they will ask for a percentage of the overall net receipts. . . . It's actually un-doable commercially, it doesn't work. . . . On a track you will also have a producer who will need a royalty, and possibly an advance, and also a featured artist who will want a royalty and an advance. So actually, any share of net receipts based on the label's net receipts . . . is just unworkable as a commercial model. . . . And for the first time ever we are turning samples down based on the deals being just too difficult to manage commercially. (Morey and Reid 2020)

The UK arms of the major companies were generally more open to negotiation and to offering terms that were more acceptable to UK artists and labels, while independent labels and publishers will generally request smaller advances and lower percentages of publishing (Morey and Reid 2020). Although Reid did describe one of the major companies as 'avaricious', she attributed the harsher deals offered by the US majors to the sheer scale of their operations, the size of their catalogues, the number of clearance requests that they receive on a weekly basis and the time it would take to negotiate each one of them: 'It's not productive for them commercially to do that, so they just issue the quote and work on the basis that if fifty percent of them are accepted then they make more revenue than if they go back and negotiate on a hundred different deals' (Morey and Reid 2020).

In regard to the size of advances to clear the master and the percentages of publishing requested, these appear to have remained relatively consistent over the last decade. Several of the artists and producers interviewed between 2011 and 2012 reported £10,000 as being a fee quoted for the master clearance of a substantial sample and Reid confirmed that the publishing split can be 90 per cent or even 100 per cent in favour of rightsholders of the original work in those instances (Morey and Reid 2020).

---

[23] Reid clarified that these deals are feasible in the United States where some publishing income flows to record companies, but not in the UK where it is split between writer(s) and publisher (Morey and Reid Personal Communication 2020).

Responses to the costs of sampling

The combination of prohibitive upfront clearance costs and loss of both artist royalties and publishing rights has led to a number of different approaches among the producers and artists interviewed, in order to maintain a sampling aesthetic within their work.[24] For instance, Andy Carthy (Mr Scruff) will record himself playing drums as a simple stereo recording so that he has to work within the constraints of the timbral, tonal and spatial balance, as he would with a phonographic sample (Morey and Carthy 2011). Others such as Paul Hammond and Dean Honer use a sample as a starting point to build other parts around before discarding it (Morey and Hammond 2011; Morey and Honer 2011). Another artist talked about continuing to sample without seeking clearance because the music involved was not going to generate sufficient income for it to be worthwhile for rightsholders to sue for infringement; if one of his records was to gain sufficient interest to be picked up and re-released by a large dance label, then he would look for clearance at that point (Morey and Anon 2011). Sample replay specialist Mark Summers spoke of a Dutch artist who takes the same view, although Summers added that he believed the use of algorithms to detect copyright infringement on platforms such as Soundcloud and YouTube made this approach both more risky and less prevalent than it used to be (Morey and Summers 2020). Another interviewee, the DJ and producer Denney, experienced the downside of this approach after seeking retrospective sample clearance when his track was already released but picked up by a large UK dance label, losing most of his publishing and significant artist royalties as a result (Morey and Denney 2017), and Saranne Reid noted that retrospective clearance of samples will usually be considerably more costly than clearance prior to release (Morey and Reid 2020).

Sample replays

Replaying the sample – commissioning a recreation that is as close to the original as possible – has the advantage of not infringing the master copyright and therefore incurring none of the costs associated with its clearance. Publishing clearance still needs to be agreed to, and the terms for clearing the publishing would be in the same range as when an original recording had been sampled

---

[24] For a full discussion of this, see (Morey and McIntyre 2014: 52–5).

and as discussed by Reid earlier: a percentage (up to a 100 per cent) required by the rightsholders of the original work and, particularly if that work is owned in the United States, a potential demand for a percentage of overall net receipts for the new track (Morey and Reid 2020). There can also be significant costs involved in obtaining a replay, as outlined by O'Riordan: 'getting a very accurate re-record of an old-sounding sample' can cost between £2000 and £5000 (Morey and O'Riordan 2020). Even if the replay does not create a significant saving in upfront costs, there is also the certainty it provides of having a usable master and of avoiding potentially protracted negotiations, or the difficulties of locating rightsholders in the case of more obscure records (Morey and O'Riordan 2020). However, when dealing with substantial samples and major rightsholders, Reid argues that the potential savings, both in upfront costs and ongoing royalty payments for use of the original master can be considerable:

> What people are doing nowadays much more than they used to do . . . is they will re-sing the vocal because sample fees are so high now, they are extortionate. If you go to [named major record company] now with a gigantic [sampled] acapella, they will charge you . . . a 15% royalty with a 15 grand [£15,000] advance. (Morey and Reid 2020)

Although sample replays are not a recent development (Mark Summers started his replay company, Scorrcio, in 1996 after successfully replaying a sample for one of his own releases), both Reid and Summers noted an increase in their use. Reid estimated that replays now account for around 30 per cent of her clearances and Summers reported a 30–40 per cent increase in the number of commissions he had received in the last five years. Both Reid and Summers also pointed to an increase in the number of replays of just the vocal performance, or acapella, as mentioned by Reid earlier, rather than a complete section of a record, and another advantage of a replay is that artists and producers can ask for just the parts that they would like to use in their new track, rather than having to attempt to mask or filter out parts of the original sample that are not wanted (Morey and Reid 2020; Morey and Summers 2020). In terms of the restrictions created by the COVID-19 lockdown, neither of them have reported being affected by it; Reid has seen no reduction in her sample clearance work and continues to clear samples on behalf of major and independent rightsholders. Summers, who is based in Kiev, and prior to that was a resident of Barcelona, has created replays for clients all over Europe and the United States, and has employed vocalists and musicians from all over the world to help him complete his replays for more than two decades, and therefore remote working is very much an established part of his sample recreation process. Summers also suggested that with the lockdown preventing DJ/producers from performing and touring, producing new records in their home studios was one of the few commercial activities left open to them, and he anticipated increased productivity, if anything (Morey and Summers 2020).

An interesting recent development discussed by Summers was that he had been commissioned to replay samples on records that had originally been released in the late 1990s and early 2000s. Two examples were by two of the UK's most successful big beat artists, with one of the records reaching Number 1 in the country in 1999. In both cases, the replays commissioned were not of the main sample, but of smaller secondary samples (Morey and Summers 2017). Discussions between interviewer and interviewee at the time led to speculation that the reason for the labels' desire to clear these secondary samples so long after their initial release was a response to more stringent enforcement of copyright in the 2010s in comparison to the late 1990s (Morey and Summers 2017). In fact, the reason for these retrospective replays was more prosaic; Reid, who by coincidence, had been responsible for clearing all of the samples on one of the records in question before its original release, offered the explanation that the replay allowed both label and artist to have more control over their master, as well as more of the royalties from any future exploitation such as synchronisation or reissues. However, this retrospective replaying of samples, regardless, of its motivation, has implications for the sound of sampling, as will be argued.

The aura of the sample and the future of sampling

While some of the producers interviewed had used sample replays in their work and intended to use them again in the future, others ruled out the idea on aesthetic grounds. DJ, producer and label owner Bob Bhamra felt that employing replays 'misses the point of using samples in a track' and that he didn't 'want to be in a covers band' (Morey and Bhamra 2012). Andy Carthy, for whom the constraints of samples were an important part of their appeal, spoke about why he was drawn to samples and would never consider replays:

> [What] attracts you to a sample is the whole tone, and it's capturing a moment in time. It's a product, obviously of the musicians, the studio environment, the mic placement, the recording technology, the way that was mixed, the way

that was mastered, the way it was pressed on vinyl. Then the additional kind of compression and stuff which comes from sampling it – which stylus I use, which preamp I use, which, you know, audio interface I use, what kind of quality I sample it in, then how I EQ it and further process it. There is kind of such a *layer* of processes even before I sample something – get to that point – how on earth am I going to replicate that? (Morey and Carthy 2011)

Carthy's comments lead to the idea of the sample having an a*ura*, to borrow Walter Benjamin's much quoted application of the word, that the sample replay cannot. Most of the interviewees attested to the sonic, rather than melodic or rhythmic, qualities of a sample being fundamental to their selection of it. Vanessa Chang, also with Benjamin in mind, argues that 'the historically inscribed aura of the original holds a redefined, but necessary, place in the practice [of sampling]' (Chang 2009: 143), and if there is an aura to a sample, then we may have reached a point where this begins to be removed from the music we have access to. The costs of clearing the master can be prohibitive, which leads the artist or producer concerned to commission a replay instead, and specialists have been busy providing such replays for decades as a result. The practice of replaying samples is on the increase, as is the replay of a single aspect, such as a vocal, rather than a section of the whole track. While this allows producers to incorporate an appropriated musical idea more seamlessly into their own work than if they were having to work with the full master, something else is potentially lost by this approach as is again argued by Carthy:

Also half the attraction to me of samples is the kind of the bits in there that you don't really want as well. . . . There might be, you know, a bass line which you're trying to filter out but you'll still get the top end harmonics coming through and things like that . . . you still have shadows of what you're trying to lose, even if you're trying to selectively remove something from a finished recording, which actually I really like. . . . So I quite like the fact that you only have a limited amount of control over a sample. And that's half the fun of it because you're trying to put things together that were never meant to be together. (Morey and Carthy 2011)

In addition, as Summers' earlier examples demonstrate, labels can and will replay the samples of canonical records in order to have more control over and derive more income from their masters. Without wishing to denigrate the considerable skill and craft of sample replay specialists, it appears that there is a shift in the present from making records using phonographic samples to employing sound-alike cover versions of those same samples, as well as replacing samples on records from the past. Artists and producers using samples chose those samples because of their specific sonic signature; Tara Rodgers, borrowing from Barthes, describes this as 'the grain' of the sample – a combination of musicianship, recording environment and production techniques, all of which are specific to a particular time and location (Rodgers 2003: 318; Barthes 1990: 296). The phonographic sample, as the *original*, possesses an aura that the sample replay does not; however well executed the replay may be, it can only ever be a very close approximation.

Conclusions

Returning to Csikszentmihalyi's systems' model of creativity, while also thinking about Norman's concept of affordances and constraints, it can be seen how an increasingly strict approach to copyright management changes each of the aspects within the model (Csikszentmihalyi 1988, 1999; Kerrigan 2013; Norman 1998: 12–13): the *individual* artist or producer either needs to take significant steps to disguise a sample if used, commission a replay or have big enough pockets – their own or their label's – to clear a phonographic sample. Members of the *field*, such as labels, are aware of the costs and issues around sampling and will either avoid records with samples or protect themselves from any legal action at considerable cost to the artists in terms of seeing financial benefit from their creation. Meanwhile the recreation of samples within past releases, and the continuing move towards sample replays, has the potential to diminish the authenticity and identity of works within the *domain*. If the future of sampling is a further move away from phonographic samples to replays of particular lines or parts, or of replays of the samples used in catalogue tracks, then the catalogue or *domain* as a whole is potentially diminished going forward. The parts of a phonographic sample that are not immediately apparent to a listener still impart something additional and distinct to a new track, and in a streaming age, when older versions of tracks containing samples become superseded by updated versions incorporating replays, that certain something may become increasingly lost. Perhaps this is not so far away from the analogue versus digital debate that has engaged record producers for decades; for the *warmth* of digital read the *aura* of the sample. But there is arguably something more fundamental at stake here – a way of music-making and of working with sonic material which may become permanently inhibited. At the same time, constraints are not the same as restraints, and the constraints of copyright management have also produced affordances in the form of new approaches to sampling practice that preserve the idea of a sampling aesthetic, even if they are not entirely true to the origins of digital sampling practice.

How successfully has the CDPA kept up with practice in terms of sample clearance and the industrial management of copyright? The widely applied reading of the Act that *any* sampling of a copyrighted sound recording is infringement and requires clearance is arguably more hard-line than the letter of the law, which allows for the question of substantiality. Given that the Anglo-American model of copyright has tended to favour the interests of rightsholders over creators and that UK rightsholders have, for example, successfully lobbied for the extension of length of term for sound recordings relatively recently, a liberalisation of UK copyright law in regards to sampling looks unlikely any time soon. Some have argued that the rights in a sound recording should be extended to cover the authorial contribution of those involved who may not be credited as co-writers, such as performers,[25] but given that the majority of music catalogue is in the hands of three very large corporations who would see a reduction in income from their rights ownership if this were to be implemented, its introduction is equally unlikely. The big players in the music industry seem to find UK copyright law fit for purpose, or at least fit for their purposes, as it stands, and it would probably take a paradigm shift in the way recorded music is consumed and monetised for that to change.

References

Arnold, R. (2001). 'Content Copyrights and Signal Copyrights: The Case for a Rational Scheme of Protection', *Queen Mary Journal of Intellectual Property*, 1, no. 3: 272–9.

Barthes, R. (1990). 'The Grain of the Voice'. In S. Frith and G. Goodwin (eds), *On Record: Rock, Pop and the Written Word*, 293–300. London: Continuum.

Benjamin, W. (1936). 'The Work in the Age of Mechanical Reproduction', in *Illuminations*, trans. H. Zohn. New York: Shocken.

Bently, L. (2009). 'Authorship of Popular Music in UK Copyright Law', *Information, Communication & Society*, 12, no. 2: 179–204.

Bridgeport Music, Inc. v *Dimension Films*, 2004 FED App. 0279P (6th Cir.) (2004).

---

[25] See, for example, (Bently 2009: 179–204).

Brodin, M. (2006). 'Bridgeport Music, Inc. v Dimension Films: The Death of the Substantial Similarity Test in Digital Sampling Copyright Infringement Claims – The Sixth Circuit's Flawed Attempt at a Bright-Line Rule', *Minnesota Journal of Law, Science and Technology*, 6, no. 2: 821–63.

Chang, V. (2009). 'Records that Play: The Present Past in Sampling Practice', *Popular Music*, 28, no. 2: 143–59.

Collins, S. (2006). 'The Greater Right of the Wrong', PhD, Macquarie University, Sydney, Aus.

Copyright Act of 1976, 17 U.S.C. § 107 [Online]. Available from: http://www.copyright.gov/title17/92chap1.html#107, accessed 27 April 2011.

Copyright, Designs and Patents Act (1988). London: HMSO.

Csikszentmihalyi, M. (1988). 'Society, Culture and Person: A Systems View of Creativity'. In R. J. Sternberg (ed.), *The Nature of Creativity: Contemporary Psychological Perspectives*, 325–9. New York: Cambridge University Press.

Csikszentmihalyi, M. (1999). 'Implications of a Systems Perspective for the Study of Creativity', In R. Sternberg (ed.), *Handbook of Creativity*, 313–35. Cambridge: Cambridge University Press.

Fink, M. (2005). 'Beck – Breaking The Narrative', *Paste Magazine*, 16. Available online: http://www.pastemagazine.com/action/article/1816/feature/music/beck, accessed 27 April 2011.

Gibson, J. (1966). *The Senses Considered as Perceptual Systems*. London: Unwin Bros.

Grand Upright Music, Ltd. v Warner Bros. Records Inc., 780 F.Supp. 182 S.D.N.Y. (1991).

Harrison, A. (2017). *Music: The Business*, 7th edn, Kindle edition. London: Virgin Books.

IFPI (2016). *Global Music Report 2016*, London: IFPI.

Kerrigan, S. (2013). 'Accommodating Creative Documentary Practice within a Revised Systems Model of Creativity', *Journal of Media Practice*, 14, no. 2: 111–27.

Laing, D. (2004). 'Copyright, Politics and The Industry', S. Frith and L. Marshall (eds), *Music and Copyright*, 2nd edn, 7–85. Edinburgh: Edinburgh University Press.

McLeod, K. (2002). 'How Copyright Law Changed Hip Hop', *Stay Free Magazine*, issue 20. Available online: http://www.stayfreemagazine.org/archives/20/public_enemy.html, accessed 28 April 2011.

McLeod, K. and P. DiCola (2011). *Creative License: The Law and Culture of Digital Sampling*, Durham: Duke University Press.

Morey, J. (2012). 'Copyright Management and its Implications for the Sampling Practice of UK Dance Music Producers', *IASPM Journal, The Digital Nation: Copyright, Technology and Politics*, 3, no. 1: 48–62.

Morey, J. and Anon (2011). *Discussing the Development of Sampling Practice and Approaches to Sampling*, Unpublished.

Morey, J. and B. Bhamra (2012). *Discussing the Development of Sampling Practice and Approaches to Sampling*, Unpublished.

Morey, J. and A. Carthy (2011). *Discussing the Development of Sampling Practice and Approaches to Sampling*, Unpublished.

Morey, J. and J. Denney (2017). *Discussing the Development of Sampling Practice and Approaches to Sampling*, Unpublished.

Morey, J. and P. Hammond (2011). *Discussing the Development of Sampling Practice and Approaches to Sampling*, Unpublished.

Morey, J. and D. Honer (2011). *Discussing the Development of Sampling Practice and Approaches to Sampling*, Unpublished.

Morey, J. and P. McIntyre (2014). 'The Creative Practice of Contemporary Dance Music Producers', *Dancecult*, 6, no. 1: 41–60.

Morey, J. and J. O'Riordan (2020). *A UK Music Law Specialist's View on Sampling and Sample Clearance*, Unpublished.

Morey, J. and S. Reid (2012). *Sample Clearance in Practice*, Unpublished.

Morey, J. and S. Reid (2020). *Recent Developments in UK Sample Clearance Practice*, Unpublished.

Morey, J. and M. Summers (2017). *Developments in Sample Replaying*, Unpublished.

Morey, J. and M. Summers (2020). *Further Developments in Sample Replaying*, Unpublished.

Norman, D. (1998). *The Design of Everyday Things*. London: MIT Press.

Osborne, R. (2017). 'The Thicke of It', *Pop Bothering Me*, 3 May. Available online: http://richardosbornevinyl.blogspot.co.uk/2017/05/the-thicke-of-it.html, accessed 11 June 2017.

Passman, D. S. (2011). *All You Need To Know About The Music Business*, 7th edn. London: Penguin.

Passman, D. S. (2019). *All You Need To Know About The Music Business*, 10th edn. London: Penguin.

Ponte, L. M. (2006). 'The Emperor has no Clothes: How Digital Sampling Infringement Cases are Exposing Weaknesses in Traditional Copyright Law and the Need for Statutory Reform', *American Business Law Journal*, 43, no. 3: 525–60.

Reynolds, S. (2013). *Energy Flash*, Kindle edition. London: Faber and Faber.

Rodgers, T. (2003). 'On the Process and Aesthetics of Sampling in Electronic Music Production', *Organised Noise*, 8, no. 3: 313–20.

Toynbee, J. (2006). 'Copyright, The Work and Phonographic Orality in Music', *Social and Legal Studies*, 15, no. 1: 77–99.

VMG Salsoul, LLC v Ciccone, 824 F.3d 871 (9th Cir. 2016).

Webber, A. (2007). 'Digital Sampling and the Legal Implications for Its Use After Bridgeport', *St. John's Journal of Legal Commentary*, 22, no. 1: 373–415.

3

Emerging frontiers

Platform regulation of mashups in and beyond an EU context

Alan Hui

Music sampling has long been the subject of conflict between copyright laws and musical appropriation (Vaidhyanathan 2003; Lessig 2008; McLeod and DiCola 2011). Mashups are distinguished from other sampling by the use of extensive samples from two or more recognisable, popular and copyrighted music recordings, and the surprising juxtapositions of samples into a seamless whole (Sinnreich 2010; Brøvig-Hanssen 2016; Hui 2018). As such, mashups are a natural target of copyright law.

As an appropriative practice, mashups challenge 'notions of individual creativity or authenticity in art' (Myers 2007: 220) that underlie copyright's rewards for and control of creative expression. Copyright rewards creators and rightsholders with exclusive rights, but can hinder sampling artists. Though mashup *videos* are also entrenched in this conflict, this chapter focuses on mashup *music*. Over a decade ago, Lawrence Lessig wrote about Apple iTunes' takedown of Girl Talk's mashup album *Night Ripper*, an emblematic case of digital copyright restraining online creativity (Lessig 2008). Lessig foresaw the encroachment of copyright laws and platform regulation on what he referred to as 'Read/Write culture'. While he recognised a need for online protection of creator interests and industry investment, he feared that copyright would hamper mashups online and other emerging creative forms created from existing content.

This chapter explores how platform regulation extends this conflict to online platforms. Although mashup music was initially found on radio and in clubs, it is increasingly being shared via platforms, especially YouTube, Facebook and SoundCloud. As mashups were distributed and made available online, they gradually became intertwined with platform regulation which restricts unlicensed, unauthorised but possibly lawful mashups. While content identification makes online copyright enforcement effective, it also makes sharing of mashups difficult, sometimes impossible. The chapter taps into empirical research from the University of Oslo's MASHED project conducted in 2019, shedding light on mashup producer experiences and the unintended influences of law and platform regulation.[1] This included semi-structured interviews with thirty producers and a survey of ninety-two producers, mostly EU and North American residents.[2] In relying on empirical research, the chapter reflects the assertion that 'often problems within the legal system, best practice insights and the effect of policy shifts can only be examined using in-depth, qualitative methods' (Webley 2010: 948).

Building on this empirical research, this chapter also considers developments in content identification and EU law in three substantive sections. The first recounts how platform regulation has denied copyright exceptions for mashups. The second explains why licensing increases platform regulation and hinders sharing of unauthorised mashups. The third explores how 2019 developments in EU law entrench sample licensing and platform regulation of mashups.

Platform regulation denied copyright exceptions for mashups

Platform regulation now includes content identification, which detects copyright material in uploaded content, and content moderation, which applies rules when copyright material is detected. Content identification enables a compromise between rightsholders that wish to control, monetise and track copyrighted material, and platforms that wish to enable access for their users. Content identification presents opportunities to minimise transaction costs for rightsholders enforcing copyright and platform operators managing copyright liability at a large 'scale' (or volume)

---

[1] Thanks to all the producers who spoke with us and to my colleagues – Ragnhild Brøvig-Hanssen, Ellis Nathaniel Jones, Irina Eidsvold-Tøien and Milos Novovic – for their feedback. Any mistakes remain my own. Thanks also to Ragnhild and Ellis for taking the lead in conducting our interviews and survey; Elisabeth Staksrud for survey design assistance; and Eirik Jakobsen, Oskar Holldorff and Ole Kristian Bekkevold for interview transcription. I acknowledge the Norwegian Research Council's support of the RITMO Centre (project number 262762) and the MASHED project (project number 275441), led by Brøvig-Hanssen, at the University of Oslo.

[2] Another article reports full results and methodology (Brøvig-Hanssen and Jones forthcoming 2022). See the MASHED project website for our full survey, interview template and a more detailed description of our method: https://www.uio.no/ritmo/english/projects/mashed/mashupscopyright/

of activity (Gillespie 2018; Suzor 2019); for example, YouTube users uploaded 500 hours of content per minute in 2019 (US Copyright Office 2020: 187). As the US Copyright Office recognises, requiring 'all content owners to have enforcement teams on retainer is guaranteed to leave many small, individual creators without an effective mechanism' (US Copyright Office 2020: 72). While larger platforms can afford dedicated systems, including YouTube Content ID and Facebook Rights Manager, smaller platforms can deploy third-party systems, like Audible Magic. Copyright holders usually provide a library of reference files, which are turned into digital fingerprints for efficient content matching.

Content identification and content moderation typically work together. When content identification finds a match, the platform automatically applies a default moderation rule chosen by the rightsholder to allow or deny content access. When access is allowed, the rightsholder can usually choose whether to monetise or monitor the access. Content moderation can also deny access by blocking before upload, takedown after upload and stay down (blocking re-uploads of taken-down content). Sometimes, access is partly allowed and partly denied, for example, with the video allowed and the audio muted.

Although mashup producers (and other users with a good faith belief that their use is lawful) can dispute them, moderation rules remain influential. Our survey shows that only 41 per cent of producers disputed moderation rules (Brøvig-Hanssen and Jones forthcoming). Of these, 45 per cent were successful. 59 per cent never disputed these rules and our research suggests why. 23 per cent believed 'distributing' their mashups was illegal while 47 per cent considered it to be a grey area.[3] Belgian mashup producer DJ Poulpi is concerned that the music industry and copyright laws do not assist creators who are mashup producers: 'the big record companies are all about "no. No way". . . . I'm 100 per cent aware that I don't own the rights to *any* of these tracks.' Others, like Austrian producer DJ Schmolli, want to avoid attracting 'the YouTube people to your channel and see which copyright laws I'm actually breaking'.

How content identification amplifies copyright enforcement

Content identification is not a neutral tool. It creates an opportunity for efficient copyright enforcement online but poses a threat to downstream creators wishing

---

[3] Here, the survey used a lay meaning of 'distributing', analogous to 'communication to the public' and 'making available to the public' in the Information Society Directive (European Parliament 2001, art. 3). It was not used to indicate 'distribution to the public by sale or otherwise' (article 4).

to rely on copyright exceptions. Our survey demonstrates that almost all mashup producers surveyed experienced content moderation of their uploads. Only 2 per cent had 'never' experienced a notice or takedown, with 68 per cent responding 'often' or 'sometimes'.

Content identification can often discern whether copyright material has been used but not the purpose of a use. In short, content identification is not purpose detection. Although copyright enforcement is pervasive online, copyright exceptions are often not invoked. Content identification does not bring to scale copyright exceptions, which guarantee free use for certain purposes. In the EU context, purposes include 'caricature, parody or pastiche' and 'quotations for purposes such as criticism or review' (*Information Society Directive*, art. 5(3)(d) and (k)).

Purpose detection could counterbalance content identification at scale, if it were to become more sophisticated. There is some literature on parody detection based on the use of charting music on YouTube videos (Jacques et al. 2018; Erickson, Kretschmer and Mendis 2013; Weese et al. 2017). However, these studies show that existing parody detection approaches require improvement. By seeking videos with the word 'parody' in the title, they wrongly include non-parodies and exclude parodies which use alternative markers – such as 'spoof', 'satire' or 'lampoon' – or no marker. Though this chapter discusses content identification in relation to copyright, it is also applied to content perceived by some to be extremist, offensive, child-friendly or misleading. Since 2020, major platforms have implemented policies to shield parody from regulation of manipulated and misleading media (Bickert 2020; Reddit 2020), though there is little published information about how their parody detection systems operate. Beyond parody detection, some content identification can find audio quotations, but cannot detect the purpose of the quotation. As this chapter discusses later, Dubset specialises in identifying samples but cannot detect purpose and assumes samples require a licence.

Without effective purpose detection, pervasive content identification favours copyright enforcement over copyright exceptions. Without automated tools to bring copyright exceptions to life on platforms, users are not equipped to dispute platform regulation defaults.

How content identification threatens producer-operated platforms

One response to platform regulation of mashups is for producers to operate their own platforms. A mashup producer based in the UK we interviewed (who

Copyright owner	URLs	Last request date
RIAA member companies (EMI Music North America, Sony Music Entertainment, Universal Music Group, Warner Music Group and their associated record labels)	104	Feb 24, 2017
IFPI	58	Sep 19, 2017
scpp	25	Mar 27, 2017

Figure 3.1 Blocking requests for webpages on Mashup Site A's old domain from Google Transparency Report. Photo courtesy of Alan Hui

is referred to as Producer A) started a platform dedicated to mashups (which we refer to as Mashup Site A).[4] As Producer A explained, the platform 'came about because a lot of mashup producers were sick of the constant takedowns and account deletions, meaning if they wanted to continue, they have to move their back catalogue to yet another platform that might delete them again in 6 months'. Our interviews reveal that several producers made the tough choice to use Mashup Site A over other platforms such as YouTube, Facebook and SoundCloud. These producers sacrificed larger audiences and existing accounts to avoid blocking and takedown of their mashups.

Unfortunately for producers, operating a platform does not guarantee that mashups remain available. By not enforcing copyright, Mashup Site A became a target of platform regulation. This is evident from Google Transparency Report, a Google website disclosing each time a rightsholder (or their representative) asks Google not to deliver search results to webpages. In 2017, rightsholder representatives including IFPI, the global recording industry body with UK headquarters, asked Google not to provide search results for 187 webpages on Mashup Site A (see Figure 3.1).[5] As Producer A reported in 2019, 'We're coming up to 3 years of [Mashup Site A] and haven't removed music for copyright

---

[4] As Mashup Site A and other websites operate in a legal grey area, we preserve the anonymity of the websites and their operators by using pseudonyms in our publications (Brøvig-Hanssen and Jones forthcoming).

[5] To preserve anonymity, I omit references for Figure 1 and Figure 2.

infringement in that time.' Two months later in 2017, at IFPI's request, Mashup Site A's domain name registrar sent a DMCA notice and simultaneously delisted the site, disconnecting it from the internet. While the website was down for one day, all links to their '.com' address were broken permanently.

Moving a platform – to another online or physical location, or legal jurisdiction – does not safeguard mashups' existence either. Producer A relocated Mashup Site A to a new domain name in a flawed attempt to rely upon a Canadian copyright exception Producer A believed would permit mashups. It is often unclear which countries' laws apply to an online copyright conflict. The applicable law could be defined by where a rightsholder resides, a platform operates, a listener resides, a contract specifies, or some combination of these. When people and corporations attempt to base their activities in the legal jurisdiction most favourable to them, a practice known as 'forum shopping', this further complicates the task of determining which laws apply to a legal dispute (Novovic 2019). Producer A, based in the UK, cannot simply decide that the laws of Canada or any other jurisdiction govern all copyright disputes concerning Mashup Site A. Even Google has failed to convince the Canadian judiciary that its activities outside of Canada are immune from Canadian law (*Equustek Solutions Inc. v Jack* 2018 BCSC 610).

Assuming Canadian law exclusively applied to Mashup Site A, the Canadian user-generated content exception has conditions that many mashups may not meet. It permits uses of copyright material 'solely for non-commercial purposes' without a 'substantial adverse effect' on the exploitation of or the market for the existing work (*Copyright Act (Canada)* 1985, s 29.21 (1)). Because there is a sample licensing market, unlicensed and free mashups may create such an adverse effect. In addition, as Canadian law professor Teresa Scassa explains, '"free" does not necessarily mean non-commercial. Free content may be a means of self-promotion, or it may build or enhance reputation with a view to professional or other advancement' (Scassa 2013: 441).

At its new domain, Mashup Site A remains under tangible threat from actors other than domain name registrars. Telecommunications providers can block their customers' access to websites with the purpose of facilitating copyright infringement, a practice known as website blocking. The Canadian Federal Court ordered website blocking against a video streaming site in 2019 (*Bell Media Inc. v GoldTV.Biz* 2019 FC 1432), despite the telecommunications regulator declining to introduce website blocking regulations (Canadian Radio-television and Telecommunications Commission 2018). Search engines can

Copyright owner	URLs	Last request date
CH US Inc.	1	Jan 8, 2019

Figure 3.2 Request to take down webpage on Mashup Site A's new domain from Google Transparency Report. Photo courtesy of Alan Hui

block search results to webpages, making them more difficult to find and access. Google blocks search results under a UK-brokered code of practice (Bing et al. 2017) and, in 2019, a rightsholder asked Google to block a webpage at Mashup Site A's new domain. Figure 3.2 shows this request from CH US Inc., possibly the California-registered company by that name (California Secretary of State 2020).

The takedown of Mashup Site A by its domain name registrar took down all mashups and remixes on the platform. This blanket takedown had no regard for whether any sampling content was lawful, regardless of other content being infringing. It warns producers that search engine blocking, website blocking and domain name delisting also use content identification. Although content identification may simply identify uses of copyright material, the ensuing enforcement can set aside copyright exceptions.

Licensing increases platform regulation and further hinders sharing of unauthorised mashups

Licensing is a common practice in music communities and music industries. At its core is permission from a rightsholder to another person – a user, creator or intermediary – to make an otherwise infringing use of copyrighted music, typically granted in exchange for payment. As this section explains, licensing has been uncommon in music sampling. Even when licences have been struck between platforms and rightsholders, they have counterintuitively hindered some sampling and mashups.

The theoretical virtues of sample licensing

Licensing has enabled some sampling uses but frustrated many others. After Biz Markie, De La Soul and other artists were punished for unauthorised sampling in the so-called golden era of hip-hop – the late 1980s to early 1990s – licensing became essential for those wishing to avoid the consequences of copyright infringement. The US Sixth Circuit Court controversially opined that all sampling requires licences, which wrongly treats all unauthorised sampling as infringement and ignores lawful sampling under copyright exceptions. While opining that a two-second guitar riff sample was copyright infringement, the Court wrote, 'Get a license or do not sample. We do not see this as stifling creativity in any significant way.' (*Bridgeport Music v Dimension Films* 410 F. 3d 792 (6th Cir. 2005), 801).

Although this 'no licence, no sample' position has been rejected by some US courts (such as the Ninth Circuit in VMG Salsoul v Ciccone 2016) and criticised by scholars (see, for example, Schietinger 2005), it has some merits. While sceptical of the Sixth Circuit's reasoning, McLeod and DiCola recognise that the Court wished to 'avoid lawsuits and instead promote voluntary, well-informed transactions within the music industry' (McLeod and DiCola 2011: 222). Sanjek argues that sampling artists should respect rightsholders by licensing samples, and 'be respected in turn as equal creators' (Sanjek 1992: 621). When sample licensing is accessible, available and affordable, rightsholders maximise revenues, producers can lawfully share mashups, platforms minimise liability and all parties benefit from the lower transaction costs.

However, sample licensing has been unreliable, unpredictable or even impossible, despite some producers being willing to pay. Because copyright owners can be difficult to identify and contact and samples require multiple copyright permissions, obtaining a licence can be difficult, leading to a niche industry of sample clearance experts such as Pat Shanahan who has worked with Beastie Boys, The Avalanches and others (Newstead and Milsom 2017). Often, licences are denied or royalties requested by the rightsholders or their representatives – typically upwards of $US5,000 according to US empirical research (McLeod and DiCola 2011: 158–63) – are seen as exorbitant by the mashup producer and are usually demanded upfront. Shanahan recounts that 'publishers and labels want more and more money. It has literally knocked the smaller artists out of the game altogether. Only the ones who are very, very well off can afford to sample anymore'. (McLeod and DiCola 2011: 159) Though mashup producers have typically sampled without licences, blocking and takedowns make this more difficult and less reliable, leaving producers with a choice: license or gamble with content moderation, or worse, an infringement case.

The initial impact of licensing: content identification and takedowns

Since 2014, SoundCloud has adopted a variation of the 'no licence, no sample' position. Previously, SoundCloud was a 'producer-oriented platform' (Hesmondhalgh, Jones and Rauh 2019), offering musicians a place to find audiences without relying on a record label or music industry organisations. Following several threats of litigation from the music industry, SoundCloud struck licensing deals between 2014 and 2016 with the Sony, Warner and Universal Music Groups, and the Merlin independent music collective representative body (Ljung 2015; 2016a; 2016b; Warner Music Group 2014).

The licences reduced copyright liability for SoundCloud by permitting many uses of copyright material by its users and ensured payment to original rightsholders in many cases. However, the licences did not permit all uses, and they had a particularly adverse impact on producers of mashups and other sample-based content. Although licensing was ostensibly intended to secure more reliable copyright access, it led to widespread takedowns for mashup producers and missed revenue for rightsholders. In our survey, we asked producers which platforms with notice-and-takedown systems they saw as hindering sharing of mashups. 69 per cent named SoundCloud, more than any other platform, and 75 per cent stopped using SoundCloud altogether. Platform regulation on SoundCloud (and YouTube) discouraged some producers from making and sharing mashups altogether (Brøvig-Hanssen and Jones forthcoming).

With informed hindsight, we can revisit the Sixth Circuit's *Bridgeport* decision. The Court intended to protect rightsholders' rights to control and license while leaving leeway for sampling artists, arguing 'just as many artists and companies choose to sample and take their chances, it is likely that will continue to be the case' (*Bridgeport Music v Dimension Films*, 804). They could not have foreseen how quickly platform regulation would enforce copyright law through extensive content identification, blocking and takedown, often denying users an opportunity to risk uses in legal grey areas. In 2005, YouTube had just started and SoundCloud did not exist. The Court believed that if samples were not licensed, sampling artists could take their risk with copyright law. We can now see that mass licensing may improve access for many, but not for many sampling artists who face ubiquitous platform regulation in spite of licences between platforms and rightsholders and are pushed off platforms altogether.

The two faces of sample licensing

SoundCloud's foray into licensing has both enabled uploads and threatened mashups. Since the wave of takedowns from 2014 to 2018, SoundCloud has adopted licensing arrangements better suited to sampling. Though too late for many mashup producers, SoundCloud's partnership with sample licensing firm Dubset is notable (SoundCloud 2018). Dubset's MixBANK sample identification and clearance service has enabled SoundCloud to pre-license remixes of thirty-five million recordings from Warner, Sony and Merlin in two ways (see Figure 3.3). First, licences cover producers uploading unofficial remixes and mashups to SoundCloud (and several other major music platforms). Unlike sample licensing in the past, there are no upfront payments for these licences; royalties are paid as the remix or mashup generates revenue. Second, licences enable mashup producers and DJs to mix and sample directly from SoundCloud's library to DJ software suites from Native Instruments, Serato, Pioneer and others. This had commercial benefits for rightsholders and SoundCloud, reducing licensing costs, and improved access for producers.

The EU regulation enabling Europeans to fully use their online content subscriptions while travelling in the EU gives more reliable access to mashup producers using SoundCloud as their DJing library (*Portability Regulation* (EU) 2017/1128). Generally, SoundCloud provides different libraries in different countries. This is inconvenient for a mashup producer preparing a DJ set using

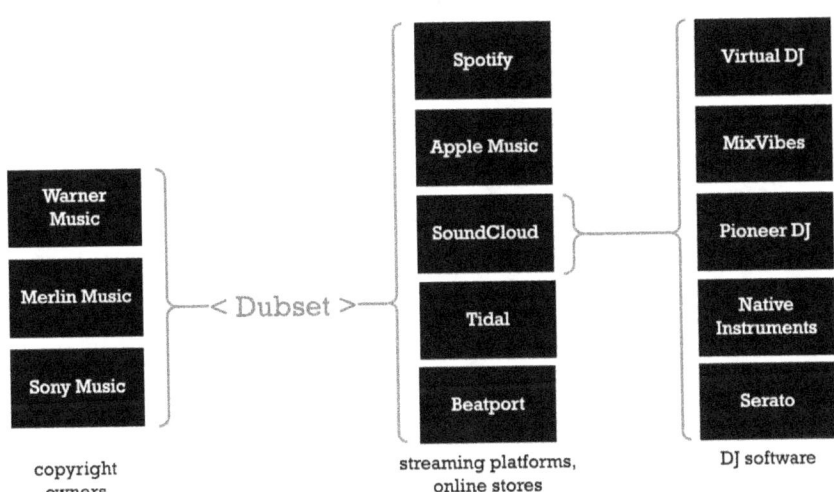

Figure 3.3 Sample licensing in action. Photo courtesy of Alan Hui

SoundCloud's library in their home country, only to find that some tracks are not available when they DJ in another country. The Portability Regulation helps to ensure that a SoundCloud user resident in a EU country has access to the same library when they visits another EU country.

Partnerships between Dubset and platforms like SoundCloud have made sample licensing easier and more accessible than before, but they also threaten mashup music and sampling. Few producers we interviewed or surveyed mentioned Dubset or their services, and none considered that it solved their sample licensing issues. One explanation is that Dubset improves sample licensing but does not enable the unpaid uses permitted by copyright exceptions. Another explanation is that Dubset has no licensing arrangement with Universal Music Group, thus excluding almost one-third of the global commercial music catalogue. With Dubset's improved sample identification, this makes copyright notices from Universal more likely to be verifiable and to lead to a takedown. In addition, it reinforces streaming over downloaded or hard copies of recorded music, making access to samples susceptible to future platform regulation or changes in licensing. This has already happened once, with Spotify cutting off its library from a third-party DJ app in July 2020 (Algoriddim 2020). This means that DJs using the Algoriddim Djay app can no longer sample directly from Spotify.

These sample licensing arrangements may extend far beyond SoundCloud and existing Dubset partners. In 2020, Dubset was acquired by Pex, a content identification firm helping rightsholders find unauthorised uses of music and video content on platforms including YouTube, Facebook, Vimeo, TikTok and DailyMotion. Pex now claims to identify and monetise samples as short as half a second and identify mashups in user-generated content across these platforms (Pex 2020).

2019 developments in EU law entrench sample licensing and platform regulation of mashups

Parallel with the evolution of sample licensing, two developments in EU copyright law affect the legality of mashups and other sampling in the EU. The first is the prominent *Pelham* copyright dispute spanning two decades in German and EU courts. The second is a new copyright directive adopted by the EU Parliament.

The Pelham judgement's threat to EU copyright freedoms

The *Pelham* dispute centred on whether Moses Pelham and Martin Haas' two-second sample of a Kraftwerk recording was copyright infringement. While stating that the sample was infringement, the German Federal Court of Justice opined in 2008 that a person 'unwilling or unable' to recreate the sounds of a sample can 'ask the rightsholder for an appropriate license' (*Hütter v Pelham* I ZR-112/06 2008; translated to English by Conley and Braegelmann 2009). This echoed the earlier US *Bridgeport* decision.

Over the next decade, several appeals resulted in the German Court referring the *Pelham* case to the Court of Justice of the European Union (CJEU). The CJEU's 2019 *Pelham* decision did not explicitly mention licensing but took away other legal options from mashup producers and sampling artists. This decision affects mashup music more than other sampling. The CJEU ruled that even extremely short samples of music recordings are potentially infringing, unless they are 'in a modified form unrecognisable to the ear' (*Pelham v Hütter* C-476/17, 2019: 87). This works against mashups which typically feature long, recognisable samples from popular music. The CJEU ruled that the broad 'free use' limitation in German copyright statute is inconsistent with the EU law and cannot permit any uses not specified in the narrower, specific-purpose EU copyright exceptions. Although member states can provide a quotation exception, the Court confirmed that such an exception is subject to a maze of conditions. The CJEU ruled that quotation and other exceptions must be 'harmonised' across EU countries, meaning that these conditions are mandatory for all EU countries. The quotation cannot use more than 'the extent required for the specific purpose', must 'enter into dialogue' with the quoted material and be 'in accordance with fair practice' (*Information Society Directive* 2001/29/EC, art. 5(3)(d); *Pelham v Hütter* 2019).

A 2020 German judgement applying the CJEU's precedent suggests that EU copyright limitations and exceptions make unauthorised, recognisable sampling not permissible or at best a grey area, but most likely an infringement (*Pelham v Hütter* I ZR-115/16 2020). Considering the two-second Kraftwerk sample again, the German Federal Court of Justice ruled that quotation, parody, caricature and incidental work exceptions do not permit sampling in this case. It leaves only a narrow window for a pastiche exception, which does not yet exist in German statute, to permit such sampling in future. At the time of writing, the UK pastiche exception – a rarity in the EU – will depart the EU with Brexit.

In sum, quotation and other copyright exceptions exist in EU law but are complex to use to defend sampling, even for some lawyers and legal scholars. For mashup producers, 2019 EU copyright reforms entrench the primacy of licensing and the complexity of copyright exceptions, at least in relation to online content-sharing by platform users in the EU.

Article 17's entrenchment of licensing and platform regulation

In 2019, the European Parliament adopted a new directive which will require platforms operating in the EU to license copyright content and increase platform regulation (*Digital Single Market Directive* (EU) 2019/790). Article 17 of the directive makes a platform (or 'online content-sharing service provider') liable when it gives the public access to copyright-protected material uploaded by its users (*Digital Single Market Directive*, art. 17). Compared to EU and US safe harbour regimes, which shield platforms and other intermediaries that take down infringing content on receipt of a valid copyright notice, this liability encourages platforms to seek a licence, and block and take down content. To avoid this liability for user uploads, a platform must seek an 'authorisation' (most likely, a licence) from rightsholders as a first resort. If a platform fails to obtain an authorisation, it must make 'best efforts to obtain' an authorisation, make 'best efforts to ensure the unavailability of specific works and other subject matter' where rightsholders have provided relevant information, and when it receives a valid notice, 'expeditiously' disable access to or remove copyright material and ensure it stays down. Although Article 17 is explicitly not a 'general monitoring obligation', ensuring unavailability will involve content identification because the scale of uploads makes purely manual identification impossible. That said, human reviewers still have a role. In their absence, as occurred during the COVID-19 pandemic, YouTube warned of 'increased video removals' and 'delayed appeal reviews' (YouTube 2020), although several producers – including DJ Earworm, bringmethemashup and Raheem D – have successfully uploaded mashups to YouTube.[6]

Article 17 also makes copyright exceptions for quotation, criticism, review, parody, caricature and pastiche mandatory on these platforms. This ostensibly offsets the stronger copyright enforcement and platform regulation required

---

[6] See https://www.youtube.com/watch?v=soBE8h3sgCE&feature=youtu.be, https://www.youtube.com/channel/UCPKTxRDHuASamyHSRM6XCNg/videos and https://www.youtube.com/user/RaheemdaplayaO4/videos

by Article 17. However, at least for the immediate future, these exceptions will not materially assist mashups or other sampling on platforms because purpose detection remains nascent. Combined with the conditions that apply to EU copyright exceptions, like quotation, it is clear that platform regulation will not automatically permit uses covered by copyright exceptions for some time.

Article 17 and the CJEU *Pelham* judgement require platforms to improve enforcement for rightsholders, but at the cost of mashup producers who wish to lawfully rely on a copyright exception or wade into a legal grey area to share a mashup. *Pelham* makes more uses of recorded music potentially infringing, and the quotation exception less permissive towards sampling. Article 17 increases enforcement against potential infringement and increasing pressure on platforms to license uses on their users' behalf, taking the choice to license away from mashup producers. SoundCloud's takedown and blocking of mashups after agreeing to licences with music rightsholders suggests that Article 17 threatens mashups and other sampling even if platforms obtain a licence. As the same time, copyright exceptions remain theoretical unless they can be brought to life on platforms. Licensing on SoundCloud increased content identification but not purpose detection on SoundCloud, and platforms abiding by Article 17 may follow the same pattern.

Conclusion

This chapter has outlined how platform regulation and copyright law strengthen enforcement and weaken exceptions. The 2019 developments in EU copyright law improve control for holders but create an uncertain future for content platforms and creators who adapt, arrange or transform prior copyright material to form new pieces. The *Pelham* decision and the absence of purpose detection converge to compromise EU copyright exceptions. Article 17 gives platforms little choice but to use content identification tools more extensively. Even if they obtain licences, rightsholders will expect content identification to track uses for calculating licence fees. If a platform fails to obtain licences, Article 17 requires it to ensure unavailability, which would require a combination of content identification and content moderation. The case of Mashup Site A suggests that this renewed emphasis on content identification may enable not only content moderation by EU platforms but also copyright enforcement beyond platforms, via search engines, domain name registrars and telecommunications providers.

These expansions of platform regulation entrench a zero-sum game between rightsholders, intermediaries and those creators who make new works from prior works.

If copyright law and platform regulation provide unjust outcomes for mashup music, licensing offers an alternative, albeit an imperfect one. Taking a utopian view, mashups might flourish under paid use. Content identification could lead to widespread, blanket permission to upload and share mashups. However, the experience of mashup producers who have used SoundCloud after mass licensing suggests that we should view Dubset-like content identification and sample licensing with caution. At stake are the freedoms – the free uses and 'tolerated uses' (Wu 2008) – that even the Sixth Circuit believed ought to be available to sampling artists if they chose to roll the dice with copyright law.

References

Algoriddim (2020). 'The Future of Streaming in Djay'. March 2020, https://www.algoriddim.com/streaming-migration.

Bell Media Inc. v GoldTV.Biz (2019). Federal Court of Canada.

Bickert, M. (2020). 'Enforcing Against Manipulated Media', *About Facebook* (blog), 7 January 2020, https://about.fb.com/news/2020/01/enforcing-against-manipulated-media/.

Bing, BPI, Google, Motion Picture Association and The Alliance for Intellectual Property (2017). 'Code of Practice on Search and Copyright'.

Bridgeport Music v Dimension Films (2005). 410 F.3d 792. 6th Cir.

Brøvig-Hanssen, R. (2016). *Justin Bieber Featuring Slipknot*, edited by Sheila Whiteley and Shara Rambarran. Oxford: Oxford University Press, https://doi.org/10.1093/oxfordhb/9780199321285.013.19.

Brøvig-Hanssen, R. and E. Jones (forthcoming 2022). 'Remix's Retreat? Content Moderation, Copyright Law, and Mashup Music'. *New Media and Society*.

California Secretary of State (2020). 'Business Search – CH US INC', 6 May 2020. https://businesssearch.sos.ca.gov/CBS/Detail.

Canadian Radio-television and Telecommunications Commission (2018). 'Telecom Decision CRTC 2018–384', 2 October 2018, https://crtc.gc.ca/eng/archive/2018/2018-384.htm.

Conley, Neil and Tom H. Braegelmann (2009). 'English Translation: Metall Auf Metall (Kraftwerk, et al. v Moses Pelham, et al.), Decision of the German Federal Supreme Court No. I ZR 112/06, Dated November 20, 2008', *Journal of the Copyright Society of the U.S.A.*, 56: 1017.

Copyright Act (Canada) (1985). R.S.C. Vol. C–42. https://laws-lois.justice.gc.ca/eng/acts/c-42/fulltext.html.

Equustek Solutions Inc. v Jack (2018). 610. Supreme Court of British Columbia.

Erickson, K., M. Kretschmer and D. Mendis (2013). 'Copyright and the Economic Effects of Parody'. III. Parody and Pastiche. Intellectual Property Office (IPO).

European Parliament (2001). *Directive 2001/29/EC of the European Parliament and of the Council of 22 May 2001 on the Harmonisation of Certain Aspects of Copyright and Related Rights in the Information Society.* Vol. 2001/29/EC, https://eur-lex.europa.eu/LexUriServ/LexUriServ.do?uri=CELEX:32001L0029:EN:HTML.

European Parliament (2017). *Regulation (EU) 2017/1128 on Cross-Border Portability of Online Content Services in the Internal Market.* OJ L. Vol. 168, http://data.europa.eu/eli/reg/2017/1128/oj/eng.

European Parliament (2019). *Directive (EU) 2019/790 of the European Parliament and of the Council of 17 April 2019 on Copyright and Related Rights in the Digital Single Market and Amending Directives 96/9/EC and 2001/29/EC.* Vol. 2019/790, https://eur-lex.europa.eu/eli/dir/2019/790/oj.

Gillespie, Tarleton (2018). *Custodians of the Internet: Platforms, Content Moderation, and the Hidden Decisions That Shape Social Media.* New Haven: Yale University Press.

Hesmondhalgh, David, Ellis Jones and Andreas Rauh. (2019). 'SoundCloud and Bandcamp as Alternative Music Platforms', *Social Media + Society*, 5, no. 4: 205630511988342, https://doi.org/10.1177/2056305119883429.

Hui, Alan (2018). '99 Problems but a Riff Ain't One: How Sampling Helps Copyright Promote Originality'. PhD thesis, Canberra, Australia: The Australian National University, 10.25911/5d6cfdb374b53.

Hütter v Pelham (2008). I ZR-112/06. Bundesgerichtshof (Federal Court of Justice).

Jacques, S., K. Garstka, M. Hviid and J. Street (2018). 'An Empirical Study of the Use of Automated Anti-Piracy Systems and Their Consequences for Cultural Diversity', *SCRIPT-Ed*, 15, no. 2: 277–312, https://doi.org/10.2966/scrip.150218.277.

Lessig, L. (2008). *Remix: Making Art and Commerce Thrive in the Hybrid Economy.* London: Bloomsbury.

Ljung, A. (2015). 'Representing over 20,000 Independent Labels, Merlin Becomes Our Latest On SoundCloud Partner', 4 June 2015, https://blog.soundcloud.com/2015/06/04/merlin-becomes-latest-on-soundcloud-partner/.

Ljung, A. (2016a). 'Announcing Our Partnership with Universal Music Group', 13 January 2016, https://blog.soundcloud.com/2016/01/13/announcing-our-partnership-with-universal-music-group/.

Ljung, A. (2016b). 'Announcing Our Partnership with Sony Music', 18 March 2016, https://blog.soundcloud.com/2016/03/18/announcig-partnership-sony-music/.

McLeod, K. and P. DiCola (2011). *Creative License: The Law and Culture of Digital Sampling.* Durham: Duke University Press.

Myers, E. (2007). 'Art on Ice: The Chilling Effect of Copyright on Artistic Expression', *Columbia Journal of Law and Arts*, 30: 219.

Newstead, Al and V. Milsom (2017). 'Why The Avalanches Took 16 Years to Make Wildflower'. Text. Triple J. Australian Broadcasting Corporation, 4 July 2017, https://www.abc.net.au/triplej/news/musicnews/the-avalanches-making-of-wildflower/8677694.

Novovic, M. (2019). 'Fighting European "Copyright Tourism": Lessons from Defamation Laws', *European Review of Private Law*, 27, no. 5: 949–71.

Pelham v. Hütter (2019). C-476/17. EU Court of Justice.

Pelham v. Hütter. (2020). I ZR-115/16. Bundesgerichtshof (Federal Court of Justice).

Pex (2020). 'Pex – The Global Video & Music Search Engine'. Homepage, 6 May 2020, https://pex.com/.

'Protecting Our Extended Workforce and the Community' (2020). *YouTube Creator Blog* (blog), 16 March 2020, https://youtube-creators.googleblog.com/2020/03/protecting-our-extended-workforce-and.html.

Reddit (2020). 'Do Not Impersonate an Individual or Entity', Reddit Help, https://www.reddithelp.com/en/categories/rules-reporting/account-and-community-restrictions/do-not-impersonate-individual-or.

Sanjek, D. (1992). 'Don't Have to DJ No More: Sampling and the Autonomous Creator', *Cardozo Arts and Entertainment Law Journal*, 10: 607–24.

Scassa, T. (2013). 'Acknowledging Copyright's Illegitimate Offspring: User-Generated Content and Canadian Copyright Law'. In M. Geist (ed.), *The Copyright Pentalogy*, 431–53. Ottawa: University of Ottawa Press.

Schietinger, J. (2005). 'Bridgeport Music, Inc. v Dimension Films: How the Sixth Circuit Missed a Beat on Digital Music Sampling', *DePaul Law Review*, 55, no. 1: 209–48.

Sinnreich, A. (2010). *Mashed Up: Music, Technology, and the Rise of Configurable Culture*. Science/Technology/Culture. Amherst: University of Massachusetts Press.

SoundCloud (2018). 'SoundCloud and Dubset Partner to Develop Next-Generation Approach to Clearing Remixes to Unlock More Value for Creators and Rights Holders'. SoundCloud Newsroom, 19 October 2018, http://press.soundcloud.com/169327-soundcloud-and-dubset-partner-to-develop-next-generation-approach-to-clearing-remixes-to-unlock-more-value-for-creators-and-rights-hol.

Suzor, N. P. (2019). *Lawless: The Secret Rules That Govern Our Digital Lives*. Cambridge and New York: Cambridge University Press.

US Copyright Office (2020). 'Section 512 Report'. US Copyright Office.

Vaidhyanathan, S. (2003). *Copyrights and Copywrongs: The Rise of Intellectual Property and How It Threatens Creativity*. New York: New York University Press.

VMG Salsoul v Ciccone (2016). 824 F.3d 871. 9th Cir.

Warner Music Group (2014). 'Warner Music Group and SoundCloud Announce Groundbreaking Partnership – Warner Music Group Official Blog'. Warner Music

Group Official Website, 4 November 2014, https://www.wmg.com/news/warner-music-group-and-soundcloud-announce-groundbreaking-partnership-20036.

Webley, L. (2010). 'Qualitative Approaches to Empirical Legal Research'. In Peter Cane and Herbert M. Kritzer (eds), *Oxford Handbook of Empirical Legal Research*. Oxford: Oxford University Press, https://doi.org/10.1093/oxfordhb/9780199542475.013.0039.

Weese, Joshua L., W. H. Hsu, J. C. Murphy and K. B. Knight (2017). 'Parody Detection: An Annotation, Feature Construction, and Classification Approach to the Web of Parody'. In Shalin Hai-Jew (ed.), *Data Analytics in Digital Humanities*, 67–89. Cham: Springer International Publishing, https://doi.org/10.1007/978-3-319-54499-1_3.

Wu, T. (2008). 'Tolerated Use', *Columbia Journal of Law & the Arts*, 31, no. 4: 617–35.

4

Music copyright, creators and fans

Enemies or friends in the digital domain?

Paul G. Oliver and Stefan Lalchev

We live in a time when digital technologies, particularly social media and streaming services, are the most effective and efficient platforms for the exposure of music (Glicksman 2020; Mercuri 2019; Wilson 2020). Market reports suggest that user-generated content is at the centre of many success stories (Roma and Aloini 2019). However, it has become clear how such forms of online success could be in an artist's best interest because, nowadays, their revenue from selling music is only a fraction of what they can potentially earn as an influencer. In order to understand how this has occurred, one needs to fully comprehend the impact of digitalisation upon the circulation and control of intellectual property rights (Liebowitz and Watt 2006). Without copyright, not one single branch of the music industry would exist (Gordon 2015). In fact, one could easily see why the contemporary music industry is perhaps best understood as a 'copyright industry' (Wikström 2009). In addition to the perspectives of music industry professionals and academics alike, one must also acknowledge that the game has changed with new players and different rules. For differing reasons, the distinction between fans and creators has become blurred, which raises important questions when analysing from a legislative point of view.

This chapter will provide a critique of how the roles, interrelations and challenges of copyright, creators and fans have evolved over the past two decades. Furthermore, it will explore the inherent conflicts between rule of law and what is in the best interests of creators, the business and the fans, as well as how current tensions may be resolved.

The evolving role of fans as creators

At the beginning of the twenty-first century, there was a significant moment of digital disruption, which forever changed the fabric of the music industry. Until this point, the music industry was making billions of dollars per year from recorded music through record sales, royalties and ancillary rights (Page 2020); however, the internet and new technologies caused a sea change in how music was created and consumed and the associated copyright laws (Rostama 2015). Napster's peer-to-peer file-sharing platform, for example, allowed music fans to access an almost unlimited digital database of users' recorded music collections, which led to a revolutionary shift in power between major record labels, publishers, artists and fans. This was a line in the sand and marked a new era of extreme creativity, innovation and change for the music industry (Tschmuck 2012).

With this new era came alternative business models that had to compensate for the unforeseen financial losses of copyright owners, but it was also a key milestone in the evolving roles of creators and fans. These two disparate roles, which were once clearly separate, were brought together as a result of the growth in the use of social media platforms, thus presenting opportunities for unique and innovative content creation, which could be easily shared without interference from gatekeepers. In other words, creativity remained a key point of separation between artists and fans, but also encouraged fan engagement, creation and the 'circulation of cultural goods' (Morris 2013: 281). Pearson (2010: 1) agrees that digital technologies have simultaneously empowered and disempowered music fans while 'blurring the lines between producers and consumers, creating symbiotic relationships between powerful corporations and individual fans, and giving rise to new forms of cultural production', whereas, Galuszka (2014: 26) refers to this changing relationship between artists, fans and the music industry as the 'new economy of fandom'.

The new opportunities for creating and sharing, freely and globally, led to a rise in popularity of the term *'user-generated content'*, also known as *'user-created content'*. In a report by the Organisation for Economic Co-operation and Development (2007: 4), user-generated content is defined as content:

1. Made publicly available over the internet;
2. Which reflects a 'certain amount of creative effort'; and
3. Which is 'created outside of professional routines and practices'.

In the past, artists were always seen as the creators, and fans were simply regarded as consumers. However, advances in digital technologies, the internet and the accessibility of audio visual creative tools have resulted in artists and fans now often working together as 'co-creators' with fans playing 'a vital role in an artist's promotional plan' (Music Ally 2018: 1). It could be stated that, nowadays, the majority of user-generated content is created by fans, commonly referred to as *'fan-generated content'*.

An interesting point of thought is whether the rise of user-generated content came as a result of the rise of social media or if it was the other way around, as some of the most successful platforms today are almost entirely based on user-generated content, such as TikTok, Twitch and YouTube. Nevertheless, its evolution and impact have been well documented, particularly over the past decade, which in turn has led to significant challenges from a legislative point of view. The diversity of user-generated content creation often results in copyright infringement, raising questions about who is liable and to what extent.

Despite content creation and sharing being made significantly easier, the content itself remains a form of intellectual property, protected by copyright. Copyright, literally meaning 'the right to copy', 'is designed to serve the interests and facilitate the creativity of musicians' (Phillips and Street 2015: 342); however, the main challenge is that 'laws governing copyright have never been able to keep fully abreast of changes in the way music is produced, communicated, bought, and sold' (Baskerville and Baskerville 2017: 22), especially via the internet. The Copyright, Designs and Patents Act 1988 (CDPA), as amended, is the official legal Copyright Act in the UK, and its protection applies to original literary, dramatic, musical or artistic works. However, it is the term *'original'* that requires attention here, as it sets the entire basis for the existence of copyright, even though its meaning is not defined in the Act. The strict legal definition of original work is nothing more than work produced by an originator (Gaines 1991). The law of copyright does not establish a definition of originality, but simply refers to it as the act of originating a piece of work, without reviewing any other aesthetic characteristics or criteria. Therefore, the manner in which legislators treat the term 'original' is not much different from the way critics and scholars do, when determining the originality of an artwork (Negus, Street and Behr 2017), which would not have been an issue, if it was not for the fact that copying, and similarity, have always been directly related to commercial music products.

User-generated content presents an even more complex challenge to legislation than simply defining the term 'original'. Undoubtedly, the decline in physical music sales at the start of the new millennium caused all sectors of the music industry to focus on trying to comprehend how digitalisation had changed the consumption habits and values of listeners (Hardy 2012; Leyshon 2014). With most rights-based attention falling on piracy, the Napster phenomenon and the music industry's attempts to fight illegal copying (Hardy 2012; Knopper 2009) resulted in the 'criminalization of sharing' (David 2010) and prosecution of individuals for downloading music accessed from other fans (Alderman 2002; Knopper 2009). While being accepted as a major threat to rightsholders, illegal downloading has been eradicated as a result of the rise of streaming platforms (Paine 2018); however, another serious issue is the significant gap in copyright legislation, which has been no less of a threat to the music industry for years.

Safe harbours and addressing the value gap

The Digital Millennium Copyright Act (DMCA), introduced in the United States in 1998, and the E-Commerce Directive, implemented by the EU in 2000, granted certain limitations to the liability of internet service providers acting as online distribution network intermediaries. Those limitations have been called *safe harbours*.

The E-Commerce Directive's 'overarching goal was to foster the development of electronic commerce in the EU', ensuring 'the free movement of information society services between Member States', as well as 'legal certainty and consumer confidence in online commerce' (Madiega 2020: 1). Intermediaries were still responsible for removing any copyright-infringing content, although the main concern for the music industry was related to the potential inefficiency of that action and the fact that such content would be expected to easily reappear online. Furthermore, there had been scope for abuse of the safe harbour exemption in this fast-moving digital domain, mainly because this concept was created back in the late 1990s, before the digital revolution, with many of the current internet companies, including social media platforms, not being foreseen at the time.

The abuse of the safe harbour exemption has created this so-called *value gap*, or *transfer of value*, which is 'a mismatch between the value that online user upload services, such as YouTube, extract from music and the revenue returned to the music community' (IFPI in Awbi 2018). In an attempt to address this value gap, in 2018, copyright reform finally reached the European Parliament, and after a year of intense discussions, campaigns and lobbying, on 26 March 2019, the music industry was able to celebrate the passing of the new EU Copyright Directive (Garner 2019; Paine 2019). One of the main reasons for such tensions around this new piece of legislation was to do with the safe harbours and the controversial Article 13, later renamed Article 17. The controversy around this article consists in opponents arguing that, while its aim is to ensure that online content creators are being fairly compensated (Europe for Creators 2019), it actually 'threatens the open internet' (Paine 2019). Not surprisingly, this part of the new Directive, making platforms 'responsible for the use of copyright-protected material in content posted by users' (Article13.org 2019) was not easily accepted by companies, such as YouTube, whose entire business models were predominantly based on that same user-generated content (Andrews 2018). The important question raised by this argument has been whether this type of copyright law enforcement protects creators or, instead, limits their opportunities to share content.

Copyright versus copyleft

Despite the continued existence of arguably robust copyright law, there are different ways that content creators can successfully duplicate or draw inspiration from previous creative works. In fact, there are two different exceptions to copyright: *fair dealing*, or its *fair use* equivalent in the United States, and *de minimis*. Both exceptions have been interpreted extremely narrowly to date by the law courts, with 'no cases in UK courts that will determine what is "fair" when it comes to quoting an artistic work' (Ward-Ure 2018). Similarly, in the United States, the *fair use* doctrine is open to interpretation, which is more subjective and can sometimes cause difficulties in terms of decision-making.

Copyright is based on the philosophy of restriction and relies, among other things, on the originality of the work; on the other hand, *copyleft* not only represents freedom but also requires freedom (Joglekar 2018). The term 'copyleft' was first coined in relation to software licensing – 'granting everyone the right to use, modify and distribute' a program 'on the condition that the licensee also grants similar rights over the modifications he [or she] has made' (Mustonen 2003: 101). This concept of 'some rights reserved' paved the way for a new type of thinking around how copyright could be more accessible in the digital domain. This subsequently inspired the *free culture* movement and the inception of Creative Commons, which took the idea of giving away free licenses and applied it to all types of online creative content. Even though this did not necessarily solve the overall problem of implementing copyright law within the digital environment, it did present an interesting alternative (Lessig 2005).

The continual advancements of digital technologies have contributed to the homogenisation of creative processes and output, juxtaposed against the rigidity of copyright laws, which has led to an exciting, yet uncertain, era for the music industry. This is fundamentally difficult to legislate for as copyright laws are designed with intent and do not change quickly; therefore, the underpinning laws are slowly being transitioned to support these new types of output.

Ultimately, just as it has become much easier to create and release creative content, it has also become easier to identify original content creators. Therefore, when a copyright infringement takes place, the original content creators may be able to prove the paternity of their works with a simple online search through the use of tagging and metadata. Similarly, as with materials, the internet is held to the same legal standards because 'copyright applies to the Internet in the same way as material in other media; e.g. any photographs posted on the Internet are protected in the same way as other artistic works; any original written work will be protected as a "literary work"' (Smartt 2017: 383).

User-generated content and the growth of social media

In the context of user-generated content, covered in this chapter, the history of related social media platforms began in 2003. Within a short period of time (2003–2006), three of the most influential social media platforms were launched: Facebook, YouTube and Twitter. And, while, at first, Facebook and Twitter were not specifically oriented towards the sharing of user-generated content – Twitter, for example, did not let users see photos or videos without leaving the platform until late 2010 – the idea behind YouTube from the beginning was to enable users to upload any video content online and reach viewers globally (Hopkins 2006). In support of this statement, the slogan 'Broadcast Yourself' remained an inseparable part of the official YouTube logo until 2011. Moreover, the launch of more platforms, such as Instagram, purchased by Facebook in 2012, and Twitch, acquired by Amazon in 2014 encouraged the sharing of content and its dissemination even further in a relatively straightforward manner. This did not require great technical expertise or equipment, with the constantly ongoing development of new features allowing different types of content-sharing and interaction between creators and fans. At the same time, new types of crowdfunding platforms emerged, such as Patreon, empowering creators to help them monetise their videos on a large scale.

While we are on the topic of user-generated content, there is one particular type of social media platform that has significantly influenced the interrelationship between creators and fans. Short-form video sharing grew to mass worldwide popularity with the Twitter-owned social network app Vine, launched in 2013. Vine was originally released as an iOS app, followed by Android and Windows Phone versions, showcasing user-generated content in the form of a few-seconds-long looping videos to be shared across different social networks, and it quickly became one of the top mobile applications (Souppouris 2013). However, the Vine model was soon adopted by several other platforms that introduced similar additional features, including the opportunity for users to upload longer videos. As a result, Vine started to lose subscribers to its competitors, and in late 2016 Twitter announced that the app would be discontinued. One platform that managed to take the short-form video concept, and further expand it to the point of reaching global success, was the Chinese-founded Musical.ly. First released in 2014, its concept was to allow users to create and share short lip-sync music videos, thus attracting millions of users globally. In 2016, another Chinese company, ByteDance, launched a different social network app, which was still focused on video-sharing. While Douyin was initially launched only for the Chinese market, in early 2017 it reached Western markets under the name TikTok. Later that same year, ByteDance acquired Musical.ly for a reported amount of close to $1 billion (Lin and Winkler 2017), and merged the two apps into one, keeping the name TikTok. With its numerous success stories and considering the key musical element in the concept behind the service, TikTok earned itself the status of one of the most influential music discovery tools in recent years.

Considering how Vine's position was usurped, it is worth acknowledging the vulnerability of platforms, particularly with regard to protecting their models. Not only does the law fail to provide protection, but the *copy-and-kill* strategy is also nothing new in the rivalry between social media platforms. Apart from the previous example of Vine and Musical.ly/TikTok, this approach has been used on numerous other occasions and, up until now, has even been used against

TikTok – for example, by the new short-form video service *Instagram Reels*, launched in the United States in August 2020 (Peterson 2020).

The aforementioned examples provide a clear indication of the rise of social media, and yet this success has come with a plethora of questions challenging legislative discussions relating to the boundaries between creators, fans and possible copyright infringements. The following three case insights will explore these copyright issues in relation to popular social media platforms and their impact on the music industry.

YouTubers and the battle for fairness

Over the last ten years, YouTubers have become a cultural global phenomenon, also having a significant influence on the music industry. The name *YouTubers* refers to 'video bloggers (vloggers) who regularly post videos on their personal YouTube channels' (Jerslev 2016: 5233).

YouTuber, Rick Beato, has been particularly vocal on the subject of free culture relating to creators and copyright issues. Beato is a musician and music teacher who presents a successful series on his personal YouTube channel called 'What Makes This Song Great?', which currently has 1.68 million subscribers and between 100,000 and 800,000 views per video (Beato 2020a). He regularly posts video tutorials of himself analysing famous pop and rock songs from the last seventy years by breaking down songs structurally and demonstrating the music theory behind the songwriting, mainly for the benefit of amateur guitarists. Recently, however, Beato has become increasingly frustrated with YouTube, who have been sending copyright-sharing claims, takedown claims and *demonetizing* his videos on behalf of copyright owners, specifically major record labels, publishers and legacy artists. YouTube demonetization occurs 'when videos or channels lose their ability to earn advertising income' (Johnson 2019). Regarding copyright-sharing claims, he has frequently expressed dissatisfaction at how many of his YouTube videos have had copyright claims made against them, resulting in them being taken down and/or demonetised. In a vlog post, Beato (2020b) talks about a specific twenty-five-second section of one of his tutorial videos where he is demonstrating how to play the melody of a Lennon–McCartney song on guitar. He argues that the way he uses a segment of this song should be classified as *fair use* and so feels that he has been unfairly treated.

Beato is one of many YouTubers who started their channels not only to be creative and connect with other music fans but also as a means of generating income. In fact, for many creators, live streaming and video content creation has become a full-time career, with the potential for economic sustainability and, in some cases, commercial success. However, because so many videos are now being demonetised for copyright infringement, YouTubers feel restricted with regard to how they can use copyrighted music as part of fair dealing, or fair use, without being issued a takedown notice from music copyright owners via YouTube. From an opposing viewpoint, however, there is a revenue stream associated with uploaded content and it seems that YouTubers are simply refusing to pay for the copyrights of creators without whom they would not have any content. While, on one hand, YouTubers might have started the channels to be creative, on the other hand, they are using material protected by copyright laws. This is the reason why YouTuber disputes rarely make it to court. When a specific video is being demonetised or blocked, the only action that a creator can take is disputing it, but if a dispute gets rejected, the creator gets a strike, and three strikes lead to the channel being taken down. Creators are aware that their chances of successfully disputing a copyright claim are low.

In another example, a lawsuit was filed in the United States by YouTuber DJ Short-E, real name Erik Mishiyev, against YouTube over allegations that the Google company did not deal properly with his counterclaims to copyright notices filed against his content, which was eventually dismissed (Cooke 2020a). The judge ruled that YouTube could deal with the claimant's counterclaims any way it wanted under the video site's terms of service. Yes, those terms of service said YouTubers could dispute copyright claims made against their channels, but the US district court Judge, William Alsup (cited in Van Der Sar 2020), noted that 'once a user submitted a counter-notice, the agreement reserved to YouTube's sole discretion the decision to take any further action, including whether to restore the videos or even to send the counter-notice to the purported copyright owner'.

The point of the new Copyright Directive is to close the value gap and to eliminate the mismatch between the revenue generated by the platforms and the money given to content creators. In the above-mentioned cases, both the video content creators (YouTubers) and the creators of the musical content, or the companies representing them, are technically co-creators of that particular piece of content. Therefore, each of them should receive a reasonable share of the revenue generated by the platform. At present, there is a conflict between creators, instead, of holding the online platform responsible for ensuring the content is not infringing upon anyone's rights. A clear way of resolving this conflict, as intended by Article 17, would be for user uploads to be 'covered by the licence the platform negotiates with rights holders' (Article13.org, 2019). As a result, YouTubers' videos will not end up being taken down or demonetised, but all creators who are in one way or another contributing to the content will also be fairly rewarded.

Twitch blurs the boundaries

Twitch has had a compelling impact on the current perception of the creator–fan relationship and, along with YouTube, has perhaps even changed the definition of both. Despite being officially presented as a video game streaming service, the Amazon-owned platform is a representation of how technological innovations have further blurred the boundaries between creators and fans, and this affects not only the video game streamers.

In 2020, Twitch signed its first exclusive deal with a music artist. Only a week after the US rapper Logic had announced his retirement from music, he signed an exclusive deal with the platform, which he has been using for years. Despite calling himself 'a nerd' who loves video games and admitting to not being a fan of social media (Stephen 2020), Logic had a partnership with Twitch that goes beyond simply gaming. The fact that his first stream under the new exclusive deal was part of the premiere of an album release clearly indicates the potential opportunities that the platform can provide for music artists.

In addition to its potential benefits to the relationship between creators and fans, Twitch has also received public attention due to discussions over copyright infringement claims related to unlicensed musical material, included in certain users' streams and uploads. Twitch does state clearly in its terms of service that it respects intellectual property and encourages any copyright owner affected by a potential infringement to contact the platform (Twitch 2020a). Furthermore, since 2014, following YouTube's example, Twitch has been using the Audible Magic software to detect and mute sections of uploaded video content which contains unauthorised third-party audio. However, the significant rise in the number of viewers, especially during the Covid-19 pandemic, has again led to important questions being asked about the licence for the used musical content and to numerous takedown requests from members of the music industry

(Cooke 2020b). In response to that, in June 2020, Twitch announced that, by automatically scanning the uploaded user-generated content, they would be deleting any clips of live streams, including some recent ones, which contain unlicensed music. While such measures could potentially be seen as drastic and frustrating by content uploaders, in fact, 'this is in line with copyright protection of musical works' (IP Sentinel 2020).

Similarly to the afore mentioned example from Twitch's terms of service, user agreements of social media platforms would normally address the consequences of any unlicenced use of third-party content. What also needs to be acknowledged here, however, is that the method of detection used has both its merits and disadvantages. While providing a quick and easy way of identifying third-party content and preventing copyright infringement, recognition software, such as YouTube's Content ID and Twitch's Audible Magic, it could still potentially target users incorrectly, 'with little recourse for appeal' (Sawers 2018). Nevertheless, at present, the use of recognition software does seem to be an effective potential solution and the technological advancements related to artificial intelligence (AI) suggest that recognition software could be implemented even more widely in the future.

In addition to policing the unauthorised use of copyrighted musical content, Twitch has also provided solutions to its user community, a way to circumnavigate the restrictions on using third-party audio without this leading to an infringement claim and possible takedown of the video or the channel respectively. First, in 2015, to not limit the streamers' creativity as a result of enforcing copyright laws, Twitch introduced the *Twitch Music Library*, providing hundreds of songs which were cleared for use on the platform. Another feature of Twitch, based entirely on third-party musical content without infringing upon copyrights, is Twitch Sings. The free-to-play singing game is part of the Twitch Services and has been made possible by the negotiated licences with different rightsholders (Twitch 2020a). Of course, the use of the licenced material is strictly limited to the Twitch Services, with the exception that streamers can still export their content to YouTube but cannot monetise the content. However, the measures taken by Twitch have set a good example of how conflicts related to the use of copyright-infringing content can not only be resolved, but perhaps even be avoided from the outset. If the main benefit of social media is that it enables users to create and share content, without the need for having any professional expertise, it cannot be expected of a new user to be aware of all the complexities of music law. For a naïve debutant, it might be easy to stumble into pitfalls and end up infringing upon other creators' copyrights, even unintentionally. Therefore, Twitch's system can serve not only to prevent this, but also to protect rightsholders.

Twitch may have been launched as a result of the rising popularity of a website's gaming category, but the way in which the service has developed over the previous years, and the inclusion of different new features, have taken it way beyond the point of being a video game streaming platform, and with every passing day, Twitch becomes more closely related to the music industry. As a consequence of the 2020 Covid-19 pandemic, music creators and companies have been compelled to examine new revenue opportunities to replace compromised income streams, and the restricted movements of consumers have supported the exploration of new experiences at home. Therefore, it is no surprise that the service is being promoted to music artists as 'a new kind of music venue' where 'musicians can unleash their creativity' and find new ways to reach their audience, with Twitch now being the place where 'fandom gets levelled up' (Twitch 2020b).

Artists becoming TikTok famous

When discussing how dynamically the music industry has changed within the context of the digital domain, there are few better examples than TikTok. Even though it has a relatively short history, with a little help from its predecessors, the short-form video-sharing platform has quickly earned itself the reputation of 'the machine that breaks music' (Fowlkes 2019). There are numerous examples of songs becoming popular worldwide and climbing the major charts as a result of their success on TikTok.

The case of the rapper Supa Dupa Humble is one such example: more than a year after the not-so-popular release of his song 'Steppin'', he noticed a sudden, yet significant, rise in the song's views online. Going through the viewers' comments he came across a name that he did not recognise – TikTok. The rapper may have had no idea about the platform's existence at the time, but that was not an obstacle as his song became a viral hit, using only the first fifteen seconds. Yet another successful case, which has already reached iconic status, is Lil Nas X. As a twenty-year-old college dropout, he had the idea to promote his song 'Old Town Road' with memes on Twitter and Instagram; however, it wasn't until the song went viral on TikTok that it became a global hit (Chow 2019). The song's record-breaking chart performance and the millions of views/streams as well as the label bidding war to sign Lil Nas X helped to provide a comprehensive testimony of TikTok's potential influence on an artist's career.

Not surprisingly, success stories like these have inspired many artists to pursue worldwide success through TikTok. Unlike Supa Dupa Humble, who had not even known about the existence of the platform, two rappers, called ZaeHD and CEO, had decided to create a song with the specific aim of *going viral* on TikTok. Initially, their social media marketing strategy worked well for the song 'All In'. However, the two rappers had not foreseen the risk of their song going viral on TikTok through an incorrectly labelled user-uploaded sample, instead of the official release. The respective hashtag was associated with tens of millions of views, but with no mention of the song or artists' names. Ultimately, ZaeHD and CEO were unsuccessful in getting the song properly labelled on TikTok, but what is especially interesting in this case is that they admitted to not being concerned about a lack of personal recognition because 'the song's success is unprecedented' for where they came from (Chow 2019).

TikTok operates mainly on user-generated content in the form of lip-sync videos, and so the use of third-party copyrighted material is almost unavoidable. As a result, the ByteDance-owned company has had a number of disputes with music copyright holders (Nicolaou 2020) over potential infringements. TikTok has licensing agreements in place with the major labels, as well as with independent distributors and other organisations, such as the UK Music Publishers Association (MPA), allowing users to legally use some musical content for their creations, although a video with a user-uploaded unlicensed musical background is not uncommon. Nevertheless, what needs to be acknowledged here is the fact that, as in the afore mentioned 'All In' case, for some artists it is not essential to be financially rewarded for the use of their music on the platform. They are simply satisfied with their music gaining popularity, with the growing potential to generate income through other revenue streams, such as fan club memberships, crowdfunding platforms, merchandise sales and other brand endorsements deals.

Conclusions and recommendations

To summarise, the internet and other digital technologies have caused a sea change in how music is created and consumed, making it significantly easier for any piece of content to be shared globally and reach an audience, with minimal interference from gatekeepers. However, while artists have always been creators, these new opportunities have also led to a rise in creation of user-generated content which has, in turn, changed expectations and thus caused a split in the demographic of fans, with some joining artists and becoming co-creators.

Copyright legislation has also had to evolve in order to remain fit for purpose, which has led to conflict, uncertainty and disagreements about specific aspects of the copyright laws and the way they are being enforced. Some music artists and copyright owners claim that certain tools or exemptions, such as safe harbours, are outdated and not applicable to the digital domain of the twenty-first century, meaning that fan-generated content is a hindrance to the artists. However, there is potentially a new rulebook for the digital world that contradicts the traditions from the physical one. Internet companies and other creators, of predominantly online content, remain of the opinion that, as an industry, we are in the midst of a digital evolution, which would not have been possible without them and, how certain copyright owners wish to enforce the law only serves to restrict creativity.

By reviewing and analysing how the interrelationships between artists, creators and fans have evolved over the past two decades, it can be noted that copyright laws lack clarity and remain uncertain as to what extent they are applicable in the context of the current digital domain. Nevertheless, the recent developments with new directives are clearly a step forward. Furthermore, new alternative approaches and technological innovations could potentially lead to a fairer enforcement of copyright law. Regardless of opinions, one thing is certain: there is no long-term benefit in copyright owners and creators continuing to pursue their toxic relationship, as they will always be fighting each other, and this can only obstruct creativity. The future of copyright law in the digital domain depends on everyone acknowledging the evolution of our industry and joining forces in finding a mutually beneficial working solution.

References

Alderman, J. (2002). *Sonic Boom: Napster, MP3, and the New Pioneers of Music*. New York: Basic Books.

Andrews, S. (2018). 'Viewpoint: Unlucky 13', *Music Week*, 3 December, 28.

Article13.org (2019). *The Final Version*, https://www.article13.org/article-13, accessed 12 September 2020.

Awbi, A. (2018). 'IFPI slams "value gap" in new Global Music Report', *PRS for Music*, 25 April, https://www.prsformusic.com/m-magazine/news/ifpi-slams-value-gap-in-new-global-music-report/, accessed 5 September 2020.

Baskerville, D. and T. Baskerville (2017). *Music Business Handbook and Career Guide*, 11th edn. California: SAGE Publications.

Beato, R. (2020a). 'Rick Beato', *YouTube*, https://www.youtube.com/channel/UCJquYOG5EL82sKTfH9aMA9Q, accessed 20 July 2020.

Beato, R. (2020b). 'The Music Industry SCAM to Rip-off YouTubers (Rant)', *YouTube*, 22 February, https://www.youtube.com/watch?v=uHh8nPj5SDY, accessed 6 April 2020.

Chow, A. (2019). 'TikTok Is Turning New Artists into Viral Sensations. But Who Actually Benefits?', *Time*, 31 May, https://time.com/5594374/tiktok-artists-money/, accessed 17 May 2020.

Cooke, C. (2020a). 'YouTuber Fails in Lawsuit over YouTube's Handling of Copyright Notices', *CMU Daily*, 17 April, https://completemusicupdate.com/article/youtuber-fails-in-lawsuit-over-youtubes-handling-of-copyright-notices/, accessed 28 July 2020.

Cooke, C. (2020b). 'Twitch Reports Sudden "influx" of Takedown Requests as Prolific Users Hit out a Copyright Claims and Channel ban Threats', *CMU Daily*, 09 June, https://completemusicupdate.com/article/twitch-reports-sudden-influx-of-takedown-requests-as-prolific-users-hit-out-a-copyright-claims-and-channel-ban-threats/, accessed 23 July 2020.

Copyright, Designs and Patents Act 1988, http://www.legislation.gov.uk/ukpga/1988/48/contents, accessed 07 September 2020.

David, M. (2010). *Peer to Peer and the Music Industry: The Criminalization of Sharing*. London: Sage.

Europe for Creators (2019). *An Open Letter to Susan Wojcicki, CEO of YouTube*, 15 March, https://www.article13.org/blog/lettertoceoofyoutube?categoryId=79632, accessed 10 September 2020.

Fowlkes, K. (2019). 'TikTok: The Good, The Bad, The Paradox for the Song Creator', *Medium*, 23 October, https://medium.com/the-courtroom/tiktok-the-good-the-bad-the-paradox-for-the-song-creator-47855be3b5d8, accessed 05 May 2020.

Gaines, J. (1991). *Contested Culture: The Image, the Voice and The Law*. Chapel Hill: University of North Carolina Press.

Galuszka, P. (2014). 'New Economy of Fandom', *Popular Music & Society*, 38, no. 1: 25–43.

Garner, G. (2019). 'Judgement Day: A Timeline of the Article 13 Debate', *Music Week*, 26 March, https://www.musicweek.com/digital/read/judgement-day-a-timeline-of-the-article-13-debate/075736, accessed 05 September 2020.

Glicksman, J. (2020). 'TikTok Continues to Launch Breakout Hits, But Can It Sustain An Artist's Career?', *Billboard*, 22 June, https://www.billboard.com/articles/business/9404479/tiktok-one-hit-wonders-career, accessed 31 August 2020.

Gordon, S. (2015). *The Future of the Music Business*, 4th edn. Milwaukee: Hal Leonard Books.

Hardy, P. (2012). *Download! How the Internet Transformed the Record Business*. London: Omnibus Press.

Hopkins, J. (2006). 'Surprise! There's a third YouTube Co-founder', *USA Today*, 11 October, http://usatoday30.usatoday.com/tech/news/2006-10-11-youtube-karim_x.htm, accessed 09 July 2020.

IP Sentinel (2020). *Twitch and Copyright Infringement Claims*, http://www.iprhelpdesk.eu/blog/twitch-and-copyright-infringement-claims, accessed 10 September 2020.

Jerslev, A. (2016). 'In the Time of the Microcelebrity: Celebrification and the YouTuber Zoella', *International Journal of Communication*, 10: 5233–51.

Joglekar, A. (2018). 'Copyright vs Copyleft – What, Why, How', *Medium*, https://medium.com/@aayushjoglekar/copyright-vs-copyleft-what-why-how-550b1639470a, accessed 21 July 2020.

Johnson, J. (2019). 'How to Survive YouTube Demonetization and Continue Making Money from Your Channel', *Uscreen*, 08 August, https://www.uscreen.tv/blog/how-to-survive-youtube-demonetization/#:~:text=YouTube%20demonetization%20is%20when%20videos,changes%20in%20YouTube's%20advertising%20algorithm.&text=Videos%20are%20removed%20from%20their%20Account%20Monetization%20program, accessed 20 September 2020.

Knopper, S. (2009). *Appetite for Self-Destruction: The Spectacular Crash of the Record Industry in the Digital Age*. London: Simon & Schuster.

Lessig, L. (2005). 'CC in Review: Lawrence Lessig on How It All Began', *Creative Commons*, https://creativecommons.org/2005/10/12/ccinreviewlawrencelessigonhowitallbegan/, accessed 23 September 2020.

Leyshon, A. (2014). *Reformatted: Code, Network and the Transformation of the Music Industry*. Oxford: Oxford University Press.

Liebowitz, S. J. and R. Watt (2006). 'How to Best Ensure Remuneration for Creators in the Market for Music? Copyright and Its Alternatives', *Journal of Economic Surveys*, 20, no. 4: 513–45.

Lin, L. and R. Winkler (2017). 'Social-Media App Musical.ly Is Acquired for as Much as $1 Billion', *Wall Street Journal*, 09 November, https://www.wsj.com/articles/lip-syncing-app-musical-ly-is-acquired-for-as-much-as-1-billion-1510278123, accessed 28 July 2020.

Madiega, T. (2020). *Reform of the EU Liability Regime for Online Intermediaries: Background on the Forthcoming Digital Services Act*. Brussels: European Parliamentary Research Service.

Mercuri, M. (2019). 'How TikTok Influenced Music Discovery In 2019', *Forbes*, 23 December, https://www.forbes.com/sites/monicamercuri/2019/12/23/how-tiktok-influenced-music-discovery-in-2019/#28f29608321b, accessed 31 August 2020.

Morris, J. W. (2013). 'Artists as Entrepreneurs, Fans as Workers', *Popular Music & Society*, 37, no. 3: 273–90.

Music Ally (2018). 'Fan Basis: Subcontracting Marketing to Your Audience', *Music Ally – Sandbox*, 197: 1.

Mustonen, M. (2003). 'Copyleft – the Economics of Linux and Other Open Source Software', *Information Economics & Policy*, 15, no. 1: 99–121.

Negus K., J. Street and A. Behr (2017). 'Copying, Copyright and Originality: Imitation, Transformation and Popular Musicians', *European Journal of Cultural Studies*, 20, no. 4: 363–80.

Nicolaou, A. (2020). 'Music Companies Threaten to sue TikTok over Copyright', *Financial Times*, 04 April, https://www.ft.com/content/1b3b78ea-32a3-4237-8b79-3595820eeb63, accessed 05 May 2020.

Organisation for Economic Co-operation and Development (2007). *Participative Web: User-created Content*, 12 April.

Page, W. (2020). 'Is the Music Copyright Business Worth More than Ever?', *Billboard*, https://static.billboard.com/files/2020/02/Is-The- Music-Copyright-Business-Worth-More-Than-Ever-1582909901.pdf, accessed 7 July 2020.

Paine, A. (2018). 'Spotify has Everything: Piracy Drops as Streaming Wins over Illegal Downloaders', *Music Week*, 2 August, http://www.musicweek.com/digital/read/spotify-has-everything-piracy-drops-as-streaming-wins-over-illegal-downloaders/073373, accessed 10 September 2020.

Paine, A. (2019). 'MEPs Back Copyright Directive, Including Article 13', *Music Week*, 26 March, https://www.musicweek.com/digital/read/meps-back-copyright-directive-including-article-13/075735, accessed 12 September 2020.

Pearson, R. (2010). 'Fandom in the Digital Era', *The International Journal of Media & Culture*, 8, no. 1: 84–95.

Peterson, T. (2020). 'There Is a Battle Going on: TikTok-Instagram Rivalry for Creators Heating Up', *Digiday*, 03 August. Available online: https://digiday.com/future-of-tv/there-is-a-battle-going-on-tiktok-instagram-rivalry-for-creators-heating-up/, accessed 12 September 2020.

Philips, T. and J. Street (2015). 'Copyright and Musicians at the Digital Margins', *Media, Culture & Society*, 37 (3): 342–58.

Roma, P. and D. Aloini (2019). 'How Does Brand-Related User-Generated Content Differ Across Social Media? Evidence Reloaded', *Journal of Business*, 96: 322–39.

Rostama, G. (2015). 'Remix Culture and Amateur Creativity', *WIPO*, https://www.wipo.int/wipo_magazine/en/2015/03/article_0006.html, accessed 23 July 2020.

Sawers, P. (2018). 'YouTube: We've Invested $100 million in Content ID and paid over $3 Billion to Rightsholders', *VentureBeat*, 07 November, https://venturebeat.com/2018/11/07/youtube-weve-invested-100-million-in-content-id-and-paid-over-3-billion-to-rightsholders/, accessed 05 September 2020.

Smartt, U. (2017). *Media & Entertainment Law*, 3rd edn. London: Routledge.

Souppouris, A. (2013). 'Vine Is Now the Number One Free App in the US App Store', *The Verge*, 09 April, https://www.theverge.com/2013/4/9/4204396/vine-number-one-us-app-store-free-apps-chart, accessed 10 July 2020.

Stephen, B. (2020). 'Logic Signs to Twitch, Exclusively', *The Verge*, 20 July, https://www.theverge.com/2020/7/20/21327589/logic-twitch-signing-deal-exclusive-partnership, accessed 23 July 2020.

Tschmuck, P. (2012). *Creativity and Innovation in the Music Industry*. Berlin: Springer-Verlag.

Twitch (2020a). 'Terms of Service', *Twitch*, https://www.twitch.tv/p/legal/terms-of-service/, accessed 29 July 2020.

Twitch (2020b). 'The Stage Is Yours', *Twitch*, https://www.twitch.tv/p/en/artists/, accessed 29 July 2020.

Van Der Sar, E. (2020). 'YouTube Fights Off Lawsuit Over "Retaliatory" Copyright Strikes', *Torrent Freak*, 15 April, https://torrentfreak.com/youtube-fights-off-lawsuit-over-retaliatory-copyright-strikes-200415/, accessed 28 July 2020.

Ward-Ure, L. (2018). 'Copyright Uncovered: Fair Use v Fair Dealing', *DACS*, https://www.dacs.org.uk/latest-news/copyright-uncovered-%E2%80%93-q3-2018-fair-use-v-fair-deal?category=For+Artists&title=N, accessed 28 July 2020.

Wikstrom, P. (2009). *The Music Industry*. Cambridge: Polity.

Wilson, Z. (2020). 'How TikTok became the New Music Tipsheet for Radio Programmers', *The Music Network*, 11 May, https://themusicnetwork.com/tiktok-music-2020-tipsheet/, accessed 30 August 2020.

5

Piracy: Past, present and future

How the recording industry can disrupt, mitigate and innovate in troubled waters

James Brandes

Internet piracy is the practice of downloading and distributing unlicensed content digitally without permission. The principles behind piracy predate the creation of the internet but it has become ubiquitous in the digital age. Piracy is thus a huge issue for the recording industry and according to the Recording Industry Association of America, costs the US economy $12.5 billion per year in lost revenue (RIAA 2020). Hence, it is fair to say that information technology has created challenging conditions that are difficult to adapt to. At the same time, technology has created new opportunities that the recording industry is now exploiting. The law has also concomitantly struggled to keep pace with these technological developments, and copyright laws designed to protect the recording industry need amelioration worldwide.

This chapter examines the evolution of piracy in the digital age, the legal framework, responses by the music business and technological solutions that have transformed the way we listen to and interact with music. It also draws on practice-based research derived from operating the Digital Copyright Consultancy,[1] an internet anti-piracy business that removes unlicensed content on behalf of prominent artists and leading independent record labels. The discourse is expanded with reference to academic articles and news stories chosen from authoritative sites on internet piracy.

Before the internet, record companies and distributors could effectively control the distribution of their content. If you wanted an album you had to

---

[1] The Digital Copyright Consultancy is an internet anti-piracy business that is run by James Brandes, the author of this chapter. It provides takedown and consultancy services for over twenty record companies.

physically buy it from a record shop which got its stock from a record company or distributor. This business model was secure, predictable and repeatable, and led to compound growth (Mulligan 2015). The technology at the time also helped. Vinyl, for instance, was extraordinarily hard to copy due to costly and time-consuming production processes that required a great deal of technical expertise. Cassette tape copying was much easier and allowed people to buy an album on cassette and make unlicensed copies for their friends and family or even curate their own music via mixtapes. The British Phonographic Industry (BPI) saw the commercial dangers of this and created the campaign 'Home Taping is Killing Music' (Peel 2008). Yet, prior to the internet, pirated music could be bought or shared in only a limited number of locations (Sudler 2013). Pat Carr of Remote Control[2] remarks: 'Tim [Wheeler] of Ash[3] walked into a shop in Tokyo, found 15 Ash bootlegs and took them to the counter. When the shop assistant insisted on payment, Tim pointed to the front cover and remarked "this is me", and the shop assistant profusely apologised' (Brandes and Carr 2020).

Music piracy became widespread due to recordable compact disc technology, which created hassle-free identical copies, and the internet, which allowed limitless dissemination. These two factors opened up a Pandora's Box and, as a result, the recording industry could no longer control the distribution of unlicensed content and thus manage the relationship between supply and demand. Despite the best efforts of record companies and distributors, anti-piracy companies[4] and even governments worldwide, internet piracy has proven extraordinarily resilient. It has adapted successfully to the changing circumstances and new technology but the utilisation of various approaches can allow the recording industry to mitigate, adapt and disrupt.

Peer-to-peer piracy

In the late 1990s several file-sharing programs came to prominence and allowed the distribution of music albums and tracks via peer-to-peer (P2P) technology.

---

[2] Remote Control is a music consultancy company run by renowned industry professional Pat Carr. Its clients include Ash, Alt-J, Idles, Laura Marling, Fontaines D.C, DMA's and Melanie C.
[3] Ash is a Northern Irish rock band formed in Downpatrick, County Down, in 1989 by vocalist and guitarist Tim Wheeler, bassist Mark Hamilton and drummer Rick McMurray.
[4] Excluding the BPI, IFPI, RIAA and other trade body anti-piracy teams, the main private anti-piracy companies that provide services for clients in the recording industry are as follows: MUSO, Audiolock, Web Sheriff, Grayzone, Linkbusters, Digital Copyright Consultancy and Leak Delete.

P2P file-sharing allows users to access and download music using a P2P software program that searches for other connected computers known as peers on a P2P network (Tiwari 2016). The first was a pioneering P2P network called Napster which was set up by Sean Parker and Shawn Fanning and generated revenue only through t-shirt sales (Lamont 2013). Initially, a major brake on consumer adaptation was limited bandwidth. We now take fast internet speeds for granted but downloading online music twenty years ago via a 56k modem was approximately 1,000 times slower than it is today. However, as internet speeds increased, Napster became exponentially more popular and in the space of just six months went from 1.1 million users to 6.7 million (Parks 2014). Napster was a real threat to the recording industry (Forde 2019) as there were no longer any limitations to the types of music that music fans could obtain as it was all freely available (Lamont 2013). The genie was out of the bottle and the genie had no intention of getting back in.

Yet, despite superficially empowering consumers, Napster encouraged mass-scale copyright infringement as its users downloaded content for free without the permission of the copyright holder. Consumers at the time seemed 'wilfully blinkered' that all songs were free via Napster (Lamont 2013). When the heavy metal band Metallica learnt that their pre-released track 'I Disappear' (Law 2020) and the entire discography had been uploaded on Napster without their authorisation, they sued Napster (West 2017). Furthermore, Metallica used a now defunct British anti-piracy agency called NetPD to identify the people who had downloaded this track without their permission (Houston 2000). In Metallica v Napster, Inc., it was ruled that Napster had to search its system and remove all copyrighted songs by Metallica (Metallica v Napster 2001). In another case, eighteen record labels united to take on Napster through the RIAA. In A & M Records, Inc. v Napster, Inc., 114 F. Supp. 2d 896, the RIAA successfully argued that Napster was guilty of contributory and vicarious copyright infringement and this was reaffirmed via appeal in A & M Records, Inc. v Napster, Inc., 239 F.3d 1004 (9th Cir. 2001). Napster argued that it could not effectively police its servers as its metadata[5] was so hard to decrypt that it made identification of infringement impossible. While this argument tried to circumvent legal arguments evinced by the RIAA, it had the effect of arguing that Napster was so badly coded that the service was irredeemably flawed because it could not be policed effectively. The corollary was that Napster was forced to

---

[5] Metadata is data that provides information about other data.

implement audio fingerprinting technology (Cohen 2001) but had to shut its P2P service when it could not achieve 100 per cent accuracy (Richtel 2001). This is impossible and something that YouTube has not achieved nearly twenty years later. Napster filed for Chapter 11 bankruptcy in May 2002 (Dansby 2002).

There were many other sites like Napster and they included Grokster, a P2P application that generated revenue through online advertisements in the user interface and was operated by a privately owned software company in the West Indies (Hornick 2005). Unlike Napster, Grokster allowed users to trade files directly between one another without these transactions passing through a centralised server. There were important reasons why Grokster operated like this. As Napster maintained a limited amount of control over the transaction of files through its server, it was ruled illegal because it should have exercised its power over the server to stop the sharing of copyright-infringing files. Grokster sought to avoid this legal obstacle. However, they were not successful and in MGM Studios, Inc. v Grokster, Ltd., 545 U.S. 913 (2005), the United States Supreme Court held that 'one who distributes a device with the object of promoting its use to infringe copyright, as shown by clear expression or other affirmative steps taken to foster infringement, is liable for the resulting acts of infringement by third parties' (MGM Studios v Grokster Verdict 2005: 19). As part of a lawsuit permitted by the MGM Studios v Grokster Supreme Court decision, Grokster agreed to pay $50 million to the recording industry (Borland 2005) and ceased operating shortly thereafter (Jardin 2005).

The Pirate Bay

The recording industry thought that it had won but then the file-sharing ecosystem transmuted yet again with the arrival of The Pirate Bay, a search engine website for BitTorrent[6] that allowed millions of people to share unlicensed albums, TV programmes and movies. The website was set up Peter Sunde, Fredrik Neij and Gottfrid Svartholm, all IT specialists and members of a Swedish think tank called Piratbyrån established to support the free sharing of information, culture and intellectual property. Thus, it is unsurprising that Pirate Bay has a long-standing history of defiance towards copyright holders and their rights agents and this was most clearly exemplified by its habit of publicly mocking their copyright notices.

[6] BitTorrent is one torrent client. The other is uTorrent.

The first raid of The Pirate Bay in 2006 was largely unsuccessful (Wired 2006). Two hundred servers were seized (BBC 2006), yet The Pirate Bay reappeared on the internet just three days after a police raid shut down the website. The raid also sparked street protests in Sweden, where The Pirate Bay owners were based at the time, and intense international interest (Libbenga 2006). The reborn website, newly relocated to servers in the Netherlands, appeared as it was before the police action but included a revamped logo that showed the site's trademark pirate ship hurling a cannon ball at the Hollywood sign (Kim 2019). However, the later trial in the Stockholm District Court (Case B 13301-06) in 2009 was far more successful. Peter Sunde et al. were all "found guilty of facilitating mass copyright infringement" (Harrison 2017: 390). Each of the three received one year in jail and fines that totalled $3,620,000 (Enigmax 2009). Yet, the torrent search engine still operates calling itself an index of digital content, and it was, once again, identified as a notorious site responsible for distributing unlicensed content (Office of the United States Trade Representative 2016).

Cyberlockers

The Pirate Bay trial seemed a critical blow for the illicit file-sharing industry but it transformed into something else again with the advent of cyberlockers, a way to download content with just one click. Unlike torrents, cyberlockers are extremely easy to use and do not require software to download unlicensed content. Internet piracy exploded in 2006 due to their simplicity and speed of download and in 2007, Alexa index listed Megaupload and RapidShare as the thirteenth and eighteenth most popular websites on the internet (Roettgers 2007). Uploading incentives and payment to uploaders based on pay per click (PPC) metrics drove the distribution of popular unlicensed content and this in turn changed free downloaders limited by download speed to premium, paying subscribers who had no limitations on speed or what they could download (Sanjuàs-Cuxart 2012). Unlike P2P, a significant number of users paid for premium membership accounts for unlimited, faster downloads on RapidShare and Megaupload (Sanjuàs-Cuxart 2012). Cyberlockers are thus extremely lucrative businesses unlike P2P and torrent search engines.

This explosion in unlicensed content led to business opportunities for entrepreneurs to pitch services to those suffering from the deleterious effects of internet piracy. Up until 2007, there was a dearth of anti-piracy businesses as unlicensed content found via torrent search engines and other P2P sites was hard to remove, with the content not being hosted on a server but transferred from computer to computer. However, all that has changed with the advent of cyberlockers as worldwide copyright laws compel them to remove reported unlicensed content which is directly hosted on their servers. Most countries have copyright laws (based on the Berne Convention) that give copyright holders exclusive rights such as reproduction and distribution rights and forbid the sharing of unlicensed content. For websites hosted in the United States, the Digital Millennium Copyright Act of 1998 (DMCA) provides safe harbour provisions under Section 512, thus protecting service providers (who meet certain conditions) from monetary damages for the infringing activities of their users and other third parties. However, to receive these protections service providers must comply with the conditions set forth in Section 512, including notice-and-takedown procedures that give copyright holders a quick and easy way to disable access to unlicensed content.

Anti-Piracy in the cyberlocker era

Between 2008 and 2011 new anti-piracy businesses were formed to remove content off cyberlockers, and they provided services alongside trade bodies such as the RIAA and BPI. The BPI, in fact, offers a free takedown service for its members via its Anti-Piracy Unit (Harrison 2017). The way those anti-piracy businesses deal with internet piracy is vastly different. Some are automated technology solutions while others are operated by individuals with legal and research experience. Automated services allow scalability and can work on an infinite number of projects whereas bespoke anti-piracy businesses that use a combination of automated and manual methodologies provide the most effective and thorough service but are limited as to the number of projects they can work on at any given time. They also tend to cost more, particularly for heavily pirated releases. The anti-piracy process involves removing unlicensed content from cyberlockers, tube sites like YouTube, torrent websites and infringing results from Google's search engine. Up until the end of 2011, Google insisted that all copyright notices sent to them had to be faxed. Google would take approximately two weeks to remove unlicensed content from its search engine. It had to create an entirely new reporting system (Masnick 2012) due to pressure from the creative industries. Removal times dropped from over one week to under three hours for Google

Trusted Partners.[7] Consequently, there was an explosion of reported URLs removed from search (Van der Sar 2016) and a pronounced improvement in the effectiveness of anti-piracy campaigns.

RapidShare and Megaupload

The pirate industry still functions, however, and has not been fatally damaged despite high-profile legal cases against torrent sites and cyberlockers. This does not diminish the battles won by the recording industry and the disruption caused. Many cyberlockers no longer operate. Some cyberlockers were cooperative with regards to dealing with copyright infringement on their servers while some were not. RapidShare was the first major cyberlocker and was cooperative with rightsholders and their agents. It was a service that took copyright infringement more seriously than most and did not offer a search engine for users to find unlicensed content on its servers (Antoniades, Markatos and Dovrolis 2009). While RapidShare was targeted repeatedly by the creative industries (Essers 2013), it did work closely with the Digital Copyright Consultancy to remove infringing content from its servers. The Digital Copyright Consultancy identified over two petabytes[8] of infringing music, films, software and pornography that RapidShare promptly deleted. In addition to that, the Digital Copyright Consultancy also helped RapidShare identify thousands of accounts guilty of repeat infringement. Despite significant efforts to remove unlicensed content (BBC 2015) and expensive lobbying efforts in Washington (Litwick 2011), RapidShare chose to shut down in 2015 (Lardinois 2015) as the site became unappealing to uploaders which in turn had a negative effect on subscriptions and, ultimately, revenue. The constant threat of legal action and the consultancy services of the Digital Copyright Consultancy disrupted the activities of thousands of pirates.

Some cyberlockers on the other hand, were forcibly taken offline. Megaupload was identified as a notorious website (Office of the United States Trade Representative 2011) and ceased operating in January 2012. The website was founded by a German national called Kim Schmitz (now known as Kim Dotcom) who had been convicted of computer fraud in 1994 and embezzlement

---

[7] Google Trusted Partners are copyright holders and anti-piracy companies that frequently submit Copyright Notices to Google.
[8] A petabyte is 1,000 terabytes, so two petabytes of unlicensed content is equivalent to 2,000 1 terabyte hard drives full of unlicensed content.

in 2003 but received suspended sentences for both charges (Gallagher (2012). At its peak, Megaupload had 50m official users (Bohas 2012), was the thirteenth most visited site on the planet (BBC 2012) and had a gross revenue of approximately $175m per year (Graeber 2012). Megaupload was indicted and charged with 'engaging in a racketeering conspiracy, conspiring to commit copyright infringement, conspiring to commit money laundering and two substantive counts of criminal copyright infringement,' (US Department of Justice 2012) by a grand jury in the Eastern District of Virginia on 5 January 2012. As a consequence of the indictment, over twenty search warrants were executed and data centres in the Netherlands, Canada and the United States of America were raided. In addition, Kim Dotcom was arrested in a dawn raid at his home (Van Der Sar 2012).

While it is true that Megaupload paid uploaders money to upload popular content and should have done a lot more to stamp out repeat infringement, they were always very responsive to copyright claims and offered a takedown tool to the recording industry and their rights agents (Anderson 2012). The armed dawn raid by agents from the Federal Bureau of Investigation (FBI) in New Zealand and the subsequent takedown of the Megaupload website without trial seemed disproportionate. What arguably led to Megaupload's downfall was the streaming service Megavideo that allowed a user to stream all Megaupload URLs, and Kim Dotcom's extravagant lifestyle which included possession of eighteen luxury cars, a $30 million mansion in New Zealand and $50 million in assets (Johnston 2012). Kim Dotcom has been fighting extradition to the United States of America for eight years and there seems to be no end in sight (Van der Sar 2019b).

The Megaupload fallout

After Megaupload was forced offline, over a dozen rogue cyberlockers voluntarily closed (Maxwell 2012), so legal pressure significantly disrupted this illicit industry. One of those rogue cyberlockers was Wupload, an uncooperative service run by a clandestine parent company in the Far East and a haven for unlicensed content (Lauinger 2013). Wupload provided monetary incentives for affiliates ($40 for 1,000 downloads) to upload popular/often pirated content to change free downloaders (capped download speeds) into premium paying members who could download content without restriction (Brandes 2012).

Uploaders made a lot of money sharing unlicensed content on Wupload and were often congratulated by Wupload's CEO on the notorious file-sharing forum, Wjunction (Brandes 2012). It was not in Wupload's interests to remove profitable pirate affiliates as they helped drive traffic/money to the site. This therefore explains why Wupload's copyright infringement department was often obstructive. For most of 2011, Wupload frustrated all legitimate removal attempts and made close to fifty misrepresentations to the Digital Copyright Consultancy that they had deleted unlicensed content when they had not (Brandes 2012). Due to their recalcitrance, the Digital Copyright Consultancy reported Wupload to their ISP, WebaZilla, on over twenty occasions as well as to the International Federation of the Phonographic Industry (IFPI) and BREIN (Brandes 2012). Wupload begrudgingly provided administrative access in mid-September 2011 (Brandes 2012). The IFPI and other agencies had similar problems with Wupload, hence the reason they were on a piracy list (Sandoval 2012).

Another service that was taken offline in 2012 was Hotfile (Van der Sar 2013). Its owner, Anton Titov, settled out of court with the Motion Picture Association of America for a sum of £4 million (Van der Sar 2014). The site was a haven for unlicensed content and 90 per cent of files downloaded through the service were thought to be infringing (Hart 2014). However, Hotfile was cooperative with rights owners and their agents and even offered them a takedown tool, thus allowing instantaneous removal of unlicensed content (Gardner 2013). Yet, Hotfile did little to stop repeat infringement (Tarantola 2012). In fact, in the case of Disney Enterprises, Inc. v Hotfile Corp., 798 F. Supp. 2d 1303, it was discovered that Hotfile had received over ten million takedown notices and yet had terminated only forty-three users in total (Disney Enterprises 2013).

The forcible closure of Hotfile considerably disrupted unlicensed file-sharing, but in recent years, there has been a spate of uncooperative sites which is a predictable consequence of cooperative sites voluntarily closing or being forcibly shut down. From a pirate's perspective, there is not much to be gained through a veneer of cooperation. Purplinx was a site that did not cooperate and was hosted by a German ISP called Contabo that often ignored copyright infringement by its clients. Purplinx ceased trading approximately one year ago. Another uncooperative site called Dbr.ee was taken offline in 2019 (Van der Sar 2019a). Dbr.ee was connected to several notorious pirate linking sites and largely refused to cooperate with rights holders and their agents (RIAA Cloudflare Notice 2019). They were so uncooperative that the Digital Copyright Consultancy repeatedly escalated copyright claims to their ISP, IP Volume, to force compliance. While content would be removed eventually, this added significant delay and reduced the efficacy of anti-piracy campaigns. If a site is uncooperative, the only imperfect solution is to remove those URLs from Google and Bing's search engine via their copyright abuse report pages.

Despite some very high-profile cyberlocker closures, many other cyberlockers became havens for unlicensed content and they included Uploaded.net, ifolder.ru, Zippyshare, Depositfiles, Letitbit.net, Bitshare and Freakshare. Only three of those sites still operate. However, despite the above-mentioned solution, internet piracy is still widespread, with hundreds of cyberlockers still using the same piracy-friendly business model pioneered by Hotfile.

Cyberlockers in 2020

Many cyberlockers offer placatory takedown access to the recording industry and their agents. One of them is Rapidgator.com, a service identified as a notorious market (Office of the United States Trade Representative 2017) that provides monetary incentives to uploaders (Maxwell 2018) and generates revenue from premium subscriptions. The most prolific uploaders of music on Rapidgator are Intmusic, NewAlbumReleases and Rlsbb. Intmusic has been around for seven years and repeatedly re-upload content on Rapidgator. NewAlbumReleases is another pirate linking site which makes money via its affiliate arrangements with cyberlockers and through advertising. While they claim via a clumsy disclaimer that they are not responsible for uploading content to cyberlockers and that they are merely a search engine, they have uploaded well over fifty thousand albums without the permission of rights holders (Brandes 2013b). Moreover, they do not remove content on request and constantly re-upload albums even when it is apparent that the content owner wants it removed (Brandes 2013b). Rlsbb is even worse and is a haven for a bewildering amount of unlicensed content. They upload to multiple mirrors which can add time to the takedown process as some services are far more cooperative in removing unlicensed content off their servers than others. Identifying the owners of Rlsbb should be of paramount importance to the recording industry, anti-piracy services and trade bodies such as the BPI. This site is a thorn in the side of the recording industry and taking legal action against the people who run this site would greatly reduce the level of music piracy out there.

Rapidgator is thus aware that Rlsbb et al. are repeat infringers, yet does little to discourage their activity as they are profitable pirate affiliates that help change free downloaders into paying premium members. Yet, Rapidgator does offer takedown access to copyright holders and their rights agents. Instantaneous removal of unlicensed content provides a level of consistency and predictability for all anti-piracy campaigns. When a cyberlocker is cooperative with takedown requests, there is no need to escalate the issue to its ISP or to payment processors it may use such as PayPal, WebMoney, Mastercard or Visa. Conversely, when a cyberlocker is not cooperative, this often means escalating the issue to ISPs and payment processors, thus adding significant delays to the takedown process. Although perhaps a controversial and unpopular viewpoint, cooperative cyberlockers are perhaps a necessary evil and should be tolerated by the recording industry.

There are, of course, existing cloud services that do not cooperate with rights holders and the recording industry needs to disrupt their activities as expeditiously as possible. Dropapk.to and Mixloads.com are rogue services that aid and abet the distribution of unlicensed music content. Information with regards to who operates those sites is hard to come by although both seem to be run by individuals who reside in Vietnam, and they have chosen an uncooperative ISP based in Columbia called Network Dedicated. The Digital Copyright Consultancy has repeatedly escalated issues to Network Dedicated but has never had a response.

Dropapk.to are also ably assisted by reselling websites such as Account Instant, Premium Key Store and Premium Voucher that sell Dropapk.to premium accounts and codes despite being aware of the fact that Dropapk.to is a haven for pirated content. Many of these services also operate from Vietnam and use services like PayPal to receive payments. Reselling websites create an additional layer of obfuscation by insulating rogue cloud services from copyright infringement claims to payment processors. Hence, it is exceedingly difficult to stop the flow of illicit cash to these rogue services. Payment processors could do more to stop flagrant copyright infringement committed by their clients. Not only is their abuse process slow and convoluted but they have also shown a reluctance to deal with resellers who are aware that they are selling premium memberships (via PayPal) to services that largely ignore copyright notices. Hitting resellers where it hurts should be a serious priority for record companies, anti-piracy businesses and trade bodies. Payment processors have indirectly profited from copyright infringement for too long. It is time that services such as PayPal et al.

were much tougher on reselling websites, but this will come only with persistent legal pressure from the recording industry.

Blocking websites in the UK

There are other ways that the recording industry has disrupted illicit file-sharing. In England, record companies have harnessed Section 97A of the Copyright, Designs and Patents Act of 1988[9] to force the largest UK broadband providers into imposing court-ordered blocks of torrent search engines. In 2013, EMI Records Ltd. sought an injunction to block '[KickAssTorrents], H33T and Fenopy' (Harrison 2017: 391). By 2017, one ISP informed Torrentfreak that their block-list had expanded to cover nearly 4,000 URLs (Van der Sar 2017). The original injunction required those ISPs to restrict access not only to the primary website but also to mirrors or web-based proxy servers. In 2015, the law firm Wiggin LLP revealed that an unopposed application costs approximately £14,000 per site (Jackson 2017). On top of the cost of legal intervention, the additional administration required to maintain the block and keep ISPs up to date with related IP address changes and new URLs costs around £3,600 per site per year (Jackson 2017). At the same time ISPs also incur ongoing costs as part of their work to introduce the blocks. Sky Broadband hinted at a mid-three figure sum for each update and then roughly half that for future updates (Jackson 2017).

Did this policy work? The answer is yes, but it took time. During an anti-piracy project, copyright notices are sent to Google in order to remove infringing results that appear via their search engine. As a result of torrent site blockades, new infringing search results appeared constantly as those torrent sites were forced to use proxies and alternative URLs (Brandes 2013a). This, in turn, created more work for copyright holders (particularly for small record companies who are not members of the BPI) and their agents. In 2013, the Digital Copyright Consultancy estimated that well over five million additional search results had been removed from Google due to sites using alternative URLs (Brandes 2013a). At the time the strategy appeared incorrect, yet there are now far fewer alternative torrent URLs and proxies. The blocking policy has

---

[9] Section 97A of the Copyright, Designs and Patents Act 1988: https://www.legislation.gov.uk/ukpga/1988/48/section/97A (accessed 12 October 2020).

worked, but there are issues. While torrent search engines help facilitate the sharing of unlicensed films, television programmes, music and pornography, it must also be borne in mind that they provide the capability to share free, public domain content. Although effective, web blocking with minimal oversight has potential censorship implications.

Piracy warnings

In addition to blocking websites, ISPs in the UK have sent approximately one million internet piracy warning emails to those they suspect of taking part in copyright infringement (Jackson 2019a). According to the BPI, the campaign led to a 26 per cent reduction in piracy (BPI News 2018) but has now been ceased because 'it served its purpose' (Jackson 2019b). This is a continuation of policies used by content owners and trade bodies over the last fifteen years. Back in 2010, two now defunct law firms called Gallant Macmillan and ACS Law represented several large music labels including Ministry of Sound (BBC 2010). They convinced their clients that they could identify who had downloaded unlicensed copies of their albums and that they would be able to obtain their postal addresses from ISPs using a UK legal procedure called a Norwich Pharmacal order that was first granted in Norwich Pharmacal Co. & Others v Customs and Excise Commissioners [1974] AC 133. Initially this procedure worked as infringers paid fines. However, BT resisted providing Gallant Macmillan with names and eventually sent a legal bill of £150,000 to Ministry of Sound. In addition, Minstry's website received a denial of service attack from Anonymous (Leydon 2010) and Gallant Macmillan voluntarily took down their site (Judge 2010), changed their name and eventually ceased trading. There was a visible PR backlash against Ministry for trying to enforce their intellectual property rights in this way (Guadamuz 2010).

There also seemed to be several legislative victories for the recording industry with the enactment of the Digital Copyright Act 2010 in the UK and HADOPI in France. HADOPI established a legal framework for a strike policy whereby repeat file sharers could have their internet connection cut off after three warnings. HADOPI had a small positive impact on music sales (Danaher 2012). Yet, it likely had less impact on music sales than anticipated as people switched to downloading unlicensed content from cyberlockers and streaming.

Streaming – A solution to internet piracy?

In recent years, many have suggested that streaming is a potential panacea for the recording industry. Streaming businesses such as Spotify and YouTube have dramatically altered the way we all interact with and consume music and some opine that it has also reduced piracy. This is debatable. YouTube's copyright abuse process has improved in recent years but it could still be augmented. If a record company has access to ContentID (a system that automatically deletes content via fingerprinting) then it is easy to remove unlicensed content. However, removing content without ContentID is not as simple. Their copyright abuse process remains clunky for record companies that do not have access to YouTube's Content Verification Programme[10] as one must report one URL at a time and say what the release is each time. YouTube's abuse process is also largely automated and it is difficult to find an individual to talk to (Vitale 2018). Furthermore, there is a cap of ten URLs that can be submitted per copyright notice. This stops small record companies from exercising control over their catalogues.

Furthermore, while content owners can earn extra income from monetising unlicensed downloads, it legitimises YouTube's large unlicensed music catalogue. This is not 'an opportunity open to other music services which depend solely on what tracks [record companies] make available to them' (Mulligan 2015: 202). It is one rule for YouTube and one for the rest because music labels dare not oppose YouTube nor can they do without it. In addition, Google AdSense payments to content owners do not compare favourably with those of other streaming services (Csathy 2020). The recording industry constantly bemoans the poor level of income relative to plays (Moskvitch 2016) yet rarely remove their content and if they do like Warner Music did in 2008 (Adegoke 2008), they eventually renegotiate and their content is back on YouTube months later (Kafka 2016). In 2017, the IFPI stated that YouTube is the single greatest threat to the renewed growth of the recording industry (Aswad 2020).

This is further exacerbated by external stream ripping sites which allow YouTube URLs to be downloaded and saved to a computer. These stream ripping sites have become extremely popular, particularly with sixteen- to twenty-four-year-olds (Cuthbertson 2016). The BPI has now indicated that it will obtain

---

[10] The YouTube Content Verification Programme allows copyright holders to submit URLs without restriction.

court orders in the UK to block stream ripping websites (Van der Sar 2020), so this is another example of the recording industry disrupting the activities of pirate sites, but surely pressure needs to be put on YouTube as well?

The recording industry is conflicted over YouTube because it can make or break an artist. Psy's Gangnam Style went viral on YouTube and was the first video to receive one billion views (Gruger 2012). We are in the age of the YouTube star and it is likely that Justin Bieber would not have risen to such prominence without YouTube (Beech 2020). Radio stations also increasingly use streaming statistics including YouTube plays as a metric to judge how popular a track is (Harrison 2017) and, according to Pat Carr, 'pop music pluggers are reluctant to plug tracks before they're nearing eight million streams on the clock' (Brandes and Carr 2020). The power that YouTube has may further explain why the recording industry is reluctant to stand up to YouTube on issues such as pay and copyright. Nevertheless, the recording industry needs to collectively stand up to YouTube, otherwise this unsatisfactory situation will continue.

Spotify has always had a much stronger stance against copyright infringement than YouTube. It is rare to find unlicensed content on Spotify. Moreover, it generally pays artists and labels more fairly than YouTube. In fact, Spotify paid $15 billion to rights holders in 2019 compared to $3 billion paid by YouTube (Hall 2020). Yet, despite the large number of free users and paying subscribers, Spotify has never posted an annual profit in twelve years and thus continues to haemorrhage money for its shareholders (Ingham 2020). Spotify still cannot successfully earn revenue at a rate that exceeds its operational costs. Jeff Bell of Partisan Records[11] stated in an interview with the Digital Copyright Consultancy that 'although live music has been decimated during the pandemic, sales and streams have increased considerably during the pandemic' (Brandes and Bell 2020) and asserted that 'even if Spotify fails, another streaming business will simply take its place' (Brandes and Bell 2020). Streaming has had in some cases a positive mitigating effect on internet piracy but it is still there and this is especially true during the Covid-19 pandemic. The Digital Copyright Consultancy has seen a considerable increase in internet piracy for record companies that have chosen to release albums and singles during this period. Many pirate linking sites such as Intmusic are uploading and re-uploading unlicensed content to cyberlockers far more frequently, thus negatively affecting the efficacy of anti-piracy campaigns.

---

[11] Jeff Bell is Label Manager at indie record label Partisan Records which has released albums by Idles, Fontaines D.C. and Laura Marling.

A tougher legal approach to internet piracy?

The injurious effects of internet piracy are the reason why the European Union (EU) created copyright legislation more appropriate for the digital age. Article 17 of the EU Directive on Copyright in the Digital Single Market seeks to radically transform and drastically curtail the distribution of unlicensed content online. It is tougher on online content-sharing service providers than previous laws but there is a liability exemption regime in Article 17(4) for online content-sharing service providers if they:

(a) made best efforts to obtain an authorisation, and
(b) made, in accordance with high industry standards of professional diligence, best efforts to ensure the unavailability of specific works and other subject matter for which the rightsholders have granted the service providers the relevant and necessary information; and in any event
(c) acted expeditiously, upon receiving a sufficiently substantiated notice from the rightsholders, to disable access to, or to remove from their websites, the notified works or other subject matter, and made best efforts to prevent their future uploads in accordance with point b (Directive EU 2019/790).

The recording industry sees Article 17 as a magic bullet with which to take aim at those facilitating the distribution of unlicensed content (Resnikoff 2018). In fact, most cyberlockers would likely fall foul of all the above-mentioned provisions; yet, according to Kathy Berry at Linklaters, 'there is likely to be an ongoing lack of legal and commercial certainty until the details are fleshed out, either by the Commission's Guidance or by European case law' (Berry 2019). Moreover, for Article 17 to work as intended, the directive needs to be transposed similarly across all member states (Daniel 2019) and there needs to be similar legislation worldwide. Without a coordinated effort, most cyberlockers will likely move to ISPs that are not in the EU. They could use uncooperative ISPs like Network Dedicated operating out of Columbia or Quasinetworks that operates from the Seychelles. It will also be interesting to see how the situation develops in the UK as Government Minister Chris Skidmore stated in Parliament that the country has no plans to implement the directive following the UK's exit from the European Union (Parliament UK 2020). The implications of this are currently unknown.

Conclusion

The recording industry has suffered due to the digital revolution and the deleterious effects of internet piracy. It is, however, adapting to this changing landscape and has had some notable legal victories against P2P sites and torrent websites, and is benefiting from the streaming revolution. Yet, the numerous cases against cyberlockers have not been quite as successful. Although it is an annoyance when cyberlockers turn a blind eye to repeat infringement, if they remove content expeditiously then this would mitigate the pernicious effects of piracy considerably. Many of these cooperative cyberlockers have been replaced with sites that do not cooperate with rightsholders and their agents. Uncooperative sites can hamper the efficacy of anti-piracy campaigns. The phrase, better the devil you know, is apt concerning cyberlockers.

The recording industry has seen the benefits of streaming. Nevertheless, it is still largely powerless when it comes to YouTube who continue to pay artists and labels comparatively derisory sums while they legitimise their unlicensed music catalogue through ContentID. The recording industry needs to collectively find a way to stand up to YouTube but this will be difficult due to YouTube's money and negotiating power. Could a major record company like Universal remove all their music from YouTube? What would happen if other labels followed suit? These questions are beyond the scope of this chapter but could be considered as areas for further research.

There has also been legislation in recent years enacted to disrupt internet piracy but there needs to be coordinated response across jurisdictions for it to be successful in the long term. Article 17 has the potential to stop a great deal of piracy but only if similar legislation is enacted worldwide.

The recording industry has disrupted and innovated in troubled waters but it can do more.

References

Adegoke, Y. (2008). 'Warner Music Pulls Videos from YouTube', *Reuters*, https://uk.reuters.com/article/industry-us-warner-youtube/warner-music-pulls-videos-from-youtube-idUKTRE4BJ1EY20081220, accessed 3 November 2020.

Anderson, N. (2012). 'Why the Feds Smashed Megaupload', *Ars Technica*, https://arstechnica.com/tech-policy/2012/01/why-the-feds-smashed-megaupload/, accessed 3 November 2020.

Antoniades, D., E. Markatos and C. Dovrolis (2009). 'One-Click Hosting Services: A File-Sharing Hideout', *Research Gate*, https://www.researchgate.net/publication/221612007_One-click_hosting_services_A_file-sharing_hideout, accessed 3 November 2020.

Aswad, J. (2020). 'Recording Industry Association Responds to Lyor Cohen: "Why Is YouTube Paying So Little?"' *Variety*, https://variety.com/2017/digital/news/riaa-posts-fiery-response-to-blog-post-from-youtubes-lyor-cohen-1202533230/, accessed 3 November 2020.

BBC (2006). 'Swedish Piracy Row Gathers Pace', *BBC*, http://news.bbc.co.uk/1/hi/technology/5047750.stm, accessed 3 November 2020.

BBC (2010). 'Lawyers to Continue Piracy Fight', *BBC*, https://www.bbc.co.uk/news/technology-11443861, accessed 3 November 2020.

BBC (2012). 'Profile: Megaupload File-Sharing Site', *BBC*, https://www.bbc.co.uk/news/world-us-canada-16657800, accessed 3 November 2020.

BBC (2015). 'Rapidshare to Close Following Long Decline', *BBC*, https://www.bbc.co.uk/news/technology-31418414, accessed 3 November 2020.

Beech, M. (2020). 'Justin Bieber Is The First Artist With 50 Million YouTube Subscribers: His Career By The Numbers', *Forbes*, https://www.forbes.com/sites/markbeech/2020/02/05/justin-bieber-by-numbers-first-artist-to-pass-50-million-youtube-subscribers/, accessed 3 November 2020.

Berry, K. (2019). 'The EU Copyright Directive – Noble Aims but Lacking Clarity', *Linklaters*, https://www.linklaters.com/en/insights/blogs/digilinks/2019/march/the-eu-copyright-directive-noble-aims-but-lacking-clarity, accessed 3 November 2020.

Bohas, A. (2012). 'The Harsh Governance of the Internet: The Closing of the Megaupload Site by the American Authorities', *Research Gate*, https://www.researchgate.net/publication/313376670_The_harsh_governance_of_the_Internet_The_closing_of_the_Megaupload_site_by_the_American_authorities, accessed 3 November 2020.

Borland, J. (2005). 'Last Waltz for Grokster, cnet', https://www.cnet.com/news/last-waltz-for-grokster/, accessed 3 November 2020.

BPI News (2018). '£2 Million Funding for "Get it Right" Campaign Announced by Government', *BPI*, https://www.bpi.co.uk/news-analysis/2-million-funding-for-get-it-right-campaign-announced-by-government/, accessed 3 November 2020.

Brandes, J. (2012). 'Hotfile in Hotwater, Megaupload in the Mire and a Hollywood Hit List . . . but is the List Fact or Fantasy? Even Mediafire, a Respected and Transparent Service, is Caught in the Crosshairs', https://zine.openrightsgroup.org/comment/2012/a-hollywood-hit-list, accessed 3 November 2020.

Brandes, J. (2013a). 'Shiver Me Timbers! Is the Torrent Site Blockade Working or have those Pesky Pirates Circumnavigated their Way Around It?', https://zine.openrightsgroup.org/features/2013/blocking-orders, accessed 3 November 2020.

Brandes, J. (2013b). 'Who Are the BPI's New Website Blocking Targets?', https://zine.openrightsgroup.org/features/2013/who-are-the-bpis-new-website-blocking-targets, accessed 3 November 2020.

Brandes, J. and J. Bell (2020). Interview for Chapter, Unpublished.

Brandes, J. and P. Carr (2020). Interview for Chapter, Unpublished.

Brodkin, J. (2019). 'Music Labels sue Charter, Complain that High Internet Speeds Fuel Piracy', *Ars Technica*, https://arstechnica.com/tech-policy/2019/03/music-labels-sue-charter-complain-that-high-internet-speeds-fuel-piracy/, accessed 3 November 2020.

Cohen, P. (2001). 'Napster Licenses Acoustic Fingerprinting Technology', https://www.macworld.com/article/1017151/napster.html, accessed 3 November 2020.

Csathy, P. (2020). 'All Eyes On Spotify's 2019 Results, But Music Industry Eyes Should Be On YouTube', *Forbes*, https://www.forbes.com/sites/petercsathy/2020/02/04/all-eyes-on-spotify-tomorrow-but-music-industry-eyes-should-be-on-youtube-today/, accessed 3 November 2020.

Cuthbertson, A. (2016). 'YouTube Download Sites Are Biggest Piracy Threat to Music Piracy', *The Independent*, https://www.independent.co.uk/life-style/gadgets-and-tech/news/youtube-mp3-converter-download-piracy-a8505131.html, accessed 3 November 2020.

Danaher, B., M. Smith, R. Telang and S. Chen (2012). 'The Effect of Graduated Response Anti-Piracy Laws on Music Sales', https://papers.ssrn.com/sol3/papers.cfm?abstract_id=1989240, accessed 3 November 2020.

Daniel, C. (2019). 'What to Make of the European Directive on Copyright in the Digital Single Market', *The Hill*, https://thehill.com/opinion/technology/440683-what-to-make-of-the-european-directive-on-copyright-in-the-digital-single, accessed 3 November 2020.

Dansby, A. (2002). 'Napster Files for Bankruptcy', *Rolling Stone*, https://www.rollingstone.com/music/music-news/napster-files-for-bankruptcy-246468/, accessed 3 November 2020.

Directive (EU) 2019/790 of the European Parliament and the Council of 17 April 2019 on copyright and related rights in the Digital Single Market and Amending Directives 96/9/EC and 2001/29/EC, https://eur-lex.europa.eu/legal-content/EN/TXT/HTML/?uri=CELEX:32019L0790&rid=1, accessed 3 November 2020.

Disney Enterprises *v Hotfile Corp*, United States District Court, Southern District of Florida, Case No. 11-20427-CIV-WILLIAMS, p16, https://ia800205.us.archive.org/35/items/gov.uscourts.flsd.373206/gov.uscourts.flsd.373206.534.0.pdf, accessed 3 November 2020.

Enigmax (2009). 'The Pirate Bay Trial: The Official Verdict – Guilty', *Torrentfreak*, https://torrentfreak.com/the-pirate-bay-trial-the-verdict-090417/, accessed 3 November 2020.

Essers, L. (2013). 'File Hosting Service Rapidshare must Scan for Copyright Infringing Files, German Federal Court Rules', https://www.pcworld.com/article/2048101/file-hosting-service-rapidshare-must-scan-for-copyright-infringing-files-german-federal-court-rules.html, accessed 3 November 2020.

Forde, E. (2019). 'Oversharing: How Napster Nearly Killed the Music Industry', https://www.theguardian.com/music/2019/may/31/napster-twenty-years-music-revolution, accessed 3 November 2020.

Gallagher, S. (2012). 'Mega-man: The Fast, Fabulous, Fraudulent Life of Megaupload's Kim Dotcom', https://arstechnica.com/tech-policy/2012/01/mega-man-the-bizarre-rise-and-sudden-downfall-of-kim-dotcom, accessed 3 November 2020.

Gardner, E. (2013). 'Warner Bros. Can't Escape Hotfile's Claim of Abusing Anti-Piracy Tool', *The Hollywood Reporter*, https://www.hollywoodreporter.com/thr-esq/warner-bros-cant-escape-hotfiles-633727, accessed 3 November 2020.

Graeber, C. (2012), 'Mega: Inside the Mansion and the Mind of Kim Dotcom', *Wired*, https://www.wired.co.uk/article/mega, accessed 3 November 2020.

Gruger, W. (2012). 'PSY's "Gangnam Style" Hits 1 Billion Views on YouTube', *Billboard*, https://www.billboard.com/articles/columns/k-town/1481275/psys-gangnam-style-hits-1-billion-views-on-youtube, accessed 3 November 2020.

Guadamuz, A. (2010), 'Ministry of Sound Gives Up P2P Claims', TechnoLlama, https://www.technollama.co.uk/ministry-of-sound-gives-up-p2p-claims, accessed 3 November 2020.

Hall, T. (2020). 'YouTube Says It's Given the Music Industry $3 Billion', *Access All Areas*, https://accessaa.co.uk/youtube-says-its-given-the-music-industry-3bn/, accessed 3 November 2020.

Harrison, A. (2017). *Music: The Business*, 7th edn, 390, 391, 399, 240. London: Penguin Books.

Hart, T. (2014). 'Some Examples of DMCA Abuse', *Copyhype*, https://www.copyhype.com/tag/abuse/, accessed 3 November 2020.

Hornic, J. (2005). 'Analysis of the U.S. Supreme Court's Grokster Decision', *Finnegan*, https://www.finnegan.com/en/insights/articles/analysis-of-the-u-s-supreme-court-s-grokster-decision.html, accessed 3 November 2020.

Houston, A. (2000). 'Metallica Fans Blocked from Napster Fight Back', https://www.campaignlive.co.uk/article/metallica-fans-blocked-napster-fight-back/136595, accessed 3 November 2020.

Ingham, T. (2019). 'Spotify Is Profitable. How Did That Happen?' *Rolling Stone*, https://www.rollingstone.com/music/music-features/spotify-profitable-how-happen-910456/, accessed 3 November 2020.

Ingham, T. (2020). 'Loss Making Spotify Will Continue to Put Growth Ahead of Profit For Next Few Years', *Music Business Worldwide*, https://www.musicbusinessworldwide.com/loss-making-spotify-will-continue-to-focus-on-growth-over-profit-for-next-few-years/, accessed 3 November 2020.

Jackson, M. (2017). 'Big UK Broadband ISPs Blocking 3,814 Internet Piracy Related URLs', *ISPreview*, https://www.ispreview.co.uk/index.php/2017/03/big-uk-broadband-isps-blocking-3814-internet-piracy-related-urls.html, accessed 3 November 2020.

Jackson, M. (2019a). 'BPI Reveal UK Broadband ISPs Have Sent 1 Million Piracy Alert Emails', *ISPreview*, https://www.ispreview.co.uk/index.php/2019/02/bpi-reveal-uk-broadband-isps-have-sent-1-million-piracy-alert-emails.html, accessed 3 November 2020.

Jackson, M. (2019b). 'Get It Right – Copyright Holders Scrap UK ISP Piracy Letters Scheme', *ISPreview*, https://www.ispreview.co.uk/index.php/2019/07/get-it-right-copyright-holders-scrap-uk-isp-piracy-letters-scheme.html, accessed 3 November 2020.

Jardin, X. (2005). 'Grokster's End and the Future of File Sharing', *NPR*, https://www.npr.org/templates/story/story.php?storyId=4994285&t=1595283607080, accessed 3 November 2020.

Johnston, K. (2012). 'FBI Claims Megaupload based in Auckland Mansion', http://www.stuff.co.nz/national/6292279/FBI-claims-Megaupload-based-in-Auckland-mansion, accessed 3 November 2020.

Judge, P. (2010). 'Revenge Attacks Take Down Lawyer and Ministry of Sound', https://www.silicon.co.uk/workspace/revenge-attacks-take-down-lawyer-and-ministry-of-sound-10319, accessed 3 November 2020.

Kafka, P. (2016). 'Here's Why the Music Labels Are Furious at YouTube. Again', *Vox*, https://www.vox.com/2016/4/11/11586030/youtube-google-dmca-riaa-cary-sherman, accessed 3 November 2020.

Kim, E. (2019). 'After 15 Years, The Pirate Bay Still Can't Be Killed', https://melmagazine.com/en-us/story/after-15-years-the-pirate-bay-still-cant-be-killed, accessed 3 November 2020.

Lamont, T. (2013). 'Napster: The Day the Music was Set Free', *The Guardian*, https://www.theguardian.com/music/2013/feb/24/napster-music-free-file-sharing, accessed 3 November 2020.

Lardinois (2015). 'RapidShare Shuts Down', https://techcrunch.com/2015/02/10/rapidshare-shuts-down/, accessed 3 November 2020.

Lauinger, T. (2013). 'Holiday Pictures or Blockbuster Movies? Insights into Copyright Infringement in User Uploads to One-Click File Hosters, North Western University, Boston', https://www.scribd.com/document/176860329/Och-Filename-Analysis-Raid2013, accessed 3 November 2020.

Law, S. (2020). '*Metallica v Napster*: The Lawsuit That Redefined How We Listen to Music', *Kerrang*, https://www.kerrang.com/features/metallica-vs-napster-the-lawsuit-that-redefined-how-we-listen-to-music/, accessed 3 November 2020.

Leydon, J. (2010). 'Ministry of Sound Floored by Anonymous', https://www.theregister.com/Print/2010/10/04/ministry_of_sound_ddos/, accessed 3 November 2020.

Libbenga, J. (2006). 'Pirate Bay Resurfaces, While Protesters Walk the Street', https://www.theregister.com/2006/06/05/pirate_bay_reemerges/, accessed 3 November 2020.

Litwick, M. (2011). 'Why Filesharing Companies Are Starting to Lobby Washington', https://mashable.com/2011/01/10/rapidshare-lobbying-interview/, accessed 3 November 2020.

Masnick, M. (2012). 'DMCA Copyright Takedowns To Google Increased 10x In Just The Past Six Months', *Tech Dirt*, https://www.techdirt.com/articles/20121211/16152021352/dmca-copyright-takedowns-to-google-increased-10x-just-past-six-months.shtml, accessed 3 November 2020.

Maxwell, A. (2012). 'Cyberlocker Ecosystem Shocked As Big Players Take Drastic Action', *Torrentfreak*, https://torrentfreak.com/cyberlocker-ecosystem-shocked-as-big-players-take-drastic-action-120123/, accessed 3 November 2020.

Maxwell, A. (2018). 'US Govt Brands Torrent, Streaming & Cyberlocker Sites As Notorious Markets', *Torrentfreak*, https://torrentfreak.com/us-govt-brands-torrent-streaming-cyberlocker-sites-as-notorious-markets-180115/, accessed 3 November 2020.

Maxwell, A. (2019). 'The Pirate Bay Lives On, A Decade After "Guilty" Verdicts', *Torrentfreak*, https://torrentfreak.com/the-pirate-bay-lives-on-a-decade-after-operators-were-found-guilty-190420/, accessed 3 November 2020.

Metallica v Napster [PDF] judgement, pp. 2–3, https://web.archive.org/web/20030706044926/http://news.findlaw.com/hdocs/docs/napster/napster-md030601ord.pdf, accessed 3 November 2020.

MGM Studios, Inc. v *Grokster*, Ltd., 545 U.S. 913 (2005), p. 19, https://www.law.cornell.edu/supct/pdf/04-480P.ZO, accessed 3 November 2020

Moskvitch, K. (2016). 'YouTube Music is Great for Record Labels, But Bad for Music Lovers', *Wired*, https://www.wired.co.uk/article/youtube-music-premium-originals, accessed 3 November 2020.

Mulligan, M. (2015). 'Awakening, The Music Industry In The Digital Age, MIDiA Research', 39, 202, https://books.google.co.uk/books?id=-0AiCAAAQBAJ, accessed 3 November 2020.

Office of the United States Trade Representative (2011). 'Out of Cycle Review of Notorious Markets', 4, https://ustr.gov/sites/default/files/uploads/gsp/speeches/reports/2011/Notorious%20Markets%20List%20FINAL.pdf, accessed 3 November 2020.

Office of the United States Trade Representative (2016). 'Out of Cycle Review of Notorious Markets', 14, https://ustr.gov/sites/default/files/2016-Out-of-Cycle-Review-Notorious-Markets.pdf, accessed 3 November 2020.

Office of the United States Trade Representative (2017). 'Out of Cycle Review of Notorious Markets', 20, https://ustr.gov/sites/default/files/files/Press/Reports/2017%20Notorious%20Markets%20List%201.11.18.pdf, accessed 3 November 2020.

NME (2001). 'Napster Stays Shut Down', https://www.nme.com/news/music/various-artists-5213-1378245, accessed 3 November 2020.

Parks, K. (2014). *Music and Copyright in America: Toward the Celestial Jukebox*, 2nd edn, 181. American Bar Association; Reprint edition.

Parliament UK (2020). 'EU Action: Written Question – 4371', https://www.parliament.uk/business/publications/written-questions-answers-statements/written-question/Commons/2020-01-16/4371/, accessed 3 November 2020.

Peel (2008). 'Thought Home Taping was Dead? Think Again . . .', *The Guardian*, https://www.theguardian.com/music/2008/jun/17/popandrock, accessed 3 November 2020.

Resnikoff, P. (2018). '84 European Music and Media Organizations Declare Their Support for Article 13', https://www.digitalmusicnews.com/2018/06/27/european-music-media-organizations-article-13/, accessed 3 November 2020.

RIAA Cloudflare Notice (2019). https://torrentfreak.com/images/riaa-cf.pdf, accessed 3 November 2020.

RIAA Piracy Impact (2020). 'The True Cost of Sound Recording Piracy to the U.S. Economy', https://www.riaa.com/reports/the-true-cost-of-sound-recording-piracy-to-the-u-s-economy/, accessed 3 November 2020.

Richtel, M. (2001). 'Napster Is Told to Remain Shut', *The New York Times*, https://www.nytimes.com/2001/07/12/technology/ebusiness/napster-is-told-to-remain-shut.html, accessed 3 November 2020.

Roettgers, J. (2007). 'Piracy Beyond P2P: One-Click Hosters', *Gigaom*, https://gigaom.com/2007/06/17/one-click-hosters/, accessed 3 November 2020.

Sandoval, G. (2012). 'MPAA Wants More Criminal Cases Brought Against "Rogue" Sites', https://www.cnet.com/news/mpaa-wants-more-criminal-cases-brought-against-rogue-sites/, accessed 3 November 2020.

Sanjuàs-Cuxart, J., P. Barlet-Ros and J. Solé-Pareta (2012). 'Measurement Based Analysis of One-Click File Hosting Services', *Journal of Network and Systems Management*, 2–3, https://www.researchgate.net/publication/225712479_Measurement_Based_Analysis_of_One-Click_File_Hosting_Services, accessed 3 November 2020.

Sudler, H. (2013). 'Effectiveness of Anti-piracy Technology: Finding Appropriate Solutions for Evolving Online Piracy', 3, https://www.researchgate.net/publication/256672699_Effectiveness_of_anti-piracy_technology_Finding_appropriate_solutions_for_evolving_online_piracy, accessed 3 November 2020.

Tarantola, A. (2012). 'MPAA Goes For Hotfile's Jugular With Summary Judgement Request', https://www.gizmodo.com.au/2012/03/mpaa-goes-for-hotfiles-jugular-with-summary-judgement-request/, accessed 3 November 2020.

Tiwari, A. (2016). 'What Is P2P File Sharing And How It Works?' *Fossbytes*, https://fossbytes.com/what-is-p2p-file-sharing-and-how-it-works/, accessed 3 November 2020.

US Department of Justice (2012), 'Justice Department Charges Leaders of Megaupload with Widespread Online Copyright Infringement', https://www.justice.gov/opa/pr/justice-department-charges-leaders-megaupload-widespread-online-copyright-infringement, accessed 3 November 2020.

Van der Sar, E. (2013). 'Hotfile Shuts Down and Takes User Files With It', *Torrentfreak*, https://torrentfreak.com/hotfile-shuts-down-and-takes-user-files-with-it-131204/, accessed 3 November 2020.

Van der Sar, E. (2014). 'MPAA Secretly Settled With Hotfile for $4 Million, Not $80 Million', *Torrentfreak*, https://torrentfreak.com/mpaa-secretly-settled-hotfile-4-million-80-million-141224/, accessed 3 November 2020.

Van der Sar, E. (2016). 'Google Asked to Remove 100,000 "Pirate Links" Every Hour', *Torrentfreak*, https://torrentfreak.com/google-asked-to-remove-100000-pirate-links-every-hour-160306/, accessed 3 November 2020.

Van der Sar, E. (2017). 'UK's Piracy Blocklist Now Exceeds 3,800 URLs', *Torrentfreak*, https://torrentfreak.com/uks-piracy-blocklist-exceeds-3800-urls-170321/, accessed 3 November 2020.

Van der Sar, E. (2019a). 'DBR.ee Shut Down By Music Industry Groups', *Torrentfreak*, https://torrentfreak.com/dbr-ee-shut-down-by-music-industry-groups-190528/, accessed 3 November 2020.

Van der Sar, E. (2019b). 'MPAA and RIAA's Megaupload Lawsuits Remain "Frozen"', *Torrentfreak*, https://torrentfreak.com/mpaa-and-riaas-megaupload-lawsuits-remain-frozen/, accessed 3 November 2020.

Van der Sar, E. (2020), 'Sites Flourish as UK Site Blocking Efforts Die Down, For Now', *Torrentfreak*, https://torrentfreak.com/pirate-sites-flourish-as-uk-site-blocking-efforts-die-down-for-now-201010/, accessed 3 November 2020.

Vitale, R. (2018). 'YouTube's Piracy Protection Efforts Are Working Perfectly (For Those Deemed Worthy Of Them)', *Forbes*, https://www.forbes.com/sites/ruthvitale/2018/08/31/youtubes-piracy-protection-efforts-are-working-perfectly-for-those-deemed-worthy-of-them/#692b1e3e7580, accessed 3 November 2020.

West, T. (2017). 'Metallica and Napster – Were they Right All Along?' *Crunch*, https://www.crunch.co.uk/knowledge/expertise/were-metallica-right-napster/, accessed 3 November 2020.

Wired (2006). 'Pirate Bay Bloodied But Unbowed', https://www.wired.com/2006/06/pirate-bay-bloodied-but-unbowed/, accessed 3 November 2020.

Part Two

Responding to the needs of the music business

6

Mediation and arbitration

An alternative forum for transnational dispute resolution in the music industries

Metka Potočnik

Commercial exploitation of musical works has rarely been confined to the domestic context. It is not often that artists[1] perform in a single country or stay offline. Instead, artists will seek audiences in multiple jurisdictions and, even more importantly, share their works via the internet. Equally, musicians will benefit not only from their music (including lyrics) but also from merchandising or endorsement deals and performance contracts. It is now common that contracts regulating the exploitation of rights are drafted in the form of 360-degree agreements (Stopps 2014), which cover all aspects of valuable assets related to the creativity and image of a musician, such as sound recordings, musical compositions, image rights, merchandising and live performance work. This presents a challenge for musicians who are not supported by large legal teams, because they face not one, but potentially multiple legal regimes, coupled with the complexities of commercialisation over the internet (mainly jurisdictional issues). It has already been argued that artists are not always well acquainted with the systems of intellectual property (IP) laws or court procedures behind enforcing or protecting their creative works (Denoncourt 2016).[2]

How, therefore, are music disputes best resolved? And what if these disputes involve multiple parties, from different regions of the world? Which law will

---

[1] This chapter explores the position of artists and other creative talent in the music industry. The umbrella term 'artists' includes performers, creatives, musicians *etc.*
[2] Findings in similar vein supported with empirical data, which the author collected in fifteen semi-structured interviews with artists, who expressed that IP law is complex and often difficult to understand; unless prompted, IP law is not high on their agenda of awareness; this empirical study is a pilot project and referenced at note 7.

regulate an international tour? In order to address some of these questions, while accepting the limitations and cost of domestic litigation, IP organisations are focusing their efforts on highlighting the benefits of 'out-of-court' dispute resolution mechanisms, offering a range of benefits to the parties of the dispute. For example, the World Intellectual Property Organization (WIPO) has been actively promoting its Arbitration and Mediation Centre (established in 1994), which operates under its institutional rules and has in recent years seen a rise in case load.[3] In the UK, the Intellectual Property Office (IPO) now promotes its Mediation Services as an alternative to court litigation.[4]

Will any 'out-of-court' solution do? 'Alternative dispute resolution' (ADR) is an umbrella term which includes mediation and arbitration. Mediation is a form of ADR, which offers the parties an 'out-of-court' forum to solve their dispute with the assistance of a neutral, the mediator. The approach is similar to contract negotiation, is less confrontational and is distinctive for its 'win-for-all' approach. Differently, arbitration is a more formal form of ADR, where arbitrators (or tribunals) resolve a dispute on the facts in front of them, under the law often chosen by the parties.

In light of the foregoing, this chapter explores the suitability of mediation or arbitration for the settlement of music disputes, while also drawing a distinction between the two ADR methods. ADR mechanisms are promoted (*e.g.* by WIPO) for numerous advantages,[5] including (1) a single procedure, or the so-called 'one-stop shop' approach; (2) party autonomy; (3) neutrality of forum (as opposed to domestic courts); (4) confidentiality of disputes (as opposed to the public court proceedings); (5) finality of awards (challenge to an award is substantially limited when compared to appeals in litigation); and (6) easy enforceability of international awards under the New York Convention (1958) (NYC) or mediation settlement agreements under the Singapore Convention (2018).[6]

Informed by empirical data,[7] it is argued here that the general preference for ADR over traditional litigation notwithstanding, there are fewer ADR

---

[3] Caseload has risen from forty-seven cases in 2009, to 179 cases in 2019 (bringing the total to over 700 mediation, arbitration and expert determination cases, with most cases filed in recent years), https://www.wipo.int/amc/en/center/caseload.html.
[4] IP Mediation, https://www.gov.uk/guidance/intellectual-property-mediation.
[5] WIPO promotes these advantages specifically in IP disputes: https://www.wipo.int/amc/en/center/advantages.html.
[6] See pages 132–141.
[7] The empirical study was possible due to the support given by the Early Research Awards Scheme at the University of Wolverhampton (ERAS): Metka Potočnik, 'Breaking Monopolies: A Feminist Approach to Intellectual Property Law in the Creative Industries' (September 2019–August 2020).

advantages for individual artists (independents, not-signed talent), who lack know-how in IP or contract law, or are unfamiliar with the ADR process. Artists who are signed by Traditional Record Labels (TRL) are more likely to have the infrastructure and support needed to gain access to ADR processes. To illustrate, an artist who has a recording contract with a TRL will have the support of the business services, accounting, marketing, public relations (PR) or access to a legal team. This pool of artists is, however, not particularly diversified in countries such as the United Kingdom or the United States (Bain 2019; Smith *et al*. 2020; Coogan Byrne 2020).[8] This chapter therefore concludes with an evaluation of the suitability of mediation and/or arbitration of contractual and IP disputes in the music industry, from the perspective of different stakeholders, including the individual artist, when they are not privy to expert legal advice. It is argued here that the individual musician is better served in mediation. Should they decide to take their case to international arbitration, it might prove to be a procedure as complex as domestic court litigation.

Music disputes

The glocal and transnational nature of music disputes

With the coming of the internet, the music industry has seen a drastic shift in how it operates (Stopps 2014). Users and artists have changed the ways in which they create, access, listen to and exchange musical works. The change in the creative environment has not, however, been matched by a change in the law relating to jurisdiction for disputes: the main protection of IP assets is still linked to territories of states. There is no single, 'world' or 'global' IP right that would cover an artist and her creative works. As soon as an artist shares her work online, she or her representatives should follow a 'glocal' strategy, which is 'a strategy of thinking globally but acting locally' (Svensson 2001: 13).

A recorded musical composition can be protected by various types of copyright (separate copyright for the music and lyrics to a song). Sound recordings of those musical works and their broadcast will each attract separate copyright. For performers, a set of related, or neighbouring rights, is provided. Because

---

[8] To illustrate the lack of diversity: (1) Bain found, for the UK that 'just over 14% of writers currently signed to publishers and just under 20% of acts signed to labels are female'. (2) Smith *et al*. found that 'women are missing from popular music'. (3) Coogan Bryne finds underrepresentation of female musicians across British Radio Stations (2019–20).

copyright is a territorial right (there is no global copyright), laws regulating the extent of protection can differ substantially. This means that artists must carefully contemplate any contractual arrangements about the use of their rights and this will often mean a detailed consideration of the interests of several stakeholders. Artists will also devise their own image; and with reputation and fame, comes the legal protection of personality or image rights (Kessler 2017). If artists are expanding outside their craft of music (*e.g.* into the fashion industry) or endorsing commercial products, issues of trademarks or designs are to be thought of. If the artists come up with ways to improve an instrument or other technical products, patents will be involved.

Contract disputes

In order to engage with exclusive rights reserved for copyright owners (reproduction, distribution, communication to the public), users need permission. Permissions to access IP-protected works are granted either by purchase or via licences. When IP is assigned (*i.e.* transfer of title), the assignee becomes the new IP rightsholder. Licenses are contracts, which give third parties the permission of the IP rightsholder to use the works protected by the IP. Licences will set duration, terms of use, remuneration, the territory and exclusivity/non-exclusivity of use, and are usually in writing. Licences, as all other contracts, are valid between the two contracting parties, and can be terminated under the terms of the contract or the law applicable to the contract. Licences or other contracts in the music industry might contain ADR clauses.

Intellectual property disputes

In cases where there is no contract between musicians, or users of particular music (*i.e.* a non-contractual dispute), or where there is an accusation of unlawful copying (*i.e.* an IP infringement dispute), IP law will play an important role. Whether there are unresolved issues of copyright authorship/ownership; the extent of exclusive rights or copyright infringement; the rights to the use of personality of the artists; or perhaps trademarks resulting from a particular artist's brand, IP disputes are, first and foremost, territorial. Although the phenomenon of music is transnational or glocal, the nature of IP rights is distinctly territorial: there is no 'world copyright'; instead, there is copyright in the UK, in China, in Nigeria, in Germany and so on.

Because IP rights are territorial, they are innately linked to a state's sovereignty and states' discretion to grant IP monopolies as per their policies.[9] Although the music industry calls for the effective resolution of disputes outside the confines of domestic courts, IP disputes have not always been deemed right for settlement outside of the supervisory court's control. Experts have considered this as a public policy limitation in their discussions on 'arbitrability', that is, whether disputes in an area of law are suitable for settlement by arbitration (Potočnik 2019; Cook and Garcia 2010).

The territorial nature of IP rights is, however, no longer a barrier to ADR mechanisms of settling disputes. It is now accepted in general, that IP disputes are arbitrable, which means that parties can resolve their IP disputes effectively outside the confines of domestic courts. There is an important limitation to this freedom however, and that is that the validity of any IP right which must be registered (*n.b.* copyright is not a registrable right)[10] will not be affected by decisions made outside national courts with the effects towards third parties (Cook and Garcia 2010).[11] In other words, decisions made by arbitral tribunals or by the parties in mediation will have a binding effect on the disputing parties alone (*inter partes*) and not on third parties (*erga omnes*).[12]

Replacing the courts: Specialised institutions

Some countries have specialised institutions, such as IP tribunals or courts, dealing with IP disputes separately. There are at present no 'creative industries' or 'music' courts, but there are some industry actors that offer some forums for dispute resolution.[13] For ADR of music disputes, parties may therefore wish to avoid 'lay judges' and, instead, appoint experts at specialised institutions accustomed to dealing with IP disputes. The most experienced in this area is

---

[9] Although all World Trade Organization (WTO) Member States are bound by the minimum of IP protection set in the Agreement on Trade-Related Aspects of Intellectual Property Rights (TRIPS), states have ample discretion to offer 'more' protection in their domestic laws.

[10] Trademarks are registrable rights (but some states also protect unregistered trademarks); patents must be registered, to receive protection.

[11] In Switzerland even with *erga omnes* effect: see PIL Art.177 (disputes involving property).

[12] For example, if an arbitral tribunal finds that a trademark is descriptive and invalid, resulting in no infringement, this will not affect the entry of this mark on the register. The validity could be revised only through an action for revocation, not through a decision by an arbitral tribunal.

[13] For example, there are several mediation commercial companies, and in the UK, one of the more well known is the Centre for Effective Dispute Resolution (CEDR), https://www.cedr.com Specifically, for TM disputes, International Trademark Association (INTA) offers mediation services, https://www.inta.org/resources/mediation/.

the WIPO Mediation and Arbitration Centre,[14] which offers services of both mediation and arbitration.

The WIPO Mediation and Arbitration Centre offers a number of ADR options. The main benefit of WIPO ADR proceedings is the participation of experts in IP matters,[15] which is not an expertise all international ADR specialists would share (Potočnik 2019).[16] Moreover, WIPO has recently issued ADR Rules and Model Clauses,[17] which should help parties avoid some of the common pitfalls of newcomers to ADR proceedings, in particular with an international element. This builds on recent increase in technology and highly technical cases (patents), which include IP issues, administered by the WIPO Mediation and Arbitration Centre.[18] In these cases, the literature supports the use of WIPO arbitration (Laturno 1996; Martin 1996). WIPO promotes the use of the WIPO Arbitration and Mediation Rules through a series of industry-targeted events[19] under the auspices of its Mediation and Arbitration Centre.

Dispute settlement through agreement: Mediation

Not to be confused with negotiations, conciliation or arbitration, mediation is a form of ADR proceedings where parties to a dispute agree to settle their dispute by communicating with each other with the skilled assistance of a mediator (a 'neutral') (Blake, Browne and Sime 2018). Mediators are independent and must remain impartial, but unlike judges or arbitrators, they will not have a final say. It is the parties that will either agree on the form of settlement, or not agree. Mediation is also praised for enabling an imaginative approach to solutions, which will often result in a 'win-for-all' outcome of the case (De Girolamo 2016).

---

[14] https://www.wipo.int/amc/en/center/background.html.
[15] WIPO's List of Neutrals, https://www.wipo.int/amc/en/neutrals/.
[16] Potočnik empirically confirmed that international arbitrators are not that 'comfortable' with IP law, but equally, they are flexible to learn its rules.
[17] (1) Mediation: WIPO Mediation Rules ('MR') (Effective from 1 January 2020); WIPO Mediation Model Clause, https://www.wipo.int/amc/en/clauses/mediation/. (2) Arbitration: WIPO Arbitration Rules (Effective from 1 January 2020); WIPO Arbitration Model Clause, https://www.wipo.int/amc/en/clauses/arbitration/.
[18] In 2019, there were 179 cases (up from forty cases in 2010), and they include disputes arising from 'licensing agreements (e.g. trademarks, patents, copyright, software); research and development agreements; technology transfer agreements; distribution agreements, franchising agreements; Information Technology agreements; data processing agreements; joint venture agreements; consultancy agreements; art marketing agreements; TV distribution and formats; film production; copyright collective management; cases arising out of agreements in settlement of prior court litigation'.
[19] https://www.wipo.int/amc/en/events/.

The legal framework

Parties are legally bound by any agreements made in their 'agreement to mediate' (or mediation contract/clause).[20] The process of mediation, when regulated, sources its rules either internationally or domestically. Internationally there are two legal instruments available for countries aiming to create a mediation-friendly environment. First, the UN Commission for International Trade and Commerce has prepared a 'template' or 'model law' on mediation (UNCITRAL Mediation Model Law (MML)).[21] To date, thirty-three countries have been influenced by the MML.[22]

The second relevant legal development from the perspective of the music industry, as a 'global' or 'glocal' industry, is the adoption of the Singapore Convention on Mediation in 2018.[23] It has always been stated that the success of international commercial arbitration[24] can be attributed to the ease of enforcement under NYC (Redfern and Hunter 2015).[25] States wishing to promote international arbitration have signed on to the standards of enforcement under NYC, and there are currently 168 signatory states. Until recently, mediation settlement agreements (MSAs) did not have an equivalent legal framework, making it more difficult to get legal recognition for any agreements reached in mediation proceedings with an international element. This has now changed, and the Singapore Convention on Mediation has already fifty-three signatories and six parties.[26] If NYC is any indication, this Mediation Convention is expected to have many more signatories in the next few years. States wishing to promote mediation in international commercial disputes will wish to offer a legal framework, which will facilitate a quick and simple enforcement of international mediation settlement agreements. The Singapore Convention prescribes rules that make a jurisdiction 'mediation friendly.'

States which have not adopted MML have their own rules, and parties wishing to understand those rules would need to consult the domestic legal framework

---

[20] See pages 134–135.
[21] UNCITRAL Model Law on International Commercial Mediation and International Settlement Agreements Resulting from Mediation, 2018 (amending the UNCITRAL Model Law on International Commercial Conciliation, 2002).
[22] Status regularly updated: https://uncitral.un.org/en/texts/arbitration/modellaw/commercial_conciliation/status.
[23] The United Nations Convention on International Settlement Agreements Resulting from Mediation (2018).
[24] See pages 136–141.
[25] See page 141.
[26] The UN keeps records of the signatories and entry into force: https://treaties.un.org/pages/ViewDetails.aspx?src=TREATY&mtdsg_no=XXII-4&chapter=22&clang=_en.

separately. In the UK, which has not followed the guidance of MML, mediation is not heavily regulated (Wechs Hatanaka 2018). Some aspects of cross-border mediation are harmonised through the EU Mediation Directive, which contains rules on the enforceability of mediation agreements, confidentiality and limitation/prescription periods.[27]

There is another set of rules that parties are encouraged to be familiar with when thinking of mediation. ADR Centres across the world have sought to help individuals and businesses wishing to make greater use of ADR mechanisms, by drafting helpful mediation rules. Examples include Mediation Rules by the International Chamber of Commerce (ICC),[28] or WIPO Mediation Rules, specifically for IP disputes.[29] These rules will apply only if both parties agree to their application.

Access to mediation

Mediation can begin only if the two parties in a legal dispute agree to solve the dispute through mediation. The agreement can be made before the dispute arises (Mediation Agreement (MA) for future disputes), or alternatively, parties can agree to settle their dispute in mediation after the dispute has already arisen (Mediation Submission Agreement (MSA)).[30] When an agreement has not been made yet, parties can request the mediation to start through the WIPO Centre (Unilateral Request for Mediation (URM)).[31] Here the case will proceed only if the other party consents to the proceedings. Accordingly, all mediation discussed here is voluntary and based on parties' consent.

Mediation agreements need not be overly formal, but in order to ensure their legal effectiveness and avoid any issues in the future, it is recommended that the parties follow institutional model clauses. To illustrate, WIPO offers a clear Model MA, which is to be inserted in the main legal agreement (*i.e.* the main contract):

> Any dispute, controversy or claim arising under, out of or relating to this contract and any subsequent amendments of this contract, including, without limitation, its formation, validity, binding effect, interpretation, performance, breach or

---

[27] Directive 2008/52/EC of the European Parliament and of the Council of 21 May 2008 on certain aspects of mediation in civil and commercial matters (OJ L 136, 24 May 2008). Situation after Brexit, is due to its uncertainty at the time of writing, not contemplated here.
[28] Effective from 1 January 2014.
[29] See pages 135–136.
[30] WIPO MR Art.3.
[31] WIPO MR Art.4. Form provided online, https://www.wipo.int/amc/en/clauses/mediation/.

termination, as well as non-contractual claims, shall be submitted to mediation in accordance with the WIPO Mediation Rules. The place of mediation shall be [specify place]. The language to be used in the mediation shall be [specify language].[32]

Mediation proceedings

Mediation proceedings are informal and confidential. WIPO Mediation Rules have only a handful of provisions that will set some procedural rules, but only in the broadest terms. Proceedings are facilitated and organised by the mediator (with the assistance of the ADR Centre if agreed by the parties) and all mediators must be independent, neutral and impartial.[33]

Mediation proceedings will begin once the Request for Mediation has been sent to the ADR Centre by the party who has initiated the proceedings.[34] After consent is established, the parties must appoint a mediator.[35] If they find it useful, more than one mediator can be appointed. Particularly in music disputes it is recommended that they also be experts in IP law, and if possible, musical experts (*i.e.* musicologists or in the business of music). When parties fail to agree on a mediator in an effective manner, the ADR Centre might have the appointing authority and name a mediator for them.[36]

Once a mediator is in place, a schedule of meetings is to be agreed with the parties.[37] Parties can choose to be represented in the mediation meetings but legal representation is not mandatory.[38] If the parties do not agree specifically on how to conduct the proceedings, the mediators have the discretion to conduct the proceedings as they find appropriate and in accordance with the applicable Mediation Rules.[39] Both the mediator, and the parties, have the duty to cooperate and conduct the mediation as expeditiously as possible.[40]

Mediators usually have the authority to meet with parties in private sessions, which will remain confidential (Blake, Browne and Sime 2018).[41] So-called

---

[32] https://www.wipo.int/amc/en/clauses/mediation/. WIPO also offers a model MSA and URM.
[33] WIPO MR Art.8; also, a ground to refuse relief under the Singapore Convention on Mediation, Art.5(1)(e).
[34] WIPO MR Art.6.
[35] WIPO procedure detailed in WIPO MR Art.7.
[36] WIPO MR Art.7(a)(v),(b).
[37] WIPO MR Art.13 (referring to a timetable for submissions).
[38] WIPO MR Art.9.
[39] WIPO MR Art.10.
[40] WIPO MR Art.11.
[41] WIPO MR Art.12.

caucus sessions are also available under WIPO Mediation Rules, which expressly stipulate that the information shared with the mediator in separate meetings is not to be disclosed to the other party, and is to remain confidential, unless express agreement to the contrary has been made.[42]

Outcome of mediation

A successful mediation ends with the parties' agreement. This is not the same as a court decision or an arbitral award. Mediators cannot impose their judgement on the parties. Instead, it is the will of the parties to reach a settlement regarding their future legal relationship. The binding nature of MSA originates with the parties' having made an agreement. This result is often referred to as a 'mediation settlement' or 'a settlement agreement'. Courts will, however, assist with the enforcement of these agreements, when one of the parties refuses to honour such a settlement. If the Singapore Convention on Mediation applies, such settlement agreements are much easier to recognise and enforce in multiple jurisdictions across the world.[43]

If mediation fails, all documentation or communication from the mediation proceedings remains confidential and cannot be used in subsequent arbitration or litigation.[44] It is also worth stating that any party can terminate mediation proceedings without any risk to its legal position at any time. All information from a failed mediation must remain confidential. Under some rules, termination of a mediation must be done in writing.[45] When the parties are mediating in the UK there are distinct obligations when mediating on the referral of the courts, and some important cost implications reinforce the parties' good faith obligation to attempt to mediate earnestly (De Girolamo 2016).[46]

Dispute settlement through private courts: Arbitration

Arbitration is another form of ADR, which sits between the more informal mediation on the one hand and the formal litigation in front of domestic

---

[42] WIPO MR Art.12.
[43] In practice, it is helpful to have access to court enforcement proceedings in any state where the debtor might have assets, which could be sold to satisfy any outstanding debt.
[44] WIPO MR Arts 15–19. Mediation is without prejudice, i.e. its contents are not to affect any subsequent legal proceedings.
[45] WIPO MR Art.19 (iii).
[46] Parties should attempt a good faith mediation, at the risk of cost sanctions: *Halsey v Milton Keynes General NHS Trust* [2004] EWCA (Civ) 576; [2004] 1 WLR 3002.

courts, on the other. There are a number of distinct advantages to arbitration, and in particular international arbitration, but there are also some specifics which might make it less accessible to individual artists. Arbitration is built on party autonomy which leads directly to greater flexibility to design arbitration proceedings. This, however, can be done effectively only if both parties have the funds and experience needed to conduct arbitration proceedings to their best interest.

The legal framework

There are distinct legal sources in arbitration, which have a clear hierarchy among them. The first, and the most important legal source is the parties' agreement to arbitrate.[47] The parties' autonomy is the cornerstone of every arbitration and can be limited only in cases of mandatory rules (Cook and Garcia 2010; Redfern and Hunter 2015), such as rules for challenging an arbitrator for conflict of interest[48] or for challenging an award.[49] The second legal source are arbitral rules, which the parties have agreed to use. Parties can choose to have their arbitration administered by an arbitral institution (*i.e.* institutional rules) or can adopt arbitral rules prepared for application in individual cases (*i.e.* *ad hoc* arbitration). Examples of institutional rules include LCIA Rules;[50] ICC Rules;[51] WIPO Rules;[52] AAA Rules[53] and SIAC Rules,[54] to name but a few. The oft used *ad hoc* arbitration rules are UNCITRAL Arbitration Rules (Redfern and Hunter 2015).[55]

The third legal source in arbitration are the domestic laws at the place of arbitration (*lex (loci) arbitri*) (Cook and Garcia 2010). Also known as the 'law of the seat',[56] these are the domestic legal rules on (international) arbitration at the legal place of arbitration. The place of arbitration, or the 'seat' is often chosen by the parties in their arbitration agreement. This law has seen its role decreasing over the years, but continues to be important (1) in its application to

---

[47] See pages 138–140.
[48] Section 24 Arbitration Act 1996.
[49] Sections 67–69 Arbitration Act 1996.
[50] London Court of International Arbitration, Arbitration Rules (2014).
[51] International Chamber of Commerce, Arbitration Rules (2021).
[52] See references at note 17.
[53] American Arbitration Association (AAA) Commercial Arbitration Rules and Mediation Procedures (2013).
[54] Singapore International Arbitration Centre (SIAC) Arbitration Rules (2017).
[55] UNCITRAL Arbitration Rules (as amended in 2010).
[56] Section 3 Arbitration Act 1996.

domestic arbitration; (2) as a support mechanism to international arbitration, when enforcement against third parties is requested through courts; (3) as a gap-fill set of procedural rules when the parties do not settle a matter expressly; and (4) as a guardian of the public interest (Redfern and Hunter 2015). The law of the seat has seen its fair share of harmonisation through the UNCITRAL Model Law instrument,[57] but some countries, like the UK,[58] have found ways to keep some of their unique legal infrastructure.

The final legal source in arbitration, which most authorities count as pivotal to the overwhelming success of international commercial arbitration since the 1960s, is the NYC.[59] This convention sets the minimum standard of the recognition and enforcement of foreign arbitral awards. This means that in most cases decisions rendered by international commercial arbitral tribunals under a valid arbitration agreement as set in Article II NYC will be recognised in any ratifying country. Domestic courts do not have the flexibility to impose barriers or obstacles to enforcement, if these are not listed in NYC. Comparatively, it is easier to get satisfaction on an arbitral award than a foreign court judgement.[60] This is because there is no comparable multilateral convention that would simplify the recognition and enforcement procedure for foreign court decisions.[61]

Access to arbitration

An arbitration can only take place if the parties agree to entrust their disputes to an independent and impartial tribunal to the exclusion of the jurisdiction of courts. There are two ways of establishing consent in arbitration: first, before the dispute has arisen (*i.e.* for future disputes, via an arbitration clause); and second, after the dispute arose (*i.e.* a submission agreement).

The content of submission agreements will be complex and will involve technical and detailed legal drafting on the part of both (all) parties involved. In contrast, arbitration agreements for future disputes are usually done in brief form and will rarely extend beyond a paragraph or two. All arbitration

---

[57] UNCITRAL Model Law on International Commercial Arbitration (1985, with amendments in 2006).
[58] If parties choose the legal seat of their arbitration to be England, the law of the seat is the Arbitration Act 1996. Scotland has a separate Arbitration (Scotland) Act 2010.
[59] The United Nations Convention on the Recognition and Enforcement of Foreign Arbitral Awards (New York, 1958).
[60] Contracting States: http://www.newyorkconvention.org/countries.
[61] There is an exception in the EU, with court decisions of domestic courts of EU Member States being easily recognised and enforced under the rules of the Brussels Regulation 1215/2012.

agreements are valid, when parties agree to take their dispute to arbitration (*i.e.* finality of arbitration), to the exclusion of national courts (Redfern and Hunter 2015).[62] Arbitration clauses are common in international commercial contracts (Redfern and Hunter 2015), but are not always carefully planned or negotiated. It is different with submission agreements, which are more difficult to negotiate, as the parties are already in a legal dispute (Redfern and Hunter 2015).

Having learned from past cases, arbitral institutions offer a number of model arbitration clauses. Any party new to arbitration proceedings is strongly encouraged to consult a model clause of an institution in order to minimise the risk of an invalid arbitration agreement. WIPO offers the following Model Arbitration Clause:

> Any dispute, controversy or claim arising under, out of or relating to this contract and any subsequent amendments of this contract, including, without limitation, its formation, validity, binding effect, interpretation, performance, breach or termination, as well as non-contractual claims, shall be referred to and finally determined by arbitration in accordance with the WIPO Arbitration Rules. The arbitral tribunal shall consist of [a sole arbitrator][three arbitrators]. The place of arbitration shall be [specify place]. The language to be used in the arbitral proceedings shall be [specify language]. The dispute, controversy or claim shall be decided in accordance with the law of [specify jurisdiction].[63]

One of the peculiarities of the music industry, or more broadly, IP disputes in general is that often the disputing parties will not be in a prior contractual relationship. While that is not common in international commercial arbitration generally, IP infringement claims will often occur outside of, or separate from, any contractual relationships. In those cases, the WIPO's recommendation for a brief form of submission agreement is uncharacteristic when compared to other institutional rules, yet a welcome instrument to parties new to music arbitration:

> We, the undersigned parties, hereby agree that the following dispute shall be referred to and finally determined by arbitration in accordance with the WIPO Arbitration Rules:
> [brief description of the dispute]
> The arbitral tribunal shall consist of [a sole arbitrator][three arbitrators]. The place of arbitration shall be [specify place]. The language to be used in the

---

[62] NYC Art.II.
[63] https://www.wipo.int/amc/en/clauses/arbitration/.

arbitral proceedings shall be [specify language]. The dispute shall be decided in accordance with the law of [specify jurisdiction].⁶⁴

For any arbitration agreement to be valid, it has to be a clear demonstration of the parties' consent to take their dispute to arbitration, to the exclusion of national courts. Arbitration agreements must also meet the requirements of Article II NYC: (1) agreements must be in writing; (2) about differences, which have arisen or may arise between the parties, regarding a defined legal relationship (contractual or not); and (3) regarding subject matter, capable of settlement by arbitration (arbitrability requirement). It is now accepted that most IP disputes are, indeed, arbitrable.⁶⁵

Arbitration proceedings

Arbitration is more formal than mediation. International businesses find international commercial arbitration particularly appealing, because it gives the parties (and their legal teams) almost complete control over the proceedings (preserving only minimum due process safeguards). Arbitral proceedings are one of the clearest examples of transnational law as it is the arbitration community that has devised a set of procedural rules that transcend the particular characteristics of common law versus civil law systems. International arbitration now has its own character, which endorses party autonomy. For parties to truly exercise their autonomy, however, they should be familiar with the process and be equal to the opposing party in their negotiation position (from the time of the contract formation).

Absent parties' agreement, arbitral tribunals conduct arbitral proceedings with great discretion. Soft laws such as the IBA Rules on the Taking of Evidence in International Arbitration (2020)⁶⁶ offer great guidance to arbitral tribunals operating in the transnational arena. Here arbitral tribunals do not act as common law courts (adversarial approach) or civil law courts (inquisitorial approach), but, instead, conduct the proceedings in an effective manner, which will result in a speedy and efficient resolution of the dispute (Redfern and Hunter 2015). Arbitrators will therefore accept written submissions, hear oral evidence (witnesses), collect written evidence and consult experts, if necessary. When needed, arbitrators can seek assistance from the courts at the seat of arbitration

---

⁶⁴ https://www.wipo.int/amc/en/clauses/arbitration/.
⁶⁵ See pages 130–131.
⁶⁶ International Bar Association (IBA) is a professional body, which has issued several codes of practice that are well accepted by the international arbitration community as good practice.

(*lex (loci) arbitri*) – for example, when third parties are ordered to do something, that is, instructed action (witnesses or freezing orders).

Outcome of arbitration

Arbitrators make their decision in writing, in an arbitral award. An arbitral award is similar to a court decision in that it will be the arbitrators dictating the terms under which one party has prevailed over the other, either fully or partially. Unlike mediation, arbitration results in an arbitral tribunal 'declaring the outcome of the dispute'. The result is an enforceable award, which means that a party which has lost its case can be forced to satisfy the award by the courts at the place of enforcement.

Arbitration is often called a 'one-stop shop' because the arbitral award is final and binding. This means that there are no appeal mechanisms to appellate arbitral tribunals which would allow the losing party to trial their case anew. Instead, a losing party can challenge an arbitral award only for limited reasons, as set out in the arbitral law at the seat of arbitration. For example, if arbitration took place in London, the seat of arbitration was England, and the Arbitration Act 1996 (*lex (loci) arbitri*) would dictate the scope of its reviews in Sections 67–69.[67]

In brief, arbitral awards will not survive a challenge if the parties' agreement has not been honoured by the arbitral tribunal (*i.e.* there is no jurisdiction to hear the dispute, as decided), or if the tenets of due process have been violated (either the parties' right to be heard has been violated or the arbitral tribunal was not independent or impartial). In general, courts will not review the evidence or merits of a case which has been decided by arbitral tribunals. State judges do not have the power to check whether the arbitrators got it right. Courts will, however, safeguard the application of mandatory domestic rules and public policy preservation (including arbitrability).[68]

Stakeholder's perspectives: An evaluation and recommendations

All ADR methods are based on consent. Party autonomy and relative equality are integral to ADR success. If the parties are not of equal power, it is argued

---

[67] Similarly, UNCITRAL ML Art.34.
[68] NYC Art.V.

here, the system will serve the stronger party. The literature posits that artists have less negotiation power than record labels (De Orchis 2015; Ormsbee 2011; Scamman 2008). This has been confirmed empirically (Potočnik 2019–20) and leads to some important considerations: (1) access to finance and legal support is unequal, (2) which results in the unequal understanding of the legal and business complexities of music disputes; and (3) artists will have the 'fear of losing out' and this will lead to a chilling effect for artists thinking of actioning a legal dispute.

Overall, it is argued here that in music disputes ADR methods are to be preferred over traditional court litigation. On balance, however, it is further argued that international arbitration is better suited for record labels (and other business organisations in the music industry), whereas individual artists (and smaller organisations) will benefit more from mediation (Ormsbee 2011; Scamman 2008). Arbitration is a formal process, which offers great flexibility on choices of applicable law, place of hearings and evidence-taking. This flexibility, however, is not free (or cheap), especially in complex cases. At the same time, cross-border proceedings can be complex, and arbitrators will have to make a decision based on the applicable law within the terms of original submissions. Once initiated, the power of the decision rests with the arbitrators, unless the parties settle early. Arbitration also suffers from qualified confidentiality in that courts have a supervisory role over the final award. Court proceedings are public (unless an exception applies (*i.e.* trade secrets and the like)).

One of the oft lauded advantages of arbitration over court litigation is the reduced cost of the legal fees attached. That does not mean that the arbitration cost is negligible. Particularly in complex cases where both parties engage legal teams to advise them on their positions in the case, and cases where more than one arbitrator is appointed, and several oral hearings are needed, the cost of legal and arbitrators' fees will be prohibitive for an emerging or individual artist, who is struggling to make a living from their work (Potočnik 2019–20). Additionally, the evidence-taking procedure, although flexible and left to the agreement of the parties, will often be expensive, unless the parties agree on restricted evidentiary procedure from the start. To illustrate, international disputes will often involve parties who speak different languages, and arbitrators from different countries. The cost of translation alone can be prohibitive for an individual thinking of bringing forth their claim of IP infringement against a party better established in the industry.

The suitability of arbitration as a dispute settlement mechanism is not to be disregarded in complex international disputes, where IP rights span numerous territories, or involve complex contractual arrangements of commercial exploitation of music works and related artists' rights (image, merchandising, *etc.*). Here, the appeal of international arbitration is clear, as the law allows parties to select their decision maker(s); the law to be used for reaching the final outcome of the case; the evidentiary procedure;[69] and the legal place of arbitration ('the law of the seat'), which will suggest which courts are to assist the arbitral tribunal, if necessary. Overall, in such cases and when handled by experienced arbitration practitioners, international arbitration is the preferred method over domestic court litigation. This is because of the 'one-stop shop' nature of international arbitration, which means that there are no appeals proceedings in arbitration, rendering arbitration a faster solution. Unlike in domestic litigation, once the final decision has been made, the supervisory body (the courts at the seat or the place of enforcement) will not have the power to review the facts, evidentiary findings or merits of the case. Beyond the limited grounds for challenging an award, national courts do not have the power to check 'whether the arbitrators got it right'.

Mediation, on the contrary, is less expensive, less formal, and completely confidential. Due to its nature, where mediators are facilitating the conversation and exchange between the parties, the imbalance in legal or business skill will not be as prevalent, and if the appointed mediator is a music expert, the independent artist will benefit from a more equal forum. Any concerns of the parties can be discussed confidentially with the mediator (in '*caucus*'), all with the aim of reaching the final resolution of the dispute, acceptable to both parties. Without the confines of initial submissions, the mediator also has creative powers of suggesting imaginative solutions to the existing problems, thereby leading to 'win-for-all' settlements in the end. The cost of legal fees can be reduced substantially, as there is no need for a formal evidentiary procedure, or the involvement of several legal teams, over a prolonged period of time. Mediation is often restricted to a shorter period, when compared to an international arbitration (Blake, Browne and Sime 2018).

Because mediation is a method of communication between the parties without a formal (and expensive) procedure attached to it, it is argued here that artists should always strive to have mediation clauses inserted in their contracts with the bigger players. These, as it is recommended here, are 'golden tickets for

---

[69] Parties can choose a purely written procedure; or opt to add oral hearings; parties also have the discretion to limit the type of admissible evidence (documents, witnesses, or expert opinions).

future conversation' that would override the power vacuum between the two parties when it is only the artists wishing to settle a dispute, with the record label avoiding the matter. Equally, a mediation clause could offer a way to renegotiate artists' position in urgent situations, such as the Covid-19 pandemic. But without an agreement there can be no mediation. In order for mediation to become the new industry standard for settlement of music disputes, it is recommended that professional bodies and organisations take a lead in promoting and facilitating mediation (*e.g.*, the Incorporated Society of Musicians for the UK).[70] This could include (1) educating artists on the power of mediation; (2) recommending mediation as the industry standard; (3) using mediation in their own affairs (with the potential of combining mediation and arbitration in a tiered ADR clause (*i.e.* Med-Arb clause)); or (4) setting up funds, to cover artists' expenses in mediation.

References

Agreement on Trade-Related Aspects of Intellectual Property Rights (Annex 1C of the Marrakesh Agreement establishing the World Trade Organization, signed in Marrakesh, Morocco, on 15 April 1994) (1869) UNTS 299 (TRIPS).

American Arbitration Association (AAA), Commercial Arbitration Rules and Mediation Procedures (2013). https://www.adr.org/Rules, accessed 17 May 2021.

Association of Independent Music (AMI), https://www.aim.org.uk/, accessed 17 May 2021.

Bain, V. (2019). 'Counting the Music Industry: the Gender Gap', https://vbain.co.uk/research, accessed 17 May 2021.

Blackaby, N., C. Partasides, A. Redfern and M. Hunter (2015). *Redfern and Hunter on International Arbitration*, Sixth edn. Oxford: Oxford University Press (*i.e.* Redfern and Hunter 2015).

Blake, Susan, J. Browne and S. Sime (2018). *A Practical Approach to Alternative Dispute Resolution*, 5th edn. Oxford: Oxford University Press.

Centre for Effective Dispute Resolution (CEDR), https://www.cedr.com, accessed 17 May 2021.

Coogan Byrne, Linda and Women in CTRL. 'Gender Disparity Data Report: An analysis of the Top 20 Most Played British Acts across British Radio Stations in the

---

[70] The UK's professional body for musicians and subject association for music. Other organisations to be considered: Association of Independent Music (AIM), which has members among the record labels and self-releasing artists; or professional bodies, such as: Music Managers Forum (MMF) as the professional association for music managers; or the International Federation of the Phonographic Industry (IFPI) (for a worldwide reach).

Period of June 2019–2020 and the Top 100 Radio Airplay chart in 2020', https://www.canva.com/design/DAEE37rIDuc/-7R8D7lzU7EMdcnv9Snw3w/view#1, accessed 17 May 2021.

Cook, T. and A. I. Garcia (2010). *International Intellectual Property Arbitration*. The Netherlands: Kluwer Law International.

De Girolamo, D. (2016). 'Rhetoric and Civil Justice: A Commentary on the Promotion of Mediation Without Conviction in England and Wales', *CJQ*, 35, no. 2: 162–85.

De Orchis, D. (2015). 'Designing Success: How Alternative Dispute Resolution Systems Can Effectively and Efficiently Manage Conflict (and Promote Relationships) Between Artists and Record Labels', *The American Journal of Mediation*, 8: 95–112.

Denoncourt, J. (2016). 'The Creative Identity and Intellectual Property', *Nottingham LJ*, 25: 39–54.

Directive 2008/52/EC of the European Parliament and of the Council of 21 May 2008 on certain aspects of mediation in civil and commercial matters (OJ L 136, 24 May 2008), https://eur-lex.europa.eu/legal-content/GA/TXT/?uri=CELEX:32008L0052, accessed 17 May 2021.

Incorporated Society of Musicians (ISM), https://www.ism.org, accessed 17 May 2021.

International Bar Association (IBA), https://www.ibanet.org/Publications/publications_IBA_guides_and_free_materials.aspx, accessed 17 May 2021.

International Chamber of Commerce (ICC) Arbitration Rules (2021), https://iccwbo.org/dispute-resolution-services/arbitration/rules-of-arbitration/, accessed 17 May 2021.

International Chamber of Commerce (ICC) Mediation Rules (2014), https://iccwbo.org/dispute-resolution-services/mediation/mediation-rules/, accessed 17 May 2021.

International Federation of the Phonographic Industry (IFPI), https://www.ifpi.org, accessed 17 May 2021.

International Trademark Association (INTA), https://www.inta.org/resources/mediation/, accessed 17 May 2021.

Kessler, S. (2017). 'The Non-Recording, Non-Artist Recording Artist: Expanding the Recording Artist's Brand into Non-Music Arenas', *Vanderbilt Journal of Entertainment & Technology Law*, 20: 515–65.

Laturno, C. A. (1996). 'International Arbitration of the Creative: A Look at the World Intellectual Property Organization's New Arbitration Rules', *Transnatl Law*, 9: 356–92.

London Court of International Arbitration (LCIA) Arbitration Rules (2014). Available online, https://www.lcia.org/Dispute_Resolution_Services/lcia-arbitration-rules-2014.aspx, accessed 17 May 2021.

Martin, J. A. (1996–1997). 'Arbitrating in the Alps Rather Than Litigating in Los Angeles: The Advantages of International Intellectual Property-Specific Alternative Dispute Resolution', *The Stanford Law Review*, 49: 917–70.

Music Managers Forum (MMF), https://themmf.net, accessed 17 May 2021.

Ormsbee, M. H. (2011). 'Music to Everyone's Ears: Binding Mediation in Music Rights Disputes', *The Cardozo Journal of Conflict Resolution*, 13: 225–58.

Potočnik, M. (2019). *Arbitrating Brands: International Investment Treaties and Trade Marks*. Cheltenham: Edward Elgar.

Potočnik, M. *Breaking Monopolies: A Feminist Approach to Intellectual Property Law in the Creative Industries*, Early Research Awards Scheme at University of Wolverhampton, (*i.e.* Potočnik 2019–20).

Regulation (EU) No 1215/2012 of the European Parliament and of the Council of 12 December 2012 on jurisdiction and the recognition and enforcement of judgments in civil and commercial matters, https://eurlex.europa.eu/legalcontent/EN/ALL/?uri=celex%3A32012R1215, accessed 17 May 2021.

Scamman, Kaleena (2008). 'ADR in the Music Industry: Tailoring Dispute Resolution to the Different Stages of the Artist–Label Relationship', *The Cardozo Journal of Conflict Resolution*, 10: 269–304.

Singapore International Arbitration Centre (SIAC) Arbitration Rules (2017). https://www.siac.org.sg/our-rules, accessed 17 May 2021.

Smith, S. L., K. Pieper, H. Clark, A. Case and M. Choueiti (2020). 'Inclusion in the Recording Studio? Gender and Race/Ethnicity of Artists, Songwriters and Producers across 800 Popular Songs from 2012–2019', http://assets.uscannenberg.org/docs/aii-inclusion-recording-studio-20200117.pdf, accessed 17 May 2021.

Stopps, D. (2014). 'How to Make a Living from Music', *WIPO Creative Industries*, Booklet no 4, 2nd edn, https://www.wipo.int/publications/en/details.jsp?id=260&plang=EN, accessed 17 May 2021.

Svensson, G. (2001). '"Glocalization" of Business Activities: A "glocal strategy" Approach', *Management Decision*, 39, no. 1: 6–18.

The United Nations Convention on International Settlement Agreements Resulting from Mediation ('Singapore Convention on Mediation') (2018), https://uncitral.un.org/en/texts/mediation/conventions/international_settlement_agreements, accessed 17 May 2021.

The United Nations Convention on the Recognition and Enforcement of Foreign Arbitral Awards (New York, 1958), http://www.newyorkconvention.org/new+york+convention+texts, accessed 17 May 2021.

UNCITRAL Arbitration Rules (as amended in 2010), https://uncitral.un.org/en/texts/arbitration/contractualtexts/arbitration, accessed 17 May 2021.

UNCITRAL Model Law on International Commercial Arbitration (1985, with amendments in 2006), https://uncitral.un.org/en/texts/arbitration/modellaw/commercial_arbitration, accessed 17 May 2021.

UNCITRAL Model Law on International Commercial Mediation and International Settlement Agreements Resulting from Mediation (2018), (amending the UNCITRAL Model Law on International Commercial Conciliation, 2002), https://

uncitral.un.org/en/texts/mediation/modellaw/commercial_conciliation, accessed 17 May 2021.

Wechs Hatanaka, A. (2018). 'Optimising Mediation for Intellectual Property Law – Perspectives from EU, French and UK Law', *IIC*, 49, no. 4: 384–412.

WIPO Arbitration and Mediation Centre, https://www.wipo.int/amc/en/center, accessed 17 May 2021.

WIPO Arbitration Model Clause, https://www.wipo.int/amc/en/clauses/arbitration/, accessed 17 May 2021.

WIPO Arbitration Rules (Effective from 1 January 2020), https://www.wipo.int/amc/en/arbitration/rules/, accessed 17 May 2021.

WIPO List of Neutrals, https://www.wipo.int/amc/en/neutrals/, accessed 17 May 2021.

WIPO Mediation Model Clause, https://www.wipo.int/amc/en/clauses/mediation/, accessed 17 May 2021.

WIPO Mediation Rules (Effective from 1 January 2020), https://www.wipo.int/amc/en/mediation/rules/, accessed 17 May 2021.

7

The acoustic trademark

Katarzyna Krupa-Lipińska

In the field of intellectual property law, analyses concerning music are usually focused on copyright law. At the same time little attention is paid to the possibility of protecting musical compositions (or their parts) in the field of industrial property law, in particular as acoustic trademarks. The reasons for it might be objective, namely, the majority of music compositions are neither created nor used as trademarks, that is, to indicate the commercial origin of goods or services. The reasons might also be subjective, namely, this kind of trademark is not very popular either among intellectual property law practitioners who might suggest such an application, or among intellectual property law scholars who, in my opinion, in principle, do not undertake elaborate research or make comments on the application and scope of protection of acoustic trademarks. In consequence, the number of acoustic trademark applications and registrations in absolute numbers is not very high. For example, in the EUIPO there were 411 of them; in the UK IPO 243; in PPO 125; and in the USPTO – 566 . If a certain musical composition was either especially created or had started to be used (in whole or in part) for commercial purposes, for instance, as a jingle or a short musical work for advertising a certain product or service on TV, the internet, or radio commercials, then its registration as an acoustic trademark should at least be taken into consideration because of the important legal advantages which trademark protection grants to its proprietors (Krupa-Lipińska 2020: 157). One of them is that, unlike other intellectual property rights which are limited in time, trademark registration in most legal systems lasts for ten years, but it may be subsequently renewed for another period of ten years, and therefore the protection stemming from that registration may last forever. Relatively strong protection of trademark law for sounds that are used commercially, among others in the form of audio (sonic, sound, acoustic) branding, is of particular importance nowadays in the digital area. Minsky and Fahey (2014) made a good point writing that

> to gain advantage on this leveled playing field, there's one powerful branding tool that has been generally overlooked – or perhaps undervalued – by most marketers: sound. With of our increasingly audio-enabled media environment, the strategic use of sound can play an important role in positively differentiating a product or service, enhancing recall, creating preference, building trust, and even increasing sales. (Minskey and Fahey 2014)

Acoustic trademarks as an example of unconventional trademarks

The vast majority of registered trademarks are word, figurative, and combined (i.e. figurative with a word element) trademarks. They are therefore called 'conventional' or 'typical' trademarks and are mostly recognised as trademarks by consumers. On the other hand, the broad definition of trademark in many countries and the EU allows it to be any sign if it fulfils the requirement of distinctiveness and appropriate representation in the register. There are therefore numerous kinds of trademarks which are called 'unconventional' or 'untypical'. They might be divided into visible signs (e.g. three-dimensional marks, colour per se marks, position marks, pattern marks, motion marks, hologram marks), and those perceived by other senses (e.g. olfactory marks, taste marks). The acoustic trademarks are classified in the group of unconventional trademarks perceived by other senses (i.e. the sense of hearing).

In the field of international law, Article 6 (1) of the Paris Convention (1883) states that 'The conditions for the filing and registration of trademarks shall be determined in each country of the Union by its domestic legislation'. Similarly, in the more recent Singapore Treaty (2006), Article 2 (1) says that 'Any Contracting Party shall apply this Treaty to marks consisting of signs that can be registered as marks under its law'. Article 15 (1) TRIPS (1994), in turn, gives the definition of a trademark as follows:

> Any sign, or any combination of signs, capable of distinguishing the goods or services of one undertaking from those of other undertakings, shall be capable of constituting a trade mark. Such signs, in particular words including personal

names, letters, numerals, figurative elements, and combinations of colours as well as any combination of such signs, shall be eligible for registration as trade marks. (. . .) Members may require, as a condition of registration, that signs be visually perceptible.

The possibility of registering an acoustic trademark in a particular legal system primarily depends on trademark definition and registration criteria in a given state. In various states (e.g. EU Member States, the United Kingdom, the United States, Canada), the definition of trademark is relatively similar. In general, it is said that it might be any sign that possesses a distinctive character, that is, that it is capable of distinguishing the goods or services of one undertaking from those of other undertakings. In certain legislations (e.g., art. 4 of EUTMR, art. 3 of EU Dir 2015/2436, Part I point 1 (1) of the UK Trade Marks Act (1994), art. 2 (1) of the Japanese Trademark Act (1959)), sound signs are explicitly mentioned as an example of permitted, registrable trademarks, while in others they are implicitly included in its general definition. Certain countries, however, do not allow for the protection of an acoustic trademark. In the WIPO questionnaire from 2006 for the document 'New Types of Trademark', only thirty-eight out of seventy-six offices responding said that they accepted musical sounds and only twenty-eight out of seventy-three offices responding said that they accepted non-musical sounds for registration as trademarks. The obstacles to registration of an acoustic trademark might come from the requirement that trademarks, in themselves, have to be perceived visually (appeal to visual sense). In case of non-musical sounds, it might also be a certain reluctance to protect them as a trademark, as was, for example, the former practice of the German Patent Office (Kur and Senftleben 2017: 100). Certain wider policy considerations are probably also present, like the ones mentioned by Advocate General Ruiz-Jarabi Colomer in the *Shield Mark BV v Joost Kist h.o.d.n. Memex* case C-283/01 (von Muhlendahl et al. 2016: 71), where he stated that certain signs should be left free for use by other traders, like direct manifestations of nature or creations of the mind that constitute the universal cultural heritage. Such signs should not be 'appropriated indefinitely by a person to be used on the market in order to distinguish the goods he produces or the services he provides with an exclusivity which not even its author's estate enjoys' (Colomer 2003: I-14327), in the sense that

> (. . .) the rights of an author of an artistic work, such as Beethoven's 'Für Elise' are to run for the life of the author and for 70 years after his death. Copyright protects the work itself. Trade marks, on the other hand, do not claim to protect

original creations: their purpose is to allow the goods or services offered by undertakings to be distinguished on the market. It may happen, however, that a sign is an original work protected by copyright at the same time, in which case it is necessary to regulate their reciprocal interrelations (. . .)'. (Colomer 2003: I-14327)

In the most recent years the world tendency, however, is to broaden the scope of registrable trademarks, including acoustic trademarks.

The types of acoustic trademarks

Acoustic trademarks are not a uniform group. The WIPO document on 'New Types of Marks' (WIPO 2006: 8) divides them into two main groups, that is, musical and non-musical trademarks, and later on the basis of whether they were created purposely to be a trademark or not. In my opinion this division may be supplemented by further distinctions and, overall, the acoustic trademarks might be classified as follows:

First group: the musical sounds. They might be further divided into musical sounds purposely created (i.e. specially commissioned) for using as a trademark and musical sounds taken from the range of existing musical scores for using as a trademark, for example, the first nine notes of 'Für Elize' by Ludwig van Beethoven, the spelled words of the Lone Ranger with Gioacchino Rossini's Overture to the opera 'William Tell' in the background (USTM no. 74639801 and USTM no. 74639802), an excerpt from Howard Hanson's Symphony 2, op. 30 (USTM no. 75591273) or a Russian folk-style tune (in an electronic version) (USTM no. 75389198-1, USTM no. 75389198-2). The musical sounds may be also divided into instrumental scores and singing.

Second group: non-musical sounds. These might be further divided into four sub-groups: first, non-musical sounds purposely created to be used as a trademark, which include sounds that cannot be found in nature, for example, a sound played on the Japanese musical instrument the 'Shakuhachi' (USTM no. 76216925) or the sound of a duck quacking the word 'AFLAC' (USTM no. 76307773); people speaking, for example, 'ooh it's so good' (USTM no. 74684280), 'you've got mail' (USTM no. 75528557), 'Hello and welcome to moviefone' (USTM no. 76316851), 'It's your time. Make the most of it' (USTM no. 76592930), a ringing cash register and a voice saying 'You've got cash'

(USTM no. 76152169); voice sounds, for example, childlike human giggles (USTM no. 76163189). Second, non-musical sounds which reproduce sounds found in nature, for example, a lion's roar (e.g., EUTM no. 005170113 and USTM no. 73553567), a wolf's howl (USTM no. 75086922), a cat's meow (USTM no. 75143671). The third sub-category are non-musical sounds reproducing ubiquitous sounds, for example, the sound of a crowd and a bell (USTM no. 76344794), the horn of a truck (USTM no. 73391897). Finally, non-musical sounds that cannot be found in nature or anywhere around and which were not originally created to be used as a trademark, for example, Tarzan's yell (EUTM no. 75326989).

Trademarks with a sound element

An acoustic trademark as such is a trademark that consists 'exclusively of a sound or combination of sounds' (art. 3 (3) (g) of EUTMIR). In many cases, trademarks – apart from the sound element – possess another element or elements constituting a combined trademark. In that case one can indicate: solely acoustic trademarks, for example, EUTM no. 001312008 (see Figure 7.1); sound trademark with a word element, for example, USTM no. 73432170; i.e. a song played and a choir singing: 'The Dreams We Share, We'll Always Remember, Remember With The Music Of Your Life' or, for example, EUTM 003553261 (see Figure 7.2); multimedia trademarks, for example, EUTM 017635293 or the Polish trademark no. R.329065 presenting football player Krzysztof Piątek's goal celebration. Multimedia trademarks are currently treated as a separate type of trademarks.

General registration requirements for trademarks

If in principle, the registration of an acoustic trademark is permitted in a certain state, it is then subject to the rules and requirements of registration prescribed for all of the trademarks and the particular rules for acoustic trademarks.

Generally, the requirement for registration of a trademark is not met if the so-called, absolute (in the public interest) or relative (in the interests of a third-party) grounds for its refusal apply. Owing to the limited scope of this chapter

The Acoustic Trademark 153

Figure 7.1 EUTM no. 001312008. Available at: https://euipo.europa.eu/eSearch/#details/trademarks/001312008

Figure 7.2 EUTM 003553261. Available at: https://euipo.europa.eu/eSearch/#details/trademarks/003553261

their analysis will be omitted. Later analysis will focus on the other issues chosen for this chapter.

The basic requirement for any trademark is that it should be distinctive so as to fulfil its principal function, that is, 'to guarantee the identity of the origin of the marked product to the consumer or end-user by enabling him to distinguish, without any possibility of confusion, the product or service from those which have a different origin' (Hasselblatt 2015: 88). In this regard a trademark should be neither too simple nor too complicated (Żelechowski 2014: 286–7). In the case of an acoustic trademark this requirement is not easy to evaluate. According to the simplicity of an acoustic trademark, non-musical trademarks are quite often not very complicated, although still possessing a distinctive character. An interesting example which might serve to illustrate this is the USTM no. 76280750 consisting of the spelled word 'D'OH' performed by the Homer Simpson cartoon character. The same may apply to certain musical trademarks: sometimes even two or three notes might be sufficient to distinguish some goods or services (e.g. the three notes in USTM no. 76302753). Different approaches are taken, however, by different intellectual property offices, for example, EUIPO refused (and General Court confirmed it) in the case of *Globo Comunicação e Participações S/A v EUIPO* (13 September 2016, T -408/15, § 51) to accept a trademark consisting of a stave with a treble clef with a tempo of 147 crotchets per minute, repeating two G sharps, which is the classic form of a ringing sound as a sound sign, because it is 'characterised by excessive simplicity and is no more than the simple repetition of two identical notes [and therefore] is not, as such, capable of conveying a message that can be remembered by consumers, with the result that consumers will not regard it as a trade mark, unless it has acquired distinctive character through use (. . .)'.

The evaluation of too high complexity of an acoustic trademark is also hard to make unequivocally. In this regard, it might be tempting to refer to the length of the musical composition applied for trademark protection. If it is too long it might be considered not to fulfil the given requirement. However, the application of this criterion also does not give precise indications. It might be argued that for a composition to be too long to be a trademark, it should significantly extend beyond a reasonable length for the consumer to associate it as a trademark. For example, it might be disputable whether a whole song (e.g. USTM no. 74158626 'Sweet Georgia Brown' lasting for more than two and a half minutes) fulfils this requirement. However, as mentioned any evaluations here would be vague, for example, the United States Patent and Trademark Office (USPTO) registered USTM no. 75389198-2 consisting of an electronic performance of a Russian folk-style tune played for one minute forty seconds. On the other hand, a few seconds seems not to be too long, like, for example, USTM no. 7593453, 75934535, 75934537, 75934538 which are the Looney Tunes Theme Song that lasts for nineteen seconds, or the musical EUTM no. 013823539:

Figure 7.3   EUTM no. 013823539. Available at: https://euipo.europa.eu/eSearch/#details/trademarks/013823539

Trademarks are registered for indicated goods and services, classified in eighty-three states in accordance with the Nice Agreement Concerning the

International Classification of Goods and Services for the Purposes of the Registration of Marks (the Nice Classification). Theoretically, acoustic trademarks may be used and registered for almost any goods or services, for instance, as a sound in their commercials (e.g. in the form of short musical compositions or parts of a larger musical composition); jingles (e.g. as radio jingles); logo themes for a film corporation (e.g. the lion's roar for Metro Goldwyn Mayer, EUTM no. 005170113, or the logo theme of Lucasfilms, USTM no. 74309951, and the logo theme of Twentieth Century Fox, USTM no. 74629287); intro music for a TV or internet programme; entertainment services (e.g. USTM no. 88129555); or as short compositions or sounds connected with goods exploration (e.g. the composition played while opening a computer program or opening a pot lid; the closing jingle for electric pressure cookers, USTM no. 88129403; the sound played while exploring toys: cars, guns, figures, glockenspiels, harmonicas, noisemakers, pianos, weapons, whistles, xylophones, action figures, candy dispensers, USTM no. 88433440, etc.); or the sound played while performing certain services (e.g. deposit notification services, USTM no. 76152168).

In many legal systems (e.g. in EUTMR and EU Dir 2015/2436) at the time of application for trademark registration, the applicant does not need to use the trademark that he/she is applying for, nor to make any official statements concerning the intent of its use. The EUTMR and EU Dir. 2015/2436 give the trademark proprietor five years to start genuine use of his/her trademark in connection with the goods and services for which it is registered, failing which certain limits and sanctions are imposed (e.g. a trademark is liable to revocation and may fall under non-use defence in infringement proceedings, unless there are proper reasons for non-use). In some other countries (in particular in the United States), the basis for filing a trademark application is either 'use in commerce' or 'intent to use', which is a bona fide intent to use the mark in commerce and requires the filing of additional form(s) and fees(s) prior to its registration.

The specific requirements for applying for acoustic trademarks

To apply for an acoustic trademark, the legislations of certain states may demand additional requirements. In many states the applicant has to indicate the type of trademark as a 'sound' and must present the acoustic trademark in the required way and file format. These two requirements will be considered in more detail.

In practice, when applying for a trademark registration, the applicant indicates the type of trademark. Even if this requirement is not explicitly mentioned in the provisions concerning trademark applications, it may be required by the intellectual property office practice to be inserted in a special space in a paper form or to be a necessary element in an electronic application. In case of an acoustic trademark the requirement of indicating its type as a 'sound', a 'sound mark' or a 'non-visual mark' is often explicitly mentioned in legal texts (e.g. in Sec. 3 (3) EUTMIR; § 807.09 TMEP – indication of a 'non-visual mark' in USTM paper application and indication of 'a sound mark' in USTM TEAS application; Sec. 31(e) of the Canadian Trademarks Regulations) or required by intellectual property office practice. This requirement has particular importance, as the musical trademarks that are represented by the notation might be mistakenly taken for a figurative trademarks. United Kingdom Intellectual Property Office (UKIPO) explicitly states in its trademarks manual that 'applications for sound marks in musical notation must clearly state that they are sound marks, otherwise the application will be examined as if it were a figurative mark' (UKIPO 2020: 2.4.6.). It might also raise some doubts for third parties when searching trademark databases. Therefore, a clear statement that the trademark applied for is a 'sound' clarifies the subject of protection and aids in searching for similar marks.

Another requirement, namely, an appropriate representation of a trademark in the register, plays a fundamental role in practice, as it indicates the protected trademark and determines the scope of its protection. In general, in states permitting registration of acoustic trademarks, the provisions of relevant legal acts or their interpretation or guidelines by the intellectual property offices indicate the permitted ways of such representation. In the following analysis certain permitted and prohibited ways are set out for presenting acoustic trademarks in the register with regard to chosen legislations.

It should be mentioned at the outset that in some legislations the appropriate representation of a trademark in the register is an element of the definition of a trademark (e.g. art. 4 EUTMR, art. 3 EU Dir. 2015/2436, Part I point 1 (1) of the UK Trade Marks Act), while others treat it as a separate formal requirement (e.g. Article 30 (2) (c) of the Canadian Trademarks Act). Setting aside theoretical classification of the given requirement, the practical question is how trademarks should be displayed in such a register. In certain legislations, the sign must be graphically represented, while others follow a more flexible approach which stipulates that such representation must be in a manner that enables the competent authorities and the public to determine the clear and precise subject matter of the protection afforded to its proprietor. The latter approach has been adopted in an amended provisions concerning EUTM (art. 4 (b) EUTMR) and the national trademarks of EU Member States upon EU Dir. 2015/2436 which is based on the so-called Sieckmann case criteria (Judgment of the Court from 12 December 2002 in Case C-273/00 *Ralf Sieckmann v Deutsches Patent- und Markenamt*, ECLI:EU:C:2002:748) in which the Court ruled that 'a trade mark may consist of a sign which is not in itself capable of being perceived visually, provided that it can be represented graphically, particularly by means of images, lines or characters, and that the representation is clear, precise, self-contained, easily accessible, intelligible, durable and objective'. The UK legislation followed the EU model regulation while it was an EU Member State, therefore in the Trade Marks Act 1994 in Part I point 1 (1) (a) one can read that in this Act 'trade mark' means any sign which is capable of being represented in the register in a manner which enables the registrar and other competent authorities and the public to determine the clear and precise subject matter of the protection afforded to the proprietor. Similarly, art. 30 (2) (c) of the Canadian Trademarks Act states that the trademark application shall contain a representation or description, or both, that permits the trademark to be clearly defined and that complies with any prescribed requirements.

Permissible representations of acoustic trademarks in the register

Notation (exclusively)

One of the most common ways of presenting musical trademarks in the register is notation. In legislations which require graphical representation of trademarks in the register it is the only way to present them unambiguously. As the Court in § 62–63 of the *Shield Mark BV v Joost Kist h.o.d.n. Memex* (C-283/01 of 27 November 2003) judgement wrote:

> (...) a stave divided into bars and showing, in particular, a clef (a treble clef, bass clef, or alto, or tenor clef), musical notes, and rests whose form (for the notes: semibreve, minim, crotchet, quaver, semiquaver, etc.; for the rests: semibreve rest, minim rest, crotchet rest, quaver rest, etc.) indicates the relative value and, where appropriate, accidentals (sharp, flat, natural) – all of this notation determining the pitch and duration of the sounds – may constitute a faithful representation of the

sequence of sounds forming the melody in respect of which registration is sought. This mode of graphical representation of the sounds meets the requirements of the case-law of the Court that such representation must be clear, precise, self-contained, easily accessible, intelligible, durable and objective. Even if such a representation is not immediately intelligible, the fact remains that it may be easily intelligible, thus allowing the competent authorities and the public, in particular traders, to know precisely the sign whose registration as a trade mark is sought.

In legislations in which graphical representation is not a constitutive element of a trademark application it can be presented in the form of notation as an alternative to an audio file (e.g. in EUTM application upon art. 3 (3) (g) EUTMIR which speaks about 'an accurate representation of the sound in musical notation'). The practice of intellectual property offices usually gives some guidelines on the format of a file required to present musical trademarks applied in the form of notation. For example, according to UKIPO Trademark manual (2020), 'musical notations may be submitted in one single JPEG file or on one single A4 sheet. "Accurate musical notation" means that the representation must include all the elements necessary for interpreting the melody, that is to say, such as, pitch, tempo, lyrics (if any), etc'.

The trade mark law provisions, however, do not make specified demands for formal representation of musical trademarks in the form of a notation, therefore different forms exist in registrations, e.g.: printed notation, e.g. EUTM 002984912:

Figure 7.4   EUTM 002984912. Available at:https://euipo.europa.eu/eSearch/#details/trademarks/002984912

e.g. EUTM 011301082:

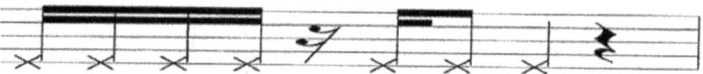

Figure 7.5 EUTM 011301082. available at: https://euipo.europa.eu/eSearch/#details/trademarks/011301082

or handwritten notation, e.g. EUTM 010265486:

Figure 7.6 EUTM 010265486. Available at: https://euipo.europa.eu/eSearch/#details/trademarks/010265486

e.g. Polish trademark R.155520:

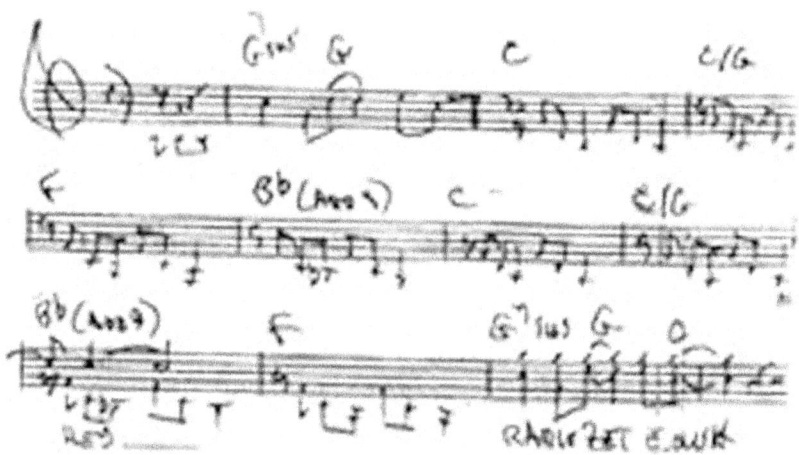

Figure 7.7 Polish trademark R.155520. Available at: https://ewyszukiwarka.pue.uprp.gov.pl/search/pwp-details/Z.227333

The notation for different instruments, ex. Polish trademark R.300795:

Figure 7.8   Polish trademark R.300795. Available at: https://ewyszukiwarka.pue.uprp.gov.pl/search/pwp-details/Z.438707

However, in each particular case the above-mentioned general examples of admissible trademark presentation are evaluated on a case-by-case basis. It is then possible that even notation will not be considered to be sufficiently clear and precise if it contains some additional elements that lack precision, for example, adding the words 'ramp' and 'seagulls/water' to notation has not been considered by EUIPO to be sufficiently clear and precise to allow for trademark registration (international application to EUIPO no. 1264210).

Audio file (exclusively)

As mentioned earlier, certain legislations are not making (or have ceased to make) graphical representation of the trademark obligatory, requiring that the trademark should be represented in the register 'in a manner which enables the competent authorities and the public to determine the clear and precise subject matter of the protection afforded to its proprietor' (art. 4 (b) EUTMR). In the case of an acoustic trademark, those requirements are met by attaching to the application only an audio file. Intellectual property offices usually prefer certain formats of audio files (mp3 is the most common one) with some limits on their magnitude and sometimes with the restriction that such applications are only permissible by electronic filing. For example, EUIPO requires an mp3 file of a maximum of 2MB, with no streaming, and the application is allowed only as an electronic application. Similarly, UKIPO requires mp3 format of a maximum of 2MB, no stream or loop, and its submission only by e-filings (no paper filing is allowed with an accompanying audio file on a physical data carrier, for example, USB stick).

The technical development naturally impacted the means on which audio files had been submitted or attached additionally to the graphical representation of an acoustic trademark. Initially, they were submitted on cassettes, later on CDs, DVDs and USB sticks. Currently, owing to the fact that many leading intellectual property offices are switching to electronic means of communication, the preferable, or the only possible, way (as in the case of the already mentioned EUTM and UKTM) to apply for an acoustic trademark by using only an audio file is by an electronic filing with attached specified electronic file format.

In audio specimens, the music trademark obviously needs to be somehow presented (performed), so it may be played on an instrument(s), sung or both sung with melody played in the background. It refers to both combined acoustic trademarks with a word element, but it seems that the same should apply to just a musical trademark if the melody (notes) were to be sung or mumbled without indicating an exact word.

It is, however, important to acknowledge that, while applying for trademark protection, an applicant needs to consider the strategy and territorial scope of its desired protection. Owing to the fact that the Madrid system[1] allows only trademarks that are graphically represented, UKIPO explains that 'where the application for a sound mark is intended to be used as the basis for an international application, the UK application must consist of musical notation'.

---

[1] With the Madrid system an applicant may apply for trademark registration in different countries – parties to the Madrid Agreement or Madrid Protocol to the Agreement – on the basis of a national application.

Notation with audio file

In accordance with musical acoustic trademarks, an application containing both notation and an audio file specimen is also permitted in certain legislations and in some even required.

The practice of submitting both notation and audio file specimens for musical trademarks is followed especially in states in which the law requires graphical representation of a trademark. In certain legislations, such as that in Poland, it is obligatory to submit an audio file specimen of an acoustic trademark, even if the application contains notation (art. 141 (2) Polish statute of industrial property of 30.06.2000 and § 4 of Polish Regulation on application and consideration of applications of trademarks of 8.12.2016, which specifies that there need to be two copies of an electronic audio file specimen).

Sonogram with audio file

At times when EU legislation required graphical representation of a trademark, the EUIPO accepted a sonogram for non-musical trademarks. It was particularly so if they were accompanied by a description, for example, EUTM no. 005170113 (lion's roar):

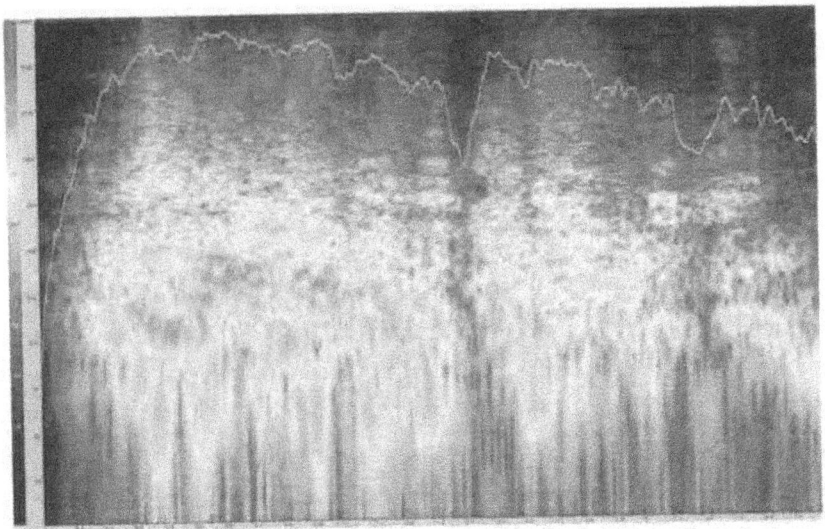

Figure 7.9 EUTM no. 005170113. Available at: https://euipo.europa.eu/eSearch/#details/trademarks/005170113

Theoretically, the audio file was optional upon Rule 3 (6) of former EUTMIR, however in practice EUIPO regularly required filing a sound recording in case of non-musical applications (Kur and Senftleben 2017: 99–100), for example, EUTM no. 005090055 (Tarzan's yell):

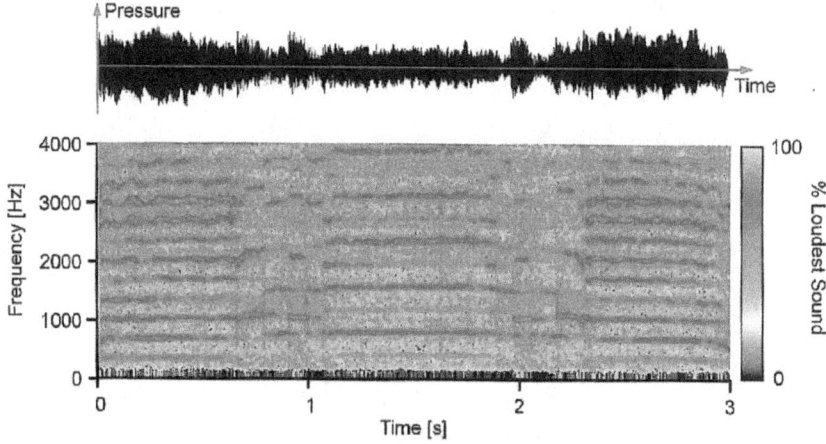

Figure 7.10 EUTM no. 005090055. **Available at:** https://euipo.europa.eu/eSearch/#details/trademarks/005090055

After amendment of the EU trademark law, sonograms should not be accepted either alone, with description or with an audio file (see further).

Trademark description with audio file

In the United States, according to § 2.52. (e) of 37 CFR, 'An applicant is not required to submit a drawing if the mark consists only of a sound [e.g. music or words and music], a scent, or other completely non-visual matter. For these types of marks, the applicant must submit a detailed description of the mark'. For example, in the description of a sound trademark played on an instrument in USTM no. 88433440 one can read that 'The mark is a sound. The mark consists of repeating, alternating musical chords consisting of A major (A, C [sharp], and E) and F minor (F, A [flat], and C [flat])' and in the case of a sung sound trademark, for example, in USTM no. 76214049 'Tell Me' and USTM no. 88129555 the description says: 'The mark is a sound. The mark consists of a sound mark comprising the word 'Oralé' sung to a melody consisting of the following musical notes: G# A# B'. Detailed description in the case of the trademark that comprises music or words set to music also means that 'the applicant should generally submit the musical score sheet music to supplement or clarify the description of the mark. (...) In a TEAS application or response, the musical score sheet music should be attached as a .jpg or .pdf file in the 'Additional Statements' section of the form, under 'Miscellaneous Statements' (§ 807.09 TMEP). Due to § 2.61 (b) CFR 'The Office may require the applicant to furnish such information, exhibits, affidavits or declarations, and such additional specimens as may be reasonably necessary to the proper examination of the application'. TMEP specifies in § 807.09 that in the case of TEAS application of a sound mark it means that:

> the applicant will be required to indicate whether it is attaching an audio file. The applicant should submit an audio reproduction of any sound mark. (...) The purpose of this reproduction is to supplement and clarify the description of the mark. The reproduction should contain only the mark itself; it is not meant to be a specimen. The reproduction must be in an electronic file in .wav, .wmv, .wma, .mp3, .mpg, or .avi format and should not exceed 5 MB in size because TEAS cannot accommodate larger files.

In the case of paper filings:

> Reproductions of sound marks must be submitted on compact discs ('CDs'), digital video discs ('DVDs'), videotapes, or audiotapes. (...) The applicant should clearly and explicitly indicate that the reproduction of the mark contained on the disc or tape is meant to supplement the mark description and that it should be placed in the paper file jacket and not be discarded. (TMEP § 807.09)

Similarly, the Canadian Trade Marks Act in paragraph 30(2)(c) states that the application must include a clear and concise description as well as an electronic recording of the sound. 'Electronic recordings must not contain any looping or repetition of the sound, nor include any sounds that do not form part of the trademark.' The example of an acceptable description is: 'The trademark consists of the sound of a lion's roar, the audio representation of which is included in the application' (Trademark Practice Notices of the Canadian Intellectual Property Office).

Non-permissible representations of acoustic trademarks in the register

In general, the representation of a trademark should be sufficiently clear and precise. The following examples are considered by certain intellectual property offices as not meeting this standard, and therefore constitute not allowed representation of an acoustic trademark in an application.

Indication of notes sequence without stave

In EU the indication of notes sequence, for example, 'E, D#, E, D#, E, B, D, C, A' has been considered by the CJEU as not fulfilling the requirement of adequate graphical representation. The Court pointed out in § 61 of case C-283/01 of 27 November 2003 *Shield Mark BV v Joost Kist h.o.d.n. Memex* that

> such a description, which is neither clear, nor precise, nor self-contained, does not make it possible, in particular, to determine the pitch and the duration of the sounds forming the melody in respect of which registration is sought and which constitute essential parameters for the purposes of knowing the melody and, accordingly, of defining the trade mark itself.

Description in words (exclusively)

Some legal systems request a description of an acoustic trademark together with an audio file. However, the sole description in words of either musical trademark, for example, trade mark no WO1215169:

The mark consists of an E5 sixteenth note, followed by a F#5 sixteenth note. then a D5 eighth note, and finally an A5 half note.

Figure 7.11 WO 1215169. Available at: https://euipo.europa.eu/eSearch/#details/trademarks/W01215169

or non-musical trademark (e.g. 'a cat's meow') should be considered as not being sufficiently clear and precise. An interesting point was made by the Court in § 59 of case C-283/01 of 27 November 2003 *Shield Mark BV v Joost Kist h.o.d.n. Memex*, namely that

> it cannot be precluded a priori that such a mode of graphical representation satisfies the requirements defined at paragraph 55 of this judgment [Sieckmann case criterions]. However, in the case of signs such as those at issue in the main proceedings, a graphical representation such as 'the first nine notes of Für Elise' or 'a cockcrow' at the very least lacks precision and clarity and therefore does not make it possible to determine the scope of the protection sought.

Onomatopoeia

In the case of non-musical trademarks existing in nature, the question of whether they may be described by onomatopoeia was also the subject of a ruling in *Shield Mark BV v Joost Kist h.o.d.n. Memex* [2003]. In the facts of the case, one of the trademarks was a Dutch onomatopoeia of a cockcrow: 'Kukelekuuuuu' and another one additionally contained an explanation that 'Sound mark, the trade mark consists of an onomatopoeia imitating a cockcrow'. The Court in § 60 of the case stated that

> there is a lack of consistency between the onomatopoeia itself, as pronounced, and the actual sound or noise, or the sequence of actual sounds or noises, which it purports to imitate phonetically. Thus, where a sound sign is represented graphically by a simple onomatopoeia, it is not possible for the competent authorities and the public, in particular traders, to determine whether the protected sign is the onomatopoeia itself, as pronounced, or the actual sound or noise. Furthermore, an onomatopoeia may be perceived differently, depending on the individual, or from one Member State to another. That is so in the case of the Dutch onomatopoeia Kukelekuuuuu, which seeks to transcribe a cockcrow, and which is very different from the corresponding onomatopoeia in the other languages used in the Benelux Member States. Consequently, a simple onomatopoeia cannot without more constitute a graphical representation of the sound or noise of which it purports to be the phonetic description.

Sonogram (exclusively)

As mentioned earlier, according to EUTM, on the basis of previous legislation upon which graphical representation constituted an element of trademark definition, the application for a non-musical acoustic trademark had to contain a sonogram and an audio file sample of the given sound. A sonogram by itself had never been sufficient to apply for an acoustic trade mark, for example, in an application for a trade mark no. WO 1291399, EUIPO did not accept the following sonogram without attachment of musical file:

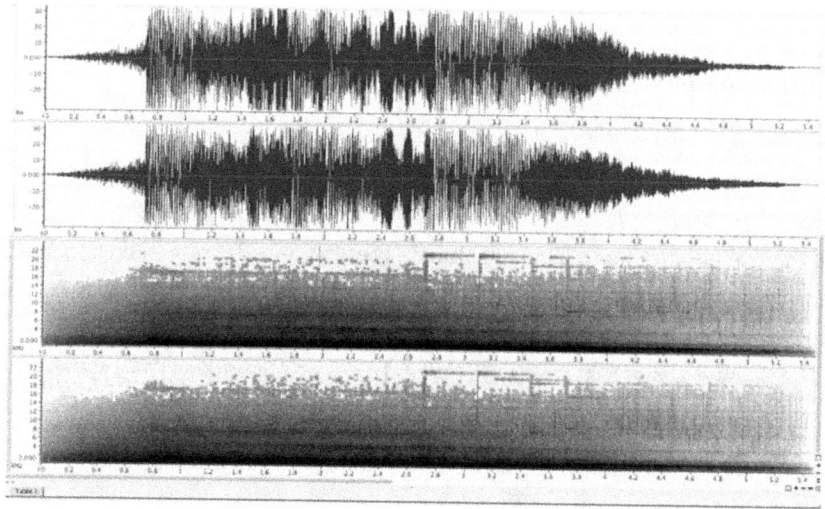

Figure 7.12 WO 1291399. Available at: https://euipo.europa.eu/eSearch/#details/trademarks/W01291399

Currently, art. 3 (3) EUTMIR states that 'in the case of a trade mark consisting exclusively of a sound or combination of sounds (sound mark), the mark shall be represented by submitting an audio file reproducing the sound or by an accurate representation of the sound in musical notation'. As the second part of the given sentence refers to 'musical' notation, it may be argued that the registration of non-musical acoustic EUTM is possible only on an audio file. The same approach should be taken by some EU Member States' intellectual property offices on the basis of their domestic regulations, for example, in Poland (Krupa-Lipińska 2020: 182).

Conclusion

The possibility of protection of acoustic trademarks has existed for a long time in many countries. However, it is only recently that this topic has increasingly become one of interest and discussion. In European legal doctrine and practice it is owing to the amendments of the EUTMR and EU Dir 2015/2436 which ceased to require a graphical representation of a trademark in the register for the requirement of its clear and precise representation. It was widely commented that the given amendment opened the door to broad registration of unconventional trademarks, including acoustic trademarks. Nonetheless, their registration had been possible before the amendment due to the fact that they were able to be represented graphically. The change from that given requirement in the case of non-musical sound trademarks should be welcomed.

The scope of protection of the acoustic trademarks depends primarily on legal rules that govern its application. In this context it is relevant to mention the forms of registration widely analysed in this chapter. In certain legislations, like in the EU and its Member States, it might be argued that submitting music files with the precise performance of the given composition limits the scope of protection only to the given performance (instruments, interpretation, etc.), while submitting an application only in notation without further indication of, for example, instruments, broadens the scope of its protection to any performance of the given notation, regardless of the instrument or instruments that it is played on. As mentioned, different legal provisions govern this requirement in different states, therefore the form of application should be carefully thought over before submission to an appropriate intellectual property office.

Acknowledgements

All visual representations used in this chapter are taken from the official, publicly available databases of the relevant country or the EUIPO in which the application was made. They are reproduced for purposes of illustration and comment.

References

Canadian Trademarks Act, R.S.C. (1985). C. T-13, amended on 1 July 2020, https://laws-lois.justice.gc.ca/eng/acts/T-13/.

Canadian Trademarks Regulations, SOR/2018-227, https://laws-lois.justice.gc.ca/eng/regulations/SOR-2018-227/FullText.html.

Colomer, Ruiz-Jarabo. *Opinion of Advocate General delivered on 3 April 2003 in Case C-283/01 Shield Mark BV v Joost* Kist, ECLI:EU:C:2003:197, http://curia.europa.eu/juris/document/document.jsf?text=&docid=48171&pageIndex=0&doclang=EN&mode=lst&dir=&occ=first&part=1&cid=4736975.

Commission Implementing Regulation (EU) 2018/626 of 5 March 2018 laying down detailed rules for implementing certain provisions of Regulation (EU) 2017/1001 of the European Parliament and of the Council on the European Union trade mark, and repealing Implementing Regulation (EU) 2017/1431, OJL 104, 24 April 2018, https://eur-lex.europa.eu/legal-content/EN/TXT/HTML/?uri=CELEX:32018R0626&from=EN.

Directive (EU) 2015/2436 of the European Parliament and of the Council of 16 December 2015 to approximate the laws of the Member States relating to trade marks, https://eur-lex.europa.eu/legal-content/EN/TXT/?qid=1506428973494&uri=CELEX:32015L2436.

Hasselblatt, Gordian N. (2015). *Community Trade Mark Regulation: A Commentary*, edited by G. N. Hasselblatt. Munchen: C.H.Beck.

Japanese Trademark Act No. 121 of 13 April 1959, http://www.japaneselawtranslation.go.jp/law/detail_main?re=&vm=02&id=3047.

Krupa-Lipińska, K. (2020). 'Zgłoszenie do ochrony dźwiękowego znaku towarowego w Urzędzie Patentowym RP'. In P. Pest and M. Winsław (eds), *Muzyka i prawo*. Wrocław: Wydawnictwo Akademii Muzycznej im. Karola Lipińskiego we Wrocławiu.

Kur, A. and M. Senftleben (2017). *European Trade Mark Law: A Commentary*. Oxford: Oxford University Press.

Madrid Agreement Concerning the International Registration of Marks (as amended on 28 September 1979), https://wipolex.wipo.int/en/treaties/textdetails/12599.

Minsky, L. and C. Fahey (2014). 'What Does Your Brand Sound Like?' *Harvard Business Review*, 07 February 2014, https://hbr.org/2014/02/what-does-your-brand-sound-like.

Nice Agreement Concerning the International Classification of Goods and Services for the Purposes of the Registration of Marks of June 15, 1957 as amended on September 28, 1979 https://wipolex.wipo.int/en/text/287437

Paris Convention for the Protection of Industrial Property of March 20, 1883 as amended on September 28, 1979, https://wipolex.wipo.int/en/text/287556.

Protocol Relating to the Madrid Agreement Concerning the International Registration of Marks adopted at Madrid on 27 June 1898 as amended on 3 October 2006 and on 12 November 2007, https://wipolex.wipo.int/en/treaties/textdetails/12599.

Regulation (EU) 2017/1001 of the European Parliament and of the Council of 14 June 2017 on the European Union trade mark, https://eur-lex.europa.eu/legal-content/EN/TXT/?qid=1506417891296&uri=CELEX:32017R1001.

Rozporządzenie Prezesa Rady Ministrów z 8 grudnia 2016 r. w sprawie dokonywania i rozpatrywania zgłoszeń znaków towarowych (Regulation on application and consideration of applications of trademarks of 8 December 2016), Dz.U. 2016, poz. 2053.

Singapore Treaty on the Law of Trademarks done at Singapore on March 27, 2006, https://wipolex.wipo.int/en/text/290013.

The Trade-Related Aspects of Intellectual Property Rights Agreement– Annex 1C of the Marrakesh Agreement Establishing the World Trade Organization, signed in Marrakesh, Morocco, on 15 April 1994, https://www.wto.org/english/docs_e/legal_e/27-trips_01_e.htm.

Trademarks Practice Notices of the Canadian Intellectual Office, https://www.ic.gc.ca/eic/site/cipointernet-internetopic.nsf/eng/wr04453.htm.

UK Trade Marks Act 1994, https://www.legislation.gov.uk/ukpga/1994/26/contents.

UKIPO (2020). 'Trade Marks Manual' from 23 August 2018, updated 6 April 2020, https://www.gov.uk/guidance/trade-marks-manual/new-applications.

USPTO (2018). 'Trademark Manual of Examining Procedure', October 2018, https://tmep.uspto.gov/RDMS/TMEP/current#/current/TMEP-900d1e763.html.

Ustawa z dnia 30 czerwca 2000 r. – Prawo własności przemysłowej (Statute on industrial property) z 30.06.2000, Dz.U. z 2020 r., poz.286, 288, 1086, http://isap.sejm.gov.pl/isap.nsf/download.xsp/WDU20010490508/U/D20010508Lj.pdf.

Von Muhlendahl, A., D. Botis, S. Maniatis and I. Wiseman (2016). *Trade Mark Law in Europe*. Oxford: Oxford University Press.

WIPO (2006). 'New Types of Trademark' document from 1 September 2006, Standing Committee on the Law of Trademarks, industrial designs and geographical indications, Sixteenth Session, Geneva, 13 to 17 November 2006, https://www.wipo.int/edocs/mdocs/sct/en/sct_16/sct_16_2.pdf.

Żelechowski, Ł. (2014). *Prawo własności przemysłowej*, P. Kostański and Ł. Żelechowski. Warszawa: C.H. Beck.

Abbreviations

CFR	Code of Federal Regulations (USA)
EU	European Union
EU Dir 2015/2436	Directive (EU) 2015/2436 of the European Parliament and of the Council of 16 December 2015 to approximate the laws of the Member States relating to trademarks

EUIPO	European Union Intellectual Property Office
EUTM	European Union Trade Mark
EUTMR	European Union trademark regulation (EU) 2017/1001
EUTMIR	Commission Implementing Regulation (EU) 2018/626
Nice Classification	Nice Agreement Concerning the International Classification of Goods and Services for the Purposes of the Registration of Marks
PPO	Polish Patent Office
TEAS	USPTO electronic trademark application
TMEP	USPTO Trademark Manual of Examining Procedure
TRIPS	The Trade-Related Aspects of Intellectual Property Rights Agreement
USTM	United States Trade Mark
USPTO	United States Patent and Trademark Office
UKTM	United Kingdom Trade Mark
UKIPO	United Kingdom Intellectual Property Office
WIPO	World Intellectual Property Organization

8

The derivative work right and the creative epistemologies of the other

Working towards a legal framework for remix

Lesley Model

The now normative practice of sampling in digitised music production conveys both shifting sensibilities and aesthetics for musical practice, but at the same time, a coinciding fine line between creativity and transgression. This chapter considers the creative strategies for music built out of samples (whose rhythmic arrangement is the point of focus) to claim that, just as these closely connect with Black musical priorities (Rose 1993), they sit difficultly within a European system of copyright. Negotiating a value for derivative expressions requires a language that can exceed copyright's existing logic, one offering space for postcolonial concerns to bear on the categories regularly invoked in copyright debates. The rationale for moving forward individual rights vis-à-vis derivative musical work rests on the basis of two points: (1) that the regulatory framework of intellectual property law, and in particular copyright, is ideologically and methodically contingent on European principles in commerce and art; and (2) that the sampling and reworking of extant musical recordings derives from the dialogic creativity characteristic of Afrodiasporic sensibilities in art.

Starting with the question of how rights are assigned in music, attention is called to the widely cited musical work-concept, and especially how this relies on a particular conceptualisation of the author (Barron 2006; Butt 2015; Goehr 1994; Rahmatian 2015; Rose 1993).[1] As a status reserved for *legitimate* productions, the musical work – and the criteria required to meet this definition

---

[1] The work-concept, which allows musical composition to be conceived in fixed and concrete terms, developed in the early-nineteenth century in relation to the printing press, the possibility for music typography and the tailing off of improvisation in classical music (Toynbee 2004).

– effectively achieves a cultural gatekeeping function in copyright. Calling into question its built-in parameters and associated hierarchies, further, calls for a look at its placement in discourse, the way it connects with the tenets of copyright's logic, namely, authorship and ownership. French philosopher Michel Foucault's model of 'discursive formations' provides a means for untangling the ostensibly natural relationships between themes and concepts in discourse; how continuity is achieved for disparate ideas, but also the 'repressive presence' of ulteriorly linked, yet excluded, components (Foucault 2002: 27–8). Foucault's approach to discourse is broadly employed in establishing the values carried by authorship – the terms it sets for defining originality and creative labour – in justifying exclusive property rights over musical expression.

Taking the structure and organisation of discourse as a lens, the focus subsequently turns to the racialised lines of the author construct. Authorship is said to act as the main indicative barometer for musical innovation, whose discursive work is represented by the Romantic authorship concept – which sees the author as essentially rooted and shaped by German idealism and Enlightenment Europe. As it brings the point of Eurocentricity to the fore, the close alignment between priorities and principles for musicianship, and the classical music canon, come into view. This chapter presumes that the discourse of Romantic authorship continues to operate discursively, represented, first, by weighing the author against traditionally Afrodiasporic sensibilities in music (African orality), demonstrated to be largely invisible in the eyes of copyright. Subsequantly revealed through examining the specific uses of sampling, looping and repetition, characteristic of dub reggae and hip hop, and connected with the Caribbean influence of 1970s New York.

The vast and varied influence of 'Black epistemologies' in popular music means that the distinct variety of creative misrecognition in question is not limited to Black musical genres. Taking the specific case of the disco edit – sampled reworks that gained smashing momentum in the early-to-mid-noughties – these are traced to the same New York music scenes, and from many of the same 'underlying generative (and) creative principles' (Irvine 2014: 15) as hip-hop, albeit with far less perceived proximity to Blackness.[2] Isolating and recognizing the epistemological terms of musical expression is thus thought a

---

[2] Disco edits grew from the techniques of turntable DJs seeking rhythmic continuity via the seamless blending of (often) two copies of the same track, resulting in an extended, danceable version. The ensuing aesthetic carried on, albeit in relation to recording technology (Brewster and Broughton 2000).

necessary move in promoting not only visibility for Afrodiasporic traditions, but also the creative strategies, aural aesthetics and compositional priorities proceeding from its influence.

Omri Rachum-Twaig's (2016) proposed adjustments to the derivative work right reveals a potential space for recognizing epistemological diversity. Twaig sees conceptions of progress and movement in art, organised within a genre theory of copyright, as necessarily contingent on an intelligible framework to expand upon; genre is the suggested basis for mapping such advancements. By taking a 'common building blocks' approach to assessing derivative work, innovation becomes relative to the creative field from which it proceeds (Rachum-Twaig 2016: 65). While not conclusively resolved to the point of application, Rachum-Twaig provides a solid basis for furthering epistemological inclusivity in copyright, in the way of the derivative work right.

It is important to point out that, while the derivative work right examined is specific to US copyright law, and although the UK treatment of derivative work falls under the adaptation right – which is said to offer less scope for blocking derivative expressions (Goold 2014) – prominent use of sampled recordings in the creation of new musical works is prohibited in both jurisdictions, and significantly, also from the same exclusionary bound up with authorship. Their mutual foundations grow out of Enlightenment Europe.

The musical work and the latent author

Copyright conceives of its musical object by way of the musical work-concept, a foundation that emerged in the late eighteenth century, as intangible expressions became designated as "things" which, despite being intangible could achieve the same type of value as material 'things', making them subject to property rights. This value is distinctly realised in the context of market exchange, wherein intangible expressions are thought to have potential value as commodities (Barron 2006).

There is some divergence regarding the origins of the musical work-concept, which, for the purposes of the argument, is worth detailing briefly. This is to a large extent a distinction of chronology, arising from different points of emphasis. For instance, in Lydia Goehr's (1994) 'The Imaginary Museum of Musical Works: An Essay in the Philosophy of Music', the musical work-concept emerges out of a felt need in the trajectory of Western music to discriminate between serious and civilised music (the classical music of the élite class), and 'less bona fide' musical expressions (associated with the popular class). For her, Romantic aestheticism combined with an established autonomy for music (from other aspects of life) is what gives way to a conception of predominantly classical instrumentation as 'works' at the turn of the nineteenth century, leading to its subsequent institutionalisation. John Butt (2015), however, dismisses this historicist account, claiming that it misses the more prolific consideration of how the 'work' arises out of synchronous conditions, including existent understandings of music, its respective social practices, and the forms that musical objects and events take. For him, attending to the way that these features coalesce provides a position for negotiating between the poles of analytic philosophy and constructivism.[3]

In terms of a fully realised musical work category, just as Rosemary Coombe suggests that 'creative practices and new norms, values, and conventions – new moral economies – grow up in the shadows of the law' (Demers 2006: 9), many critical legal theorists place the genesis of the 'work' within the development of copyright itself (Barron 2006; Bracha 2008; Rose 1993) – leaning towards an inverse causality than that suggested by Goehr. As Barron (2006) most explicitly calls into question Goehr's narrative on copyright's history, she invokes Rose (1993) to trace the DNA of the musical work to a stream of case laws occurring between the 1730s and 1770s. It's amidst these that the provisions under the 1710 Statute of Anne are said to become 'stretched' to include rights over non-literal imitations of works.[4] Rose (1993) specifically isolates the 1741 case of *Pope v Curl (1741) 2 Atk. 342* in accounting for the abstraction of literary property from its material form. Although copyright had been moving away from its sole treatment of literal copying in the years prior, Lord Chancellor Hardwicke's decision in this case is said to have established '(n)ot ink and paper, but pure signs, separated from any material support . . . (as) the protected property' (1993: 65).[5] It is between this and subsequent watershed cases that writing became effectively conceived as detached not only from the work, but also from

---

[3] Butt (2015) claims that while analytic philosophy and musical analysis veer too far towards an autonomous musical work-concept – removed from any human agency – constructivism is able to conceive of music only in relation to the culture that produces it.

[4] The Statute of Anne 1710 was enacted to secure exclusive if temporary rights over literary property, to prevent any unauthorised printing and trading of books. Proprietary rights, which were hitherto exclusively in the hands of booksellers, here become extended to give the author equal legal standing (Rose 1993).

[5] In *Pope v Curl*, London (1741) 'Lord Chancellor Hardwicke draws a distinction between the ownership of a letter, as a physical document, and the right to authorise the first publication of that letter, a right which he concludes remains with the author of the same' (Primary Sources on Copyright (1450–1900)).

the social conditions that produce it, constructing it as an unadulterated and solitary act of creation. In the absence of clear lines to distinguish the creative agency of the writer, the work itself is what, in copyright, became reified in the image of authorship.

The Copyright Act of 1842 consolidates the author's claim to property rights, as the previous utilitarian approach is superseded by Locke's concept of 'men's natural entitlement to the fruit of their labour', cementing the case for inalienable rights (Toynbee 2015: 42). Its justificatory terms, further, significantly call upon eighteenth-century German idealism (in which intellectual works are thought to be the product of individual personality). For instance, Hegel's distinction between 'disposable things of "external nature" and inalienable 'inner' capabilities represents an order in which the *real* property of value, always inevitably lies within the author (Toynbee 2015: 42). While this conception of authors' rights was initially configured in relation to literary property, it was the abstraction of the work from the book that enabled the authorship rationale's transferability over to musical composition (Barron 2006).

Romantic authorship – a concept that has gained recent notoriety within critical legal theories of copyright – problematises the assumed individualist view of creative labour, and the reciprocal notion that original works ensue from solitary intellectual exertions. Despite a loose consensus that Romanticism informed the foundation of authors' inalienable rights in the eighteenth century, the continued relevance of this scheme is contested. Both Bracha (2008) and Rahmatian (2011, 2015) denounce the more recent invocation (from the late twentieth century onwards) of Romantic authorship in copyright debates, on the grounds that it doesn't directly bear on the doctrinal logic employed in court decisions. Both attribute its resurgence to the poststructuralist movement and, specifically, Barthes and Foucault's influential texts, 'The Death of the Author' and 'What is an Author?', respectively. While Bracha (2008) argues that the authority of the author construct is misguided, he does so on the basis that nineteenth-century case laws elevate originality as a defining principle in copyright, one built out of commercial interests and not necessarily serving artists. Rahmatian (2015) similarly argues that the Romantic author critique works against individual artists by invalidating their claims to rights over works and thereby privileges the position of big enterprise. For him, the Romantic author critique is convincing and compelling because it is logically constructed, and not because it sits on 'logically valid arguments or syllogisms' (2015).

Taking these points on board, the Romantic author concept is approached cautiously in arguing that, even without having direct jurisdiction over copyright settlements, it operates discursively to condition our understandings of creativity and innovation, especially with respect to musical composition. It is thought to play a constitutive role in what Foucault terms the 'discursive formation' of copyright, namely in the way it upholds an internal dialectical structure.[6] As the main 'authority of delimitation', copyright sets the terrain for its associated themes and concepts. And since over and above anything else, these are organised around the task of managing rights for individual property owners, understandings and applications of authorship are nominated accordingly (Foucault 2002).[7] Even when conceptualisations of the author do deviate from the creative genius trope (a more extreme articulation of Romantic authorship that ascribes creativity to the elusive mental faculties of exceptional individuals) and absorb contradictory ideas, this does not render them even marginally at odds with the principles and procedures deciding who and what merit property rights. And it most definitely doesn't negate or subvert an already in place individualist orientation. The real limits of systematisation can be known only when we consider the disparate range of creative practices that amount to novel expressions – notably, in the case of music, those that proceed from an oral or folkloric mode – yet subsist outside the parameters of copyrightability (Foucault 2002). Given copyright's core function of regulating exclusive ownership for intangible expressions, its application revolves around a 'definable and durable' object, a 'determinate person', and 'a way of attributing the (object) to the person with certainty and precision' (Barron 2006: 111). While the tenacity of Romantic authorship lies in its ability to conciliate these terms, its ambiguity is put down to its fluidity and understated influence.

The often minimal recourse to moral rights in surveying originality for works is often more about denying the 'human constructivist element' in music, and probably worse, 'an elitist, culturally normative attitude to western art' (Butt 2015: 4), than the diminished role of Romantic authorship.[8] Though musical works

---

[6] Unlike 'discursive unities' – which refers to the continuity of concepts that occurs from their constitution within a singularised space – 'discursive formations' refers to the 'regularities' for relations between discursive elements, revealing the rules and specific conditions for their existence (Foucault 2002: 42).

[7] The law and order characteristic of European civilisation proceeds from Locke's *Second Treatise of Government* in which he proposed that 'by "mixing" labour with common goods a new "private dominion" would be created' (Toynbee 2004: 21).

[8] Moral rights (droits moral) – which originated in France and became part of UK copyright in 1988 – are inalienable rights for authors, intended to protect the right to be identified as the author

may be required to assume an element of autonomy to be objectively palpable, music is the result of 'human constructions through and through' (Butt 2015: 5). In other words, the work of human agency is always implicit in justifications for music as property, whether or not the associated doctrinal logic is couched in this way. Any designation of originality for the 'music itself' is thus defined by and contingent on antecedent values for authorship. 'On the one hand, the author (is) the owner of the rights in his work. On the other, his status as author guarantee(s) the status of the work: only compositions have authors' (Toynbee 2006: 83). Theodor Adorno's assessment of popular music – in which he says that it mirrors the highly standardised and pseudo-individualised music marketplace – exemplifies this point. For here, despite bypassing any consideration for authorial values, his scepticism plays into the Romantic authorship paradigm through his enunciation of values tied to the classical music canon:

> Listening to popular music is manipulated not only by its promoters, but as it were, by the inherent nature of this music itself, into a system of response mechanisms wholly antagonistic to the ideal of individuality in a free, liberal society. This has nothing to do with simplicity and complexity. In serious music, each musical element, even the simplest one, is »itself«, and the more highly organized the work is, the less possibility there is of substitution among the details. (Adorno 2009: 285)

Adorno's suggestion that each element of serious music should be 'itself' – his prioritizing of 'individuality' – presumes the same solitude behind bona fide musical artistry upheld by the creative genius trope, and respectively, Romantic authorship. This is obscured by his overemphasis on the capitalist mode of production, which effectively minimises human agency's place in musical composition. The author is subdued, but also inferred in vigorously affirming European principles in art.

Copyright's musical other

Given Adorno's positioning towards European conventions in music, his notorious critique of jazz in *'Perennial Fashion – Jazz'* is unsurprising, characterised by standardisation and clichés, right down to its improvisational segments which he calls a 'more or less feeble rehashing of basic formulas in which the schema shines

(the paternity right or le droit a paternité), and preserve their honour and reputation (the right of integrity or le droit à l'intégrité) (Toynbee 2004: 9).

through at every moment' (Adorno 1997: 122). But just as Adorno overperforms a perceived superiority for European musical aesthetics, he signals the racialised contours of the author construct. He attributes the virtues of 'serious' classical music to its ability to be complete, in the sense that all the individual elements derive their musical sense from the total completed piece (rather than from a premeditated mechanised formula). Redundancy and repetition are, on the other hand, pejoratively reserved for music whose individual elements are substitutable and inconsequential to the whole (Adorno 2009). To draw on Walter Ong's work on 'Orality and Literacy' (1982), however, this perception of *completeness* for cultural texts is structurally contingent on the 'technologizing of the written word' (or the print culture that emerges out of European Enlightenment).[9] Artistic expression is able to assume a self-containedness only via the 'time obviating technology' of print, since this is what allows for its separation from the immediate 'living world' via its fixture as an autonomous contextless object. If redundancy is thought to characterise more natural patterns of thought and expressions of orality, print establishes a mode for the more 'sparsely linear or analytic' creations brought on by Enlightenment in Europe (Ong 1982: 39). As for the monotony Adorno attributes to jazz, this has arguably more to do with its deviation from European modalities than with substandard artistry. Like other genres that descend from African traditions of orality, rhythmic repetition and 'mnemonic patterns' are key aesthetic components, mostly because these served as devices that nurture the retainment and retrievement of carefully articulated thought (Ong 1982: 39). The profound influence of West African musical tropes over American popular music since the 1950s (Toynbee 2004; Vaidhyanathan 2004) may further explain Adorno's assessment of popular music, generally. The question to consider then is how innovation in music is generally constituted and assessed – especially since repetition and variance are thought to feature in both classical European and traditional African musical forms, just in different ways and with less understanding and recognition of the syntagmatic order employed in the latter (Potter 1998).

Recent works addressing the discord between Black modes of musical expression and copyright (Hesmondhalgh 2006; McLeod et al. 2011; Toynbee 2004, 2006; Vaidhyanathan 2004) convey a causal relationship between the rising influence of black musical styles and genres (since the mid-twentieth

---

[9] Walter Ong contends that knowledge and expression are intricately bound up in the communicative resources employed by human cultures. Technologies should not be seen as 'mere exterior aids but also interior transformations of consciousness ...' (1982: 81).

century) and the increasing mismatch between popular music and copyright. It is suggested that this scheme runs the risk of consigning epistemologies rooted in African orality exclusively to black musicianship – despite a recognition of its influence elsewhere – and obscuring an understanding of new (often illicit), generative genres built out of these sensibilities. Matthew Morrison addresses the difficulty for transcending European categories of music:

> To be serious about justice and equity extends beyond creating a 'melting pot' or 'multicultural' approach within music studies to one that includes diverse methodologies, topics, and the collective efforts of both majority (white) and structurally marginalised groups (black, brown, Indigenous, and other people of colour) who reflect the messiness and richness of the culture in which we exist. (2019: 782)

Since music-making strategies develop and are expanded on over cross-cultural lines (Carfoot 2016),[10] their isolation is a necessary move in revealing the 'unique epistemic landscape of oppression' at work (Dotson 2014: 116). This point is in view of the double-edged danger of, on the one hand, distinguishing black music as its own entity and essentialising a black identity, and on the other, speaking to the hybridity of all music and downplaying colonial structures of power. These poles are described by postcolonial theorist Paul Gilroy (1993) as ontological essentialism (in the case of the former) and strategic essentialism (in the case of the latter). That said, and inasmuch as post-slave black musical expressions develop into disparate genres and forms, we can observe a commonality in their adherence to oral principles, revealed through an emphasis on performative qualities such as 'dramaturgy enunciation and gesture' (1993: 75). This is also the common denominator that positions heterogeneous manifestations against copyright.

In Toynbee's (2004, 2006) account of how oral principles transfer into the age of recording technology (in twentieth-century America), he also traces the particularly stringent difficulty for hip-hop as a genre that uses direct samples of existing works. Although both the blues tradition and hip-hop are traced to the dialogic process of 'phonographic orality' (what happens when a folk mode of music-making is enacted in relation to existing recorded material),[11] rather

---

[10] Gavin Carfoot uses the concept of 'interculturalism' to move beyond 'the discourses of discovery central in Western practices of Othering' to locate cases of in-betweenness for cross-cultural musical communication. He contends that 'structured relations of dominance and subordination' are realised in the embodiment of the cultural practices being activated (2016: 184).

[11] 'Phonographic orality' is said to emerge with the way jazz and blues musicians (from the 1920s onwards) learned and developed their craft, which – while involving some formal training – was mainly characterised by listening to and developing on existing recordings (Toynbee 2004: 126).

than merely imitating existing works, sampling directly violates copyright's terms by duplicating (part of) the sound recording's tangible form (Toynbee 2006: 90). Whatever leeway may have existed for hip-hop's sampling methods prior to 1991 (due to its relative marginality but also and because of the inaccessibility of recording technology), the court's ruling against Biz Markie's use of Gilbert O'Sullivan's 'Alone Again Naturally' cemented a precedent with the pronouncement of 'Thou Shalt Not Steal' (Behr, Negus and Street 2017; Toynbee 2006). Just as this outcome consolidated recorded material as the 'object of value in and of itself' (Théberge in Behr, Negus and Street 2017: 227), it also affirmed European musical standards through a staunch resistance to the iterative and recursive strategies of hip-hop. From here on, sampling became positioned as synonymous with 'the technical copying afforded by recording technology' (Behr, Negus and Street 2017), eclipsing a view for its role within innovative and transformative new works. Moreover, this arrangement served existing and 'legitimate' copyright holders with a market for 'packets' of recorded music' (Toynbee 2006: 90).

Epistemological alterity

As for an aggregate understanding of hip-hop, it should be seen in terms of the creative field from which it emerged and thrived. Despite a reluctance towards assigning a decisive beginning, a noted key agent in the rise of performance-based and sample-heavy musical practices (in 1970s New York) is sound-system culture, brought to the South Bronx by Jamaican DJs, and in particular, DJ Kool Herc (Brewster and Broughton 2000; McLeod et al. 2011). It is arguably from the Caribbean conventions and priorities extended by reggae and dub that a tone was set for new applications of orality in music-making.[12] And while, as mentioned, this is distinctly evidenced in hip-hop, it would be more accurate to attribute a Caribbean influence to the intervening musical cultures of which hip-hop is a part. The more salient correlation between disco and hip-hop is considered, where mutual ground is mainly characterised by the performance of the DJ.

---

[12] While Jamaican reggae is known for its absorption of disparate influences, which are redeployed in innovative ways, reggae dub is focused on reshaping and re-versioning existing works (often with an emphasis on the instrumental layout) (Brewster and Broughton 2000: 129–30).

Status, for disco DJs and hip-hop artists alike, was tied to a deep musical knowledge and repertoire, coupled with an ability to seamlessly and seductively perform these competencies for the dance floor. The creative priorities that ensue, as Borschke (2017) points out, were also substantially shaped by the media formats and technologies available, and otherwise, turntablism (but in the case of hip-hop, also a mic). Tim Lawrence traces the points of overlap:

> (D)isco/dance and hip hop/rap DJs drew on the same pool of funk, soul, uptempo R&B and imported records, developed intersecting turntablist practices, set up inclusive record pools, nurtured dance styles (breakdancing and vogueing) that blended athleticism and angularity, and produced a set of recordings that were mixed back-to-back in clubs during the first half of the 1980s. (2008: 278)

Although the performative conventions and styles may deviate for disco and hip-hop, they proceed from the same creative mode. In both cases, innovative techniques occur in relation to the performance of existing recordings, which were treated as raw material in the formation of new rhythmic combinations. With hip-hop, this involved isolating the musical break and redeploying it as the underlying loop of a track, which – more than just a repetitive trope, through its punctuation and combination with other sonic elements – became the footing for the realisation of new material (Vaidhyanathan 2004: 131). Disco edits, also organised around the break, were motivated towards landing a seamless groove that would keep the crowd excited and moving. This often involved cutting between two copies of the same record to extend the break (also characteristic of hip-hop) (Brewster and Broughton 2000). Recording technology would later provide a means for honing this already-in-place aesthetic, where 'gradual builds and long breaks would really make their mark' (Wilson 2016). The official take-off point for the 12-inch single (the re-edited version) began in 1976 with Walter Gibbons' mix of 'Ten Percent' by double exposure (Wilson 2016; Brewster and Broughton 2000). The disco edit continues to expand and carry influence even after disco's demise, specifically in relation to 'the post-disco dance scene, the art-punk scene and the nascent hip-hop scene'. While previously somewhat divided musical fields, Lawrence describes their merging as

> in part due to the fact that the preeminent DJs of the era – Ivan Baker, Afrika Bambaataa, John 'Jellybean' Benitez, Johnny Dynell, Grandmaster Flash, Bruce

Forest, Jazzy Jay, Mark Kamins Larry Levan, Anita Sarko, Tee Scott, Justin Strauss and Roy Thode along with musical host David Mancuso – were all notable for their willingness to cross genre lines. (Lawrence 2016)

In proposing that the disco edit draws its appeal on different grounds than the original recording(s) sampled, Potter's distinction between 'musematic' and 'discursive' repetition is an important point. While the former refers to 'short tropes or riffs' and is said to be more closely aligned with African sensibilities, the latter, defined by 'longer phrases set in a hierarchical or antiphonal relation to other phrases', is associated with a more European orientation in music (Potter 1998: 33). Although African and European structures of music contain elements of each, and despite the need to treat this dichotomy problematically, these patently correspond with the previously outlined and disparate principles rooted in European classical and African oral traditions. Just as the danceability of the disco edit is entrenched in its rhythmic organisation, with the looped break a foothold for the careful building up of the track's interlocking layers, it is arguably targeted at a more 'musematic' structure. The melodic and harmonic features of the disco edit augment its rhythmic core in potentially interchangeable ways. It is 'incomplete' according to Adorno's aforementioned model of serious music. Yet, in the words of New York DJ/producer Lee Douglas: 'Edits made disco' (Beta in Borschke 2017: 78).

Redefining derivative work

As productions that are organised around a 'musematic' orientation, the disco edit, like hip-hop, falls outside the definitions of originality carried by copyright. Through a primary focus on rhythm and recombination, it betrays a type of innovation that's difficult to constitute within copyright's existing categories. Authorship in music requires the fulfilment of certain traceable and clear-cut measurements of innovation, which are mainly found in the form of lyricism, melody and notation (Behr, Negus and Street 2017; Toynbee 2004), features that are privileged within European modalities of music.

In Rachum-Twaig's (2016) rationale for revising the derivative work clause in copyright, we find a sliver of fertile ground for the case of non-European strategies in music-making. For him, bringing genre theory to bear on legal conceptions of originality can better align copyright with the creative activities it regulates, particularly derivative work. While currently (and since the 1976 Copyright Act), creative uses of copying are reduced and measured according to levels of similarity – which is reflected in the almost indistinguishable functions of the reproduction right and the derivative work right – he proposes that the 'common building blocks' approach to genre justifies the recovery of a qualitative value for derivative work. More specifically, Rachum-Twaig contends that '"the common building blocks" approach allows examination of the sets of rules that apply to groups of texts and the analysis of the way these sets of rules affect the creative field and the players acting within it' (Rachum-Twaig 2016: 64). It is further ascribed with two roles: (1) to enable creativity through the provision of existing artistic conventions, also enabling for the development and transformation of these; and (2) to act as a meaning-making tool for the audience, a framework from which creative products can be understood and assessed.

By disregarding context in the assessment of creative products, copyright universalises and reaffirms European standards in art and culture. We can see this in the way that disco edits, which have seen a significant revival since the early noughties and taken a more digitised form (thereby raising their profile) (Borschke 2017), once subject to debates around creativity, become conceived within a general remix rhetoric that treads awkwardly close to technological determinism (Borschke 2017). It's all too easy to conflate the disco edit with the type of copying and quoting brought on by digitisation and remix culture, especially having gone through a period of dormancy, before storming the dance scene with an early noughties' revival. At best, such uses of sampling are associated with cultural interactivity and creative democracy; at worst, they constitute theft. Since, and more accurately, as legendary DJ and music producer Greg Wilson puts it, the 'seeds of the current re-edit movement were sown in the 80s via now classic edits by DJs like Danny Krivit (New York)' (2016), the production strategies for disco re-editors precede digitisation and progressed from a particular cultural context. Even with attempts to defend the edit's aesthetic and creative value (as with the case of Nieswant's *'In Defense of Disco Edits'* and Borschke's *'This is Not a Remix'*), we find it characterised by performance and as DJs' tools, and ultimately subordinated within existing hierarchies of musicianship. At the top of this is the composer, whose originality derives from individual novelty and is legitimated by the rights accorded to their labour; then, 'further down the pecking order, comes the performer, who plays music written by someone else' (Toynbee 2004: 123). Inasmuch as digital technology has facilitated sample-based musical works, which undeniably factors into the aesthetic for re-edited and reworked music, the disco edit emerged and formed within a 'specific colon(y) of genres' (Rachum-Twaig 2018: 70), and importantly, one in which oral sensibilities carried currency. This is the condition for its invisibility and what the influence of genre theory can bring to the fore. 'A new genre is always the transformation of an earlier one, or of several: by inversion, by displacement, by combination' (Todorov in Rachum-Twaig 2016: 67).

The final point to emphasise is that genre theory confronts the idea/expression dichotomy in copyright.[13] It provides a view that is 'indifferent to whether the use of common building blocks is of ideas or unprotected expression or whether it is of protected expressions' insofar as creative products develop new genres or add something novel to existing ones (Rachum-Twaig 2016: 86). This moves the derivative work away from the reproduction category and closer to original works. However, this is not to be mistaken as a definitive arrangement, with no consideration for first authors or a distinction between ideas and expressions; rather, it functions as a model to expand the scope of derivative work.

Conclusion

Treating recorded sounds as raw material in compositional practice, while not distinctly enshrined in the Caribbean musical tactics of 1970s New York (Musique Concrete being a case in point), took on a specific application vis-à-vis the sensibilities enunciated by dub reggae and hip-hop. This chapter sought to trace the discordance between this and subsequent uses of the sample (especially for compositions where sampling comprises the main creative labour), and the cultural disposition embodied in copyright's organisation and administration. In doing so, and in seeking to bring 'Black' musical epistemologies (and their successive uses) to light, specific attention has been paid to the conditions for their misrecognition. Through an emphasis on discourse, the musical priorities, conventions and creative labour sustained by copyright – especially in the way musical works are constituted and rewarded – have been traced to the continuing influence of Romantic authorship and European paradigms of art. Similarly, making perceptible the

---

[13] The problematic idea–expression dichotomy refers to copyright's mode of distinguishing copyrightability. Ideas are considered as communal resources of the public domain, whereas expressions are copyrightable, since they refer to the distinctive way an idea is articulated or put to use.

types of innovative activities – specifically the uses of rhythmic punctuation and mnemonic repetition – elevated by 1970s hip-hop and disco DJs and imprinting themselves on succeeding compositional values, has required a view that can exceed existing cultural–legal paradigms.

By locating the disco edit – an illicit and recently popularised sub-genre of dance music – as materialising within this creative field, then, more than just a by-product of digitised music production software, it is shown to have a clear performative and aesthetic precedent. In other words, a connection has been drawn between its misrecognition in copyright and an adherence to traditionally 'Black' musical epistemologies. The extent to which this is also the case for other uses of digitised musical sampling is equivalently difficult to discern, without consideration for its positioning within wider fields of practice. The proposed modification to the derivative work right presented by Omri Rachum-Twaig (2016) – in which he insists on a working distinction between the reproduction and derivative work right – follows from his genre theory of copyright and offers up a space for recognizing epistemological diversity in art. Although not specifically attuned to the case of derivative music, its emphasis on a 'common building block approach' provides a model from which innovate work is assessed in relation to the artistic (generic) fields from which it emerges. Copyright's scènes à faire and fair use doctrines already consider the transformative quality in uses of pre-existing works. There is therefore already a precedent for extending this course of logic to the derivative work right, a move that would raise not only the visibility of musical practices derived from the Afrodiaspora, but also its generative potential and influence on successive musical groupings.

References

Adorno, T. W. (1997). 'Perennial Fashion – Jazz'. In *Prisms*, 119–32. Cambridge, MA: MIT Press.

Adorno, T. W. (2009). 'On Popular Music: Material and Text'. In *Current of Music*, 272–342. Oxford: Polity Press.

Barron, A. (2006). 'Copyright Law's Musical Work', Special Section: Law and Music, *Social & Legal Studies*, 15: 101–27.

Behr, A., K. Negus and J. Street (2017). 'The Sampling Continuum: Musical Aesthetics and Ethics in the Age of Digital Production', *Journal for Cultural Research*, 21: 223–40.

Borschke, M. (2017). *This Is Not a Remix: Piracy, Authenticity and Popular Music*. London: Bloomsbury.

Bracha, O. (2008). 'The Ideology of Authorship Revisited: Authors, Markets, and Liberal Values in Early American Copyright', *The Yale Law Journal*, 18: 188–264.

Brewster, B. and F. Broughton (2000). *Love Saves the Day: The History of the Disc Jockey*, London: Headline Book Publishing.

Butt, J. (2015). 'What Is a "Musical Work"? Reflections on the Origins of the "work concept" in Western Art Music'. In A. Rahmatian (ed.), *Concepts of Music and Copyright: How Music Perceives Itself and How Copyright Perceives Music*, 1–22. Cheltenham: Edward Elgar.

Carfoot, G. (2016). 'Musical Discovery, Colonialism, and the Possibilities of Intercultural Communication through Music'. *Popular Communication: The International Journal of Media and Culture*, 14: 178–86.

Demers, J. (2006). *Steal This Music: How Intellectual Property Law Affects Musical Creativity*. Georgia: The University of Georgia Press.

Dotson, K. (2014). 'Conceptualizing Epistemic Oppression', *A Journal of Knowledge, Culture and Policy*, 28: 115–38.

Gilroy, P. (1993). *The Black Atlantic: Modernity and Double Consciousness*. London: Verso.

Goehr, L. (1994). 'Musical Meaning: From Antiquity to the Enlightenment'. In *The Imaginary Museum of Musical Works: An Essay in the Philosophy of Music*. Clarendon: Oxford University Press.

Goold, P. (2014). 'Why the U.K. Adaptation Right Is Superior to the U.S. Derivative Work Right', *Nebraska Law Review*, 92, no. 4: 849–95.

Foucault, M. (2002). *Archaeology of Knowledge*. London: Routledge, http://ebookcentral.proquest.com/lib/suss/detail.action?docID=1144626.

Hesmondhalgh, D. (2006). 'Digital Sampling and Cultural Inequality', *Social & Legal Studies*, 15, no. 1: 53–75.

Lawrence, T. (2008). 'Disco Madness: Walter Gibbons and the Legacy of Turntablism and Remixology', *Journal of Popular Music Studies*, 20, no. 3: 276–329.

Lawrence, T. (2016). *Life and Death on the New York Dance Floor*. New York: Duke University Press.

McLeod, K., P. DiCola, J. Toomey and T. Kristin (2011). *Creative License: The Law and Culture of Digital Sampling*. London: Duke University Press.

Morrison, M. (2019). 'Race, Blacksound, and the (Re)Making of Musicological Discourse', *Journal of the American Musicological Society*, 22: 781-823.

Potter, R. A. (1998). 'Not the Same: Race, Repetition and Difference in Hip-Hop and Dance Music'. In *Mapping the Beat: Popular Music and Contemporary Theory*, 31–46. Oxford: Blackwell Publishers Inc.

Rachum-Twaig, O (2016). 'A Genre Theory of Copyright', *Santa Clara High Technology Law Journal*, 33: 34–89.

Rose, M. (1993). *Authors and Owners: The Invention of Copyright*. Cambridge, MA: Harvard University Press.

Rose, T. (1994). *Black Noise: Rap Music and Black Culture in Contemporary America*. Hanover: Wesleyan University Press.

Toynbee, J. (2004). 'Musicians'. In S. Frith and L. Marshall (eds), *Music and Copyright*, 123–38. Edinburgh: Edinburgh University Press.

Toynbee, J. (2006). 'Copyright, The Work and Phonographic Orality in Music', *Social & Legal Studies*, 15, no. 1: 77–99.

Vaidhyanathan, S. (2004). *Copyrights and Copywrongs: The Rise of Intellectual Property and How It Threatens Creativity*. London: New York University Press.

Wilson, G. (2016). *From Segues to Stems: A Potted History of the DJ Manipulator*, https://boilerroom.tv/from-segues-to-stems/, accessed 20 December 2020.

The US Compulsory Licence

A lesson in technological development and legislation shaping the music market

Ralph W. Peer

Intellectual property regimes can be a one-sided bargain. In exchange for an author or inventor sharing the fruits of their labour with the public, the state grants them a limited monopoly over its use. The limitations of the monopoly, such as its duration and its boundaries, are also set by the state. The ultimate form of limitation is the compulsory licence. It originated in the Crimean War, when the British army found the demands of patent holders of military supplies too costly, and in turn the government legislated that the patent holders were to be compelled to licence their patents at the rates set by Parliament (Johns 2010: 274). The irony here is obvious: with one hand the state bestows protection, while with the other, it derogates from it in order to serve the public good. Today, compulsory licensing measures are often used in supplying generic forms of pharmaceuticals to those in need (World Trade Organization 2020); however, the US Congress, in conferring protection to the replication of musical compositions in 1909, implemented a compulsory licensing system which continues to this day.

The compulsory licence system originated from fears of monopolisation of both copyright ownership and the patenting of methods of consumption. By compelling copyright owners to allow replication, whatever form it could take, to license their works, such fears were calmed. The licence though did come with conditions and an ambit that did not allow for direct copying, instead requiring that a user make analogous but not identical usage, a unique aspect of the compulsory licence in the creative realm. This led to the development of a lucrative 'cover' market which technological developments have since negated.

The requirement also diminished other aspects of a work's copyright – notably the right of arrangement. As technology progressed, the compulsory licensing system was surpassed, leading to multiple revisions which, while taking into account the technology of the day, could not read the future. The latest of these has dichotomised the mechanical right; for the first time one method of exploitation has become favoured over another, bringing about a state of affairs which the original compulsory licence sought to avoid.

This chapter examines key legal cases, legislation and legislative reports concerning the mechanical right and compulsory licence. The concurrent evolution of the mechanical right and the compulsory licence is qualitatively analysed in the context of shifts in technology which have influenced the consumption of music and the major corporations within the marketplace.

The meaning of replication within music

Within each musical recording there are two separate elements which are protected by copyright and related rights: the sound recording and the composition of the underlying musical work. Broadly speaking, record companies control rights in sound recordings, while music publishers control the underlying compositions. Each of these elements is then protected by various rights, including the right of the copyright owner to allow or prevent reproduction, performance or making available to the public, and using one or both elements for the creation of new (aka derivative) works.[1] In the United States, one of these elements is subject to the compulsory licence, while the other is not.

While it is easy to distil the mechanical right to the 'right of reproduction', in understanding its evolution, it may help to take a purposeful approach: How does music make its way into the ears of the consumer other than by means of a live performance? The answer is: by means of some form of replication, whether by piano roll or digital stream; when Beethoven wrote his symphonies, he could not have foreseen an audience which would have perfect, digital copies of their performance to be enjoyed in the confines of their own headphones.

When the right of reproduction was first conceived the ownership of the composition, or 'raw material' (*Edward B. Marks Music Corp. v Colo. Magnetics, Inc.*: 285) of a sound recording was considered the more valuable right. Coupled

---

[1] E.g. putting a song in a movie soundtrack

with the fear of an entity which would buy up copyrights in musical compositions and hold patents in the machines which reproduced the compositions to the ear of the consumer, Congress foresaw the spectre of a musical monopoly which could be brought to heel through a compulsory licence system. As we will see, technology, hand in hand with the compulsory licence, has shifted the balance and conspired to make sound recordings the more valuable of the two elements.

The mechanical right is born

The year 1909 saw the first omnibus revision of United States copyright law since the 1790 Copyright Act crafted by the country's founders. Such was the need for revision that even President Theodore Roosevelt felt it necessary to implore Congress to modernise the country's regime in a 1905 address:

> Our copyright laws urgently need revision, [sic] They are imperfect in definition, confused and inconsistent in expression; they omit provision for many articles which, under modern reproductive processes, are entitled to protection; they impose hardships upon the copyright proprietor which are not essential to the fair protection of the public; they are difficult for the courts to interpret and impossible for the Copyright Office to administer with satisfaction to the public. (House of Representatives, Committee on Patents 1909)

Prior to 1909 the 1790 Act had been amended piecemeal. The original text had bestowed on the authors of 'any map, chart, book or books (the sole right) to print, reprint, publish, or vend the same' (Original Copyright Act 1790). In 1831 Congress for the first time included 'musical compositions' on the list of works protected; however, it was not until 1897 that their performance was recognised as an individual right (Copyright Office 1973).

It was against such a backdrop that the mechanical right was born. In the House report presenting the new Act, Congress itself noted:

> The whole system, in the light of an interpretation by the courts, call for a revision. The courts are more and more called upon to consider these questions [of reproduction rights]. And besides this, the reproduction of various things which are the subject of copyright has enormously increased. The wealth and business of the country and the methods and means of duplication have increased immeasurably. The law requires adaptation to these modern conditions. It is no longer possible to summarize it in a few sections covering everything copyright

that protection to the honest literary worker, artist, or designer shall be simple and certain. (House of Representatives, Committee on Patents 1909)

While the need for such protection was clear, reservations were also present:

> It was at first thought by the committee that the copyright proprietors of musical compositions should be given the exclusive right to do what they pleased with the rights it was proposed to give them to control and dispose of all rights of mechanical reproduction, but the hearings disclosed that the probable effect of this would be the establishment of a mechanical-music trust. It became evident that there would be serious danger that if the grant of right was made too broad, the progress of science and useful arts would not be promoted, but rather hindered, and that powerful and dangerous monopolies might be fostered which would be prejudicial to the public interests. This danger lies in the possibility that some one company might secure, by purchase or otherwise, a large number of copyrights of the most popular music, and by controlling these copyrights monopolize the business of manufacturing the selling music producing machines, otherwise free to the world. (House of Representatives, Committee on Patents 1909)

Congress then recognised two competing interests: first, new technology necessitated a new form of copyright, and second, the concern about monopolisation of that right through the interplay with a second form of intellectual property – the patent. If an entity could patent the dominate method of consumption, while simultaneously holding copyrights, the musical marketplace would be constricted and the public would suffer. To ameliorate these concerns, the mechanical right was granted, but Congress immediately derogated from it by making it subject to a compulsory licence. By allowing anyone to mechanically reproduce a copyrighted composition in exchange for a statutorily set fee a vibrant market in recorded music could exist even if a single entity dominated copyright ownership as it would be compelled to license its copyrights to anyone that wished to use them. Further, the fear of monopolisation of 'the business of manufacturing the selling of music producing machines,' (i.e. the method of consumption) was assuaged by as the compulsory license applied to all forms of replication. Therefore, even if a patented form of consumption dominated the market, technology could advance and a new form could take its place under the same auspices.

These two prerequisites were clearly articulated in the 1909 Act:

> . . . as a condition of extending the copyright control to such mechanical reproductions, That whenever the owner of a musical copyright has used or

permitted or knowingly acquiesced in the use of the copyrighted work upon the parts of instruments serving to reproduce mechanically the musical work, any other person may make similar use of the copyrighted work upon the payment to the copyright proprietor of a royalty of two cents on each such part manufactured.
(An Act To Amend And Consolidate The Acts Respecting Copyright)

While Congress simultaneously created a new right, they also immediately hobbled it though this is not to say the mechanical right was toothless and without boundaries. What is allowed within those boundaries though, such as the recording of multiple versions of a composition, or the making of new arrangements, and their economic importance, has changed with time as technology has developed.

Boundaries of the compulsory licence

A work may be subject to the compulsory licence only after the copyright owner has 'used or permitted or knowingly acquiesced to' the mechanical reproduction of the work. Thus, a copyright owner gained an exclusive right to dictate who would first record their work and through what medium it would be distributed to the public, known as the right of 'first fixation'. It is important to note that the definition of such mechanical reproduction in the 1909 Act specifically refers to mechanical reproduction upon the 'parts of instruments serving to reproduce mechanically the musical work', meaning that if a copyright owner had published the work in sheet music, a compulsory licence for the creation of piano rolls did not immediately follow (*Standard Music Roll Co. v Mills*: 360).

An early case examining this portion of the Act was *Aeolian Co. v Royal Music Roll Co.* Aeolian had been granted a mechanical licence to manufacture 'music rolls or records' which the court noted exhausted the right of first fixation and meant the underlying copyright was now subject to the compulsory licence. However, this did not mean that those making use of the compulsory licence could

> thereby secure the right to copy the perforated rolls or records [produced under the original licence]. He cannot avail himself of the skill and labor [sic] of the original manufacturer of the perforated roll or record by copying or duplicating the same, but must resort to the copyrighted composition or sheet music, and not pirate the work of a competitor who has made an original perforated roll. (*Aeolian Co. v Royal Music Roll Co*: 927)

'Similar use' then did not extend to creating identical copies of medium of the first use. The implication is that in order for an entity to make use of the compulsory licence, they must make their own version, whether a new recording or piano roll, of the musical composition in a medium.

The year 1917 saw the case of *Standard Music Roll Co. v Mills*. Mills had licensed Standard 'to use the copyrighted musical composition in the manufacture of its sound records in any form whatsoever' (*Standard Music Roll Co. v Mills*.: 360) for the popular song 'Waiting for the Robert E. Lee'. Standard had produced the ubiquitous music rolls; however, in addition to the rolls, Standard also supplied printed lyrics of the song for people to sing along to, perhaps an early form of karaoke.

In current copyright law, words and the musical compositions behind them enjoy separate copyright protection, therefore Standard's actions would appear to be a clear infringement. Prior to the 1909 Act, Standard's actions would have been allowed. An earlier case of *Witmark v Roll Co.* had held precisely this as the lyrics at issue had not been separately subject to copyright as a literary work. However, in Standard the court acknowledges this change in the law under the 1909 Act:

> A song is now copyrighted as a musical composition, both the words and the music are protected; and, as these do not constitute an indivisible whole, the owner may limit the use of his copyright either to the music or to the words, or he may allow both to be used. (*Standard Music Roll Co. v Mills*.: 362)

However, the court notes a wrinkle in the Act due to the recent popularity of the phonograph, which unlike piano rolls had the ability to reproduce a sound recording itself which may then include a rendition of the song's lyrics:

> Just how the reproduction is to be made, and whether it is to be confined to the music or shall extend to the words also, is in the first instance left for the owner to determine. But after he has determined it, and has granted a license to one person, he thereby opens the field to all others to do the same, or a similar, thing. If he license [sic] one person to reproduce both words and music by the phonograph method, other persons may reproduce them both by using the phonograph. (*Standard Music Roll Co. v Mills*.: 363)

While Standard enunciates the modern understanding of copyright – that within a single musical work multiple rights are engendered and licensed – applying such a rule is less straightforward in modern consumption methods. A streamed file will doubtless contain lyrics sung alongside musical instruments, but the lyrics themselves will not be separately licensed (assuming no visual representation of the lyrics takes place). The digitised data copied and distributed will contain the information of the composition, the lyrics, and the sound recording, but only one of these elements is subject to the compulsory licence, and no licence for the lyrics themselves is required unless displayed separately.

Eighty years after *Standard*, the Court of Appeals of the Second Circuit heard *ABKCO Music, Inc. v Stellar Records, Inc.* Stellar produced a new form of karaoke device termed the 'Compact Discs + Graphics' (CD+G). Unlike other karaoke discs at the time, which used video files that combined music and lyrics into a single video file, Stellar's CD+Gs worked as traditional Compact Discs (CDs) when put in a CD player; however, when attached to a CD player with video output (akin to a modern day Bluray player), the media displayed the lyrics on the video screen as a static image. From a technological perspective, no new work was being created – the audio track playing would be that of a recording duly authorised under a mechanical licence, while the lyrics were kept apart. Therefore, under Stellar's logic, no licence to create a new work from the previously copyrighted elements was required, as the CD+Gs constituted 'phonorecords' under the compulsory licence. The court did not agree:

> A time-honored [sic] method of facilitating singing along with music has been to furnish the singer with a printed copy of the lyrics. Copyright holders have always enjoyed exclusive rights over such copies. While projecting lyrics on a screen and producing printed copies of the lyrics, of course, have their differences, there is no reason to treat them differently for purposes of the Copyright Act. (*ABKCO Music, Inc. v Stellar Records, Inc.*: 64)

The weakened arrangement right

Under the 1909 Act one of the rights of a copyright owner was the right to 'make any arrangement or setting of it or of the melody of it in any system of notation or any form of record in which the thought of an author may be recorded and from which it may be read or reproduced': (An Act To Amend And Consolidate The Acts Respecting Copyright 1909). *Standard* answered the question as to whether such 'similar use' included the separate reproduction of a song's lyrics, but with regard to other aspects of a composition – its melody, style, tempo, etc. – how far did such similar usage extend? Technology had quickly eclipsed the piano rolls at issue in *Standard*. The phonograph, with its ability to perfectly reproduce the performance of a musical composition, meant the courts would have to define 'similar use' in this new context.

Edward B. Marks Music Corp. v Foullon, in 1948, took up the question. Marks sued United Masters for creating a new version of their copyrighted work 'Malagena' which was then pressed on acetate records and sold. Marks alleged infringement of their exclusive right to make an arrangement of the work.

The court's decision is somewhat capricious, at first acknowledging that under the statute a separate, exclusive right is granted to the copyright holder to create arrangements; however, such a right was curtailed within the compulsory licence by requiring a new arrangement be made in order for it to be a 'similar use'. In writing the 1909 Act, Congress' primary focus had been the replication of works through piano rolls and, as seen in *Aeolian*, some form of protection extended to the skill and creativity of the screever in producing such rolls. This meant that no two rolls produced by different companies would be identical, but could still be similar enough for a listener to perceive the same work being reproduced.

This limited the arrangement right of the original copyright owner as technology progressed. If a compulsory licencee may make 'similar use' of a work after it has been pressed to a record, then it follows that they must have the latitude to record their own version of the song.

Consider the incentives of competitors within each medium. In order to compete with a successful piano roll version of a work, the party under a compulsory licence would try to make their version as identical to the previous, successful version as possible. However, in records, courts had held that competing phonograph producers were barred from directly copying one another under the equitable doctrine of unfair competition.[2] Therefore, the only avenue to compete was through differentiation with the hope they would capture a market beyond that of the original.

Such was the case of *Leo Feist, Inc. v Apollo Records, N.Y.* in 1969. Apollo had produced a compilation titled 'The Swinging 20's Go Latin', which contained 'New Latin dance arrangements' of popular titles from the era (*Leo Feist, Inc. v Apollo Records*: 32). Feist and other copyright holders had refused Apollo's payment of royalties under the compulsory licence and sued arguing that the new versions infringed their arrangement right.

---

[2] See, for example, *Metropolitan Opera Ass'n v Wagner-Nichols Recorder Corp.* 199 Misc. 786 and *Capitol Records, Inc. v Greatest Records, Inc.* 43 Misc. 2d 878

The court was not convinced. Apollo's use of the word 'arrangements' constituted no more than 'ambivalent promotional opinions', and that 'arrangement' could connote 'merely the tempo or rhythm' of a piece had been altered, or that 'Latin treatments' could mean more than an artist's interpretation of an original arrangement (*Leo Feist, Inc. v Apollo Records*: 40). The court, though, abstained from defining any sort of boundary which would delineate a new infringing arrangement and the none-infringing 'treatment' which took place here.

It is here, though, that the compulsory licence in musical compositions distinguishes itself from others. When used in any other form, both pertaining to copyright (e.g. retransmission of copyrighted works, or blanket licences for public performance) or otherwise (e.g. medical patents), compulsory licences do not allow or encourage the creation of *new* derivatives of the original. Instead, such licence generally amplifies the availability of the protected original element, without altering it.

However, the US compulsory mechanical licence goes a step further; by requiring the creation of a new derivative work based on a previously copyrighted musical composition, as a condition of coming under the auspices of the compulsory licence, the right of a copyright owner over arrangements of their work is *de facto* weakened.

The decline of the cover market

In this grey area between direct copying and creating a new arrangement is the 'cover'. Generally, this will be a recording of a musical composition by an artist after a first recording has already been distributed to the public. In the modern music market, the cover is conspicuously absent, but this is no accident. Technology's development has led to microphones, mixing boards, and all else required in the recording process becoming widely accessible, and digitisation has made the costs of duplication practically nil.

Consider the work 'Summertime', written as an aria by George Gershwin in the 1930s for the opera 'Porgy & Bess'. The work first found fame after being recorded by Billie Holiday in 1936, reaching number twelve on the US charts (Wilson). Some thirty years later the same song reached number ten in a recording by Billy Stewart, and was subsequently recorded by Ella Fitzgerald, Janice Joplin, and, punk-ska band Sublime in the 1990s (Wilson).

Before digitisation, recording each of these versions required significant investment – costs for studio time, engineers, mixing and mastering are prohibitively high without confidence in the ability to sell the records, and on top of this are the costs associated with physical reproduction and distribution. But if the expenses were incurred in recording a previous 'hit', it would more likely be commercially successful. Therefore, labels were incentivised to rerecord such hits as covers and make use of the compulsory licence for their underlying compositions.

With the removal of such costs in the digital age, no such incentive exists. This is not to say the right to make covers has completely gone by the wayside. The most likely way in which a younger reader may have experienced such covers was in the early days of streaming services before licences for sound recordings had been secured from major record labels. On many of these streaming services, genre-specific playlists included cover recordings so close to their more famous originals that many consumers did not appreciate the idea that they were listening to a sound-alike and not the original version made famous by a pop star instead of session singers hired to imitate.

The decline of the compulsory licence to produce a cover version is also due in large part to the infinite library on offer in the streaming age – both due to consumer choice and search algorithms, it is unlikely that a lesser known artist's rendition of a song will be found and consumed. This further negates the economic incentive to produce cover versions.

The 1976 Act

By 1955 it was clear that the US copyright system had not kept pace with new technology, and Congress provided funds to the Copyright Office to produce a comprehensive set of reports on the copyright regime and give recommendations for its revision (United States Government Publishing Office 1963: 166).

One such report examining the compulsory licence was published in 1961. It makes clear how the compulsory licence has undermined 'the fundamental principle of copyright that the author should have the exclusive right to exploit the market for his work' (Register of Copyrights 1961: 35), describing its provisions for a copyright owner as 'severe' (Register of Copyrights 1961: 35) in negating their control of those who go on to record their compositions, and that the two-cent royalty acted as an economic constraint on the market by establishing a ceiling[3] for mechanical licence royalties.

'The danger of a monopoly . . . in 1909 was apparently the sole reason for compulsory license', (Register of Copyrights 1961: 35) the report goes on, but this was clearly no longer the case. Instead of a concentration of record labels, publishers, and writers, there existed hundreds of such businesses (Register of Copyrights 1961: 35).

By this point there were two factions: record labels and recording artists on one side, and publishers and songwriters on the other. The record labels argued that the compulsory licence meant the public was provided with 'a variety of recordings of any particular musical work', that it enabled smaller record companies to 'compete with the larger ones by offering other recordings of the same music', and that it benefited copyright owners by giving their works greater public exposure through multiple recordings of the same composition (Register of Copyrights 1961: 34).

The Copyright Office, however, countered all of these assertions by pointing out that these benefits would not necessarily be lost with the abolition of the compulsory licence. In such a market, while a copyright owner would be free to engage in exclusive licensing, this would not necessarily be in their interest. As such the three benefits enumerated would continue, with the exception that a copyright owner could refuse a licence to a record company it considered untrustworthy or which would produce a low-quality product (Register of Copyrights 1961: 34).

The report concluded that the compulsory licence 'should be eliminated' (Register of Copyrights 1961: 36) as it was no longer required as a bulwark against the spectre of a great music monopoly. The Copyright Office saw 'no other public interest' (Register of Copyrights 1961: 35) in maintaining the system.

Despite the recommendations, record companies were successful in their efforts to maintain the compulsory licence system and it found a new home in section 115 with some minor alterations (Abrams 2009: 225). The notification system was updated so that if a copyright owner could not be found, a notice of intent was sent to the Copyright Office at least thirty days prior to the use. The licence did not have to pay royalties to the Copyright Office, and if a copyright

---

[3] In some cases, it also was cited as a limit for recovery of damages in litigation. See *G. Ricordi & Co. v Columbia Graphophone Co.* 263 F. 354

owner was located or became aware of the use, the owner could only claim future royalties and not retroactively (An Act For The General Revision Of The Copyright Law, Title 17 Of The United States Code).

The 1976 revision also saw the granting of federal copyright protection to sound recordings; however, at no juncture does it seem that a compulsory licence was contemplated in this area. Perhaps the multitude of record labels active at the time made such considerations seem far off. Regardless, Congress could not have foreseen a situation in which a single means of exploitation would offer a consumer the entirety of recorded music, as streaming has today.

The failure of the 1976 Act in the digital music market

Spotify was launched in the United States in 2011, ushering in the streaming era (Reisinger 2011). The service quickly grew, reaching 1 million subscribers by 2011, and 24 million active users two years later (*Eight Mile Style, LLC v Spotify USA INC.*: Para. 65) Until this point, technology had steadily increased access to recorded music; however, streaming is the apex of such expansion – for the first time the consumer was offered access to the effective entirety of the world's recorded music, and in order to provide such access, the licensing strictures of the 1976 revision proved inadequate.

In the twenty-first-century music industry structure, record companies provide sound recordings to distributors who then provide them to digital service providers (DSPs). DSPs are incentivised to work with as many distributors as possible in order to grow the recordings available on their services and therefore attract the largest range of consumers. This incentive appears to have undermined concerns of remunerating the copyright owners of the underlying musical compositions embodied in the recordings, as 'in a race to be the first to market . . . Spotify made the deliberate decision to distribute sound recordings without building any internal infrastructure to license compositions properly' (*Eight Mile Style, LLC v Spotify USA INC.*: Para 77).

In order to ameliorate its liability, Spotify entered into an agreement with Harry Fox Agency (HFA). The HFA was established in 1927, and while never statutorily recognised, it has since been the de-facto mechanical licensing entity in the United States, working as an administrator between labels and music publishers. HFA maintains a database of musical compositions and, when a record label wishes to exploit such compositions, it will facilitate a licence between the two parties, normally at a rate below that statutorily defined. While at first this may seem strange, rightsholders are willing to accept a rate below the statutorily defined one as the HFA bears the costs of administering the licences. At the time of their agreement, HFA was owned by the National Music Publishers' Association (NMPA), the rights holding community's trade organisation.[4]

Under the agreement, Spotify would provide data to the HFA of recordings available on the platform and their usage. The HFA, in turn, would then match the recordings to the musical compositions in its database and facilitate mechanical licences with rightsholders (Masnick 2020). However, the arrangement was fraught with issues, most notably that 'At the time that Spotify hired HFA, HFA had a database with less than the number of recordings and compositions available in the Spotify library' (*Eight Mile Style, LLC v Spotify USA INC.*: Para. 79). This, alongside the needs of other DSPs, led to more than 60 million notices of intent (NOI) being sent to the Copyright Office (Israelite 2018), and royalties not finding their way to copyright owners of the musical compositions.[5]

In 2015, HFA was acquired by private equity group Blackstone for $20 million (Christman 2015). As a condition of HFA's sale, a portion of the sale price was held in escrow until any liabilities against HFA were resolved (*Eight Mile Style, LLC v Spotify USA INC.*: Para. 79). As the seller, the NMPA was then motivated to resolve any such liabilities.

A so-called 'settlement' was reached between the NMPA and Spotify in April 2016 (Music Law Updates 2016). Unlike most settlements though, the NMPA and Spotify agreement was not preceded by the filing of a lawsuit or any contentious process (Future of Music 2016). Not all rightsholders were satisfied with the terms of the settlement, however, and took to the courts.

The largest of these actions resulted in a reported settlement of $43.4 million (Levine 2017); however, other cases are still ongoing. No dispute is as emblematic of the situation than the recent filing of *Eight Mile Style, LLC v Spotify*. Eight Mile Style (EMS) is the company of famous rapper Eminem and controls the

---

[4] HFA is now owned by SESAC, a performing rights society in the US which is in turn owned by the Blackstone Group (Christman 2015).
[5] Recall that under the 1976 Act, if a copyright owner could not be found an NOI would be filed with the Copyright Office, but there was no obligation to pay royalties to any party or keep them in escrow. If a copyright owner was found they could not back claim.

copyrights to his works including the hit 'Lose Yourself'. In its complaint EMS alleges that Spotify and the HFA worked to defraud EMS by backdating the NOI sent to EMS's administrator Kobalt. Such backdating would render an NOI ineffective and the consequent usage an infringement. Furthermore, EMS questions why an NOI would be necessary when finding the copyright owner of such well-known compositions was easily within Spotify and HFA's competency. EMS even claims to have correspondence in which HFA acknowledges EMS as the copyright owner. Despite this Spotify and HFA had placed 'Lose Yourself' in a category of works for which copyright owners could not be found, meaning that royalties from its streams were not being paid.

Beyond Spotify's relationship with the HFA and its sale were other seismic rearrangements of the music market. First, the ubiquitous file-sharing of the early 2000s had significantly altered consumer expectations, as the price of a sound record product and its availability were no longer considerations to a consumer in the piracy age. Second, Spotify rewarded record companies for licensing their sound recordings with shares in the company's equity, thereby aligning the interests of previously contentious parties and potentially giving rise to a conflict of interest (Ingham 2018).

The Music Modernization Act

On 11 October 2018 the Music Modernization Act (MMA) was signed into law. While reforming many aspects of the musical copyright regime with regard to mechanical licensing, the legislation makes a profound shift in introducing a *blanket* mechanical licence for digital forms of exploitation. In a compulsory licensing system, all works have the *potential* to be licensed according to the terms set in statute; in contrast, under a blanket licence all works *are licensed* to those entities which meet a criteria. The new blanket licence will be administered by a Mechanical Licensing Collective (MLC), which will collect and receive mechanical royalties and establish a publicly available database of musical works. Further, the MLC will also be authorised to distribute unclaimed royalties based on market share. Importantly, the MLC will be paid for by the licence DSPs (US Copyright Office 2018).

With regard to non-streaming consumption the compulsory licence remains intact. In doing so, a new class within copyright has been created, whereby one method of exploitation, digital streaming, is treated differently than others. This formalises the prior arrangement of the HFA and Spotify. Through hiring the HFA to administer Spotify's mechanical licensing and by sharing liability with them, this main purveyor of streaming technology was able to secure favourable treatment in ameliorating liability.

Under the MMA the DSPs then are given immunity while other forms of musical consumption are not. Musical copyrights are then no longer neutral as to the medium of exploitation. This bifurcation will lead to the entrenchment of streaming as the primary model of consumption in the years to come.

In favouring a format of consumption, incentives to develop new formats are reduced, and, if new formats do come about, these will be at an inherent disadvantage when seeking licences. As was attempted in the *ABKCO Music* case, a new format, whatever form it may take, may not fall within the confines of a 'digital phonorecord delivery' under the MMA, and ironically would then be forced to licence under the 1976 provisions. As new mediums often precipitate new entrants into a market, it is also less likely that the current DSPs will face competition from newcomers, thereby confining consumer's choice as to the purveyor of their streaming service.

The future of technology and music under the MMA

The compulsory licence was born from the confluence of technological progress, the need to protect creativity embodied in such progress, and fears of monopolisation through patent and exclusive licences. However, technology and market movements have outpaced it to the point of contradiction – bringing about a state of affairs the compulsory licence strove to avoid. A dominant mode of consumption has emerged with aligned interests to those of the copyright owners. The copyright owners, though, are not the proprietors of musical compositions, as Congress had feared in 1909, but those who own sound recordings. The streaming model, which was possible only because of the compulsory licence, has also made its provisions untenable, thereby necessitating the shift to a blanket licence, but only for this method of consumption. Technology has undermined Congress' 1909 vision of a vibrant market in which multiple sound recordings are produced from a single musical composition, and the values of the copyright elements of a song have shifted.

Conclusion

Intellectual property regimes will always be reactive to the current circumstance and cannot take into account the unknown future technological developments which will act as vehicles for creativity. Nowhere is this clearer than in the US mechanical rights regime. Arising from fears of monopolisation, the compulsory licence was meant to lead to diversification of both musical output and consumption methods, and its conditions worked to shape the market for nearly a century. Digital technology upended this and brought about a state of affairs untenable with the then current legislation. Like previous revisions of copyright law, the MMA is reactive to the conditions of the day, but ironically will solidify a method of musical consumption within the market through unequal treatment of licencees. This is not to say the legislation is inherently flawed or that Congress committed a folly more so than it has in previous revisions, but it will likely hamstring the development of new means of musical consumption.

References

ABKCO Music, Inc. v Stellar Records, Inc., 96 F.3d 60.

Abrams, H. (2009). *Copyright's First Compulsory License*. Santa Clara High Tech Law Journal 26/2, http://digitalcommons.law.scu.edu/chtlj/vol26/iss2/2, accessed 29 July 2020.

Aeolian Co. v Royal Music Roll Co., 196 F. 926.

An Act For The General Revision Of The Copyright Law, Title 17 Of The United States Code, And For Other Purposes (1976). Washington, DC.

An Act To Amend And Consolidate The Acts Respecting Copyright. (1909). Washington, DC.

Christman, E. (2015). 'SESAC Buys The Harry Fox Agency', *Billboard.com*, https://www.billboard.com/articles/news/6620210/sesac-buys-the-harry-fox-agency, accessed 29 July 2020.

Copyright Office (1973), *Copyright Enactments*. Washington, DC.

Edward B. Marks Music Corp. v Colo. Magnetics, Inc., 497 F.2d 285.

Edward B. Marks Music Corp. v Foullon, 79 F. Supp. 664.

Eight Mile Style, LLC v Spotify USA INC (2020). Civil Case No. 19-CV–00736. District Court for the Middle District of Tennessee Nashville Division.

Future of Music (2016). 'All of the Problems with the Spotify/NMPA Settlement', http://futureofmusic.org/blog/2016/05/27/all-problems-spotifynmpa-settlement, accessed 29 July 2020.

G. Ricordi & Co. v Columbia Graphophone Co. 263 F. 354.

House of Representatives, Committee on Patents (1909). *The House Report 1 On The Copyright Act Of 1909*.

Ingham, T. (2018). 'Here's Exactly How Many Shares The Major Labels And Merlin Bought In Spotify – And What Those Stakes Are Worth Now – Music Business Worldwide', *Musicbusinessworldwide.com*, 2018, https://www.musicbusinessworldwide.com/heres-exactly-how-many-shares-the-major-labels-and-merlin-bought-in-spotify-and-what-we-think-those-stakes-are-worth-now/, accessed 29 July 2020.

Israelite, D. (2018). 'Written Testimony of David M. Israelite, President and CEO, National Music Publishers' Association Before The Senate Judiciary Committee for Hearing Titled: "Protecting And Promoting Music Creation For The 21St Century"', https://www.judiciary.senate.gov/imo/media/doc/05-15-18%20Israelite%20Testimony.pdf, accessed 29 July 2020.

Johns, A. (2010). *Piracy*. Chicago: University of Chicago Press.

Leo Feist, Inc. v Apollo Records, N.Y., 300 F. Supp. 32.

Levine, R. (2017). 'Spotify Settles Class Action Lawsuits Filed By David Lowery and Melissa Ferrick With $43.4 Million Fund', *Billboard*, 26 May 2017, https://www.billboard.com/articles/business/7809561/spotify-settles-class-action-lawsuits-filed-by-david-lowery-and-melissa, accessed 29 July 2020.

Masnick, M. (2020). 'Harry Fox Agency Scrambles To Fix Spotify, Streaming Licencing Mess', *Hypebot.Com*, https://www.hypebot.com/hypebot/2016/03/harry-fox-agency-scrambles-to-fix-spotify-streaming-licencing-mess.html, accessed 29 July 2020.

Music Law Updates (2016). 'Spotify Settles NMPA Mechanicals Claim', http://www.musiclawupdates.com/?p=6788, accessed 29 July 2020.

Original Copyright Act, 1790.

Register of Copyrights (1961). *Report of the Register of Copyrights on the General Revision of the U.S. Copyright Law*. Washington, DC: U.S. Government Printing Office.

Reisinger, D. (2011). 'Spotify (Finally) Launches In The U.S.', *CNET*, https://www.cnet.com/news/spotify-finally-launches-in-the-u-s/, accessed 29 July 2020.

Standard Music Roll Co. v Mills, 241 F. 360.

United States Government Publishing Office (1963). *Congressional Record – House (January 10)*. Washington, DC.

U.S. Copyright Office (2018). 'Music Licensing Modernization', *Copyright.Gov*, 2018 https://www.copyright.gov/music-modernization/115/, accessed 29 July 2020.

Wilson, J. 'Jazz Standards Songs and Instrumentals (Summertime)', *Jazz Standards*, http://www.jazzstandards.com/compositions-0/summertime.htm, accessed 29 July 2020.

Witmark v Roll Co., 221 Fed. 376.

World Trade Organization (2020). 'TRIPS and Public Health: Compulsory Licensing of Pharmaceuticals and TRIPS', *Wto.org*, https://www.wto.org/english/tratop_e/trips_e/public_health_faq_e.htm.

Part Three

The developing commercial landscape

10

Blockchain

Hero or hindrance for the music industry from a legal perspective

Charlotte O'Mara

Technological change for the music industry has brought about a revolution, 'a revolution in potential – potential that has not, as yet, been realised'
(O'Dair 2016b: 5).

This chapter will look at the advantages of blockchain for musicians and the music industry from a legal perspective, focusing on some of the main issues facing the industry and how blockchain technology could address these; the challenges and disadvantages it poses and finally, possible prospects for the future of blockchain in the music industry. Some of the long-standing issues facing the industry today have arguably been exacerbated by the globalisation, and technologically advancing nature, of our world today. The main problems that this chapter will focus on and the advantages and challenges that blockchain can bring to them are: lack of a comprehensive music rights database which results in songwriters, artists and rightsholders not always obtaining recognition for their work and costly and time-consuming licensing issues; imperfect royalty distribution with lengthy time gaps between consumption of music and payment reaching the rightsholders or in some cases getting 'lost', and the lack of transparency in calculations of royalties; numerous middlemen wanting a share of the income generated by music resulting from years of intermediaries strengthening their positions and bargaining power over artists and songwriters and increasing their hold on the industry. This chapter will

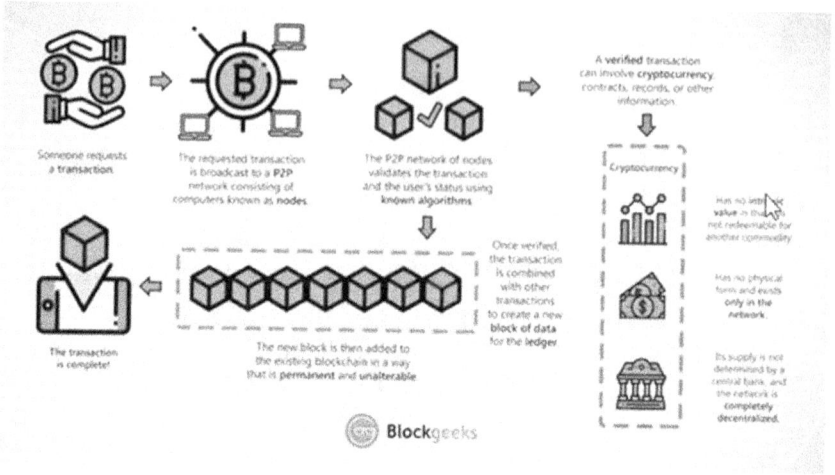

Figure 10.1 How blockchain works. Diagram courtesy of www.blockgeeks.com

also look briefly at jurisdiction and complications when music crosses borders; and data protection.

What is blockchain?

A blockchain operates by distributing a cryptographically secured ledger[1] between multiple participants. Every time a record is added to a blockchain, that record receives a cryptographic hash and the agreement from every participant to add it to the distributed record. As a result, any historical record is immutable, transparent and can be compared between ledgers, and thus any tampering can be discovered (Dotson 2020). Blockchain technology also allows payments to be made, via cryptocurrencies, peer-to-peer without a third party (decentralised) (O'Dair 2016a).

In the music industry, a blockchain-based network could allow for a tamper-free, immutable, transparent database of intellectual property rights in the music, containing rightsholder information as well as licensing or transferring of contractual obligations (Carretta 2020: 40). Such clarity and transparency in information may lead to easier identification, and thus higher remuneration

---

[1] Cryptography relates to the process of converting ordinary plain text into unintelligible text and vice versa. It is a method of storing and transmitting data in a particular form so that only those for whom it is intended can read and process it. Cryptography may be used to protect data from theft or alteration and for user authentication. https://economictimes.indiatimes.com/definition/cryptography

for such uses given to the correct rightsholders. Further, it is argued that smart contract technology[2] within the blockchain platform could allow for an automated and fast, efficient payment mechanism to the rightsholders of the works of music directly from fans to music creators (Rethink 2015).

The emergence of blockchain technology has provided hope for possible solutions to some of the problems faced by the music industry, both historical and emerging. Blockchain-based platforms such as Choons, Ujo, Peertracks, Dot Blockchain, Mycelia, Musicoin, Opus, Blokur and others have been causing a stir in various corners of the industry as the technology holds the potential to allow songwriters, artists and rightsholders greater protection and control over authorship, ownership and rights management of their Intellectual Property in their works of music (Works) and fair, transparent remuneration for copyright holders in the music industry on a global scale (Carretta 2020) by creating a new decentralised transparent database and marketplace for rightsholders to directly enter into transactions with individual users (Tam 2018), reducing the monopoly of intermediaries.

Technology and law have always been closely connected and the law is currently endeavouring to keep pace with the rapidly changing habits of consumers and their consumption of and access to music (Carretta 2020), highlighted by the lengthy debate surrounding Article 17 of the European Directive on Copyright in the Digital Single Market (DSM Directive 2019) over the use of protected content by digital service providers and also by the $20 million settlement between Spotify and the National Music Publishers' Association (NMPA) over unpaid royalties (New York Times 2016), in part due to difficulties in determining to whom they must be accounted.

All these issues require a solution, which is transparent and fair, and which can keep up with technological advances, stay relevant, and facilitate legal systems to keep pace. A new framework to assist in addressing these issues is required. Blockchain could, it is argued, provide such a technological framework for legal systems to build on. Some believe that blockchain technology could be 'at the same level as the World Wide Web in terms of importance' (Mougayar 2016: xix). However, blockchain still attracts much debate with regard to its practical constraints (Tam 2018).

This chapter will explore these various issues facing the industry in more detail and consider how these issues might be addressed or potentially aggravated by blockchain.

---

[2] *Smart contracts* are lines of code that are stored on a blockchain and automatically executed when predetermined terms and conditions are met. https://www.ibm.com/blogs/blockchain/2018/07/what-are-smart-contracts-on-blockchain/

Blockchain: advantages for musicians and the music industry

'If blockchain technology can help the commercial and contractual relationships in music keep pace with technology and the communication between artists and fans then it could be truly revolutionary.'

(Nick Mason Pink Floyd in O'Dair 2016a: 3)

Blockchain technology does not change the legal fundamentals surrounding the protection of copyright and related rights, for the use and exploitation of intellectual property. Instead, it potentially introduces a new method through which the rights in such intellectual property can be protected and remunerated. It offers a new way or framework to deal with those legal factors and to protect authorship, copyrights, neighbouring rights and, in general, the music usage and licensing in the internet era as well as potentially shifting control back to the creative. The EU Directive on Copyright in the Digital Single Market (DSM Directive 2019) calls for protection of Works, proportionate remuneration for creatives and transparency (DSM 2019: arts 17–20). The potential of blockchain technology in enabling this should not be underestimated.

Lack of a comprehensive music rights database and how blockchain might address this

'When the technology industry comes calling to ask what music needs to solve its data issues, the music industry doesn't often know. They are too busy fighting among themselves about their share of the pie!'

(Kenswil in Rethink Music 2015: 21).

Currently, there is no single database that documents ownership of all song and recording copyrights. There are numerous databases globally, often with conflicting or incomplete information, with no central authority to settle conflicts (O'Dair 2016a). In Europe alone, there are over twenty-eight collection societies collecting public performance and mechanical royalties in around twenty-eight different markets (PWC 2018). As a result, this lack of transparency and of a centralised system leads to slower and often inaccurate royalty payments, complex administration of rights systems for artists, songwriters, labels and publishers, with payments sometimes taking years to reach the rightsholders and sometimes the wrong ones.

> This is arguably THE BIG problem in the industry which has an impact on other issues the industry faces. Without a comprehensive music rights database, identifying rightsholders and maintaining and updating accurate information about who owns what rights in which songs and recordings can be difficult, time-consuming and sometimes impossible. This in turn can make copyright protection of artists' creative works difficult often leading to costly legal disputes. (O'Mara and Cooke 2020)
>
> The complexity of music copyright with many layers of rights embodied in a single sound recording corresponds to multiple rightsholders and licensees among whom the profits must be split, making the ability to correctly identify the owner of copyright and related rights essential, as well as ensure the protection of authorship in the market. (Carretta 2020)

The lack of a complete, international, reliable database containing information on Works and rightsholders makes it extremely difficult to identify the correct party to contact in order to negotiate use of Works and licensing terms. This affects the entire music supply chain, including digital service providers such as Spotify, trying to pay artists and rights owners (Walden 2018).

Thus, monetizing the rights associated with these Works can be an extremely lengthy and laborious process with those wishing to license first facing the difficult task of identifying who actually owns the rights, and if successful in this, seeking permission via possibly a number of entities before approval is or isn't granted by one or more rightsholders. Consequently, often those potentially seeking to license music don't, or use it without permission – thus, no one gets fairly paid because it takes too much effort and is far too complicated. The question of royalties and monetizing rights is considered in more detail later, but they are interlinked and there is a long-held belief that fixing the problems of the music industry is more difficult because of the lack of a global, easily accessible and comprehensive music rights database which could significantly ease other issues in the industry including those discussed later (O'Mara and Cooke 2020). Previous attempts to address this data problem have failed (the Global Repertoire Database; the International Music Joint Venture; the International Music Registry) arguably due to the cost and time required to collate the necessary information and the co operation and enthusiasm of the main players involved stalling (disputes over control of such a global database and fears over main players such as major music publishers and collection societies becoming obsolete perhaps sealing the fate of these efforts). Some argue that the enormity of the task is too great or impossible (Deahl 2019a). Others foresee possibilities through a not-for-profit element to those undertaking the work which could facilitate cooperation between organisations currently holding the data required and minimise antitrust concerns (Rethink Music 2015).

Blockchain has been described as a revolution in how to keep track of rights (Fairfield 2014). Potentially the creation of a networked database for music copyright ownership where rights ownership in both the underlying words and music of a song and in the sound recording of a song could be stored on the blockchain via a cryptographic hash (essentially producing a digital fingerprint). It is claimed that once uploaded, the information stored on the blockchain cannot be changed but can be updated instantly and automatically and there is no central control – it is decentralised – and it forms a public ledger for all users to see (O'Dair 2016a). Alternatively, private blockchain ledgers can be created with access limited solely to those enabled to do so. The 'hash' function allows creatives to prove authorship and to prove that a creative work existed at a given time without revealing the actual contents (Tsiilidou and Foroglou 2015). It is envisaged that metadata embedded into every piece of music could include terms of use, copyright holder information, payment details and costs (Rogers 2015), forming part of the blockchain entry structure.

Some see the gradual placing of copyright data on the blockchain leading to the creation of one copyright database for music providing easily accessible and transparent information of the correct rightsholders of Works for all. This could potentially ease, or go some way in, solving Spotify's issues, for example, around identifying copyright holders in songs, as well as ensuring artists and rightsholders are correctly identified, assisting in copyright protection of their Works, decreasing the number of copyright disputes and facilitating payment directly to the correct rightsholders for use of their Work. SACEM, ASCAP and *PRS for Music*[3] are working on a joint initiative using blockchain technology to match, aggregate and qualify existing links between ISRCs (standard recording codes) and ISWCs (standard musical work codes) in order to confirm correct ownership information and resolve conflicts (O'Mara and Cooke 2020). More detailed credits on blockchain data

---

[3] Society of Authors, Composers and Publishers of Music (SACEM) in France; American Society of Composers, Authors and Publishers (ASCAP) in the United States; Performing Right Society (PRS for Music) in the United Kingdom.

may assist session musicians, backing vocalists and other contributors to a recording in claiming their 'moral right' or credit and recognition for their work (O'Dair 2016 b).

Imperfect royalty distribution and how blockchain might address this

'Since the turn of the millennium, people trying to make money from . . . music have struggled with significant challenges. Music can be streamed and downloaded at the click of a button but payments to the people who actually make that music can be slow and opaque.'

(O'Dair in Allison 2016)

IFPI figures released show a 22.9 per cent increase in streaming revenues worldwide and an 8.2 per cent increase in record industry income globally equating to a total income of $20.2 billion (IFPI Report 2020). However, despite its being a seemingly very healthy industry financially, many artists argue that they are not seeing a fair share of this revenue. Citigroup Report states that in 2017, artists captured just 12 per cent of the music revenue with most of the value leakage driven by the costs of running a myriad of distribution platforms augmented by the costs (and profits) of the record labels and intermediaries (Citigroup Report 2018). As the business has transitioned from sales of CDs to MP3 downloads and then streaming, it has become increasingly difficult to keep track of the number of data points that are needed to pay royalties to the correct people (McIntyre 2017).

Royalty payments involve songwriters, artists, and rightsholders entering into various contracts with sometimes a number of third parties such as music publishers, record labels and distributors. Collective Management Organizations (CMOs) aim to ensure the payments are being received by the correct parties, but to track every play on every platform is challenging (Carretta 2020). Royalties can take years to reach the rightsholders, often with deduction of fees by a number of these third parties along the way (Rethink Music 2015). Further, royalties are often directed to the incorrect people (Rethink Music 2015) or end up in the 'black box' of lost royalties because the correct rightsowners cannot be identified due to the lack of a comprehensive industrywide music rights database, as discussed earlier.

With instant data, instant access to music and instant payment systems such as PayPal at our fingertips, this slow royalty payment process does not make sense.

The recent practice within the industry of secret non-disclosure agreements between labels and publishers with digital service providers in relation to streaming and digital deals and of major labels having equity ownership shares in most streaming services (Rethink Music 2015) makes for an opaque system which often keeps creatives in the dark, making it difficult for them to audit royalties and assess whether they are being accounted to them by the labels and publishers and CMOs correctly (O'Mara and Cooke 2020).

The Ivors Academy and The Musicians' Union have recently called on the government to assist in bringing about a music ecosystem that is transparent and fair – they argue that streaming royalties for artists and songwriters – the creatives – are woefully insufficient from 'an old, broken industry' (Crispin Hunt (The Ivors Academy) 2020). Voices within the industry argue that it should be possible in a digital world for royalties to go directly and transparently to the music creators, the artists and the rightsholders instead of through a slow, inefficient, and opaque chain of collection societies, record labels and publishing administrators.

Blockchain could remove the need for artists to trust intermediaries to pay royalties fairly and efficiently due to the transparency of blockchain ledgers and because payments would no longer need to pass through intermediaries at all, thus perhaps helping the industry keep up with technology with faster, frictionless payments (Howard 2020). Spotify's Mediachain has been hailed as a potential saviour of the industry for these reasons and Ujo, a New York-based company, provides a decentralised database of music ownership where artists can not only upload their works and earn 100 per cent of their sales and tips with no fees but also automatically split payments with collaborators of each project (Madeiras 2020).

Smart contracts

According to songwriter, artist and advocator of blockchain, Imogen Heap, 'When someone buys a piece of music or plays a piece of music, ultimately in the future there will be no need for a middle, centralized service. The fan will be immediately paying the artist' (Heap in Reed 2017). Blockchain advocators argue that another essential element of blockchain technology, 'smart contracts', (first proposed by Nick Szabo in the 1990s) could assist with transparency and allow music revenue to be split at source (O'Dair 2016b). Smart contracts are not a legal contract but a self-executing computer code that includes the operational terms of an agreement between two or more parties, with the operational terms being written into and executed by the lines of code. If a particular amount of money X is paid to a virtual wallet Y, it automatically triggers a specific action, for example, shipment of a commodity – a track. Smart contracts do not rely on a costly and time-consuming verification process by any third party since they process by themselves (Tschmuck 2017).

In the music industry, smart contracts can be used to automate royalty payments, to manage ownership rights, to enforce copyrights and to license musical works and sound recordings. Smart contracts allow for faster payment enabling the industry to keep up with the speed of changing consumer habits. They allow music royalties to be administered almost instantaneously. Wright and De Filippi assert that smart contracts are 'one of the first truly disruptive technological advancements to the practice of law since the invention of the printing press' (Wright and De Filippi 2015). This 'smart contract' element of blockchain technology could help to hand back to the artist or songwriter control over pricing and terms of use of music such as licensing to the creators of the music – the artists and songwriters. Rights in music could be bought, sold and licensed with this secure smart contract payment system with all transactions tracked and backed by blockchain systems. The Open Music Initiative and Imogen Heap's Mycelia are examples of enabling rightsowners to transfer or sell rights on the market openly and securely through the use of blockchain (Hoppe 2019). Further, the low transaction costs of cryptocurrencies on blockchain make micropayments possible, which is helpful in the streaming era (O'Dair 2016a).

In October 2015 Imogen Heap in collaboration with Ujo released Tiny Human on Ethereum blockchain with all relevant metadata and music licensing policies including revenue splits, defined in the smart contract, allowing fans to pay the artist and creators directly. All revenue streams were visible on Ujo Music's webpage providing transparency (Tschmuck 2017). The transparency of blockchain with smart contract technology could potentially help ease or at least lessen the endless legal disputes within the music industry over royalty payments.

Numerous intermediaries wanting a share of the income and how blockchain might address this

'The current lack of transparency appears to benefit middlemen, but creators, consumers, and others in the music industry value chain should no longer passively accept this.'

(Kenswil in Rethink Music 2015: 10)

The music industry has been dominated by big recording labels, major music publishers, big name producers and CMOs as well as other large organisations who have gained enormous economic power within the industry (Carretta 2020). Major record labels, for example, receive a significantly greater share of licensing revenue from streaming services than the artists. As highlighted earlier, data provided to artists and songwriters with their royalty payments is often opaque (Rethink Music 2015). As a result, they often don't understand the payments and accountings that they receive. One reason for this lack of transparency may be that it benefits intermediaries (Rethink Music 2015).

Perhaps the most radical and controversial aspect of how blockchain technology could affect the record industry is its potential to cut out or at least reduce or shift the role of the middleman (O'Dair 2016b and Wright and De Filippi 2015). As highlighted earlier, an advantage of blockchain is the removal of layers of intermediaries with the potential payment of royalties directly to artists and songwriters, and the terms of use of their music remaining in the control of the creatives. By cutting out the intermediaries, the artist, songwriters and other rightsholders should get more of the money. Blockchain-based music platform Opus, for example, leverages two different peer-to-peer networks to remove middlemen completely and provide a fully decentralised streaming platform (Madeira 2020), and Peertracks allows artists to write their own licence and set their own financial terms. Smart contracts could allow artists and songwriters to set the terms of use of their music as well as the price of such use.

If artists, songwriters and rightsholders do not have to rely on an intermediary to license Works and collect royalties with the assistance of smart contracts, transaction costs could be reduced without the need to pay extra for intermediaries' fees, thus reducing the cost to the eventual consumer of the music (Tam 2018) while perhaps increasing income for the creatives. This points to Rogers' 'Fair Trade' music argument, discussed further later, and how blockchain could enable a fair compensation scheme (Rogers 2015).

Blockchain: challenges and disadvantages

Despite the promise and potential of blockchain to address some of the issues facing the music industry, as discussed earlier, some foresee various problems ahead. A key question to consider when looking at the issue of building a comprehensive music rights database is who would take the lead and who would enter the data onto the blockchain. Labels and Collective Management Organizations (CMOs) such as SACEM, ASCAP and *PRS for Music* are already exploring joint initiatives, as mentioned earlier; industry giant Warner Music Group is investing in a new blockchain network (Madeira 2020); and Spotify has now acquired Mediachain, a blockchain-based media rights attestation network.

There are, however, differing views on the amount of control within the industry already held by labels, digital service providers and CMOs. Given this, would these influential organisations who already hold much of the control, and in many cases much of the income within the industry, be trusted by others in the industry to take this lead and keep the interests of the creatives at the forefront of the task? While some argue for the need to have the major players on board for blockchain to be adopted (Rogers 2015), the question perhaps arises about how such players will use the technology given their past history on fair play, perceived or otherwise.

Following on from this, the question arises as to who would verify the information entered onto a blockchain database and how this would be done. There are questions about piracy and those uploading fake information or incorrect data by mistake – how could it be amended if blockchain is immutable? While blockchain may not aim to wipe out piracy and may not even really be used to address piracy (Dredge 2017), it is argued that blockchain makes piracy more of a problem (Deahl 2019b). Some existing music platforms, such as Audius, host user-uploaded content built on blockchain. The tasks of hosting and making uploaded content available is spread among people registered as node operators.[4] Unlike platforms such as YouTube, there are some with no

---

[4] A node operator runs software that keeps a full copy of the blockchain and broadcasts transactions across the network. (O'Mara and Burnie 2020)

content ID system to catch potential infringement (Deahl 2019b). Governance and blockchain is certainly one of the important questions surrounding this technology (O'Mara and Burnie 2020). If blockchain is immutable and there is no way for such platforms to remove the infringing material, questions arise as to how such infringement can be stopped and who would be liable. Would a node operator or uploader be liable for such infringement?

The immutability of blockchain thus throws up a number of questions – not only about liability for infringing material but also in relation to how to correct incorrect information, how to deal with conflicts over data and with information in flux, for example, whether a final master recording uses certain performers (Silver 2016) and how samples would be identified. Experts point out that although marketed as immutable, with any code, it can be broken, and it could be possible to override blockchain provided this was by a trusted source. This possibility of overriding, however, could potentially destroy the entire security of blockchain (O'Mara and Burnie 2020).

Such problems could perhaps in time be overcome or the industry might decide that the benefits of blockchain technology outweigh the potential downsides. Authorship and rightsholder identity information set into blockchain may not, for example, prevent recordings being illegally uploaded to streaming platforms by third parties, but it would at least mean that artists and rightsholders would be properly acknowledged (O'Dair 2016b). Proposals have been made that at the time of uploading data to the blockchain, proof of ownership in some form from those representing the Work would be required. Benji Rogers envisages a 'Fair Trade Database' owned by all who interact with it where each song or entry of data would have minimum viable data (MVD) attached to it – to include, for example, identification for each song or recording of the songwriters, performers and rightsholders before it could be verified for entry on the blockchain (Rogers 2015).

Further issues arise over back catalogue releases already owned by a major label and how such large and potentially confusing amounts of data could be uploaded onto blockchain. Including heritage artists' information and indexing all music from the past would be a huge task requiring cooperation from many entities – labels, publishers, CMOs, copyright holders – who may or may not be willing to cooperate, and confidentiality issues would undoubtedly arise. A solution could be for the technology to be used solely for new artists who have not yet signed deals with labels or publishers or at the time of signing their first deals or releasing their first records, for example, as a simpler way of setting up a database (Dredge 2018).

Despite these potential pitfalls, there is hope that blockchain could significantly address the database issue. Tschmuck believes that the relevance of blockchain technology for establishing a global music rights database should not be underestimated (2017). Despite sceptical comments, there is optimism and belief that perhaps there is a chance that the music industry too will eventually recognise the long-term value of a global music rights database and from this the potential for an equitable distribution of money in the industry (Silver 2016). The potential solution blockchain technology offers to the current slow, inefficient and opaque royalty payment process seems like an obvious way forward for the industry. However, concerns have been expressed over smart contracts and their regulation.

It is not clear how governments intend to legislate for blockchain-related technologies and address their compatibility or lack thereof with the existing regulatory framework (FCA Discussion Paper 2017). Smart contracts are not contracts and not necessarily smart (O'Mara and Burnie 2020). They are a code that implements the operational or business logic of a contract. There would also need to be a separate legal agreement between the parties – issues governing the smart contract such as governing law, warranties and dispute resolution may need to be addressed in a standard separate contract – so perhaps they are not as efficient as would initially appear. The administration of smart contracts can be complex and a huge amount of time may be required to set them up (O'Dair 2016b), particularly if they take up too much data themselves. What happens if the smart contract does not actually execute what the parties intend or if a smart contract containing an error is created leading to an unexpected result or the wrong money is paid? The rigidity of smart code does not easily allow for flexibility and discretion over contractual terms, thereby limiting parties (O'Mara and Burnie 2020). How disputes over such issues could be resolved has yet to be established. Further, blockchain may offer transparency; however, transparency in relation to royalty income is not always embraced by all, even some creatives because 'the music industry is built on people pretending to be bigger than they are' (Howard 2015). Creators and performers of music getting most of the income from the music they create and perform sounds to many like an ideal solution. However, there are potential stumbling blocks. The process of disintermediation that blockchain technology could enable is likely to be resisted by those intermediaries themselves (O'Dair 2016b). It currently seems unlikely that the major players in the industry such as large labels, music publishers and CMOs would happily sit back and just accept this peer-to-peer sharing or allow the data they hold, that could make blockchain so valuable due to its transparency, to be held on potentially such a publicly available platform. Such distrust would have to be overcome to achieve cooperation to place the relevant data on the blockchain (O'Dair 2016b).

Further, to have the chance to achieve commercial success and make a name for themselves, many artists turn towards big intermediaries such as record labels, producers, music publishers, CMOs and streaming platforms for economic support and sponsorship in the market (Carretta 2020). There are a multitude of artists on their own in a big pond of many other artists trying to do the same thing and getting fractions of money for each individual stream. For many creatives, it is the intermediaries who help them raise their heads above the parapet and who can make the difference between unknowns and global stars.

Some see the middlemen remaining but in an altered or reduced role (Rogers 2015). It could be argued that CMOs are needed to negotiate the terms of use of music with, for example, large broadcasting organisations. Others point out that manufacturing, distribution and marketing will still be required, roles which artists themselves may not have the time or the inclination to take on (O'Dair 2016b). However, the different revenue split may favour the artists as revenue could be split from source via smart contracts between all parties, not through intermediaries first. Others perhaps see the role of intermediaries shifting to that of verifying companies, that is, verifying the information uploaded to the blockchain (Tschmuck 2017). There do seem to be opportunities for intermediaries as well as creatives in embracing the efficiencies and transparency of blockchain and benefiting from the economic advantages of this if all parties are willing to trust each other and work together in adopting blockchain (Carretta 2020).

There remain further emerging challenges presented by blockchain technology in the music industry such as those surrounding jurisdiction. Failing to obtain a proper licence to exploit a Work may lead to a copyright infringement claim. Determining where to go to obtain the licence and which type of licence is required can be difficult. Such licences and rights granted, often administered on a territorial basis, may differ between jurisdictions. The lack of a centralised database to identify the licence required and the rights granted in which jurisdiction for each musical work may complicate matters. It may be difficult for a string of code to easily capture data in relation to these issues. Blockchain experts are working on this issue and it may be that jurisdiction lies with where the use originates or where the main traffic of use is coming from; however, this is still to be determined (O'Mara and Burnie 2020).

Further, there is the issue of data protection. Depending on how the blockchain is structured, the identities of the parties to a transaction are not always disclosed, which could go some way to protecting privacy. However, the immutability of the blockchain poses separate data privacy and personal information concerns. One right under the General Data Protection Regulations (GDPR) is the right to be forgotten, another is the right to modify or update information. Once information is recorded to the blockchain ledger, it is hard to remove, which poses problems under the GDPR. In addition, there is the possibility that a permissioned music blockchain network could be established which controls access to it and the income (Silver 2016), thus, perhaps being neither transparent nor easily accessible and potentially defeating the reason blockchain has been viewed as such a hero in some parts of the industry.

Blockchain potential for the future

'We need to streamline the system and save money where we can and give that back to the artists so they can shape their own futures.'

(Heap 2016)

If the technical pitfalls and legal issues, as there are with any new technology, surrounding blockchain can be resolved, its potential advantages for the music industry and the legal framework which underpins it could be game-changing. As discussed earlier, blockchain has the potential to provide a comprehensive, accurate database of music rights ownership information and to act as a new royalty distribution mechanism for the music industry, transforming the role of intermediaries.

> In addition to rights ownership information, making it easier and simpler for the correct rightsholders to be identified and thus paid, the royalty split agreed for each work could be added to the database. Imagining a world where blockchain is widely adopted by the industry, each time a payment is generated for a given work, the money would be automatically split through the use of smart contracts according to the set terms, and each party's account would instantly reflect the additional revenue. (Rethink Music 2015)

In their report on Fair Music: Transparency and Payment Flows in the Music Industry, Rethink Music detailed an example of how this could work in practice:

> This entire process would take place in less than one second, allowing all parties to access their money immediately after it is generated. Further, this payment system is fully trackable and would ensure that royalties are not held by third parties, such as labels and publishers, before being passed to the artist and songwriter. This would eliminate concerns about accidental or intentional underpayment of royalties. (Rethink Music 2015: 28)

Thus, blockchain offers the chance for a simpler, more straightforward, more transparent way perhaps. However, for now there does seem to be some way to go. It is argued that 'this technology needs to reach mass use by a significant number of rightsholders and cover large amounts of copyright protected works in order to unleash its full potential. Only time will tell whether blockchain will be widely adopted by the industry and by consumers and in turn for the law to accept and adapt to such technological changes' (Carretta 2020:52).

Conclusion

We have seen that blockchain does not offer a fix-all miracle for some of the major problems hindering the music industry. Blockchain certainly has its potential problems from a legal perspective, and for its implementation in the music industry to be successful there are a number of obstacles to be overcome. At present there appears to be some resistance to its adoption within the industry on a larger scale for various reasons including perhaps the fact that the technology is still in its early 'teething' stages and that it takes time to shift well-worn, outdated legal frameworks. However, blockchain may offer a way forward for the industry and the potential to shift into the same gear as the technology that surrounds it. Potentially, it could offer creators of music the chance of direct control of, and fair remuneration for, their Works; protection of their copyrights and correct identification of their authorship; and thus a greater chance of being able to make a living out of creating music.

It is perhaps the potential and the possibilities this technology offers to the music industry and its legal framework which is the most exciting and valuable aspect. '**Blockchain does not lead to any one specific "solution" for** the music industry. It leads to a new set of possibilities, and new business models, and new opportunities for the music industry' (Barry in Dredge 2017).

References

Allison, I. (2016). 'Pink Floyd: Blockchain Technology in Music could be "truly revolutionary"', *International Business Times*, 8 July 2016, https://www.ibtimes.co.uk/pink-floyd-blockchain-technology-music-could-be-truly-revolutionary-1569649, accessed 30 March 2020.

Carretta, S. A. (2020). 'Blockchain Solutions for the Online Music Industry: Revolutionising the Value Chain Through Better Protection of Artists' Rights, A Creation of a Fairer Music Ecosystem and Frictionless Royalties Payment'. *Stockholm Intellectual Property Law Review*, 3, Issue 1: 40–53.

Citigroup Report (2018). 'Putting the Band Back Together: Remastering the World of Music', https://ir.citi.com/NhxmHW7xb0tkWiqOOG0NuPDM3pVGJpVzXMw7n+Zg4AfFFX+eFqDYNfND+0hUxxXA, accessed 7 June 2020.

Deahl, D. (2019a). 'Metadata is the Biggest Little Problem Plaguing the Music Industry', *The Verge*, 29 May 2019, https://www.theverge.com/2019/5/29/18531476/music-industry-song-royalties-metadata-credit-problems, accessed 7 June 2020.

Deahl, D. (2019b). 'New Blockchain-Based Music Streaming Service Audius Is a Nightmare', *The Verge*, 9 October 2019, https://www.theverge.com/2019/10/9/20905384/audius-blockchain-music-streaming-service-copyright-infringement-piracy, accessed 7 June 2020.

Directive (EU) 2019/790 of the European Parliament and of the Council of 17 April 2019 on copyright and related rights in the Digital Single Market, and amending Directives 96/9/EC and 2001/29/EC (DSM Directive 2019).

Dotson, K. (2020). 'A Note to Launch Blockchain-Based Music Royalty Investment Platform', *Silicon Angle*, 5 June 2020, https://siliconangle.com/2020/06/05/anote-music-launch-blockchain-based-music-royalty-investment-platform-july-28/?utm_medium=email&_hsmi=89403181&_hsenc=p2ANqtz-9kwU7HtTWM2ZM3OhhVHbrKamDY5Za784L6Uw518APEc3pxkmqzv6TykvpIDRzhGueRKmFK055HS7-o_X4bfjijGVVReA&utm_content=89403181&utm_source=hs_email, accessed 16 June 2020.

Dredge, S. (2017). 'Technology on Its Own Is not the Whole Picture', *MusicAlly*, 3 August 2017, https://musically.com/2017/08/03/blokur-blockchain-music-technology/, accessed 30 March 2020.

Dredge, S. (2018). 'Gareth Emery of Blockchain Music Startup Choon "We're Committed to Radical Transparency"', *MusicAlly*, 5 February 2018, https://musically

.com/2018/02/05/gareth-emery-blockchain-music-startup-choon/, accessed 30 March 2020.

Economic Times (2020). https://economictimes.indiatimes.com/definition/cryptography, accessed 6 September 2020.

Fairfield, J. (2014). 'BitProperty', *Southern California Law Review*, 88: 805. 5 October 2014, https://papers.ssrn.com/sol3/papers.cfm?abstract_id=2504710, accessed 30 March 2020.

FCA Discussion Paper (2017). DP17/3 on 'Distributed Ledger Technology', https://www.fca.org.uk/publications/feedback-statements/fs17-4-distributed-ledgertechnology.

Gopie, N. (2020). 'What Are Smart Contracts on Blockchain', *IBM*, 2 July 2018, https://www.ibm.com/blogs/blockchain/2018/07/what-are-smart-contracts-on-blockchain/, accessed 6 September 2020.

Heap, I. (2016). 'Decentralising the Music Industry with Blockchain?', *MyCelia*, 14 May 2016, http://myceliaformusic.org/2016/05/14/imogen-heap-decentralising-the-music-industry-with-blockchain/.

Hoppe, D. (2019). 'How Blockchain Will Change the Music Industry', *gammalaw*, 14 August 2019, https://gammalaw.com/how-blockchain-will-change-the-music-industry/, accessed 7 June 2020.

Howard, G. (2015). 'We Have the Push, Now We Need the Pull: A "Blockchain and the Arts" State of the Union', *Forbes*, 7 October 2015, www.forbes.com/sites/georgehoward/2015/10/07/ we-have-the-push-now-we-need-the-pull-a-blockchain-and-the-arts-state-of-the-union/#88cd44028279, accessed 30 March 2020.

Howard, G. (2020). 'Blockchain Powered Initiatives Pays Musicians In Two Hours Rather Than Two Years', *Forbes*, 29 May 2020, https://www.forbes.com/sites/georgehoward/2020/05/29/blockchain-powered-initiative-pays-musicians-in-two-hours-rather-than-two-years/#667d1b7d4ef8, accessed 16 June 2020.

IFPI Global Music Report (2020). 'IFPI Issues Annual Global Music Report', 4 May 2020, https://www.ifpi.org/news/IFPI-issues-annual-Global-Music-Report, accessed 9 July 2020.

Internet Society (2020). 'Blockchain', https://www.internetsociety.org/issues/blockchain/?gclid=CjwKCAjwtqj2BRBYEiwAqfzurzwz5fSzHafcP_uqdBVAkpPZkjrxejyYSO3EsT4n3afC2K2ulKyaJBoCW58QAvD_BwE, accessed 30 March 2020.

ISO/TC 307, 'Blockchain and Distributed Ledger Technologies', www.iso.org/committee/6266604.html, accessed 7 June 2020.

Madeira, A. (2020). 'Blockchain to Disrupt Music Industry and Make It Change Tune', *Cointelegraph*, 6 June 2020, https://cointelegraph.com/news/blockchain-to-disrupt-music-industry-and-make-it-change-tune, accessed 9 July 2020.

McIntyre, H. (2017). 'Spotify Has Acquired Blockchain Startup Mediachain', *Forbes*, 27 April 2017, https://www.forbes.com/sites/hughmcintyre/2017/04/27/spotify-has-acquired-blockchain-startup-mediachain/, accessed 7 June 2020.

Mougayar, W. (2016). *The Business Blockchain: Promise, Practice and Application of the Next Internet Technology*. Hoboken: John Wiley & Sons.

O'Dair, M. (2016a). 'Music On The Blockchain', Report Nr. 1 Blockchain for Creative Industries Research Zuleika Beaven, David Nelson, Richard Osborne, Paul Pacifico, Clusters Middlesex University.

O'Dair, M. (2016b). 'The Networked Record Industry: How Blockchain Technology Could Transform the Consumption and Monetization of Recorded Music', University of the Arts London.

O'Mara, C. and J. Burnie (2020). 'Cryptoassets, Blockchain and Financial Services Lawyer', *Discussing Blockchain and Its Challenges*. Interview: Unpublished.

O'Mara, C. and C. Cooke, co-founder CMU (2020). *Discussing the Potential of Blockchain in the Music Industry*. Interview: Unpublished.

PwC (2018). 'Blockchain: Recording the Music Industry: How Blockchain Technology could Save the Music Industry Billions', https://www.pwc.co.uk/entertainment-media/publications/blockchain-recording-music-industry.pdf, accessed 30 March 2020.

Reed, M. (2017). 'Bjork: The New Kid on the Blockchain', *Lawdit Music*, https://www.lawditmusic.co.uk/bjork-the-new-kid-on-the-blockchain/, accessed 30 March 2020.

Rethink Music (2015). 'Fair Music: Transparency and Payment Flows in the Music Industry', Berklee Institute of Creative Entrepreneurship, https://static1.squarespace.com/static/552c0535e4b0afcbed88dc53/t/55d0da1ae4b06bd4bea8c86c/1439750682446/rethink_music_fairness_transparency_final.pdf, accessed 30 March 2020.

Rogers, B. (2015). 'How the Blockchain and VR Can Change the Music Industry (Part 1)', *Cuepoint*, 24 November 2015, https://medium.com/cuepoint/bc-a-fair-trade-music-formatvirtual-reality-the-blockchain-76fc47699733#.c9nbnhs7b, accessed 30 March 2020.

Rosic, A. (2020). 'What Is Blockchain Technology? A Step-by-Step Guide for Beginners', *Blockgeeks*, 'https://blockgeeks.com/graphics/'><img src='https://blockgeeks.com/wp-content/uploads/2019/05/transactioncycle.jpg' alt='Transaction Cycle' 540px border='0' /></a' https://blockgeeks.com/guides/what-is-blockchain-technology/, accessed 16 September 2020.

Silver, J. (2016). 'Blockchain or the Chaingang? Challenges, Opportunities and Hype: The Music Industry and Blockchain Technologies', *CREATe Working Paper* 2016/05, www.create.ac.uk/publications/blockchain-or-the-chaingang-challenges-opportunities-and-hype-the-music-industry-and-blockchain-technologies/.

Sisario, B. (2016). 'Spotify Reaches Settlement with Publishers in Licensing Dispute', *New York Times*, 17 March 2016, https://www.nytimes.com/2016/03/18/business/media/spotify-reaches-settlement-with-publishers-in-licensing-dispute.html, accessed 30 March. 2020.

Tam, T. (2018). 'Music Copyright Management on Blockchain: Advantages and Challenges', 29.0000000000000 ALB. L.J. SCI. & TECH. 201, http://www.albanylawjournal.org/archives/pages/article-information.aspx?volume=29&issue=1&page=201, accessed 5 June 2020.

Tapscott, D. and A. Tapscott (2016). *Blockchain Revolution. How the Technology Behind Bitcoin Is Changing Money, Business, and the World*. New York: Portfolio.

The Ivors Academy Official Press Release (2020). 'The Ivors Academy and Musicians' Union Launch Keep Music Alive Campaign to Fix Streaming Now', *Pressparty*, 11 May 2020, https://www.pressparty.com/pg/newsdesk/BASCA/view/211824/.

Tschmuck, P. (2017). 'The Music Business in the Blockchain', *Music Business Research*, 28 February 2017, https://musicbusinessresearch.wordpress.com/2017/02/28/the-music-business-in-the-blockchain/, accessed 30 March 2020.

Tsilidou, A. L. and G. Foroglou (2015). 'Further Applications of the Blockchain', Conference paper, Researchgate, May 2015, https://www.researchgate.net/publication/276304843_Further_applications_of_the_bl ockchain, accessed 30 March 2020.

Walden, J. (2018). 'What A Blockchain For Music Really Means: Dispelling the Myths and Explaining How We Can Actually Build One', *Mediachain*, 25 April 2015, https://blog.mediachain.io/what-a-blockchain-for-music-really-means-e2f8dc66d57d, accessed 30 March 2020.

Wright, A. and P. De Filippi (2015). 'Decentralized Blockchain Technology and the Rise of Lex Cryptographia', Working paper, *SSRN*, 20 March 2015, https://papers.ssrn.com/sol3/papers.cfm?abstract_id=2580664, accessed 30 March 2020.

11

Greening the live music industry

Teresa Moore

The music industry has used its voice to call on governments to act on climate change and the environment since at least 1970 and the Amchitka benefit concert that launched Greenpeace. The UK's 'Music declares an Emergency' launched in 2019 is the most recent campaign by the industry to draw attention to the issue. On the ground live music and music festivals in particular have been grappling with the environmental impacts caused by staging live music events. At times, it has appeared that the festival industry has been ahead of legislation in formulating and evaluating the problems and finding solutions which have then been more widely adopted. While Covid-19 stopped the industry in its tracks, the environment has undoubtedly benefited and those engaged in improving the environmental impact of live events have started the conversation about how to do it faster once the industry gets back on its feet.

This chapter will focus on key environmental issues faced by those staging live music events and the relationship between developments in EU and UK environmental legislation and industry practice. It will concentrate most on the music festival sector where the regular use of green field sites, and the scale of these events, bring many of the environmental impacts into sharp relief. It will examine the issues and innovative solutions developed by festival organisers and their teams and will pose the question as to whether it is the industry or legislation that is really driving the change to more environmentally friendly live music events. Finally, it will look at the environmental issues created by some of the rapid changes to the industry brought about by the 2020 Covid-19 pandemic and the emerging solutions.

The growth of live music and its impact on the environment

The social consumption of music through live performance has been a dynamic sector of growth in the music industry for more than a decade. Globally, live music has been forecast to show a compounded growth of 3.3 per cent annually, generating $31 billion in revenues by 2022 (PWC 2018). The contribution from live music to the UK economy topped £1 billion in 2018 when 4.9 million people attended UK music festivals alone (UK Music 2019).

This economic growth has occurred against a backdrop of increasing concern about climate change and our impact on the environment. As a result, there has been a growing recognition within the industry that live music events create a significant environmental impact. Music festivals used 7 million tons of fuel, generated 25,800 tons of waste and created a carbon footprint of 24,261 tons in the UK alone in 2018 (Vision 2025, 2020). In short, the economic growth of the live music industry is at odds with its environmental sustainability. The now widely recognised model of sustainability derived from the UN's sustainable development goals (UN Agenda 21, 1992) shows that where there is an imbalance between economic, environmental and social impacts, there can't be long-term sustainability (Raj and Musgrave 2009; Henderson 2011).

The industry response – campaigns and actions

Single use plastics

Many music festivals, having recognised the environmental impact of their events, have been at the vanguard of initiatives to improve their environmental record even though there is sometimes no national legislation or local regulations requiring them to do so. They have sought to address the impacts of water and energy use, transport and waste created by their events, all of which we look at in more detail later in the chapter. In addition, there have been a number of recent campaigns to draw attention to specific issues of which we have only just started to become aware. One of these, which is a big concern of environmentalists, has been the damage done to wildlife and the oceans through discarded, often single-use, plastic waste. The single-use plastic water bottle was identified as a particular anathema from the environmental damage done to the sheer waste of resources. It takes three times the amount of water it can hold to make a single-use plastic bottle and the cost of a bottle of water is up to five hundred times more than tap water (RAW Foundation 2018). An early initiative to eliminate plastic water bottles from their festival came from Shambala Festival, UK, which introduced a reusable bottle scheme in 2014. Discarded single-use plastic tents have been a ubiquitous problem at large music festivals and singled out for attention by organisers. They create a huge amount of waste, with an estimated quarter of a million discarded tents in 2018 alone (AIF 2018). Eco Action Partners, the organisation behind the Love Your Tent campaign, which has worked with the Isle of Wight Festival UK for many years, set up their campaign in 2012 to draw attention to tent waste at music festivals and change audience behaviour. Both were early interventions by music festivals to address the plastic waste problem at their events and to highlight more widespread concern about the issue to their audiences at a time before any legislation to deal with plastic waste was on the table. Recently in 2018 and partly in response to what is being called the 'Blue Planet 2 effect',[1] over sixty music festivals signed up to the UK's Association of Independent Festivals (AIF) campaign 'Drastic on Plastic' to end the use of all single-use plastics at music festivals by 2021. The first draft of legislation to ban some single-use items, plastic straws and stirrers, but not including single-use plastic water bottles, was prepared by the UK Government in 2018 (UK Government 2018) with the planned introduction in 2020.

Food and food waste

What we eat, where it comes from and its impact on the environment has been of concern to the industry for some years. Roskilde Festival in Denmark, the largest festival in mainland Europe, estimates that over one million meals are served during their festival. Festival organisers concerned about the level of methane emissions from livestock have moved towards providing vegetarian or vegan alternatives to meat. Sweden's heavy metal music festival 'Way Out West' went further and introduced the first meat-free heavy metal festival in 2013, and increasing numbers of events have since gone meat-free.

What happens to the food waste has also been a focus, and in the Nederland Digital Festival an Amsterdam-based dance music festival has created a circular food court where inedible food waste and compostable serveware are turned into compost onsite rather than going to incineration.

---

[1] 'The Blue Planet Effect' is named after the David Attenborough programme first shown in 2017 which highlighted the devastating impact of plastic waste pollution in our oceans on its wildlife.

But that's not the only story on food waste. There is a huge problem of edible food waste left at events by food traders and on festival campsites by audiences. In the UK, festival industry organisations responded with the Eighth Plate initiative founded in 2015 by A Greener Festival and the National Catering Association (NCASS). Named in recognition of the estimated one in eight of the world's population which go hungry, it is a food salvage and redistribution scheme which also highlights the issue of edible food waste at music festivals. Eighth Plate collected twelve tons of edible food waste from five festivals in their first year of operation, creating over 28,500 meals. To put these initiatives in perspective, legislation on food waste is currently minimal. The EU's revised waste directive of 2018 calls on member states to reduce food waste while the UK Government has only recently announced that it would launch a pilot scheme to tackle food waste in 2019/20 (UK Government 2018).

It could be argued that these various initiatives simply reflect widespread concern across society and are not particularly significant, but the music industry sees it somewhat differently. Since that first benefit concert for Greenpeace, the music industry has sought to use its influence to take action on climate change through special concerts and campaigns.

Artists, too, are becoming more vocal in their concern about the environmental impact of live performance and touring. Whether it's a concern about the overall CO_2e[2] footprint of touring, or the impact of single-use plastics, the issue is gathering momentum among major artists. Following early pioneers of greener touring, Pearl Jam who developed a plan to reduce their CO_2 emissions back in 2003 and Radiohead who undertook a carbon audit of their 2007 tour, Billie Eilish, Cold Play, Massive Attack and 1975 all made declarations in 2019 about reducing the environmental impact of their tours and performances.

Artist green riders

Artist riders, the list of additional requirements added to an artist contract with a tour venue or festival, have sometimes received bad press. Alongside items relating to product sponsor endorsements and lists of favourite foods and snacks, Kanye West is reported to have included a requirement for a barber's chair in his dressing room, Rihanna had specific scented candles in hers, and, famously, Van Halen are said to have banned all brown M&M's from their dressing rooms. A small number of artists, though, have used the artist rider to help address their environmental concerns and have added green or enviro-riders to their

---

[2] CO_2e refers to CO_2 or equivalent greenhouse gas emissions.

contracts. Artists such as Jack Johnson have included green measures such as recycling, energy efficiency and carbon offsetting in their tour venue contracts (Blankfield Shultz 2008). This, though, has often been seen as another whim of the artist, enforceable only by those with a name.

In 2019, A Greener Festival, a not-for-profit formed in 2006 to help events and festivals to understand their environmental impacts, attempted to make green riders more universal by launching their artist green rider initiative in partnership with Paradigm Agency (formerly Coda Agency). The rider was developed as a blueprint for use by agents and their roster of artists rather than it being left to individual artists to create and apply their own green riders.

The stated aims of the green rider are to:

- Reduce single use plastics
- Source good food with low environmental impact and high social benefit
- Reduce and balance emissions and to eliminate waste

It was designed to help artists reduce their environmental impact from live events and touring and also to encourage a stronger collaboration with promoters and venues in tackling the environmental impacts created by live performance. Acceptance of green riders across the industry, though, is still at an early stage and there are currently a number of issues to overcome. These range from fears that additional terms will impact bookings for lesser known artists to lack of infrastructure to support green rider terms. Further there is a view by the industry that only headline artists have the power to drive change and enforce these riders.

Venues and the corporates

Many venues staging music events around the globe are making changes to the way they do business from ethical purchasing policies for their productions and operations to measures to reduce waste and energy consumption. Sparks Arena in New Zealand and SECC in Glasgow are just two examples of the growing number of green arenas and venues staging live music events. At the corporate end of the live music industry the two biggest global players, Live Nation and AEG, have both made extensive commitments to reach carbon zero impact by 2050. Live Nation's 'Green Nation' coalition across all Live Nation-owned and -operated venues, clubs, theatres and festivals, is 'committing to new environmental goals'. AEG, through its 2019 annual report AEG '1 Earth', set out new goals to reach zero carbon emissions by 2050.

On the face of it then it would appear that the live music industry and festivals in particular have been at the forefront of innovation and change responding to the climate change issue and the environmental impact of staging live events.

Legislative context and frameworks

International agreements

To fully understand the policies and targets that the live music industry has been setting itself, these need to be looked at in the context of a hierarchy of international agreements and related legislation on climate change. The Kyoto Agreement at the first 'Earth Summit' in 1992 which became law on 16 February 2005 has been instrumental in galvanising the global community to address climate change by creating the world's only legally binding treaty to reduce greenhouse gas emissions. This agreement initiated the Kyoto protocol, the first running from 2008 to 2012, and committed the international community to agreed targets to reduce greenhouse gas emissions. The second protocol, the Doha amendment, which came to an end in 2020, targets a 20 per cent reduction in emissions shared between the twenty-nine countries and the EU. This, together with the Conference of the Parties or COP,[3] the governing body of the UN Climate Change Convention (UNFCCC), have driven the international agenda on climate change.

The annual COP meetings continue to push the agenda on climate change action and serve to determine the focus, new goals and agreements for the global community. They have been responsible for driving the legislative agenda on climate of the participating countries and the EU. Through a series of directives, the EU has done much to introduce comprehensive and consistent environmental legislation across its member states, formerly including the UK, often creating higher targets in the process.

Legislation

Individual countries are expected to introduce legislation which will support and implement the UN protocols. In the case of the EU, it set up the Climate

---

[3] COP26 which was scheduled for 2020 coinciding with the end of the 2nd protocol had to be postponed until 2021 due to the Covid-19 pandemic as has most of the live music industry.

Change programme in 2000 but only agreed to a climate change programme in 2008. This resulted in the creation of a series of EU directives which provide the framework, scope and criteria for individual member countries to create their own national legislation. This has meant that while the time frames for the enactment of national legislation may vary, ultimately the EU aims for consistent legislation across the member states so that the EU climate targets can be met. The EU has stated that by 2050 it aims to become the world's first climate-neutral continent. In 2019, the UK also updated its legally binding targets under the Climate Change Act 2008, to net zero greenhouse gas emissions by 2050. There are, however, questions about how these targets will be enforced. At a national scale there are signs that targets will be enforced, and there is some evidence that courts are willing to intervene. A landmark case brought against the Dutch government by environmental group, Urgenda, ended with a supreme court ruling in 2019 that the government must cut emissions by 25 per cent on 1990 values by 2020 (Kaminski 2019). How enforcement will filter down to individual organisations particularly those that operate globally such as Live Nation and AEG is less clear. Currently, self-regulatory systems of audit, certification and self-assessment are the checks and balances most frequently adopted by organisations to evaluate their own environmental performance.

Live Nation and AEG, along with many other organisations in the live music industry, have aligned their green policies with this target and, as we have seen, aim to reach zero carbon emissions by 2050. One of the problems in practice, though, as many festivals and event organisers discover, is that the supporting infrastructure needed to achieve this ambition may not be available and often its development can lag a long way behind the legislation. For example, the infrastructure to support plastic waste recycling, or in some countries recycling in general, has been slow to develop. Festival and event organisers who have done much to develop waste separation strategies onsite at their events are sometimes shocked to find that when they follow the supply chain their separated waste is all sent to incineration or their plastic waste is bundled and shipped overseas. Not only does this process increase the events emissions as a result of transporting the waste but there is also a growing unease about simply shifting the waste problem to another country. It could be that enforcement of organisational targets if and when it comes will help to speed up the development of the necessary infrastructure.

Self-regulation certification schemes

While the UN protocols have filtered down to legislation at a national level, as an industry live music through the festival sector had already started to implement environmental practices in the early 2000s, in some cases before, in order to green their events. Festivals such as Glastonbury in the United Kingdom and Burning Man in the United States have had protecting the environment at the core of their values. Many of these festivals were looking for ways in which to monitor and evaluate the effectiveness of the measures they had put in place as

Instrument	Organisation	Summary
International UN Accords and Agreements	Kyoto Agreement 1992 Annual UN Conference of the Parties (COP). (COP26 Glasgow 2021)	International agreements which set actions and targets. Protocols 2nd (2013–2020)
EU Directives and Legislation	EU and Member Countries	Provides a legislative framework for member states to create their own laws. e.g. European Green Deal targets for 2030
US National and Federal Laws	US and the States	Code of Federal Regulations e.g. EPA Waste Management Regulations
National Legislation	Individual countries	Introduces national legislation which incorporates actions and targets agreed at the UN Conferences e.g. UK Climate Change Act 2008 (amended 2050 target 2019)
Self-Regulation Audit and Certification	ISOs 14001, 20121 EMAS (EU Eco-Management and Audit Scheme A Greener Festival Award	Independent organisations provide external verification Schemes to assess the environmental impact of live music events Carbon emissions (CO2e) calculated.
Self-Regulation Self-Assessment	Julie's Bicycle Creative Green Tool.	Individual organisations provide online self-assessments tools and carbon emission calculators

Figure 11.1 Summarises the hierarchy of regulation and self-regulation currently in place. Image Courtesy of Teresa Moore

well as sharing knowledge and good practice (Berridge, Moore & Ali Knight. 2019). In 2007, A Greener Festival launched a certification scheme creating an external audit and verification system designed specifically for music festivals which helped to establish festival industry benchmarks and provide recognition for the festivals' efforts. Later developments such as event standards BS8901 and ISO 20121 created for the 2012 Olympics have also been used by the live music industry. EMAS, the European eco management and audit scheme, is similar but has a wider application.

Self-regulation, self-assessment

Beyond certification schemes, organisations such as Julie's Bicycle in the UK have created online self-assessment tools and calculators without an external verification process for use by the wider creative industries as well as the live music industry.

Key environmental impacts and legislation

Understanding the broader environmental impacts of staging live music events and how legislation applies to them is crucial for an event organiser. The following sections focus on the key environmental impacts and issues which directly affect live music and the festival sector, applying relevant legislation and practice to review whether these have kept in step.

Live music energy sources and energy usage

Live music events use energy to power everything, from the venue, the sound and lighting for the production to supplying power to the bars and food traders and lighting for car parks and campsites. In the UK energy makes up 77 per cent of the onsite CO_2e footprint of music festivals (Show Must Go On Report 2020). UN policy has focused on shifting energy sources from fossil fuels to renewables and the EU's 2012 Energy Directive set a target of 20 per cent from renewables by 2020. In practice, where a venue or outdoor site has access to the energy grid of the country, switching to renewable sources is a little easier, provided those sources are well developed. Festivals such as the Cambridge Folk Festival in the UK and the Oya Festival in Norway have been able to access green power from the grid for some years. Internationally, though, only 17 per cent of A Greener Festival assessed events were wholly powered by renewable sources although a further 36 per cent were partially powered by renewables (AGF 2019). While the picture is changing, events on green field sites with no access to the grid have had a particular problem and temporary power has typically been supplied by diesel generators. Although industry suppliers have been developing alternative temporary power sources such as solar and HVO, a form of renewable biodiesel, for some years, these have still not been widely adopted. The most recent EU Energy Directive, which came into force in 2020, stipulates that all newly manufactured engines should reduce emissions by up to 90 per cent which means that new generators must also be compliant and will likely speed up the switch to non-diesel generators.

The source of energy has also been a focus for the industry and its suppliers, but it is only relatively recently that smart power or the efficient use of energy has become as important a concern for events trying to reduce energy emissions. The evidence shows that live music has been a little slow to understand the advantages of energy efficiency when event organisers can save considerable sums of money on their energy bills as well as reducing their energy impact (AGF 2019). Surprisingly perhaps, until recently many event organisers didn't know how much power they were using, and it is only by understanding an event's power usage that it can be managed and reduced. Across Europe and the UK, Smart Power has now taken off and new providers have moved into the event power industry to provide power management as well as supply services. The EU amended energy efficiency targets to 32 per cent of total energy by 2030 in the Directive ((EU) 2018/2002), and in this respect the industry is being driven by legislation.

Water use and conservation

Water management is another key aspect of staging live events, particularly those on green field sites, and involves the provision of drinking water, water for food traders, washing facilities, showers and toilets and the handling of wastewater and sewerage. There is legislation concerning water, its distribution, quality and disposal, which directly relate to live music events. Most predate the climate change legislation we have looked at so far, which is not surprising given the importance of water and water management to the populations' health and well-being. The EU's Directives of 1989, 89/106/EEC relating to construction products including water distribution networks, the 1998 Directive 98/83/EC on the quality of water intended for human consumption and the UK's Water Industry Act 1991, which covers the illegal disposal of water counted as waste are particularly important to outdoor music events.

Spillage and pollutants, which can enter the water system via drains or the water table, are a particular challenge, and recent legal cases brought against festivals have shown that the EU and UK authorities take water very seriously. Environment agencies in the UK as in other countries will visit festival sites to test the water, particularly if there is a water course running through, or adjacent to, the site. Some festival organisers will have a system for monitoring the water quality of nearby rivers, lakes and even local seawater so that they can take immediate steps if there is any change in water quality. Accidents involving water contamination caused by the event can result in prosecution and heavy fines. In 2015, the Glastonbury Festival was taken to court and, though found not to have been negligent, was fined £31,000 for a water pollution incident which involved the leakage of untreated sewerage from one of the festival's storage tanks (UK Government 2018).

More positively, festivals have developed innovative solutions with regard to water issues that affect them most without there being any legal requirement to do so. The Boom Festival, which operates in a particularly arid area of Portugal where water conservation is of great importance, has developed its own water filtration system using natural methods of plant filtration to turn the festivals grey water, water from sinks and shower blocks, back to drinking water.

Travel and transport

Reducing emissions from audience travel has been a goal of the live music industry for many years but has proved to be one of the most difficult. In 2006, A Greener Festival recognised (A Greener Festival 2006) that transport to and from festivals was of environmental concern, and in 2009 Julie's Bicycle published a study on audience travel to live music events. Globally, transport emissions have continued to rise as road traffic and aviation have grown. In 2016, road transport emissions contributed to over 20 per cent of total emissions in the EU (EU Transport Policy 2019). The EU has introduced a series of directives and policies to 'green' road transport, focusing on the level of emissions and sources of energy used and developing regulations for the manufacture of cars and lorries as well as advocating alternative modes of transport. The live music industry has largely focused on changing travel behaviour. A series of measures have been tried to encourage the use of public transport through deals with rail and bus companies, providing additional facilities for bicycles and pricing incentives for car share. Yet, international festival audience travel data gathered by A Greener Festival in 2019 shows that car occupancy rates average 2.8 people while cars and camper vans account for over 50 per cent of audience travel to green field sites. This has been largely unchanged in over a decade. Surprisingly perhaps, travel by car to urban festivals, where more public transport options are available, still accounts for over 30 per cent of audience travel. In some countries, car travel is so firmly entrenched that a wider societal change is necessary. For events such as Burning Man located in the Nevada desert in the United States, the wholesale adoption of electric or clean fuels are perhaps the only solution likely to reduce emissions.

Travel and transport emissions, however, are not just limited to audience travel, and the industry has started to look at areas such as trader and production supplier transport, artist travel and even onsite transport in order to do what they can to reduce emissions.

It would be fair to say that so far neither the live music industry nor government legislation has succeeded in reducing transport emissions and it is only through new technologies that we are likely to see any real long-term reductions.

Waste

The issue of waste at live music shows, while not producing the highest amount of CO_2e emissions, creates the most visible environmental impact of staging an event. Currently, every aspect of the event contributes to the waste problem: from the audience to the artists, from the build to the production, from the sponsors to the crew and beyond. Music festivals in particular have been grappling with the problem for many years. Glastonbury introduced its 'Love the Farm Leave No Trace' pledge in 2008 after a particularly bad experience with the amount of waste left after the 2007 festival. Media coverage of the aftermath of festivals often includes graphic images of mountains of waste left behind and discarded single-use tents at some of the biggest music festivals has become an annual story. This phenomenon is not just limited to the United Kingdom, but can be found at festivals across Europe, the United States and Australia. At the same time, festival audiences have consistently put waste at the top of their concerns about the impacts of festivals (Moore 2013; A Greener Festival 2012, 2008, 2006).

It could be said that there is no better illustration of the attitude behaviour gap (Kollmus and Agymen 2002) between festival audiences, their professed environmental concerns about music festivals' impacts and their actual behaviour onsite.

Over the years, festival organisers have led the way in trying to tackle the problem using both displacement strategies on site and behavioural change strategies before and during their events to tackle the problem. While there is not much doubt that the economic cost of disposing of the waste has been as much of an incentive as the environmental impact it creates, organisers have introduced many practices which are now commonplace at many types of events. Festivals such as OpenAir St Galen in Switzerland introduced waste separation over twenty-five years ago and launched their scheme "Trash Heroes" in 2003 (OpenAir St Galen 2017) to clean the site and raise awareness of the waste problem through a variety of communication techniques.

By contrast EU legislation which incorporates the concepts of separation, recycling and prevention through behaviour change was introduced through the EU Waste Directive in 2008 while the UK's version was introduced only in 2011.

More recent developments in policy and legislation such as the UK Waste Strategy 2018 and the EU Waste Legislation 2019 provide clear indications that governments may now be driving the agenda on waste, signposting the direction that festivals and venues need to take. A particularly interesting recent development is the EU's Green Deal and the Dutch government's initiative to join with music festivals to test out the circular economy principle which is now central to both the EU's and UK's strategies on waste.

Green deal and circular economy

The Green Deal is the EU's strategy to address climate and environmental challenges facing the global community.

> The European Green Deal is a response to these challenges. It is a new growth strategy that aims to transform the EU into a fair and prosperous society, with

a modern, resource efficient and competitive economy where there are no net emissions of greenhouse gases in 2050 and where economic growth is decoupled from resource use. (EU Green Deal 2019)

Where the EU refers to the decoupling of economic growth from resource use, it is referring to the circular economy, an alternative economic model which is central to the Green Deal. Currently, the dominant model is consumerism and the linear economy – in short, the 'make, use, dispose' model which is recognised to be responsible for squandering resources and generating the waste problem that we now have. The circular economy, on the other hand, advocates that greater value be placed on resources so that we maximise their use through reuse and recovery to create a closed loop system where nothing is viewed as waste and everything becomes a resource.

Dutch government and festival partnership

The Dutch government has embraced the Green Deal and is pushing ahead with the circular economy. However, one of the challenges of changing an economic system on a national scale or even within a city such as Amsterdam is that it is difficult to know what the issues and effects will be once you have started. Perhaps it is not surprising then that in looking for a way to test new economic principles the Dutch government has chosen to work with music festivals. Music festivals have been called living labs where experimentation and innovation are fostered. They are in effect micro economies where all the infrastructure and supplies

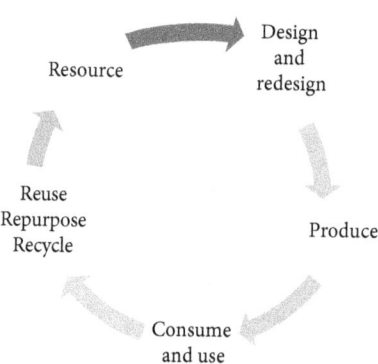

Figure 11.2 The Circular Economy. Image Courtesy of Teresa Moore

are brought in to create temporary areas the size of large towns. In addition, they have been testing different ways of dealing with their waste problem for many years, advocating recycling, reuse and repurposing of materials. Where better then to test a circular economy by creating a circular event? The festival industry has responded with enthusiasm and in October 2019 festivals from across Europe and the UK signed an agreement to introduce a circular model to limit the generation of waste and reuse materials at their events. The festivals involved are the following:

Amsterdam Open Air, Best Kept Secret, Boardmasters, Body & Soul, Boomtown, Down the Rabbit Hole, DGTL, Eurosonic-Noorderslag, Into the Great Wide Open, Lollapalooza Berlin, Lowlands, Mañana Mañana, Milkshake, North Sea Jazz, Roskilde, Shambala, Vierdaagse Feesten, We Love Green and Zwarte Cross.

This initiative is highly significant and could herald a much closer alignment between government, legislation and the music festival industry to bring about change.

And then there was Covid-19

If Covid-19 and the 2020 lockdown has shown us anything about the relationship between the environment and the live music business, it is that the imbalance between economic success and damage to the environment as a result of that success can be so quickly turned on its head. What has been an economic cliff edge for the live music industry has been a welcome respite for the environment, with zero waste, zero emissions from transport and power, zero ecological damage and so on. Ironically, the measures needed to restart the industry safely are likely to increase the environmental impact of events. There is concern about new single-use plastic waste problems created by the disposal of the PPE used by staff and audience and that the work to replace disposable plastic cups with reusable cup schemes will be undone due to contamination worries. Social distancing favours car use over public transport. These are just a few of the environmental concerns being voiced. On the other hand, the advent of more digital events and so-called hybrid events with limited live attendance have been advocated as a solution which will both reduce the impact on the environment and offer an alternative business model. Without research we don't know how environmentally friendly this type of event is and we don't know whether hybrid events can provide a sustainable business model. No one wants to see an end to live music. So, as we reimagine our live music events, the trick now must surely be to find a business model which brings these two elements of sustainability into balance to improve the impact of both on their audiences and society at large.

Conclusions

This chapter started by highlighting recent economic and environmental data which showed how live music's growth and economic success over the last two decades had come at an environmental cost. It has looked at specific problems as well as the key environmental impacts of staging live music and industry initiatives to introduce greener practices. As we have seen, legislation has sometimes lagged behind with change being driven by the industry.

There are signs, however, that legislation is catching up. The focus on the Circular Economy in recent EU legislation and the UK's waste strategy, both issued in 2018, placing circularity at the top of the agenda takes us to a new level challenging fundamental economic models of consumption. The fact that the Dutch government has recognised that music festivals can play a major part in testing circularity could see in a much closer alignment between government, legislation and the music festival industry. This, in turn, could raise the level of ambition and bring about faster change. And this is where the conclusion to this chapter would have ended had we not experienced the 2020 pandemic.

It is uncertain to what extent we will pick up where we left off post Covid-19. There is a chance to rethink the live business model while the industry is paused. The result of the pandemic may be that our live music industry may never look quite the same again.

References

A Greener Festival (2006). https://www.agreenerfestival.com/knowledge-base/, accessed 20 June 2020.

A Greener Festival (2008). https://www.agreenerfestival.com/knowledge-base/, accessed 20 June 2020.

A Greener Festival (2012). https://www.agreenerfestival.com/knowledge-base/, accessed 20 June 2020.
A Greener Festival (2019). 'Juicy Stats', https://www.agreenerfestival.com/consultancy-research/juicy-stats-2019/, accessed 20 June 2020.
Association of Independent Festivals (2018). *Drastic on Plastic Campaign*, https://aiforg.com/initiatives/drastic-on-plastic/, accessed 25 May 2020.
Berridge G., T. Moore and J. Ali-Knight (2019). *Promoting and Assessing Sustainability at Festivals*. In *Green Events and Green Tourism: An International Guide to Good Practice*, 18–30. Oxon: Routledg.
Blankfield Shultz, K. (2008). 'Jack Johnson's Low-Impact Tour', *Scientific America*, 1 September 2008, https://www.scientificamerican.com/article/jack-johnsons-low-impact-summer-tour/, accessed 26 June 2020.
Circular Economy (2008). https://www.ellenmacarthurfoundation.org/circular-economy/concept, accessed 26 June 2020.
Climate Change Act (2008). http://www.legislation.gov.uk/ukpga/2008/27/contents, accessed 20 December 2020.
EU Green Deal (2019). https://ec.europa.eu/info/sites/info/files/european-green-deal-communication_en.pdf, accessed 26 June 2020.
EU Road Transport Policies (2019). https://ec.europa.eu/clima/policies/transport/vehicles_en#tab-0-0, accessed 2 July 2020.
Festival Vision 2025 (2020). The Show Must Go On Update 2020, https://www.vision2025.org.uk, accessed 30 June 2020.
Glastonbury Water Pollution Case (2015). https://www.gov.uk/government/news/glastonbury-festival-fined-for-causing-pollution, accessed 2 July 2020.
Henderson, S. (2011). 'The Development of Competitive Advantage through Sustainable Event Management', *Worldwide Hospitality and Tourism Themes*, 3 (3): 245–57.
Kaminski, I. (2019). 'Dutch Supreme Court Upholds Landmark Ruling Demanding Climate Action', *The Guardian*, 20 December 2019, https://www.theguardian.com/world/2019/dec/20/dutch-supreme-court-upholds-landmark-ruling-demanding-climate-action, accessed 29 August 2020.
Kollmuss, A. and J. Agyeman (2002). 'Mind the Gap: Why do People Act Environmentally and What Are the Barriers to Pro-environmental Behavior?', *Environmental Education Research*, 8 (3): 239–60. doi:10.1080/13504620220145401
Moore, T. (2013). *Tent Waste*, https://www.agreenerfestival.com/knowledge-base/, accessed 5 July 2020.
Openair St Galen Sustainability (2017). https://www.openairsg.ch/wp-content/uploads/2017/11/OASG_Nachhaltigkeitsbericht_2017_EN_LAY_v2.pdf, accessed 25 July 2020.
Price Waterhouse Cooper (2018). 'Global Entertainment and Media Outlook, 2018–2022 Report', https://www.pwc.be/en/news-publications/2019/global-entertainment-media-outlook-2019-2023.html, accessed 14 May 2020.

Raj, R. and J. Musgrave (2009). *Event Management and Sustainability*. Oxon: CABI Publishing.

RAW Foundation (2018). 'Plastic-Free Festivals Guide', http://rawfoundation.org/making-waves/wp-content/uploads/2018/03/Festival-Guide-20182.pdf, accessed 20 July 2020.

Single Use plastic Banning the Distribution and or Sale of Plastic Straws Stirrers and Plastic Stemmed Cotton Buds in England (2018). https://www.gov.uk/government/consultations/single-use-plastic-banning-the-distribution-andor-sale-of-plastic-straws-stirrers-and-plastic-stemmed-cotton-buds-in-england, accessed 25 July 2020.

UK Government Food Waste Pilot (2018). https://www.gov.uk/government/news/action-to-reduce-food-waste-announced, accessed 20 July 2020.

UK Music (2019). 'Music by Numbers', https://www.ukmusic.org/research/music-by-numbers/, accessed 14 April 2020.

12

Branding and endorsement

The growing importance of branding and the developing legal framework

Emma Harding

Sponsorship and endorsement are becoming increasingly more prevalent in the music industry and offer potential for enhanced earning capacity if woven into strategy. It is widely recognised that an emerging recording artist with an engaged and growing online following on platforms like Spotify and Instagram is of significant value. A strong online following not only helps drive streams, but it also correlates with increased sponsorship and endorsement opportunity, which signifies that having a strong social media presence is an area of growing importance.

This chapter outlines the key legal principles of image rights and it explores the salient terms of most branding agreements. It will ask experts if the ubiquity of social media and commercialisation online have changed artist and management responsibilities regardless of branding aspirations. I investigate why artists are particularly valuable to brands and explains the most common types of branding deals available. Looking to the future, I question if there is a reduced role for a record label.

The confidential nature of branding agreements combined with the reality that disputes rarely go to court (which would then become a matter of public record) means there is a current lack of tangible cases to refer to. Disputes are not uncommon, but the parties usually settle behind closed doors. The lack of public cases means this topic has relatively low visibility to people outside the business. As such, this chapter draws on autoethnographic research gained through working as a lawyer in the UK music industry specialising in endorsement-related matters, and interviews with expert industry practitioners.

Over the last five years working at music law firm SSB Solicitors, I have seen a significant increase in the number of branding deals available and deals being offered to artists much earlier in their career. Furthermore, the deals with high-profile artists have become more complex, evidenced through the level of detail contained within contracts.

Throughout this chapter, the umbrella term 'branding agreement' is used to capture the plethora of licensing arrangements in which an artist can license certain intellectual property rights which may include their name, logo, photo, image, likeness, voice, music and so on, and the perspective is from the artist's unless otherwise specified. The terms 'artist' and 'brand' are used to differentiate between the musician and the advertiser, although it is acknowledged that the musician is also a brand in their own right.

Image rights

'Image rights', sometimes referred to as 'personality rights' or 'publicity rights', are a person's proprietary right in their personality which allows them to control the commercial use of their name, likeness and other personal indicia including physical characteristics associated with them. Image rights are not codified under English and Welsh law like they are in the United States. Instead, in the England and Wales, the unauthorised use of a person's name and image can be actionable by other means including through contract law, trade mark infringement, passing off, defamation and malicious falsehood, breach of confidence, breach of advertising rules and breach of privacy (*Douglas and others v Hello! Ltd and others* 2005). Although the law in England and Wales does not strictly recognise image rights in the same way as the United States, it is the writer's view that this may change in the future as celebrities explore more ways to monetise their image rights.

Key terms of branding agreements

For a branding agreement to function, there needs to be a grant of rights (or a 'licence') between the parties. Artists should set strict parameters around the licence of their image rights and other intellectual property rights granted in the contract. Exercising care and skill when negotiating the contract allows (depending on bargaining position) for an immeasurable amount of freedoms and restrictions to be decided between the parties in whatsoever granular detail they desire. For insight, examples of such granularity may include disallowing certain endorsed products to be reduced by more than half price in a sale, permitting the sale of certain endorsed products to luxury store outlets only, and imposing a cap on the number of times a sponsored post on Instagram can reach the same end-user per day.

Artists may want to consider limiting the brand's use of their image rights to a certain period of time, media (common channels include online, television, radio, out-of-home, on-pack and in-store), territory and a particular campaign or product category (this is especially important if the brand is a large corporation with many subsidiaries or if it sells a variety of products). For example, instead of granting image rights for utilisation in connection with the brand itself, rights could be limited to a specific campaign relating to its fashion range or, more specifically, its sunglasses range. This would in theory keep the artist open in the marketplace for product categories outside of sunglasses.

The 'term' as it is commonly known usually denotes the period in which the licensed rights can be actively and publicly used. Certain post-term rights may be carved out such as a reasonable sell-off period for physical goods or an archival right for historical posts to be kept on a timeline (provided there is no paid amplification post-term). If the term has no cut-off point, the brand could use the licensed rights indefinitely. Not only does this preclude artists from negotiating a better deal to reflect their success and their market value in the future, but it also dissuades competitors from offering the same artists a similar deal in the future. Furthermore, if a campaign proves to be a success and the rights clause is limited, there is room to renegotiate, for example, by extending the term for an additional year. I represent an artist whose branding agent saw the artist's image rights being used on an app, the media of which was not granted in the contract, and she was able to negotiate a sizeable sum from the brand as compensation.

There is a cost applied to each branding deal which not only represents the value of the artist endorsement within that certain product-category space, but it also represents reputational risk, overexposure and dilution of their market value. In an interview with Sarah Hurwitz, Account Director at FUSE, a marketing agency for music partnerships and experiences, Hurwitz explained: 'For an artist who enters into too many deals, their social media channels end up being saturated with sponsored posts and brands consider it unlikely that additional posts will have any cut-through' (Harding and Hurwitz 2020).

In the same interview with Danielle Sammeroff, Director at FUSE, Sammeroff elaborated on the practicalities of limiting media and territory rights in a collaboration agreement:

> For brands, the extra channel cost primarily comes from the synchronisation side and if there needs to be cost saving, consider whether geo-locking content to active markets is possible without negatively impacting the campaign. Limiting the media rights and territory will not significantly change the artist's fee as it ultimately locks them out in the category regardless of focus markets for the campaign. With the nature of the internet it's still possible consumers could come across ad content showing the artist promoting two competitor brands which looks incredibly inauthentic which devalues the partnership. (Harding and Sammeroff 2020)

It is for this reason most branding agreements with a term imposed contain exclusivity obligations to prevent the artist from endorsing two competing brands in the same product category at the same time. The word 'endorsement' can have a very broad interpretation and when defined in the context of an exclusivity obligation, it should not be disproportionate. In its simplest of definitions, it can mean making it publicly known that a person uses or supports a product, service or brand. I was privy to a negotiation which fell apart because the brand's exclusivity clause was too overreaching – the brand insisted that in the hypothetical situation of an artist going to a restaurant with a friend, the artist would need to ensure their friend would not drink a competitor product because that drink's container could be placed on the table. It would be worthwhile to connect the exclusivity obligations to a specific product category and to an exhaustive list of competitors. Be mindful to allow for certain exemptions too such as allowing the artist to attend or perform at events or live shows sponsored by a competitor and allowing the artist to grant synchronisation licences to a competitor.

Artist approvals are often a point of contention in a negotiation. The brand will assume control of the project because it is their campaign, but artist approvals act as a safeguard for the artist to ensure their intellectual property is used in a manner they are happy with, and any services they perform run to their liking. While it is commonly accepted that an artist should have approval right for any photographs and video footage of them, if the artist is in a strong bargaining position, they may require additional approvals. For context examples of approval rights I have seen built into contracts include approval on security and glam personnel, styling, photographers, directors, the storyboard and script of video content, the music used in video content, press releases, slogans, hashtags, the stage design for performances, the packaging and labelling of products, samples of fabric and samples of finished products, point of sale promotions, display advertisements and so on. A client of mine once requested approval on the size range of a fashion line she co-designed and approval on the models used for marketing to ensure they were diverse in race, culture and sizing. Occasionally the brand may request an approval right with respect to any changes made to the artist's appearance.

Social media enables artists to customise how they represent themselves to the world and it allows them to promote their values and interests. If a brand partners with an artist who has a strong identity, it can help manage public perceptions. 'Used in the right way sponsorship can give brands personality and provide physical demonstrations of them living what they breathe' (Wylie 2020). A successful partnership is symbiotic where both parties benefit from the goodwill reputation of the other and share similar associations. The Lewis Capaldi and Greggs partnership (Paradigm 2020) and the Nike and Ellie Goulding partnership (Joseph 2013) exemplify this synergy.

It is therefore unsurprising that in most branding agreements with a term imposed, each party usually asks for a right to terminate the contract if the other party is brought into public disrepute or scandal (this is in addition to customary contract termination rights which can be triggered if a party commits a material breach of contract or if a party ceases trading or becomes insolvent). The brand may ask for the right to terminate if the artist is charged with a criminal offence (historic behaviour already in the public domain, mere behaviour reported in the press or behaviour that offends a small portion of the public should not be regarded as conclusive of such an offence). Interestingly, brands have generally become more supportive of talent involved in political activism and agree that any related criminal charges or negative press should not give rise to termination. In recent years, particularly since the Harvey Weinstein offences came to light and the #metoo movement of 2017, it has become easier to embed an artist termination right into the contract if the brand or an executive of the brand is publicly accused of sexual harassment or discrimination. It was widely reported in 2018 that Beyoncé terminated her joint venture Ivy Park with Sir Philip Green after allegations of racial abuse and sexual harassment (Okwodu 2018). These allegations may have given Beyoncé the right to buy out Green's stake in their co-founded company through a mechanism in their contract. Another ethical rights clause, depending on the type of deal, is assurance from the brand that no child labour is used in the manufacturing process and artists may even obtain in their contract the right to personally inspect factories to ensure working conditions are satisfactory.

The fee, not to be forgotten, is another key term of any branding agreement. An artist can be remunerated in a number of ways, most commonly by way of a flat fee or a gift. Sophie Ellis Bextor received a discount in lieu of payment when she purchased a Danz Spas hot tub (Boffard 2014). As an alternative payment structure, a start-up brand may be inclined to offer the artist equity in lieu of a fee. The Chainsmokers are the biggest non-founder stakeholders in a small batch spirit brand called JaJa Tequila (O'Malley Greenburg 2019). If an artist designs a product range, they would expect to receive a minimum guarantee that will be offset against a share of revenue, which can increase when certain sales thresholds are met. In an interview with Eve Hutson, director of the Brand Department, a business development agency focused on brand licensing, collaborations, franchising, and investment opportunities, Hutson shared her experience: 'Any income over and above the minimum guarantee rewards the artist on the actual success of the product range. Some of these ranges can be really well received and we see them run on for years and even decades' (Harding and Hutson 2020).

The contract should clarify if expenses are inclusive or exclusive of the fee, especially if there is a live performance or if music clearance is required. If music is being licensed, artists should consider if they own the rights to that music or if those rights vest in their publisher and record label. If there is a performance, it may be helpful to liaise with the tour manager to set out the production requirements and costs. It would be sensible to ensure any costs relating to the hospitality rider, travel, accommodation and per diems are paid on top and the appropriate class of travel and accommodation is agreed for the artist and for the crew. Artists may expect a private dressing room with a private toilet and shower in accordance with their hospitality rider and styling, glam and personal security expenses to be paid on top and if so, this should be agreed in writing. Diligent artist managers ask for a substantial amount of the fee to be paid upfront to mitigate the risk of cancellation and to cover expenses.

The value of social media to artists

In an interview with Lily Crockford, Manager at Crockford Management, a management company representing both emerging and legacy talent, Crockford described the prominence of social media in the music world:

Crockford Management, like so many other management companies, has launched a digital agency to serve their clients. It's a full-time job, there are so many platforms, hashtags, handles, there is a constant demand for new content, and it needs to be different every time. The content that's posted on each platform needs to be tailored for that specific platform, every artist now has about six to eight websites. Labels do help with digital marketing but only around a release and it's vital the artist remains active online outside of this to keep traction. We use the data to plan a tour and we use socials to promote a tour, which is more effective than sticking a poster at a venue and hoping fans might see it. As a manager you can use an artist's social following as a negotiating tool, for example I have negotiated better billing for a festival based on following. The more press we lose and the harder it becomes to pitch to radio, the more emphasis there is on social media because there are fewer ways to promote an artist. (Harding and Crockford 2020)

In an interview with Danny Roberts, Head of A&R at MADE Records, Roberts described the benefits from a label perspective if a potential new signing has a strong brand identity and online following:

The A&R process has changed a lot over the years. An A&R can still stumble across a new act in a number of different ways but the first thing 99% of A&Rs will do is scan the artist's socials to build a picture. An A&R can learn a huge amount about the state of a project within five minutes of 'detective work'. Facebook: Is there a team already involved (a manager/ a publicist/ a label)? Instagram: Does the artist have a strong aesthetic with a growing and loyal fanbase? Is there consistent high-level engagement from fans? Is the artist providing different content across different platforms and is the level of engagement genuine? The best ideas normally come from the artist. A label is best when implementing an already established vision so if the artist is already showing signs of this, treating themselves as a brand already, this will always make a positive impression. Having said that, a great song is a great song and artists can be signed without social media traction. (Harding and Roberts 2020)

The value of artists to brands

It is not new for brands to associate themselves with musicians, but it can be deduced that the advent of social media has acted as a catalyst for the upsurge in branding opportunities. An artist's authenticity, credibility and fan base online makes them especially desirable to brands who can use programmatic advertising to reach their target demographic online with accuracy. Not only are paid partnerships useful for a brand to mould their identity, they are cleverly constructed and data-driven and can involve huge sums of investment from the brand. Some artists collaborate with brands in their capacity as social media influencers. In an interview with Elliot MacNay, a specialist in the advertising technology industry, MacNay explained Influencer Marketing:

> Influencer Marketing is where an advertiser will leverage individual influencers or a network of influencers, usually through a platform to promote their products, services and marketing campaigns. Based on the demographics, behaviours and interests of the audiences that the influencers reach, brands can decide which influencers tailor best to the wide range of different audiences with specific attributes based on the needs of the advertiser. For influencers, accessing the audience data is a walk in the park because it's readily available on their Instagram and other social accounts. In fact, all campaign performance insights are readily available on social platforms. The audience-insights cover metrics like clicks, likes, comments, saves and shares. If it's a video: views, completed views, viewability and more. If the advert clicks through to a site where users can purchase, brands can also see what their CPA (cost per acquisition) is for the campaign. Brands also get audience insights for the campaign along with the performance metrics. (Harding and MacNay 2020)

Current scope of branding activities

It is not possible to provide the reader with an exhaustive list of every type of branding deal available because some deals are bespoke, tying in with the unique qualities of the talent, and as technology develops new branding opportunities emerge. An example of a branding opportunity that was not available five years ago is the sponsorship of an existing Spotify-operated playlist. Brian Benedik, Spotify's VP–Global Head of Sales remarked: '[the sponsoring of popular Spotify playlists] makes it easier for [brands] to reach specific types of consumers performing specific activities' (Morrison 2017). Another example is the Tuborg 'Open To More' 2020 campaign which launched an AR filter featuring brand signifiers synchronised with The Chainsmokers' music and had it pushed out to fans for them to share an interactive experience (Elbjørn 2020).

Technological developments have also enabled artists to monetise their image rights themselves without the need to partner with a brand by working with a platform or a developer. For example, in 2017 Jessie Ware started her podcast

'Table Manners with Jessie Ware' (Zoladz 2020), in 2018 Paloma Faith launched an Alexa Skill called 'Bedtime with Paloma' (Palomafaith.com 2018) and in 2019 UB40 launched an app with a premium subscription service (ub40.global 2019).

There is still plenty of money to be made via the more traditional types of branding deals too such as synchronisation licences, product placement and tour sponsorship. Synchronisation licences may increase in frequency and adapt to include new media use such as micro-influencer use and stories use. Product placement in music videos (despite MTV no longer broadcasting music videos on television) is still commonplace and it can fund the production in its entirety.

Product placement is attractive to brands because the placement is not removed after a certain time frame and it enables the brand to become intrinsically linked to pop culture. The Diet Coke product placement in the Lady Gaga – Telephone ft. Beyoncé music video is an example of product placement at its best: creative, innovative and timeless. There is currently no regulation of product placement in the United States. Product placement in television programmes made for UK audiences is regulated (Ofcom.org.uk undated) but product placement in music videos falls outside of the scope of these regulations although this could change as the UK Government is minded to appoint Ofcom as the regulator for Online Harms, and following changes to the Audiovisual Media Services Directive (.gov.uk), Ofcom's role will be expanded to include the regulation of video-sharing platforms.

The sponsorship of tours and events can be hugely beneficial to an artist and may help to cover shortfall in touring income. During the first Covid-19 lockdown in the United States and the United Kingdom brands adapted quickly and began to sponsor artists' live performances on their stories and sometimes even posted to them backdrops featuring their brand logo. Country singer Morgan Wallen livestreamed a Jack Daniels concert on his Facebook and Instagram pages (Hespen, 2020) and Triller hosted the 'Co-Triller' festival online which garnered far-reaching press (Bossi 2020). In an interview with Andy Bibey, Director of New Pin Management and Touring, Bibey commented:

> Artists directly benefit from brands sponsoring their live shows and tours, which could include signage rights, sponsored meet and greets and VIP experiences. These large sponsors offer an alternative revenue stream that can strengthen the overall tour income. (Harding and Bibey 2020)

The Harley Davidson sponsorship of The Struts' 2020 tour is a striking example of an effective sponsorship and very rock 'n' roll. Frontman Luke Spiller drove the new Harley Davidson electric motorcycle onto the stage (Buban 2020).

Another type of branding agreement is an 'appearance' agreement. The artist may be offered an incentive to attend or perform at an event or it may be requested by a brand as a deliverable as part of a wider collaboration arrangement. Examples of private events include presenting at a corporate conference or singing 'Happy Birthday' at a party. Examples of public events include attending a fashion show, a product launch or an afterparty, and perhaps posting about it too or being photographed outside. In 2012 Rihanna made headlines for earning £5 million for turning on the Christmas lights at Westfield shopping centre, Stratford (Renshaw 2012).

An endorsement deal commonly means a short-term, one-off endorsement arrangement which may involve the artist wearing or using a brand's product for a public appearance or posting about it on their social media account. Where artists are required to endorse a product or service on their social media account which they have been paid for, gifted or otherwise incentivised, it is necessary they disclose the commercial nature of the endorsement to their followers clearly and prominently (asa.org.uk undated). This is usually achieved by tagging a post as '#ad' or as a paid partnership. If obvious disclosures are not given by the artist, the artist may be breaching consumer protection law for misleading the public, violating the social media platform T&Cs and breaking advertising regulations. The branding agreement usually requires the artist to make certain disclosures, too, because if the brand has editorial control over the content, they become liable for that post too (asa.org.uk 2020).

In the United States, the Federal Trade Commission is empowered to prohibit unfair and deceptive advertising. In the UK, the Competition and Markets Authority (CMA), Trading Standards/ The Department for the Economy in Northern Ireland and the industry regulator Ofcom (who delegates to The Advertising Standards Authority (ASA) for the regulation of online advertising through the CAP Code) are empowered to protect the public from unfair and deceptive advertising practices. In 2019 the CMA launched a public investigation into disclosures from celebrities and required them to sign undertakings that they would abide by practices against misleading advertising (gov.uk 2019).

In 2018, a Snapchat post by DJ Khaled prompted US organisation The Truth in Advertising Inc. along with other advocacy groups to publish an open letter to his legal representatives. The letter argued:

> By marketing alcohol to the millions of minors who follow DJ Khaled on social media, he and his sponsors are violating the policies and procedures put in place by social media platforms to ensure such content is not shown to those under the age of 21, as well as self-regulatory agency codes. . . . The deceptive impact and societal harm resulting from these risky and irresponsible ads cannot be overstated. (The Truth In Advertising Inc. 2018)

Another type of branding agreement is a 'collaboration' agreement also sometimes referred to as a 'brand ambassador' agreement. These usually include a term of engagement exclusivity and numerous deliverables. In the interview with Eve Hutson, Director of the Brand Agency, Eve explained:

> A brand ambassador agreement is usually a straight up fee-based relationship where the artist is paid to promote a product for a set period of time. They are photographed or filmed with the product, the assets are used as part of TV, print or digital campaigns and this is often supplemented by social media and sometimes also personal appearances to which consumers, press and key retail buyers are invited. In some instances, we see an additional element to the relationship where the artist is seen to design their own product which is part of the range but not frequently. (Harding and Hutson 2020)

An example of this type of partnership is Dua Lipa's appointment as YSL's Beauty Fragrance Ambassador (Rodulfo 2019). In an interview with Nicola Langley, Account Manager at FUSE, we discussed common deliverables in collaboration agreements. Langley commented:

> Service days are usually a key requirement. If this is the case the contract should specify the number of days required, the length of the day, the location and timing and specifics on glam and styling. The length of a service day is usually exclusive of time for travel and glam/grooming and styling though this may be a negotiation point with the artist. Other deliverables can include social posts, press commitments, personal appearance commitments, live shows, interviews, artist quotes and fan experiences. (Harding and Langley 2020)

A more multifaceted type of branding agreement is one where the artist is involved in the design process of a product range. 'The artist helps to design a product their followers will aspire to own, working with the brand to ensure its commerciality to manufacture, and appeal against trend forecasting and so on' (Harding and Hutson 2020). This will be supplemented with key commitments such as promoting the product range on social media, attending a launch and participating in press activities. An example of this type of partnership is the capsule of backpacks that Zayn Malik designed for The Kooples (GQ 2018).

'Investor' agreements are more complex still. They may require the artist to invest their own money to create a new business as a long-term investment vehicle which could be jointly owned with an investor or owned by the artist and licensed to an investor. If the artist has equity in the company, it is likely they will go the extra mile to promote it. An example of this type of arrangement is the Kanye West Yeezy shoe line. It is reported West owns 100 per cent of Yeezy and Adidas is is responsible for the production, marketing and distribution of the shoes (Forbes 2020). Forbes reported:

> West receives a royalty around 15% of Yeezy revenue from Adidas. Upon closer inspection, it appears some expenses are carved out of that slice, bringing his actual cut closer to 11%. At that rate, he would have received royalties of over $140 million from Yeezy sales last year. (O'Malley Greenburg undated)

By comparison, Bloomberg reported: 'West's entire music catalogue – from 'The College Dropout' to 'Jesus is King' and everything in between – is worth about $110.5 million' (Alexander and Bhasin 2020).

While West's situation is extraordinary, branding deals are not exclusive to superstars. For example, in 2019 The House of Vans elected to partner with Loyle Carner (Byers 2019), who is known primarily for his music rather than being in the media spotlight.

What is the future? Is there a reduced role for the record label?

The nature of social media as a global direct-to-fan database coupled with an artist's ability to create and distribute content online at relatively low cost has undoubtedly made it easier for an artist to self-release and make a living this way. Music managers have explained to me their artists feel pressure to develop a strong online following to seek branding opportunities and to promote their music. However, gaining traction online is not easy for everyone and having an agent or a label to help navigate the complexities of social media and its algorithms can be valuable. It follows there is still a hunger for the expertise and funding a label has to offer and even if the artist has had some success on their own, it's likely a label can scale that.

Major record labels have expanded their branding departments in recent years, which signifies they foresee sponsorship and endorsement as a growing area for modern day recording artists, whether it's through product placement, sponsorship, endorsement or utilising new technology like podcasting or vodcasting to capitalise on the artist's existing fan base. In 2018 Sony Music UK launched 4th Floor Creative as a new division comprising brand partnerships, sync, visual creative, digital and audience development and podcasting (sonymusic.co.uk undated). It is widely accepted that if an artist signs a major label record deal, they would be expected to pay the label a passive share of ancillary income (such as merchandise income, branding income and live) and appoint the label as their non-exclusive representative for procuring branding deals. Potential branding income is a key factor when labels forecast a new signing and sometimes one branding deal can swing the balance on an artist's profit and loss account. For a label, receiving a passive share of branding income is particularly attractive because the income does not recoup against an advance and it is perceived as direct income.

Conclusion

Macro-economic changes in technology have changed the way music is consumed and by the same token, as observed in this chapter, technological developments bring new and more frequent sponsorship and endorsement opportunities. This chapter has highlighted the importance for an artist and their team to understand the scope of branding opportunities available, to tailor each deal to complement the artist's values, music career and ecosystem, and to negotiate terms strategically in order to maximise branding revenue potential.

There is every indication that branding agreements will continue to develop in chorus with technology and may continue to serve as an additional revenue stream for artists and labels. Consequently, it will continue to be an area of growth for some time to come.

References

Alexander, S. and K. Bhasin (2020). 'Kanye West Vaults from Broke to Billions with Yeezy in Demand', 24 April 2020, www.bloomberg.com/news/articles/2020-04-24/kanye-west-vaults-from-broke-to-billions-with-yeezy-in-demand.

ASA.org.uk (Undated). 'An Influencer's Guide to Making Clear that Ads Are Ads', undated, www.asa.org.uk/uploads/assets/uploaded/3af39c72-76e1-4a59-b2b47e81a034cd1d.pdf

ASA.org.uk (2020). 'Recognising Ads: Advertisement Features', 5 February 2020, www.asa.org.uk/advice-online/recognising-ads-advertisement-features.html, accessed 10 August 2020.

Boffard, R. (2014). 'The Value of Celebrity Endorsements', BBC, 11 December 2014, www.bbc.co.uk/news/business-30392829, accessed 10 August 2020.

Bossi, A. (2020). 'Migos, Marshmello and Others to Perform For Triller's Upcoming Digital Music Festival', *Forbes*, 2 April 2020, https://www.forbes.com/sites/andreabossi/2020/04/02/migos-marshmello-and-others-to-perform-for-trillers-upcoming-digital-music-festival/#5eb832d46c9e, accessed on 10 August 2020.

Buban, G. (2020). 'Getting up to Speed with Luke Spiller before The Struts Roar into their Tour de California', *Digital Beat Mag*, 7 February 2020, www.digitalbeatmag.com/getting-up-to-speed-with-luke-spiller-before-the-struts-roar-into-their-tour-de-california, accessed 10 August 2020.

Byers, R. (2019). 'The South London Rapper on His New Album and Launch Last Night at House of Vans', *Wonder Land*, 19 April 2019, www.wonderlandmagazine.com/2019/04/19/loyle-carner-album-interview/, accessed 10 August 2020.

DCMS (2020a). 'Department for Digital, Culture, Media & Sport, Online Harms White Paper', 12 February 2020, www.gov.uk/government/consultations/online-harms-white-paper/online-harms-white-paper, accessed 10 August 2020.

DCMS (2020b). 'Department for Digital, Culture, Media & Sport, Requirements for Video Sharing Platforms in the Audiovisual Media Services Directive', 24 July 2019, www.gov.uk/government/consultations/requirements-for-video-sharing-platforms-in-the-audiovisual-media-services-directive, accessed 10 August 2020.

Douglas and others v Hello! Ltd and others (2005). EWCA Civ 595.

Elbjørn, K. (2020). 'Tuborg Open Returns with The Chainsmokers to Help Fans across the World Discover Exciting New Music', 1 July 2020, www.carlsberggroup.com/newsroom/tuborg-open-returns-with-the-chainsmokers-to-help-fans-across-the-world-discover-exciting-new-music/, accessed 10 August 2020.

Forbes (2020). 'The World's Highest-Paid Celebrities', *Forbes*, www.forbes.com/profile/kanye-west/#146daa4956f1, accessed 10 August 2020.

Gov.uk (2019). Federal Trade Commission Act, Incorporating U.S. SAFE WEB Act amendments of 2006, Competition and Markets Authority, 'Celebrities pledge to clean up their act on social media', 23 January 2019, www.gov.uk/government/news/celebrities-pledge-to-clean-up-their-act-on-social-media, accessed 10 August 2020.

GQ (2018). 'You Need these Ultracool Zayn Malik-Designed Bags', *GQ*, 19 September 2018, www.gq-magazine.co.uk/article/bc/you-need-these-ultracool-zayn-malik-designed-bags, accessed 10 August 2020.

Harding, E. and A. Bibey (2020). *Tour Sponsorship Explained*. Interview: Unpublished.

Harding, E. and L. Crockford (2020). *If An Artist Releases a Record and There Is No One Following Them Online to Hear It, Does It Make a Sound?* Interview: Unpublished.

Harding, E. and S. Hurwitz (2020). *Discussing Key Terms of Branding Deals.* Interview: Unpublished.

Harding, E. and E. Hutson (2020). *Discussing Branding Deals.* Interview: Unpublished.

Harding, E. and N. Langley (2020). *Discussing Branding Deals.* Interview: Unpublished.

Harding, E. and E. MacNay (2020). *Influencer Marketing and Ad Tech Explained.* Interview: Unpublished.

Harding, E. and D. Roberts (2020). *How Important Is Social Media for an Artist?* Interview: Unpublished.

Harding, E. and D. Sammeroff (2020). *Discussing Key Terms of Branding Deals.* Interview: Unpublished.

Hespen, M. (2020). 'Morgan Wallen Facebook Live Friday Night', *979 Kick FM*, 21 May 2020, https://979kickfm.com/morgan-wallen-facebook-live-friday-night/, accessed 10 August 2020.

Joseph, S. (2013). 'Nike and Ellie Goulding Unite to Inspire Runners', 16 April 2013, https://www.marketingweek.com/nike-and-ellie-goulding-unite-to-inspire-runners/, accessed 10 August 2020.

Morrison, M. (2017). 'Spotify Opens Its Popular Playlists to Sponsors', *AdAge*, 26 May 2017, www.adage.com/article/digital/spotify-expands-ad-formats-sponsored-playlists/304174, accessed 10 August 2020.

Ofcom (Undated). 'Product Placement on TV', *Ofcom*, www.ofcom.org.uk/tv-radio-and-on-demand/advice-for-consumers/television/product-placement-on-tv.

Ofcom (2016). 'Guidance Notes, Section Nine: Commercial References in Television Programming', *Ofcom*, 20 May 2016, https://www.ofcom.org.uk/__data/assets/pdf_file/0014/33611/section9_may16.pdf, accessed 10 August 2020.

Okwodu, J. (2018). 'Beyoncé Makes a Stand for #MeToo by Cutting Ties With Topshop', *Vogue*, 16 November 2018, www.vogue.com/article/beyonce-buys-out-ivy-park-topshop-owner-philip-green-me-too, accessed 10 August 2020.

O'Malley Greenburg, Z. (2019). 'Chainsmokers On Fire: The World's Highest-Paid DJs Are Spinning Celebrity Into A Rock-Star Portfolio', *Forbes*, 6 December 2019, www.forbes.com/sites/zackomalleygreenburg/2019/12/06/chainsmokers-on-fire-the-worlds-highest-paid-djs-are-spinning-celebrity-into-a--rockstar-portfolio/#564008764eb1, accessed 10 August 2020.

O'Malley Greenburg, Z. (undated). 'Kanye West Is Now Officially a Billionaire and He Really wants the World to Know', www.forbes.com/sites/zackomalleygreenburg/2020/04/24/kanye-west-is-now-officially-a-billionaireand-he-really-wants-the-world-to-know/#6c9f17e97b9e, accessed 10 August 2020.

Palomafaith.com (2018). 'Paloma's Bedtime', 3 January 2018, https://www.palomafaith.com/palomas-bedtime/. accessed 10 August 2020.

Paradigm (2020). 'Case Study: Lewis Capaldi and Greggs', *Paradigm*, www.paradigmagency.com/files/Lewis.Capaldi.Case.Study.pdf, accessed 10 August 2020.

Renshaw, D. (2012). 'Rihanna to earn £5m for Pushing a Button', *NME*, 16 October 2012, www.nme.com/news/music/rihanna-173-1252391, accessed 10 August 2020.

Rodulfo, K. (2019). 'Dua Lipa Is The New Face Of YSL Fragrance', 4 June 2019, https://www.elle.com/beauty/a27716098/dua-lipa-ysl-beauty-ambassador/, accessed 10 August 2020.

Sony Music (Undated). '4th Floor Creative', https://www.sonymusic.co.uk/label/4th-floor-creative/, accessed 10 August 2020.

Truth In Advertising (2018). www.truthinadvertising.org/wp-content/uploads/2018/03/3_29_18-Ltr-re-Khaled-Deceptive-Advertising_Redacted.pdf, accessed 10 August 2020.

UB40.global (2019). 'Be the First to See Our Brand New UB40 App!!', *UB40 The Official Site*, 21 February 2019, https://ub40.global/news/updates/be-the-first-to-see-our-brand-new-ub40-app/201902875/, accessed 10 August 2020.

Wylie, C. (2020). 'The Power of Purpose – Sponsorship's Missing Pillar', 24 June 2020, www.sponsorship.org/the-power-of-purpose-sponsorships-missing-pillar, accessed 10 August 2020.

Zoladz, L. (2020). 'How Jessie Ware Cooked Her Way Into a Musical Fantasy', *New York Times*, 22 June 2020, https://www.nytimes.com/2020/06/22/arts/music/jessie-ware-whats-your-pleasure-table-manners.html, accessed 10 August 2020.

13

The artist/manager relationship

Jules O'Riordan, a.k.a. Judge Jules, and Les Gillon

The relationship between an artist and manager is typically a complex and multi-dimensional one. The different layers of this relationship may well include the personal, the financial, the psychological, artistic and commercial aspects of their collaboration, with all of those different interacting layers operating within an overarching contractual framework. Geoffrey Hull indicates some of the key attributes and areas of management activity, particularly in the case of artists in the early stages of their careers.

> Personal managers are in charge of developing all aspects of a performer's career. To that end they must possess good 'people skills' to be able to work closely with the artist and others in all of the income streams. They must also possess significant knowledge of the industry and have contacts within the industry to be able to create the kinds of opportunities that the artist needs to develop a significant career. In the early stages the personal manager will work with the artist to develop a good live act and performance, giving the performer feedback and constructive criticism. (Hull 2011: 147)

In the first part of this chapter we examine this relationship and the legal context that has developed in support of its operation within business models forged in the popular music industry of the post-war twentieth century.

In the second part of the chapter we look at the evolving nature of the relationship between artist and manager in the twenty-first century. Specifically, we consider the way that technological innovations in music dissemination and forms of consumption within the music industry have led to the adoption of new roles and areas of activity in music industry management.

Part one: The management agreement

The complexity of the relationship between artist and manager underlines the need for it to be framed within a clear and comprehensive management agreement. A recognition of the delicate power balance between artist and manager forms the backdrop to the overall negotiation of a management agreement: while it is protecting the manager's interest, it is also clarifying certain very important points from the artist's perspective. While the popular image of the music manager has sometimes been of a rapacious exploiter of the naïve artist, that is very much a residual caricature with its roots in the early years of the rock and pop industry. At that time, music industry figures such as Allen Klein (Goodman 2015) and 'Colonel' Tom Parker (Nash 2003), with their reputations for intimidation and psychological manipulation, enjoyed shares of artist income that would be unthinkable today. Such figures may still loom large in the public imagination, but those stereotypes do not reflect the reality of music management in the twenty-first century.

In fact, the power equilibrium between artist and manager is more of a balancing act and the negotiation of a management agreement is vital in order to protect the interest of the manager. Unlike the artist, managers own no intellectual property: instead, they are dependent on 'selling' their professional services to their clients in return for commission. Typically, when a manager takes on a new artist, there is a bedding-in period before any contract is signed, of perhaps three to six months, after which it is commonplace for a lawyer to draft a contract on behalf of the manager.

When a draft contract is presented to an artist, it has almost invariably been drafted by the manager's lawyer, rather than originating from the artist or their representative. However, experienced managers recognise that it is important for the artist to be legally represented at this point. Without the safeguard of independent legal advice, the legal principle of undue influence might allow the artist to challenge the validity of the management agreement, as it could be argued that the manager used their position of greater knowledge and power to make the artist sign an agreement that was not in the artist's best interests.

For that reason, legal representation of the artist is essential, particularly in cases where the artist may be relatively inexperienced. It would be very unwise for a manager to allow their artist to negotiate the management contract on their own, because of possible non- enforceability of a contract down the line. If no third-party lawyer were involved, it might allow the artist to exercise a right to apply to the courts to walk away from the contract at some future point. A court may well decide that in such a situation, the manager is in the position of exercising undue influence, as in the case of *O'Sullivan v Management Agency and Music Limited* (1985).

Of course, specialist music industry legal representation cannot be bought cheaply and artists at the start of their careers may well be relatively impoverished. The UK Musicians' Union offers very basic legal advice to members, but experienced managers will usually offer to make a contribution of a capped amount towards the costs incurred by the artist for legal representation in management contract negotiations. The payment would generally be recoupable from the artist's future income from the entertainment industry.

This may seem altruistic on the part of the manager, but it is actually in their own best interests, as it guarantees that the artist gets the contract properly negotiated, thereby creating a robust agreement that is less vulnerable to future legal challenge.

The most lengthy strands of back-and-forth between the parties involved in the negotiation of a management agreement are typically the management term duration and the 'deductibles'.

The management 'term' is the period during which the manager is the artist's exclusive manager. The term duration of a management agreement is typically two to five years, depending on how developed an artist's career is at the date of signing, and therefore how much speculative chance the manager is taking. The negotiation of the term is reflective of a risk and reward scenario; the more unknown an artist is, the more there is a moral and commercial justification for the manager having a longer period of time over which to make a success of that artist's career. The reality is that, as good a talent spotter as a manager might be, in truth there are so many variables (and, indeed, so much luck) involved in whether an artist goes on to be successful. Therefore, where an artist's career is less developed, a longer management term is reasonable. Consequently, it is commercially normal for at least a three-year management term to be negotiated with an unknown artist: some may consider that to be the bare minimum and may push for a five-year term. In the case of a particularly experienced and well-connected manager who stands a greater chance of making the right strategic decisions for advancing the artist's career, it could be argued that there is even greater commercial justification for the contract term to be longer. Of course, the management term must be seen in the context of the rights of the artist. A manager will struggle to hold an artist to their contract against their will, in restraint of trade, but a fair and well-drafted management agreement acts as powerful leverage for the manager in settlement negotiations.

One eventuality that could potentially trigger termination on the part of the artist arises from the fact that management agreements are frequently not between an artist and a named person, but between an artist and a management corporate entity, that is, a management company. From a contractual perspective, a company is considered a person in the same way that a human being is considered a person. However, from the perspective of the artist, it is unlikely that the company enticed the artist through the door and persuaded them to sign up. That relationship will have been forged and maintained by an individual within the company. Consequentially, management agreements often contain 'key person'[1] clauses that tie the relationship to a named individual who is the artist's de facto manager.

It becomes more complicated if the person who enticed the artist on board is an employee of the company rather than a director. A departing employee could trigger termination on the part of the artist. Therefore, a management agreement should insist that somebody whose connection to the company is more permanent, such as a director or a founder of the company, is identified as a key person (or at least one of the key persons) within the contract.

If there is a significant personnel change within the management company, there are other legal factors to consider. If the leaving staff member is an employee and has been the person with whom the artist has had a relationship, then the likelihood is that under the staff member's employment contract there will be some form of restrictive covenant preventing them from taking artists away.

In such a case, the management company could enforce their restrictive covenant against their former employee to prevent them from poaching their artist, but there are a lot of legal constraints around restrictive covenants. Such restrictions must be reasonable, proportionate and not amount to restraint of trade as seen in *Esso Petroleum Co Ltd. v Harper's Garage (Stourport) Ltd.* [1968]. As a general legal principle, restrictive covenants are unlikely to be enforceable if they last longer than six months and the broader an impact they have on the restricted party, the less likely they are to be upheld by the courts. Nonetheless, a management company faced with potentially losing their artists might understandably be keen to enforce relevant restrictive covenants, even in

---

[1] Key person clauses mean that if the particular person who is the effective day-to-day manager of the artist leaves the management company, then the artist would be entitled to terminate the term of agreement.

the case of an artist who was not of huge commercial value to the company; as such a defection might lead to a loss of face and create a problematic precedent.

Other major elements to be settled in the management agreement are the 'deductibles', namely the costs that can be offset by the artist against the manager's commissionable income. The rate of commission which a UK music manager would expect to receive is typically 20 per cent of the artist's gross income, minus fixed deductions of pre-agreed expenses for all income streams except live performances. Live commission is charged on touring profit, for reasons we will explore later. (It is important to note that in the United States, different approaches to the management term, fees and deductions apply). There is inevitably extensive negotiation to be undertaken in order to reach a position in the management agreement regarding which artist costs can be offset before the management charges commission upon that gross income.

In relation to income streams such as songwriting, recording of tracks, endorsements and other commercial opportunities, without some degree of control within the management agreement, there would be no limit to the costs which could be offset by the artist against artist income before calculating the management commission. For example, if an artist decides that they wants to boost their brand image or break into new markets by engaging hugely expensive PR companies or social media companies, it would be an expense that is not necessarily reasonable for the manager to stand behind before receiving their fee. The frequently accepted position in management agreement negotiations is that such expenses would not reasonably be included as 'deductibles'. The possible exception might be artists self-releasing their own records, as opposed to those signed by a record label. Sometimes, artist lawyers negotiating management agreements get lost in a jungle of fighting the corner of their artist clients without looking at the commercial realities of being a manager. In order for a manager to earn £20,000 a year, which is a relatively modest income, their artist needs to be making a profit of £100,000. The number of artists in the UK (or, indeed, in the world) who are making that amount of money is fairly limited.

In some cases, management contracts may specifically ring-fence certain areas of the artist's career as sitting outside the management agreement. This is likely to happen only in the case of artists who have a particular pre-existing strength in a certain area; for example, they may have side-line businesses that they run themselves for which they feel that they do not require management involvement, nor pay the commission associated with it. As we will see in the second part of this chapter, the new digital music industry landscape has increasingly led to the establishment of artist-run labels. Consequently, this kind of ring-fencing arrangement may become more common as musicians become more entrepreneurial in their approach to their careers. Paul Pacifico, CEO of the Association of Independent Music argues that 'artists today are pretty much by definition music entrepreneurs and owner-operated companies, building their businesses and their brands' (Coleman 2018). One of the most visible aspects of this new entrepreneurialism is the phenomenon of artists running their own record labels. In the second part of the chapter, we discuss the implications of this for the relationship between artist and manager, and its impact on the structure of management agreements.

In UK management contracts, revenues from live performance are the exception to the general rule that management commission is levied on the artist's gross income. Live commission is charged on touring profit. This is because, as we have seen, for other income streams there are many justifiable questions about which expenses can be deducted from gross earnings. In the case of live performance and touring, the categories of costs that can be incurred are finite and fairly straightforward: travel, accommodation, backline,[2] booking agent's fees and possibly a tour manager, or merchandising costs. However, a management agreement may include wording intended to introduce a degree of proportionality to these. For example, the agreement may stipulate that travel costs to live performances have to be 'reasonable'; if artists choose to fly first-class around the world when their gross touring fees do not justify the expense, then it would not be proportionate to offset the cost of first-class flights. Contractual wording of that nature may be useful in controlling profligacy, but in general there is little dispute about what categories of touring costs can be deducted. Apart from reasonableness of travel costs, another key area for discussion might be commissioning of monies withheld by overseas taxation authorities as withholding taxes for foreign performances, but that perhaps falls more within the realm of accountancy than law. Overall, negotiating a management agreement frequently requires extensive discussion between the representatives of the two parties, but the resultant management agreement should, once signed, bring an end to any conversation about what is deductible in the calculation of commissionable income.

The manager has a fiduciary duty to act in the artist's best interests. This is a default position under common law, but it is also frequently set out in

---

[2] 'Backline' refers to on-stage amplification or other musical equipment used in live performance.

the management agreement. It is not necessarily the position under common law that the manager has to act in the artist's best interests in a general sense, but it is certainly the case that the management must act in the artist's best interest from a financial perspective. So, for example, the payment of excessive fees to an associated or subsidiary company might breach that duty as in the case of *Elton John v Dick James Music & This Record Company* [1991]. As we consider the current evolutionary trends in the artist–manager relationship in the second part of the chapter, this theme becomes more complex, but without explicit agreement regarding a more collaborative business partnership, it might be a breach of the manager's fiduciary duties towards the artist to in any way profit from a transaction in which the manager purported to be independent.

As Millet L. J. commented in a judgement regarding fiduciary duty:

> Where the fiduciary [manager] deals with his principal [artist], in such a case he must prove affirmatively that the transaction is fair and that in the course of the negotiations he made full disclosure of all facts material to the transaction.
>
> It is therefore essential that the pitfalls and possible conflict of interest in a manager's involvement in his artist's career beyond a commission entitlement are fully negotiated and outlined in the management agreement. (*Mothew v Bristol and West Building Society: Respondant* [1996])

This area of fiduciary duty is one that we will return to, as we consider the evolving and expanding role of management in the new digital music industry landscape.

Another key third-party role in an artist's career is that of the booking agent. There are a limited number of managers who serve as booking agent as well as manager. Such cases are relatively rare (although it is the case for one of the authors of this chapter, in his role as an artist). Where the dual manager/agent role occurs, there are interesting conversations to be had about what would represent a reasonable level of commission. Typically, a booking agent charges a commission of 10 per cent to 15 per cent of gross income, while a management commission is frequently 20 per cent of net touring income. This raises the problem of how to combine those two commission entitlements and reach a fair and comfortable middle ground. Establishing a mutually agreeable rate of commission is not the only reason why the combined manager and agent roles happen only rarely. In certain jurisdictions, for example the United States, agents need to be licensed, and most management agreements specifically disclaim the fact that the manager is serving as a booking agent, because they are not licensed to do so.

Part two: Novel forms of artist/manager relationship

So far, we have described long-standing elements of the relationship between artist and manager, negotiated and then detailed within the management agreement. However, disruptive technology, which has shaped popular music in the digital age, has provoked a change and expansion of the roles of music managers, as increasing numbers of artists 'self-release', rather than being signed to a record label. The Music Managers Forum (2019) report, *Managing Expectations*, based on a survey of more than 180 managers, found that many had taken on roles that in the past had been performed solely by record labels; 65 per cent managed PR and promotion and 76 per cent oversaw social media for their artists. In addition, 74 per cent had invested their own money in clients' careers. Increasingly, it appears that managers are becoming both financial patrons and record label administrators for their artists.

Historically, and up until a decade ago, the only conduit for artists to get their music to market was a record label, whether it was one of the major labels or a small 'indie'. A label provides a comprehensive set of services for the artist, doing everything from coordinating the recording of the tracks to delivery of the master recordings, and in many cases providing a recording budget as well. The label will also have an A&R function so that the artist has a point of contact within the label who will help in the development of their recording career, plus a marketing department to promote and advertise the records. In return, the traditional record company business model is for the label to retain between 70 per cent and 80 per cent of the proceeds and for the artist to receive between 20 per cent or 30 per cent, although certain smaller labels, who are less able to offer advances or large marketing budgets, operate on a 'net receipts' profit share basis.

However, with the evolution of the new digital music market, an alternative means of getting recorded music to market emerged. 'Label Services' providers developed out of the distribution companies historically used by labels to get physical products (CDs and vinyl) to wholesalers and into shops. As digital music consumption expanded, those companies increasingly began to provide services for artists who were releasing records independently of a record label. Some of the first artists to successfully take advantage of this alternative model were heritage acts; household name artists such as Kylie Minogue or the Pet Shop Boys, whose records would receive significant 'fan love', but who were not necessarily highly valued by record labels that were more focused on younger or newer artists. Because such artists have a well-established and often very loyal fan base, self-releasing via label services was a viable option. Indeed, for an artist with an established fan base there is a powerful commercial advantage to releasing via label services. While the traditional record label deal typically involves an 80/20 split in favour of the record company, a label services deal reverses that split, with the artist receiving 80 per cent of the proceeds.

If heritage acts led the way in releasing their material via label service deals, then they were swiftly followed by others, some of whom saw it not only as a commercially savvy option, but also as a political statement of creative independence. For UK black music artists in the grime genre, who had often worked within collectives and developed fan bases from pirate radio and YouTube, the option of independence was a good fit – Skepta being a notable example. In 2005, he founded Boy Better Know as a record label with his brother, in order to release his own material and tracks by collaborators. Enormous success followed. Since then, the model has become increasingly common in the UK black music market and other key genres such as dance music and indie rock have followed suit.

This change has enormous implications for the relationship between artist and manager, and for the management agreements that formalise those relationships. While the label services entity takes a much smaller cut of the artist's income, the corollary is that they offer a less comprehensive set of services than a traditional record company. At their most basic level, they simply upload the artist's music to all the digital portals (Spotify, Apple Music, Deezer etc.). At the other end of the scale are label services entities like the Orchard, ADA and AWAL Plus that have developed into a hybrid of digital distributor and record label, with in-house marketing teams and recoupable marketing budgets for those artists whom they choose to actively support. Nevertheless, even in those comparatively rare cases, the artist receives much less support, staffing and infrastructure in releasing their records than they would receive under a traditional record company deal.

That effectively places the burden of running a record label entirely upon the artist, and though artists may be good at making records, it does not necessarily follow that they are good at running a record label or good at 'the music business' in general.

> Since an artist needs time for his core competencies, music making and performing, it makes sense to get support from professional management, if this is affordable. Instead of the former long-time relationship with a record label, artists can now enter shorter-term collaborations with record companies as well as with other partners in the value-added network. Since the artist is centre stage in the new digitized music economy, she or he can benefit from very different income streams, as pointed out above. In this respect, music making is a 360-degree task in the early twenty-first century that covers economic and legal aspects in addition to the core artistic competencies. (Tshmuck 2016: 26)

As Tshmuck points out, in this complex digital music economy, the need for professional management is important, particularly for artists whose talents lie elsewhere. And when an artist is in need of someone within their orbit who would be good at running the record label, the manager is the obvious first port of call.

It is important to point out the enormity of the task of running a record label, should the manager agree to take on that role: namely, the challenge of successfully releasing and marketing a record in a digital music market overflowing with products. In April 2019, Spotify founder Daniel Ek told investors that there were more than 50 million tracks available on Spotify and that the number was growing by nearly 40,000 per day. He added: 'In Quarter 1, we saw a 20% increase in the number of artists streamed on our platform year-over-year and a 29% increase in the number of artists with at least 100,000 listeners' (Ingham 2019). The role of record label boss is demanding, time-consuming, and requires very good contacts and a high level of commercial expertise.

This extension of the manager's role into that of effectively being a record label boss raises questions about whether the manager should be rewarded differently to the commission-based remuneration that we have described up to this point. Arguably, there are two ways in which managers can reasonably be rewarded for taking on this kind of work, containing activities that are over and above their normal duties. One is an increase in commission and the other is receipt of longer-term equity in the intellectual property of the label.

Where an increase in commission is to be the means by which the manager is recompensed for the extra work involved in running a label, it would be unreasonable to suggest that a manager should get an across-the-board increase in commission on artist activities. Rather, the increase in commission should be directly related to the income from the record label, given that this is where the extra work is being undertaken.

As label management is a fairly new addition to the portfolio of possible tasks a manager might be asked to perform, not every manager will identify it as a likely scenario at the point when the management agreement is being negotiated. But a manager should certainly address the issue before they get actively involved in the running of a record label. Unless a clear basis is negotiated and agreed before any 'label running' work is undertaken by the manager, it will likely be difficult for the manager to change the commission basis retrospectively.

Another impact of the move to a label services arrangement is the way it might affect permitted 'deductibles' in management commission calculation. If a manager is commissioning on label services released records, then it is reasonable for the artist to deduct those expenses that are directly associated with the release of those records. There are only a limited number of categories of record label expenses, and one of the most significant outlays relates to marketing costs. However, it is necessary to draw a clear distinction between defined label-related costs and those of any, more 'general' artist marketing, PR or branding, which would potentially benefit the artist well beyond the term of the management agreement, so a clear distinction needs to be established between marketing costs of the label and marketing expenses related to the artist.

The second possible way of recompensing the manager for being a label boss is through a share in the intellectual property rights of the record label. Given their investment of additional time over and above the services a manager would traditionally have provided, there is a strong argument for a higher rate of commission, but perhaps less of a case for shared ownership of intellectual property. However, it is a different situation when a manager makes a financial investment, be it in the record label or, indeed, in some other aspect of the artist's career relating to recordings. As we have seen, many managers, if not bankrolling their artists, end up at least contributing to the costs of making recordings. Sometimes a manager will provide financial support in the form of a loan which may, subject to the terms of the management agreement, be repayable on demand. However, the reality of the situation may be the impossibility of extracting payment from an artist who has no resources to repay the loan. If, under a label services arrangement, a manager is actually contributing to the cost of running a business and sharing some of the consequent risk, then there is an argument for the manager to have some degree of ownership, that is, longer-term equity in the intellectual property of its recordings, or at least a longer-term income right in recordings exploited by the label.

Such an arrangement could potentially be more beneficial to a manager than the traditional 'sunset clause', under which intellectual property created during the managerial term is still commissionable after the contract has terminated. A sunset clause relates to, among other things, artist compositions that have been written and recordings that have been made during the management term, released and/or first commercially exploited during that term, or within a limited period afterwards. In many European agreements the sunset period is often five or six years at full 20 per cent rate of commission followed by five or six years at half rate of commission. But, depending on the relationship between the parties and what was negotiated, in a scenario where the manager took on the role of label boss in return for some ownership of copyright, there would be no percentage tail-off, and the manager would enjoy a much longer-term right to income in relation to that copyright. Such a longer-term approach is not unprecedented, as in the United States there are instances of managers insisting upon a right to commission in perpetuity, even without taking on the extra work of running a record label on behalf of their artist. As the role of personal management increasingly conflates with that of record label management, it strengthens the case for the manager having a longer-term equity in the intellectual property of recordings.

Conclusion

In the music industry of the twenty-first century the artist–manager relationship is characterised both by continuity and by change. On one hand, the management agreement formalises the relationship within stable principles of responsibility, equity and transparency. On the other hand, negotiation of those agreements is increasingly taking place within the context of a business environment that has the potential for revision and expansion of the definitions and expectations around management duties. Some might argue that, in order to facilitate these extensions to traditional management roles, there is a case for making changes to the law on fiduciary duties. However, while existing law requires transparency, openness and 'informed consent', it does not expressly prevent a manager's involvement in other artist income streams, so for that reason we would argue that a change to the law is not necessary. Clearly, these are fast-emerging areas of negotiation that relate directly to the changes in technology that have led to the development of label services as a significant means by which artists release their recorded material. As a growing reality of the industry, the implications of any extended roles need to be understood by managers, and increasingly it will need to be part of the established conversation at an early stage in the artist/manager relationship.

References

Coleman, A. (2018). 'In The 21st Century, To Be a Musician Is To Be an Entrepreneur', *Forbes*, 19 Januaery 2018, https://www.forbes.com/sites/alisoncoleman/2018/01/19/in-the-21st-century-to-be-a-musician-is-to-be-an-entrepreneur/, accessed 23 December 2020.

Elton John v Dick James Music & This Record Company (1991). FSR 397.

Esso Petroleum Co Ltd v Harper's Garage (Stourport) Ltd (1968). AC 269.

Goodman, F. (2015). *Allen Klein: The Man Who Bailed Out the Beatles, Made the Stones, and Transformed Rock & Roll*. New York: Houghton Mifflin Harcourt.

Hull, G. P., T. Hutchinson and R. Strasser (2011). *The Music Business and Recording Industry: Delivering Music in the 21st Century*, 3rd edn. New York: Routledge.

Ingham, T. (2019). 'Nearly 40,000 Tracks Are Now Being Added to Spotify Every Single Day', *Music Business Worldwide*, 29 April 2019, https://www.musicbusinessworldwide.com/nearly-40000-tracks-are-now-being-added-to-spotify-every-single-day/.

Mothew (t/a Stapley and Co) v Bristol and West Building Society (1996). EWCA Civ 533, 24 July 1996.

Music Managers Forum (2019). *Managing Expectations*, https://themmf.net/site/wp-content/uploads/2019/10/Managing-Expectations-MMF.pdf, accessed 24 August 2020.

Nash, A. (2003). *The Colonel: The Extraordinary Story of Colonel Tom Parker and Elvis Presley*. New York: Simon & Schuster.

O'Sullivan v Management Agency and Music Limited (1985). QB 428.

Tshmuck, P. (2016). 'From Record Selling to Cultural Entrepreneurship: The Music Economy in the Digital Paradigm Shift'. In Patrik Wikström and Robert DeFillippi (eds), *Business Innovation and Disruption in the Music Industry*, 13–32. Cheltenham: Edward Elgar Publishing Limited.

Index

ABKCO Music, Inc. v Stellar Records, Inc. 196, 204
acoustic trademark 6
ad disclosures 256, 257
Adorno, Theodor 179, 184, 187
advertisement 148, 149, 156
AEG 233, 235
AEG "1 Earth" 233
Aeolian Co. v Royal Music Roll Co. 194, 197
alternative dispute resolution (ADR) 127, 128, 142
Amchitka benefit concert 1970 229
American Society of Composers, Authors and Publishers (ASCAP) 214, 219
ancillary rights 259
App 88, 255. *See also* mobile applications
appearance agreements 251–2, 256–7
Apple 8, 16, 271
approval rights 250–1
arbitral award 141
    challenge to 141, 143
    in writing 141
arbitration 14, 136
    access to arbitration 138
    ad hoc 137
    advantages of 142, 143
    agreement to arbitrate 137–40
    arbitrability 131, 140, 141
    clause 138, 139
    confidentiality 142
    finality of 138, 141, 143
    institutional rules 137
    law of the seat 137, 143
    legal framework 137
    lex loci arbitri 137, 141
    model clause 139
    one-stop-shop 143
    outcome 141
    party autonomy 137, 140, 141, 143

    proceedings 140
    rules 137
    seat 137, 138
    submission agreement 138, 139
arbitrators 137
    conflict of interest 137
    discretion to conduct proceedings 140
arrangement. *See* rights within copyright
Article 17 (of the European Union Digital Single Market Directive) 76, 77, 86, 91, 115, 116, 211, 212
artificial intelligence (AI) 92
artist green riders 233
aura 46, 61–4

Beastie Boys (the) 51
Beato, Rick 89
Beggars Group 36, 38, 46
Berne Convention for the Protection of Literary and Artistic Works 6, 105
Black epistemologies in popular music 174
Black Lives Matter 38
Blackstone 202
blanket licence 198, 203–4
blocking websites 111, 112
Blue Planet 2, 231
Blurred Lines 12, 13
brand ambassador agreements 250–1, 256–7
branding 5, 7, 8, 274
branding agreements 247–59
    approvals 250–1
    deliverables 257
    expenses 252
    fees 252
    grant of rights 248–52
    service days 257
    types of branding agreement 254–8

BREIN   108
Bridgeport v. Dimension Films
    judgement   51-4, 56, 65, 67,
    71-2, 75
British Phonographic Industry
    (BPI)   101, 105, 109, 111-13
Brøvig-Hanssen, Ragnhild   64, 66, 72
Burning Man   240

Canadian Intellectual Property
    Office   150, 165
Capitol   52
Carthy, Andy   46, 58, 61
case law   7
chilling effect   142
circular economy   241, 244
clearance (of samples)   46, 51, 52,
    54-9, 64
CO2e emissions   233
collaboration agreements   250-1, 256-7
collection societies (CMOs)   212, 213,
    215, 216, 218-22
commission   264, 267, 268, 270, 273-5
Composition (musical)   190-6, 198-204
compulsory licences or licensing
    of musical composition   190-
        201, 203-5
    of patents   190, 193, 198
Conference of the Parties (COP)   234
consent   141
    to ADR   141
content creators   86-7, 90
content ID   220
content identification   65-70, 72, 74
content moderation   65-7, 71, 77
contract(s)   7, 8, 11, 264-7, 275
contract law   1, 4, 7, 8
copyleft   86
copyright   1, 4, 6, 9, 10, 12, 19, 21, 27-31,
    33, 34, 37, 38, 40-4, 46-54,
    56, 58-60, 63-72, 74-8, 82-7,
    89-95, 100-15, 173-8, 180-2,
    184-7. See also exceptions;
    online enforcement
    under Canadian law   69
    under European Union (EU)
        law   67, 73-7
    under United Kingdom law   70
    under United States law   71, 78
Copyright, Designs and Patents Act 1988
    (CDPA)   6, 27, 30, 31, 43, 53,
    54, 64, 84, 111
Copyright Act of 1842   177
copyright holders   103, 105, 106, 110,
    111, 113
copyright industry   28, 41
copyright infringement   47, 52, 56, 58,
    84, 87, 90-2
copyright legislation (US)
    1790   192
    1831   192
    1909   190, 192-7, 200, 204
    1976   199, 201, 204
    copyright directive of 2019   38
    Music Modernization Act   203-5
copyright notices   90
copyright owner   27
copyright protection   92
cost of ADR   142
counterclaims   90
cover   190, 198, 199
Covid-19   16, 20, 114, 229, 243-4
Creative Commons   87
creative content   87
creators   82-4, 86-91, 93, 95
cross-border
    proceedings   142
cryptocurrencies   210, 217
cryptographic hash   210, 214
Csikszentmihalyi, Mihaly   48, 63, 65
cyberlockers   104-7, 109, 110, 112,
    114-16
    Dbr.ee   108
    Dropapk.to   108
    Hotfile   108, 109
    Megaupload   104-7
    Mixloads.com   110
    Pay Per Click   104
    Purplinx   108
    Rapidgator.com   109, 110
    RapidShare   104-6
    Wupload   107, 108

data protection   210, 223
database   209, 211-15, 219-23
decentralised   210, 211, 214

'deductibles' 265, 267, 268, 274
Deezer 272
Def Jam 51
de minimis 50, 51
demonetisation 89
Department for Digital Culture, Media and Sport (DCMS) 6, 17, 19
derivative work. *See* rights within copyright
design agreements 252, 257–8
DiCola, J. 50, 51, 64, 71
Digital Copyright Act 2010 112
Digital Copyright Consultancy 100, 101, 106, 108, 110, 111, 114
digital disruption 83
digital domain 85, 87, 93, 95
Digital Millennium Copyright Act (DMCA) 85, 105
Digital Performance Right in Sound Recordings Act 1995 32
digital service provider (DSP) 201–4
digital technologies 82–4, 87, 94
digitalisation 82, 85
disputes 10, 12–16, 90, 94
distinctiveness of a trademark 149, 150, 154
Dixie Chicks 15–17, 24, 25
DJ Kool Herc 182
DJ Short-E 90
Drake 13
Dubset 73–4, 78
Dutch government and festival partnership 241–3

E-commerce Directive 85
economic growth 230
Edward B. Marks Music Corp. v Colo. Magnetics, Inc. 191
Edward B. Marks Music Corp. v Foullon 197
Eight Mile Style, LLC v Spotify USA 201–2
Eighth Plate 232
Ek, Daniel 273
EMAS 237
endorsement agreements 256
energy sources and usage 238

environmental impact 230
Ethereum 217
EU Directives 235, 238–40
EUIPO. *See* European Union Intellectual Property Office
EU Mediation Directive 134
European Green Deal 240
European Union (EU) 85–6
European Union Intellectual Property Office 148, 161–4, 167–8
European Union Trade Mark (EUTM) 150, 154–8, 167–8
  non-permissible representation 165–8
  permissible representation 158–64
EUTM. *See* European Union Trade Mark
exceptions 65, 67, 69–71, 74–7
  parody 67, 75–6
  quotation 67, 75–7

FAC. *See* Featured Artist Coalition
Facebook 64, 66, 68, 74
Facebook Rights Manager 66
fair dealing 86, 90
Fair Internet for Performers (FIFP) 40, 44
'Fair Trade' 219, 220
fair use 86, 89, 90
fan-generated content 84, 95
fans 82–5, 88–91, 95
featured artis coalition (FAC) 41
fiduciary duty 269, 270
file sharing 203
first fixation. *See* Rights within copyright
food waste 231
Frith, Simon 27–9, 41, 44, 45
'Für Elise' by Ludwig van Beethoven 150, 151

Glastonbury Festival 239, 240
glocal 129, 133
Google 9, 24, 105, 106, 109, 111, 113
governance, governing 220, 221
grant of rights 248–51
A Greener Festival 234, 237, 240
Greenpeace 229
grime 272

HADOPI   112
Harry Fox Agency   201–4
HFA. *See* Harry Fox Agency
Hook, Peter   2, 15
hybrid events   243

image rights   248–51
immutable, immutability   210, 220, 223
influencer   82, 253–4
Instagram   87, 89, 93
intellectual property   13, 18, 19, 82, 84, 91, 130
   disputes   130
   office   21
   specialised institutions   131
intellectual property law   1, 4, 9, 14, 173
intermediaries   10, 209, 211, 215, 216, 218, 221–3
International Federation of the Phonographic Industry (IFPI)   28, 29, 32, 33, 35, 36, 42, 45, 101, 108, 113, 215
internet   83–7, 94–5
investor/equity agreements   258
ISRC   214
ISWC   214
Ivors Academy (The)   216

Jack Johnson   233
jingle   148, 156
Julie's Bicycle   239
jurisdiction   177, 210, 222–3
jurisprudence   4, 13

Karaoke   195–6
key environmental impacts   237

label services   271
legislation   85–6, 95
legislative context and frameworks   234
Lennon, John   10, 12
Leo Feist, Inc. v Apollo Records, N.Y.   197, 198
licensing agreements   94
licensing of samples   65, 67, 69–77
Lil Nas X   93–4
linear economy   242
live music industry   5
Live Nation   233, 235

Live Nation "Green Nation"   233
live sponsorship   255–6
live streaming   90
logic (rapper)   91
Lose Yourself   203
lyrics   195–6

McLeod, K.   51, 52, 64, 71
make available to the public. *See* rights within copyright
Malagena   197
management agreement   264–70, 274, 275
management term   265
manager   263–70, 272–5
marketing   271–4
mashup music   64–78
mashup producer
   bringmethemashup   76
   DJ Earworm   76
   DJ Poulpi   66
   DJ Schmolli   66
   Girl Talk   64
   Raheem D   76
Mechanical Licensing Collective   203
mediation   128, 132
   access to mediation   134
   advantages of   143
   agreement   134
   agreement to mediate   133
      caucus   136, 143
   confidentiality   135, 136
   legal framework   133
   model clause   134
   outcome   136
   proceedings   135
   request for   135
   schedule of meetings   135
   settlement agreements   133, 136
   submission agreement   134
   termination   136
   unilateral request for mediation   134
mediator   135
   appointment   135
   independence, neutrality, impartiality   135
   metadata   214, 217
   minimum viable data   220
#metoo   251

Microsoft   9
MLC. *See* Mechanical Licensing Collective
mobile applications   88
monopoly or monopolization   190–3, 200, 204–5
   mechanical-music trust   193
moral right(s)   178, 215
multimedia trademark   152
Musical.ly   88
musical trademarks   150–1, 154–5, 158–67
Music declares an Emergency, (UK)   229
music disputes   127, 130, 143
   contract disputes   130
   intellectual property disputes   130, 131
   nature of   129
Musicians' Union (The)   37, 41, 216, 265
music industry   82–3, 85–7, 89, 91, 93
music law   1–5, 9, 10, 14, 15, 19
Music Managers Forum   271
music sampling. *See also* mashup music
Mycelia   217

National Music Publishers' Association   202
negotiation power   142–4
New York Convention for Recognition and Enforcement of Foreign Arbitral Awards   128, 133, 138
Nice Classification   155–6
NMPA. *See* National Music Publishers' Association
node operators   219, 220
NOI. *See* notice of intent
non-musical trademarks   150–2, 154, 161–8
notice of intent   202–3

Ofcom   255–6
online copyright enforcement   65, 66, 68, 72, 76
Ono, Yoko   12, 25
OpenAir St Galen festival Switzerland   241
Open Music Initiative (The)   217
Opus   218

Panayiotou v Sony Music Entertainment   7
Patent   190, 192–3, 198, 204
Pearl Jam   233
P.E.S.T.   5
peer to peer (P2P)   101, 102, 104, 116
   Grokster   103
   Napster   102, 103
Peertracks   218
Pelham v. Hütter litigation   74–7
performance agreements   251–2, 256–7
Performances and Phonograms Treaty   35
personal rights   248–51
phonograph   195
phonographic sample   46, 58, 63
phonorecord   196
   digital phonorecord   204
piano roll   191, 195, 197
   music roll   194–5
piracy   10, 21, 22, 100–2, 104, 105, 108, 109, 112–16, 219. *See* file sharing
   anti-piracy   100–2, 104–6, 109, 110, 116
   copyright infringement   102, 104, 106–8, 110, 112, 114
   piracy warnings   112
   unlicensed content   100, 101, 104–10, 112–15
pirate   194
   pirate linking site   108, 109, 114
   Intmusic   109, 114
   New Album Releases   109
   Rlsbb   109, 110
platform regulation   64–78. *See also* content identification; content moderation
podcasts   254–5, 259
policy   150
Polish Patent Office   148, 163
Pope v Curl (1741)   176
PPE (personal protective equipment)   243
PPO. *See* Polish Patent Office
product placement   255
PRS for music   214, 219
public enemy   52

publicity rights 248–51
public performance. *See* rights within copyright
publisher (of musical compositions) 191, 200–1
publishing industry 5

Rachum-Twaig 175, 184–7, 189
radiohead 233
recognition software 92
record 194, 197
 acetate 197
record company. *See* record label
recording industry 5, 11, 100–3, 106, 107, 109–16
Recording Industry Association of America (RIAA) 33, 34, 36, 100–2, 105, 108
record label 13, 15, 16, 18, 19, 191, 199–203, 258–9, 268, 271–5
representation of a trademark in the register 149, 150, 157–68
 audio file (exclusively) 161–2
 description in words (exclusively) 166–7
 indication of notes sequence without stave 166
 non-permissible representation 165–8
 notation (exclusively) 158–61
 notation with audio file 163
 onomatopoeia 167
 permissible representation 158–65
 sonogram (exclusively) 167–8
 sonogram with audio file 163–4
 trademark description with audio file 164–5
revenue 82, 85, 90, 93–4
rightsholders 11, 46, 47, 51, 55–60, 64, 85, 91–3
rights within copyright
 reproduction right 27, 29, 31, 33, 35, 40
 the right of first fixation 194
 to make a derivative work 191, 198
 to make an arrangement 191, 194, 196–8
 to make available to the public 27, 29, 30, 35, 38, 40, 42, 191

 to perform to the public 191–2, 197, 198
Romantic authorship 174, 177–9, 186
royalty, royalties 27, 32, 35–8, 40, 42, 209, 211–13, 215–18, 221, 223

safe harbours 85–6, 95
sample clearance 46–8, 51, 53–6, 58, 60, 64
sample replays 46, 59, 61, 63
sampling 173, 174, 182, 185–7
self-regulation 236
similar use 195–7
Singapore Convention on Mediation 128, 133, 136
single use plastics 230
Skepta 272
smart contracts 211, 216–18, 221–4
social media 82–5, 87–9, 91–2, 94, 247, 249, 251–8
Society of Authors, Composers and Publishers of Music (SACEM) 214, 219
Sony Music Entertainment 8, 16
SoundCloud 64, 68, 72–4
sound recording 191, 192, 196, 199, 201, 203–4
spotify 9, 17, 113, 114, 201–4, 211, 213, 214, 216, 219, 254, 272, 273
Standard Music Roll Co. v Mills 194–5
streaming (of music) 5, 16, 17, 19, 21, 25, 29, 30, 33, 35–42, 44–6, 107, 112–14, 116, 191, 195, 199, 201, 203–4
streaming services 82, 85, 91, 93
styling 250, 257
Symphony 2, op. 30 by Howard Hanson 151
synchronisation licences 255

takedown claims 89–91
TEAS. *See* USPTO electronic trademark application
Tencent 8
term 249
termination rights 251
territoriality 130, 131
territory 4, 8, 12, 259
third-party content 91–2, 94

Index   283

TikTok   84, 88–9, 93–4
Tiny Human   217
torrent   104–6, 111, 112, 116
    BitTorrent   103
    KickAssTorrents   111
    The Pirate Bay   103, 104
touring   267, 269, 270
transnational
    arbitration rules   140
travel and transport   239
'Travis Scott'   13
Twitch   84, 87, 91–3

Ujo   216
UKIPO. *See* United Kingdom Intellectual Property Office
UK Waste Strategy   244
UNCITRAL Arbitration Model Law   138
UNCITRAL Mediation Model Law   133
unconventional trademarks   149
unfair competition   197
United Kingdom Intellectual Property Office   148, 159, 162
United States Patent and Trademark Office   148, 164–5
United States Trade Mark   154–7, 164–5
unlicensed music   91–2, 94
UN sustainable development goals   230
use of a trademark   156
user-generated content   82–8, 92, 94
USPTO. *See* United States Patent and Trademark Office
USPTO electronic trademark application   157, 164–5
USTM. *See* United States Trade Mark

value gap   85–6, 90
venues and corporates   233
video sharing   87–9, 93
visual perception of a trademark   150
vloggers   89

Warner Music Group   9, 24, 219
waste   240
water use and conservation   238
William Tell' opera by Gioacchino Rossini   151
WIPO. *See also* World Intellectual Property Organization   6, 30, 32–5, 46, 47, 128
    Arbitration Model Clause   139
    Arbitration Rules   139
    Mediation Model Agreement   134
    Mediation Rules   134
    Submission agreement   139
WIPO ADR Centre   128, 134, 135
    appointing authority   135
Witmark v Roll Co.   195
World Intellectual Property Organization   150, 151

YouTube   64, 66–8, 84–7, 89–92, 103, 105, 113, 114, 116, 219
    ContentID   66, 113, 116
    Content Verification Programme   113
    stream ripping   113, 114
YouTubers   89–91

zero carbon emissions   235

www.ingramcontent.com/pod-product-compliance
Lightning Source LLC
Chambersburg PA
CBHW052153300426
44115CB00011B/1651